# We Shall Be All

*(abridged edition)*

The Working Class in American History

*Editorial Advisors*
  David Brody
  Alice Kessler-Harris
  David Montgomery
  Sean Wilentz

*A list of books in the series appears at the end of this book.*

# We Shall Be All

## A History of the Industrial Workers of the World

*Abridged Edition*

Melvyn Dubofsky

*Edited by Joseph A. McCartin*

University of Illinois Press

Urbana and Chicago

The photographs reproduced in this book appear courtesy of
the Walter P. Reuther Library, Wayne State University.

Library of Congress Cataloging-in-Publication Data
Dubofsky, Melvyn, 1934–
We shall be all : a history of the Industrial Workers of the World /
Melvyn Dubofsky ; edited by Joseph A. McCartin.— Abridged ed.
p.   cm.
Includes bibliographical references and index.
ISBN 0-252-02595-4 (acid-free paper) / ISBN 978-0-252-02595-2
ISBN 0-252-06905-6 (pbk. : acid-free paper) / ISBN 978-0-252-06905-5
1. Industrial Workers of the World—History. I. McCartin, Joseph
Anthony. II. Title.
HD8055.I4D83    2000
331.88'6—dc21    00-008215

1 2 3 4 5 C P 10 9 8 7 6

# Contents

# Editor's Introduction

Very few books in American social or labor history have stood the test of time as well as this one. More than thirty years after its publication in 1969, Melvyn Dubofsky's history of that hardy band of working-class radicals, the Industrial Workers of the World (IWW), remains the definitive account of its subject. This book's endurance is all the more remarkable considering how the field of labor history has changed since its publication. Over the past generation, in part because of the influence of studies like this one, labor history claimed its place as a legitimate academic subdiscipline in departments of history. Contributing to the rise of this field, hundreds of scholars, publishing thousands of books and articles, helped shape a new labor history in the years since the 1960s. Those scholars helped recover the untold stories of ordinary workers, rank-and-file labor activists, and radicals. More than a few participants in this scholarly renaissance directed their attention to the Wobblies (as IWW members were called). But none has yet attempted to duplicate or surpass Dubofsky's comprehensive, archive-based history of the IWW. This book has introduced more readers to the history of the Wobblies than any other.

Reasons for this book's enduring influence are not difficult to find. In addition to the massive research and careful analysis that informed its engaging prose, the popularity of this account can be attributed to at least three factors. Surely among these factors was the timing of its appearance. What more propitious moment than 1969 for the appearance of a full-length study of an unabashed radical movement—a movement that offered a vision of racial equality, that pioneered the techniques of nonviolent civil disobedience and direct action so central to the insurgent politics of the 1960s?

Dubofsky's history of the IWW appeared at just the moment when proponents of the New Left and the civil rights and antiwar struggles, having suffered the disillusions and defeats of 1968, began to cast about for models of an authentic American radicalism that could sustain them over the long haul and rescue them from encroaching despair. In Dubofsky's IWW, they found joyful champions of what the New Left called participatory democracy, ardent visionaries of what the civil rights movement called the beloved community, and principled foes of what antiwar activists dubbed the military-industrial complex. They also found radicals undaunted by crushing defeats, men and women who had come to believe that "in the struggle itself lies the happiness of the fighter," as one IWW die-hard once put it.

But Dubofsky's account could scarcely be characterized as an effort to find a usable past for 1960s activists. This book was first and foremost a careful work of history, not a prescription for social change or an ideological brief. Indeed, it was Dubofsky's fealty to detail, balanced historical context, and measured judgment, and his unwillingness to bend his narrative in the service of any particular agenda, that constitutes a second reason for this book's lasting popularity.

As the following chapters make clear, Dubofsky refused to romanticize the Wobblies, to posthumously recruit them for the political battles of the day, or to settle for merely reinforcing their place in American mythology. Rather, he sought to probe beneath the IWW legend and to understand the movement and its leaders, their contradictions and failings, warts and all. The IWW's radicalism, as depicted in this account, defied simple categorization. Nor did it offer clear answers to the dilemmas that confronted radicals at the end of the 1960s, when this book first appeared. The Wobblies of whom Dubofsky wrote were presented as complex and sometimes contradictory figures who simultaneously embraced a radical vision and a realistic concern with the here and now that workers struggled with every day. They believed they could fight for concrete gains in the real world without sacrificing their ultimate vision of an industrial democracy administered at the point of production. Yet when forced to choose between the dictates of their revolutionary rhetoric and the immediate demands of their rank and file, Wobbly leaders usually opted for a pragmatic approach. It is ironic, given the Wobblies' incendiary reputation, that it was their decision to forgo grand radical gestures and instead concentrate on practical, job-centered organizing during World War I (a conflict the IWW opposed on principle) that led to the organization's repression. So effective were the Wobblies at organizing workers and leading them out on strike during the war that the United States government used nearly every means in its power to destroy the IWW in 1917.

By illuminating precisely such ironies as this one in the IWW's story, Dubofsky avoided casting the Wobblies in the role of mere radical icons or heroic martyrs. Rather, they emerge as real men and women, both flawed and admirable. Their principled political commitments, Dubofsky made clear, did not give the Wobblies pat answers to the problems of organizing workers in their time. Nor did the passion or purity of those commitments rescue them from the costs of poor political analysis, the chaos of bitter factional strife and administrative incompetency, and the opposition of powerful forces beyond their control. Ultimately, the Wobblies who emerge in these pages are all the more compelling—and their contributions to American radicalism, labor organizing, and democracy all the more apparent—because their imperfections and contradictions are so well illuminated.

Yet the final—perhaps the most obvious—factor contributing to the enduring popularity of this book is surely its subject. Few stories in American history can match the one told here for stirring passion, pathos, romance, and tragedy. Few casts of historical figures can match the color or fiery eloquence of the Wobbly band, which included such figures as "Big Bill" Haywood, Elizabeth Gurley Flynn, Arturo Giovanitti, Ben Fletcher, and Father Thomas J. Hagerty.

But it is not only the dramatic character of the Wobblies and their story that have made them compelling figures through the years. They and their movement raised questions that have not yet been answered adequately, posed challenges that have yet to be met, and suggested alternatives that have yet to be consigned forever to the ash heap of history. Wobblies questioned whether a democracy was worthy of the name if it did not empower its poorest, its most maligned and marginalized. They challenged workers to build an inclusive labor movement capable of achieving that empowerment. And they envisioned a society of tolerance and material abundance administered for the benefit of all, a world in which international solidarity would make war obsolete.

The Wobblies' vision continues to challenge those who share their dream of equality and justice. Nor is there any reason to believe that they will soon be forgotten. Indeed, the developments of recent decades arguably make the Wobblies' story more relevant than when this book was first published. The Wobblies anarcho-syndicalist suspicion of government and its reform initiatives may have seemed somewhat anachronistic in the 1960s in an America reconstructed by the New Deal and the Great Society. But that critique seems eminently more plausible in an era marked by the dismantling of the welfare state, the paralysis of labor law reform efforts, and the growing power of transnational corporations. The Wobblies' disparagement of the limitations of the American Federation of Labor's "pork chop unionism" may have seemed unreasonable in an era when powerful unions were achieving generous contracts for an increasing proportion of American workers. Yet that critique seems far more apt in an era when organized labor is able to deliver less power and fewer benefits to a shrinking slice of the American work force. If the Wobblies' story does not furnish obvious strategies for reversing such trends as these, it at least provides inspiration for those who would resist the globalization of unaccountable corporate power, redeem the unmet promises of democracy, and achieve dignity and security for the poor and neglected.

✳  ✳  ✳

This is not the same book Melvyn Dubofsky published thirty years ago. In an effort to make this narrative more accessible to a new generation of readers, especially undergraduate students, I have abridged his account of the Wobblies' history. Although I have retained the original narrative and chapter structure of the book, I have excised roughly one-third of the original text along with Dubofsky's scholarly annotation. At times this effort led me to trim sentences, combine or cut entire paragraphs, or shorten quotations. However, I have not eliminated any significant episode from Dubofsky's 1969 narrative. I have attempted to make my cuts in a way that keeps faith with the careful tone, colorful detail, and complex analysis that informed the original book. To minimize distractions, I have not drawn attention to my cuts by the use of ellipsis points (except when I have shortened quotations). At the end of this volume, I have appended a bibliographical essay surveying recent works on the IWW.

I have made a special effort to preserve the nuances of Dubofsky's original analysis. Yet careful readers will note that I have altered Dubofsky's language when it was dated by current standards of usage. I have also eliminated most historiographic and theoretical references from this abridged account. In my judgment, removing such references (which would naturally seem outdated to today's readers) makes the text more accessible without materially altering Dubofsky's original argument. Of course, for those who seek the finer points of IWW history, there is no better starting place than Dubofsky's original volume.

✳  ✳  ✳

I would like to thank several people for their help in preparing this volume. Without the support of Richard Wentworth at the University of Illinois Press this abridged edition of a labor history classic would have been impossible.

Thanks also to managing editor Theresa L. Sears and copyeditor Carol Anne Peschke for their help in preparing this volume. Thomas Featherstone helped me locate Wobbly photographs in the holdings of the Walter Reuther Library at Wayne State University. My brother and fellow historian, Jim McCartin, helped me digitize the original text that I edited into this book. My wife, Diane Reis, and daughters Mara and Elisa brightened my work with their love. And Melvyn Dubofsky left me free to make whatever decisions I felt appropriate in abridging his work while providing steady support as both a mentor and a friend. For this, and for his guidance over the years, I owe him a large debt of gratitude.

# 1

## A Setting for Radicalism, 1877–1917

The history of the Industrial Workers of the World (IWW) can be understood only in relation to the economic and social changes that between 1877 and 1917 transformed the United States into the world's leading industrial nation. IWW members, whether American-born or foreign-born, were first-generation immigrants to that industrial society. Hence they mirrored the perplexities and confusions, the strivings and ambitions of a generation compelled to contend with a world it had never made, a world it sometimes barely understood.

With the end of the Civil War, Americans shifted their energies from waging battles to building steel mills, digging coal, packing meat, and constructing cities. In the process of accomplishing all this, they created a new urban nation. In 1870 only about one of every four Americans lived in what the Census Bureau defined as an urban area; by 1900 the proportion had increased to more than two of every five, and by 1920 more than half the population resided in urban areas.

Americans also built immense industrial combinations. Between 1897 and 1904 the so-called first American trust movement spawned its corporate colossi. Wall Street analyst John Moody in 1904 reported the existence of 318 active industrial trusts with a capital of over $7 billion, representing the consolidation of over 5,300 distinctive plants in every line of production. The acme of industrial combination came in 1901 when J. P. Morgan purchased Andrew Carnegie's iron and steel holdings, merging them with his own Federal Steel Company to form United States Steel, the first billion-dollar corporation in American history.

While America's total wealth increased enormously, its distribution remained uneven. The more wealth Henry George discovered, the more dismal poverty he perceived, leading him to conclude that progress and poverty went hand in glove. Jacob Riis also found no signs of affluence among his "Other Half" in New York's slums. Nor did Jane Addams at Hull House, nor did Lillian Wald at her settlement house on Henry Street. The nation's great wealth, so impressive in the aggregate, was being distributed very unevenly among the groups making up American society.

Although the standard of living improved for most American workers between 1877 and 1917, poverty remained a fact of life for most working-class families and a condition of existence for many, if not for most. Robert Hunter, in his classic study *Poverty,* published in 1904, reported that not less than 14 percent of the people in prosperous times, and not less than 20 percent in bad times, suffered from dire poverty, with unemployment causing the bulk of the distress.

Other observers of working-class life in early twentieth-century America found conditions reminiscent of the worst features of nineteenth-century industrial England. At a twine factory in New York City, a social worker watched the women file out at day's end: "Pale, narrow-chested, from hand to foot . . . covered with fibrous dust. . . . They were the types of factory workers—pale, haggard feeders of machines—like those described in the days of a century past in England."

Yet not all workers labored for a pittance. For the skilled, who were always in scarce supply, a seller's market guaranteed high wages. And the influx into industry of millions of non-English-speaking immigrants created numerous well-paid supervisory plant positions for those who could read and write English. Native Americans and acculturated immigrants could move from the blast furnace or the work bench to the foreman's post. And their children could wear a white collar in place of the blue one. Their skills and their relative scarcity also enabled these workers to establish potent trade unions.

And what of the workers who did not qualify for membership in labor's aristocracy? Occupying a position somewhere between the elite and the lumpenproletariat, these workers probably received just enough from the system in good times to keep them contented. As long as the promise of improvement beckoned and opportunity for it existed, the great mass of American workers had no irreconcilable quarrel with capitalism.

But if most workers benefited to a greater or lesser degree from American capitalism, a significant minority appeared to be bypassed altogether by industrial progress. Of these, none had a stronger grievance against the system than African Americans. Freed at last from the bondage of chattel slavery, they found new forms of economic subservience waiting for them. At a time when industry cried for workers, black men saw themselves in desperate, unsuccessful competition for factory employment with the immigrant millions from eastern and southern Europe. The black man thus typically remained in the Southland of his birth, there to work a white man's land with a white man's plow, a white man's mule, and a white man's money. When industrial America finally did call him, it was too often to serve as a strikebreaker.

The new immigrants fared better than African Americans, but they too were second-class citizens in relation to native whites. Every survey of immigrant earnings shows that the latest arrivals ranked at the bottom of the economic ladder, the less industrialized their country of origin the lower their earnings in America. Only the African American's presence kept the Italian, the Pole, and the Slav above society's mudsill.

Although most immigrants found life in the New World sweeter than what they had known in the Old, sometimes they concluded, as did a Rumanian immigrant, "This was the boasted American freedom and opportunity—the freedom for respectable citizens to sell cabbages from hideous carts, the opportunity to live in those monstrous dirty caves [tenements] that shut out the sunshine."

One native American group with higher status than African Americans or immigrants also fared ill in the land that bred it. If the first half of the nineteenth century had been the golden age of the farmer in America, then the second half was the time of testing. The farms of New England, New York, and Pennsylvania now had to compete with the vast, fertile prairies of the West. From the noncompetitive farms of the Northeast, the foreclosed farms of the South and West, and from some successful farms everywhere, thousands of young men were pushed off the land. Eventually many of them drifted into the growing ranks of migratory workers: the men who followed the wheat harvest north from Texas to Canada; picked the fruits, vegetables, and hops of the West Coast; labored in the mines, construction camps, and lumber camps of the West, always ready to move on with the job to a new region, a new camp, a new life. But the region, the camp, and the life too often turned out to be the same as the old: primitive, brutal, lonely, drudging, and poorly paid.

From such as these—oppressed American blacks, immigrants disillusioned with America's promise, native-born Americans forced off the land—the Industrial Workers of the World attempted to forge a movement to revolutionize American society. Blacks, immigrants, and migratories always served as the major objects of the IWW's efforts and (such as they were) the sources of its strength. Of the three groups, the migratories were to prove the most militant, revolutionary, and loyal.

If American capitalism in the best of times provided just adequately for most citizens and hardly that well for millions more, in the worst of times it failed to provide even the fortunate with jobs, income, and security. Industrial depressions and recessions occurred like clockwork in the half-century following Appomattox: first from 1873 to 1878, then again in 1883–85, 1893–97, 1907–9, and 1913–15. Always the story was the same: poverty in the midst of plenty. Idle people and idle capital. Sullen discontent and sporadic protest by the workers, gnawing fear by the middle and upper classes, and harsh repression by the authorities.

Desiring a measure of security in a time of economic fluctuation, workers sought to organize. The founders of the modern American labor movement learned the cardinal lesson of industrial society: the imperviousness of its basic problems to individual solution. For workers, this knowledge dictated the pooling of strength in trade unions and the creation of a national labor movement.

The wonder of labor history in the late nineteenth century is not that unions emerged but rather that they were so weak and that so few workers joined them. But a little reflection shows why. Although American society was hardly classless, it lacked the traditional bonds that tied European workers together into a class characterized by common patterns of thought and behavior. Indeed, America's working class was most notable for its religious and ethnic heterogeneity. Native-born workers had nothing but contempt for Irish Catholic immigrants, and Irish workers in turn looked down upon the late-coming Poles, Slavs, and Italians. Whites feared blacks; Jews suspected Gentiles. Employers easily played off one group against another and shrewdly mixed their labor forces to weaken group solidarity.

What judicious mixing could not accomplish, economic conditions and the law did. Too many workers had only their brawn to sell, and in a labor market periodically flooded by immigrants, brawn commanded a low premium. Better to win approval of one's boss by avoiding labor agitators and their unions than to lose one's job to a greenhorn or a scab! Those with skills to sell faced other barriers to union organization. American law sanctioned employers' anti-union devices but outlawed basic trade union tactics. The American judiciary, it has been said, tied one hand (and sometimes both) behind the worker's back before sending him into the Darwinian ring to fight a more powerful adversary.

The whole American environment seemed to conspire against the labor movement. From 1877 to 1893 social mobility was writ large. Everywhere one looked, evidence emerged of poor boys who had "made good." Perhaps they were the exception, but men live by fantasies as much as by reality, and if the reality of great wealth eluded a worker, he could still dream about it for his son.

So when times were good and opportunities abounded, the ambitious worker showed slight interest in trade unions or in any institution that threatened to alter America's social structure. With depression, however, opportunities shriveled and dreams faded, driving the worker into the embrace of the union organizer, but unions, barely able to survive in prosperity, often collapsed at the first hint of depression.

The first important national labor organization to appear in industrial America was the Knights of Labor. Organized initially as a local secret society in 1869, made public and national in 1878, it invited all producers to join. Only capitalists, lawyers, gamblers, and drunkards were excluded from membership. Proclaiming universality of membership as its guiding principle, and solidarity—"An injury to one is the concern of all"—as its motto, the Knights functioned as a conventional labor organization. Most members were wage workers who joined to fight for higher wages and better working conditions.

As the only prominent national labor organization in existence, the Knights grew rapidly during the prosperous years from 1879 to 1886. By 1886 membership approached one million, and some middle-class Americans came to fear the organization's Grand Master Workman, Terence Powderly—a mild-mannered, narcissistic, administratively incompetent, constitutionally ineffective, teetotaling bumbler—much as later Americans feared the post–New Deal generation of powerful labor leaders.

But the Knights lacked real substance and power. Their membership diminished after 1886 as rapidly as it had previously increased. By 1888 the organization, if not dead, was certainly dying. The age demanded planning, executive ability and a rational grasp of the issues. The Knights lacked all three.

Some elements in the labor movement did dwell on efficiency and results, notably the national trade unions, which in 1886 reorganized themselves as the American Federation of Labor (AFL). A rival national labor center competing with the Knights for members and for survival, the AFL lived and eventually thrived while the Knights declined and died.

What happened was that the trade unions recognized and acted upon what *was;* the Knights proposed what *could be.* The Knights, one historian wrote, "tried to teach the American wage-earner that he was a wage-earner first and a bricklayer, carpenter, miner, shoemaker after; that he was a wage-earner first and a Catholic, Protestant, Jew, white, black, Democrat, Republican after. This meant that the Order was teaching something that was not so in the hope that sometime it would be." But the AFL affiliates organized carpenters as carpenters, bricklayers as bricklayers, and so forth, teaching them all to place their own craft interests before those of other workers.

More and more after 1900, as the AFL under Samuel Gompers's leadership grew and prospered, it sought to sell itself to employers as the conservative alternative to working-class radicalism. It could do so because its members were by and large the workers most satisfied with the status quo. In return for the good treatment accorded to the skilled elite dominant in the AFL, the federation became in time one of the strongest defenders of the American system. So long as wages rose, and they did, hours fell, and they did, security increased, and it appeared to, the AFL could grow fat while neglecting millions of laborers doomed to lives of misery and want.

Here the IWW entered the picture, for it offered to do what the AFL declined to attempt: organize the blacks, the new immigrants, and the workers in mass-production industries where craft lines dissolved under the pressures of technology. The IWW, like the Knights before it, told men and women that they were workers first and Jews, Catholics, whites or blacks, skilled or unskilled second. The IWW would also try to teach "something that was not so in the hope that sometime it would be."

Workers, however, were not the only Americans dissatisfied with the prevailing industrial order. This was also the era of populism, progressivism, and the rise of American socialism: The Age of Reform. While it lasted, all manner of things seemed possible in America. Myriad reformers hoped to transform America into a just and good, if not "Great," society.

Arising out of the agrarian depression of the 1880s and 1890s, populism presented the first effective challenge to thirty years of political complacency and drift. Discontent united the Populists. They agreed that production for profit, not for use, made the few rich at the expense of the many. They sensed that to compel workers to obey "natural" laws of supply and demand turned them into just another commodity, like lumps of coal or sacks of flour. Populists saw no sense in an economic order that forced farmers off the land because they produced a surplus yet could not feed hungry millions, they saw less sense in a system that laid off millions of workers because they could not consume what they had produced, and they found no sense at all in a political order that repressed the discontents of the masses but did little to curb the excesses, follies, and even tyrannies of great wealth. Populists instead proposed to keep the farmer on the land, the worker at the bench, and to return government to the service of the many, not the few.

Although populism died after the Democratic defeat in 1896 and the return of prosperity, reform survived. Progressivism followed. More urban, much more successful economically and socially, and much less alienated, Progressives nonetheless were well aware of the inadequacies and injustices rooted in American society. Through reform of the prevailing order, which they considered by and large to be satisfactory, Progressives sought to eliminate the occasion for future working-class uprisings or Populist revolts.

Progressive-era reforms included a little something for everyone: stricter antitrust laws and business regulation for the small manufacturer, merchant, and farmer; lower tariffs for the agrarians of the South and West, and also for consumers; and rural free delivery, postal savings banks, federal farm land banks, and other measures for the nation's farmers. Nor were workers and immigrants excluded from the bounty of progressive reform. For them, Progressives provided factory and social welfare legislation. Child labor was restricted, women workers gained new legal protection, factories were made safer and cleaner, workers gained compensation and liability laws, some states moved in the direction of minimum-wage legislation, and many cities began to tidy up their noisome slums.

Progressivism did of course terminate in a conservative cul de sac. But that was not the intention of most reformers. The capitalism they sanctioned was clearly not that of J. P. Morgan, Henry Frick, or George F. Baer; they favored a vague, undefined democratic version. Perhaps capitalism was not compatible with the progressive reformers' notions of a democratic and just society, but they could not know that until the nation had tried their reforms. Many reformers for a time had more in common with Socialists than with the businessmen and major party politicians of the period.

Indeed, during the progressive years socialism enjoyed its only period of sustained nationwide political success. Socialists benefited from the nation's awakened social conscience. To citizens alarmed about unrestrained and unregulated industrial capitalism, only the Socialist party offered a complete blueprint for a fundamentally different and, it believed, better America.

Socialism in this period also became Americanized. Previously thought of as the importation of European intellectuals and workers, the Socialist party's complexion appeared to change after 1900. Eugene Debs, its outstanding leader, though the child of immigrant parents, was himself American to the core, born and bred in the Midwest. Countless other prominent native Americans followed Debs into the party: The muckraking journalist Charles Edward Russell, Walter Lippmann, Florence Kelley, Frances Perkins, Upton Sinclair, John and Anna Sloan, Theodore Dreiser, and Max Eastman were only a few of the many Americans who found in socialism an antidote to their alienation from American society.

Americanization brought the Socialist party votes. Debs's presidential campaigns of 1904, 1908, and 1912 spread socialism's message broadcast. Locally, where the possibilities of electoral victory were greater than at the national level, Socialists did exceedingly well. By 1911, as they captured the cities of Berkeley, Scranton, Bridgeport, Butte, and Schenectady, among others, articles were appearing in popular magazines voicing alarm at the "rising tide of socialism."

Political success, however, only obscured basic weaknesses. Within the Socialist party, factionalism and personality clashes ran riot. Although factions and individuals usually united or divided on specific issues without much attention to ideological consistency, a right (reformist) and a left (revolutionary) wing struggled for party ascendancy. More important than factionalism was the party's inability to widen its ethnic appeal beyond a limited number of new immigrants—Jews, most notably—and its consequent abysmal failure to win mass support from Catholic workers. American socialism never captured the primary bastion of the labor movement the AFL, as most European Socialists had done in their native lands.

While the age of reform lasted, millions of Americans challenged the old capitalist order. The system as described fifty years earlier by Marx and Engels was dying throughout the industrial world, the United States included, and various social groups were struggling to shape the economic order to come. None was absolutely certain of what the future would hold, but all wanted it to accord with their conceptions of a just and good society. In America, many options then appeared to exist, for in the 1890s and early 1900s the triumph of the modern corporation and the corporate state did not seem final or inevitable. Among the Americans who opted for an alternative to the capitalist system were the many Western workers who became the backbone of the IWW.

# 2

## The Urban-Industrial Frontier, 1890–1905

Nowhere in the late nineteenth century were the economic and social changes that produced American reform and radicalism so rapid and so unsettling as in the mining West. There, in a short time, industrial cities replaced frontier boom camps and heavily capitalized corporations displaced grubstaking prospectors. The profitable mining of refractory ores (gold and silver) and base metals (lead, zinc, and copper) required railroads, advanced technology, large milling and smelting facilities, and intensive capitalization. "The result," in the words of Rodman Paul, "was that [by 1880] many mining settlements were carried well beyond any stage that could reasonably be called the frontier. They became, instead, industrial islands in the midst of forest, desert, or mountain." During the 1890s and early 1900s, continued economic growth carried Western mining communities still further beyond the frontier stage.

Elsewhere in America it took as long as two centuries for the transformation from handicraft economy to machine production, from individual proprietor to impersonal corporation, from village to city. Even with this slow pace of development in older communities, the shock of change had proved unsettling to millions. In the West, where communities grew from villages to industrial cities, mining enterprises evolved from primitive techniques to modern technology, from the small business to the giant corporation, if not overnight, at least within a generation, and this transformation proved even more disruptive of old habits and traditional attitudes.

As early as 1876, Colorado, though sparsely settled and far distant from the nation's primary industrial centers, had been colonized by corporations and company towns. Leadville, for example, stood as a monument to the urban frontier in America. Eighty air miles southwest of Denver, nearly 2 miles above sea level, surrounded by towering mountain peaks and shrouded in low-lying clouds (from which it derived its other name, Cloud City), it was by 1880 the metropolis of a Lake County mining community with 35,000 people. Leadville had had a varied history. Gold, discovered in 1858, had first attracted to the mountain settlement called Oro City all the odds and ends of society commonly found in rowdy mining camps. Oro City was at first no more urban or industrial than the California mining camps immortalized in the stories of Bret Harte and Mark Twain. As had happened in many of California's boom camps, dreams of fortune founded upon gold soon dissolved. In Oro City this occurred in 1876, the year Colorado was admitted to the Union. In 1878, however, newly unearthed rich sources of another mineral caused Oro City to be renamed Leadville. Within three years, the population soared from 200 to 14,280.

Now publicized as the greatest silver camp in the world, Leadville became by 1880 a leading producer of lead-silver ores, products requiring large-scale processing, intensive capitalization, and skilled labor. Within a few years Leadville had developed into a middle-sized urban settlement with a heterogeneous population, a varied social structure, a thriving economy, and ample educational and cultural institutions.

Cripple Creek, a once isolated region hidden by Pike's Peak, grew more rapidly than Leadville. In 1891 Bob Womack, the legendary Western cowpuncher and prospector, discovered gold in Poverty Gulch, though he himself died poor. That same year W. S. Stratton, a local building contractor, struck the Independence vein on the site of what later became Victor, Colorado; unlike the cowboy Womack, Stratton the entrepreneur died rich, leaving a fortune of $20 million. By 1893 Cripple Creek was known far and wide as the greatest gold camp in America. Its gold output, valued at $1,903 in 1891, increased to more than $2 million by 1893 and rose each year thereafter until it peaked at $18,199,736 in 1900. By then Cripple Creek proudly was advertising its ten thousand inhabitants, three railroads, trolleys, electric lights, hospitals, and schools.

Montana repeated the Colorado pattern. Its production of ores, valued at $41 million in 1889, made it the nation's leading mining state, while Butte, "the richest hill in the world," had become America's copper capital. Idaho, on a lesser scale, recapitulated the developmental pattern of Montana and Colorado. And Arizona, in the 1890s and early 1900s still a territory (it did not become a state until 1912), proved remarkably similar in social evolution to its northern neighbors. At Bisbee, near the Mexican border and hard by Tombstone, where the Earps shot it out with the Clantons at the O.K. Corral, Phelps Dodge Corporation built an industrial city. Like company towns everywhere, it had its corporation-owned church, hospital, store, and homes.

The industrial cities of the mining West represented in microcosm the emerging conditions of life in urbanized, industrial America rather than the simpler social arrangements of the passing frontier. These mill and smelter towns, with their shoddy company houses and stores, their saloons, and their working-class populations, bore a distinct resemblance to their Eastern industrial counterparts, with this additional difference: In the West the very rapidity of economic growth brought greater unrest, conflict, violence, and radicalism.

The high costs associated with discovering, extracting, processing, and transporting metal ores led inevitably to large-scale business operation. The large corporation could more easily finance its own geological surveys and then exploit its findings more fully and cheaply. As prices declined and the cost of extracting ores from deeper beneath the earth's surface rose, only operations able to spread fixed capital costs over increased productivity could survive. Large corporations were also in a better position than their smaller competitors to exact favorable rates from railroads, smelters, and refineries. So, in the West as in the East, large corporations devoured smaller, less efficient, or less capitalized firms.

In constructing its mining empire in the Arizona territory, Phelps Dodge colonized a region known more for its badmen and buttes, its Apaches and U.S. Cavalry, than for its mineral riches. But Phelps Dodge had the capital and the business skills requisite to turn a barren frontier into an industrial citadel. Unlike small local enterprises, Phelps Dodge worked the deeper refractory ores and erected its own refining and transportation facilities. The company literally built the cities of Bisbee and Warren, while the neighboring community of Douglas, a refining center, bore the company president's name. Between 1885 and 1908 Phelps Dodge extracted over 730 million pounds of copper from its famous Copper Queen mine at Bisbee, reaping dividends of over $30 million.

Not satisfied with economic hegemony in the Warren district, Phelps Dodge gained control of copper production further north at Morenci. There it established an even larger, more efficient smelting operation. Large-scale investment raised Morenci's production from about seven million pounds in 1897 to over eighteen million in 1902, and twenty-four million by 1908. By 1910 the Arizona territory was a world leader in copper production; only seven years later, on the eve of World War I, a handful of companies, led by Phelps Dodge, controlled the new state's mining economy.

Corporate concentration had far-reaching implications for Western workers. As national corporations replaced local enterprises, Western workers and labor leaders suddenly began fondly to recall how easy it had once been to see the head of a local concern and work out amicable arrangements to settle most disputes. Giant corporations, by contrast, did not allow local managers to make ultimate labor policy, and workers and union spokesmen could rarely interview the general officers, who were usually situated in distant cities. Local managers would refuse to settle disputes, claiming they could not go beyond their instructions from the home office. The home office in turn would pass the buck back to its local agents. Workers and union negotiators were caught uncomfortably in the middle.

The workers who filled the industrial cities of the West shared a common language, a certain degree of ethnic similarity, and a tradition of union organization. Unions organized by miners in the 1860s on the Comstock Lode in Nevada had grown and prospered, defending existing wages in bad times and obtaining increases in good times. From there the union idea had spread to other mining districts.

Ethnic ties increased union solidarity. Census statistics disclose that, unlike other American industrial centers of that era, all the major mining districts in Colorado, Idaho, and Montana were dominated by native-born majorities. Moreover, the foreign-born came largely from the British Isles (including Ireland) and Scandinavia and were hardly representative of the more recent waves of immigration. A look at the names published in the Western Federation of Miners (WFM) directory of officers printed regularly by the *Miners' Magazine* demonstrates the overwhelmingly Anglo-Saxon origins of the organization's local and national leadership.

The miners, foreign-born and American, were also skilled workers. Cornishmen who had mined lead in their home country were brought to America for their known skills. Irishmen, too, were recruited primarily as skilled miners. And many a native-born American had long since forsaken prospecting and the hope of striking it rich for the steadier returns of skilled wage labor. There is every reason to believe that as mining became more complex and costly, mine and smelter operators preferred skilled, regular workmen to "pioneers" or "frontiersmen" and that wage differentials attracted European and Eastern miners to the American West. John Calderwood, the first union leader at Cripple Creek, entered the coal mines at the age of nine and thereafter devoted his life to mining, including brief attendance at mining school. Ed Boyce, the first successful president of the WFM (1896–1903) and an Irish immigrant, worked as a miner from 1884 until his election to the union presidency; his successor, Charles Moyer, had been a skilled worker in the Lead, South Dakota, smelter complex. And the most famous of all mountain West labor leaders, William D. "Big Bill" Haywood, entered the mines as a teenager and worked in them until his election as secretary-treasurer of the WFM in 1901.

Although the workers of the mountain West were not wild and woolly frontiersmen, they did differ in important respects from their counterparts in the East and in Europe. Fred Thompson, former editor of the IWW's *Industrial*

*Worker,* has expressed these differences as he remembers them from his own experiences as a "working stiff": "Their frontier was a psychological fact—a rather deliberate avoidance of certain conventions, a break with the bondage to the past. . . . Individuality and solidarity or sense of community flourished here together, and with a radical social philosophy." Thompson ascribes Western working-class uniqueness to the inherent character or personality of the worker. He believes the Western working force was made up of men who had consciously chosen to cut loose from unprofitable farms, strikebound Eastern factories, or the security of immigrant enclaves.

Although Thompson apparently perceives a direct relationship between the extent of footlooseness and the growth of radicalism, other factors are more important in accounting for Western differences. First, labor was scarcer in the West, and this scarcity encouraged footlooseness (not vice versa); workers moved where wages were highest and conditions best. Second, ethnic divisions were not as sharp in the West. Though employers attempted to recruit heterogeneous work forces to reduce labor solidarity, they did not succeed as completely as they did in the East. When eastern and southern Europeans were introduced into the Western work force, they never dominated a community quite as they had in the coal-mining and steel-making communities of Pennsylvania; instead, they were quickly either socially ostracized or integrated into the Western community of English-speaking workers. (Ethnic conflict was not altogether absent among Western workers; no two nationalities disliked each other more intensely than Cornishmen and Irishmen.) Third, social institutions were not as firmly established in the West. Finally, most Western workers lived in mining communities, where men derived their sustenance by daily risking their lives in the bowels of the earth. Western mining centers shared with mining communities the world over the group solidarity and radicalism derived from relative physical isolation and dangerous, underground work.

Owing largely to the ethnic composition and solidarity of Western mining communities and to the reliance of local merchants and professionals upon miners' patronage, workers and local businessmen were not at first split into hostile factions. Local businessmen and farmers often supported the miners in their struggle for union recognition and higher wages. In Idaho's mineral-rich Coeur d'Alenes the local residents—farmer and merchant, journalist and physician, public official and skilled worker—sympathized with striking miners.

Into these mining communities the modern corporation intruded to disrupt the local peace and to drive a wedge between workers and their non-working-class allies. The 1890s were an uneasy decade for American businesses, and for none more so than mining, milling, and smelting. The falling price of silver, the depression of 1893, the repeal of the Sherman Silver Purchase Act, and the inherent instability of extractive industries made mine owners and smelter operators eager to reduce production costs and consequently less tolerant of labor's demands. Mining corporations formed associations to pressure railroads by threatening to close down mining properties and cease shipments unless shipping rates declined. But capitalists found it easier to make savings by substituting capital for labor.

Technological innovations increased productivity but in so doing diluted the importance of traditional skills and disrupted established patterns of work. Although technological change did not usually decrease total earnings, it tended to lower piece rates and to reduce some formerly skilled workers to unskilled positions with lower earning potential. In Bill Haywood's hyperbolic language, "There was no means of escaping from the gigantic force that was relentlessly crushing all of them beneath its cruel heel. The people of these dreadful mining camps were in a fever of revolt."

Haywood exaggerated only slightly. The modernization and corporatization of the mining industry indeed aggravated the miners' traditional job grievances. If technological innovation did not irritate miners, company-owned stores, saloons, and boarding houses charging noncompetitive prices did. If miners accepted changing job classifications and skill dilutions, they refused to tolerate false economies achieved by providing insufficient mine ventilation and timbering and by cutting down on other safety measures.

Whatever their grievances, Western miners discovered that only through organization could they obtain redress. Employers, however, failed to appreciate the benefits of union organization. Hence for a decade and a half, miners and mine owners struggled for economic power and security.

Modern miners' unions first emerged in Butte in 1878, when on June 13 local workers organized the Butte Miners' Union (later to become Local 1 in the WFM, its largest and richest affiliate) to defend workers against proposed wage reductions and to maintain the $3.50 daily minimum for underground workers. The union grew rapidly, succeeded in its defense of prevailing wage rates, and accumulated a full treasury. Labor leaders trained in Butte and money accumulated there were later to play a prominent role in union organization elsewhere.

Not for another decade, however, did an association of miners' unions develop. Then, in 1888 or 1889, Idaho miners in the Coeur d'Alene camps of Burke, Gem, Mullan, and Wardner formed the Coeur d'Alene Executive Miners' Union. Here violent labor conflict was to occur, and here labor organization began to cross state lines as Butte miners provided legal counsel and strike funds for their Idaho comrades.

Before the 1880s the immensely rich Coeur d'Alene district was hidden in a northern Idaho mountain wilderness. The whole area, consisting of a narrow east-west belt 30 miles long and 10 miles wide, was surrounded on all sides by the peaks of the Coeur d'Alene Mountains. The main canyon was barely wide enough to contain a railroad, and subsidiary canyons leading to the main mine sites were even narrower. Such mining towns as Gem and Mullan consisted of a single street, with homes and saloons backed up against mountain walls.

In 1887, a narrow-gauge railroad finally made its way into the main canyon, inaugurating the growth of large-scale mining. Three years later the Northern Pacific and the Union Pacific reached the district, making operations even more profitable. With the railroads came new investors. The most productive local mine, the Bunker Hill and Sullivan, was purchased in 1887 by the Portland, Oregon, capitalist Simeon G. Reed. Not long thereafter, Reed sold out to a San Francisco–New York capitalist combine organized by John Hays Hammond, a world-famous mining engineer.

But large-scale investment also brought to the region new mine managers eager to discipline local labor. Almost as soon as Simeon Reed had assumed ownership of the Bunker Hill, his resident manager advised, "I want the privilege to employ one confidential man, who quietly and unostentatiously reports to me all about our employees. . . . His salary would be a trifle compared with the services he might render us." And so labor spies came to the district. Two years later, Reed's next manager, Victor Clement, reported that local mine owners had formed an association for mutual benefit and protection, particularly in dealing with railroads and smelters. But Clement added, "Will also endeavor to regulate many abuses in the labor question."

The labor "abuses" referred to were caused by the policies of the Coeur d'Alene Executive Miners' Union. This local labor organization, generally moderate in its attitudes and policies, sought to maintain the union shop, minimum wages for underground workers regardless of skill, and its own union-financed hospitals and medical services.

Mine managers, faced with competition from other nonunion lead-silver districts as well as with railroad and smelter rates they considered too high, decided to crack down on labor. In order to reduce labor costs through increased productivity, they had introduced air drills, an innovation that forced many miners to accept less skilled jobs.* But the unions had insisted upon and won a $3.50 daily minimum for all underground workers. Obviously the mine

* A single miner with an air drill could produce considerably more per unit of time, thus increasing the demand for less skilled workers (muckers) to shovel the ore more rapidly—a prime reason the unions made two men to a drill a major bargaining demand.

owners could not reduce costs sufficiently while local unions remained so powerful. Employers again looked to private detectives to assist them in breaking labor's hold on the district; in this endeavor they turned to Charlie Siringo, the self-proclaimed "Cowboy Detective." Given employment at the Gem Mine under the assumed name of Allison, Siringo joined the local union. Ingratiating himself with union men by his generosity, Allison/Siringo won election as recording secretary of the Gem local of the Coeur d'Alene Executive Miners' Union.

Knowing in advance what to expect from the unions, the mine owners promptly cracked down on their workers. On New Year's Day, 1892, district mines announced an impending shutdown to remain in effect until local railroads reduced their shipping charges. Within two weeks of the announcement every district mine had closed, leaving unemployed workers to contend with a subzero northern Idaho winter. Although managers hoped their action would lead to fairer rates from the railroads, they were equally certain that a winter of discontent would weaken the local unions and make a wage reduction easier to effect. So on March 27 employers reduced the minimum wage for underground work from $3.50 to $3 a day.

Winter unemployment, however, had failed to weaken the union's will or its power. Miners still demanded the "traditional" $3.50, no less! Informed by Siringo that the unions would not compromise, the owners withdrew their wage offer of March 27, and rather than work their mines at what they deemed too high a cost (especially given the depressed market for lead-zinc ores), they decided to keep them closed until June 1.

At this point, April–May 1892, the miners and their unions remained in control of the primary sources of local power. Few, if any, local men would scab. The major district newspapers, the county government whose sheriff and deputy were union men elected by union votes, and the local justices of the peace, who also were either union men or sympathizers, supported the miners' unions. Similar support came from many area merchants, doctors, lawyers, and even farmers. Moreover, the Butte Miners' Union had amassed a $5,000 cash loan for the Coeur d'Alene miners, and it had also assessed its own members $5 monthly for a strike fund.

Yet the employers possessed two important and, in the last analysis, determining weapons: money and influence. Unable to control the local law or to sway the district's non-working-class population, they approached federal judges and the governor of the state for assistance. From one such judge, James H. Beatty, mine owners in May 1892 obtained an injunction that forbade union members to trespass upon company property, interfere in any way with mining operations, or intimidate company employees. In effect, this and subsequent injunctions restricted picketing and all union efforts to induce strikebreakers to leave the mines. But court decrees could not provide labor to work the mines.

At this point the labor conflict took a strange and violent turn. From March through early July the unemployed miners had maintained a united but peaceful front. Knowing their employers were unable to secure an adequate supply of strikebreakers, the union men quietly waited for their bosses to surrender. But on July 11 the strike-lockout stalemate was unexpectedly altered. *What* happened on that day is clear; *why* it happened is not. Union members, who had been peaceful and law-abiding for three months, suddenly armed themselves, formed into an attacking force, and seized two mines. During the attack two men were killed, six were injured, and company property was destroyed. The circumstances of the July 11 incident are suspicious, to say the least. Only a few days before, employers had learned from Governor Willey that President Harrison had turned down their request for troops because the Coeur d'Alene district was peaceful. Allegedly, the mine owners had been taken by surprise, enabling the miners to capture the two mines so easily. Yet Siringo was at the time a trusted union member who would certainly have had knowledge of a premeditated union attack, and he would just as certainly have passed such knowledge on to his employers well before July 11. His role as a company spy was not discovered until that very day (July 11), when he made a hasty and ignominious escape from union headquarters and fled the district. Yet Siringo who had been reporting to the employers regularly on union tactics, forwarded no advance notice of the most important single step allegedly planned by the miners.

Whatever the circumstances, the events of July 11 decisively altered the local balance of power, turning it away from the unions and toward the mine owners. If the employers neither planned nor provoked the violent attack, they were nevertheless its only beneficiaries. Immediately after the July 11 union attack, mine owners demanded aid from Willey and from Idaho's congressional delegation. With each passing hour the employers appeared to become more frantic, as did Willey's own attorney general, who telegrammed Idaho's U.S. senators: "The mob must be crushed by overwhelming force. We can't retreat now." Still more panicky a little later, he added, "Gatling guns and small howitzers . . . should be sent. The woods may have to be shelled. Nothing but overwhelming force will . . . prevent serious fight." Under these circumstances—an outburst of violence by long-suffering workers (or perhaps instigated by their employ-ers) and a great deal of rhetorical blood and thunder drummed up by employ-ers and state officials—Willey and the mine owners obtained from the White House the federal troops they desired.

Within three days of the initial union "outbreak" (which passed as sudden-ly as it had come), federal troops had the situation well in hand. At Governor Willey's suggestion, the military authorities acted decisively, arresting over 600 men, 350 of whom were held in custody between July 16 and 20. The arrestees included top union officials, justices of the peace George Pettibone and Wil-liam Frazier, and Peter Breen, the liaison between the Butte Miners' Union and the Coeur d'Alene unions, who had been extracited from Montana. Where once employers had complained to the governor about a union-created "reign of terror," miners now railed against the "terror" inflicted on them by a pow-erful government-business alliance.

There was some justice in the miners' complaints, for the federal troops on duty in the Coeur d'Alenes clearly made themselves a union-busting tool for employers. State and federal officials offered the imprisoned union men their freedom, but only on condition that they implicate their organization in the July 11 violence and renounce future union activity. To a man, the prisoners refused the offer, insisting instead that they had broken no law and would not sign an anti-union declaration even if it meant an additional ten years in prison.

Federal and state authorities meanwhile prosecuted a select group of pris-oners. In two separate federal trials, Judge Beatty found seventeen union men guilty of violating his injunctions; thirteen of them he declared guilty of con-tempt of court, a civil offense, and sentenced to short terms in the Ada Coun-ty jail, but he found the other four guilty of criminal conspiracy, sentencing them to two years' imprisonment at the Detroit House of Correction. Almost simultaneously the state brought murder charges against forty-two strikers. But here the prosecution had to depend upon a jury verdict (Beatty had handed down his decisions from the bench), and it lacked the evidence to convict. Losing the first in a planned series of murder trials, the state never tried an-other defendant. Even Beatty's verdicts did not go unchallenged. James H. Hawley, attorney for the miners' unions, appealed Beatty's criminal convic-tions to the United States Supreme Court, which in March 1893 overturned them. The Supreme Court majority declared that Beatty had abused his au-thority by using federal power to punish men for violation of what could only be considered a state law.

The mine owners lost more than the legal cases arising out of the Coeur d'Alene conflict. Despite their use of strikebreakers, injunctions, and troops, they also failed to break the local unions. By 1894, in fact, miners' unions had reestablished themselves more strongly than ever in all but one (Bunker Hill) of the district mines. Most important, the owners' aggressive anti-union tactics served to bring into the open conditions that would plague Western labor relations for the next decade. The first war of the Coeur d'Alenes demonstrated the degree to which miners' unions dominated the local community, its news sources, its law agencies, its sympathies. Employers as a result resorted to strikebreakers. But imported workers only increased community hostility toward employers and led to yet sharper conflict. The ensuing violence, in turn, permitted employers to request and usually to obtain state and federal assistance. Troops, martial law, and trials followed inevitably, and whatever the immediate result, a heritage of hatred and class resentment was left behind.

The Coeur d'Alene labor leaders, imprisoned in Ada County Jail, had ample time to consider mine labor's plight. They perceived, with the advice of their lawyer, Hawley, that the dominance of the mining industry by national corporations had drastically altered the miner's existence, and they soon agreed among themselves that only a national organization of hard-rock miners could defend labor's rights against powerful interstate corporations. Hence agitation for a new labor organization began in earnest in March 1893. Soon thereafter, the Butte Miners' Union issued a call to Western hard-rock miners to convene in Butte on May 15. On that day, delegates from Idaho, Nevada, Utah, Colorado, Montana, and South Dakota arrived in Butte. Within five days they adopted a constitution, elected permanent officers, and created the Western Federation of Miners (WFM).

The infant WFM, in the spirit of other labor organizations of the era, grandiloquently proclaimed as its purpose "to unite the various miners' unions of the west into one central body; to practice those virtues that adorn society and remind man of his duty to his fellow men; the elevation of the position and the maintenance of the rights of the miner."

Reading such modest goals in 1893, no one could have foreseen that four years later a WFM president would call for union rifle clubs and for the establishment of a dual Western labor organization, nor that seven years later the WFM would endorse socialism, nor that in 1905 it would found the IWW. Indeed, the WFM almost died in infancy. When its second convention met in 1894, the organization was barely viable, and 1895 proved no better: That year two presidents of the WFM failed to complete their terms in office. The prospect for 1896 looked equally bleak. But the 1896 convention elected Ed Boyce as president, and his firm leadership, combined with the return of prosperity, restored life to the organization. By 1899 the WFM had entered a period of brief but impressive growth.

But as it grew, the WFM more often came into conflict with its business opponents and their allies in the courthouses and statehouses, and even in the White House. For a full decade, 1894–1904, violent labor conflict shattered the peace of the mountain states. From the fires of these struggles emerged the radicals who ultimately founded the IWW.

# 3

## The Class War on the Industrial Frontier, 1894–1905

Born in the aftermath of a violent labor conflict in which the combined power of private business, state authorities, and federal troops had subdued rebellious miners, the Western Federation of Miners (WFM) matured during a series of even more explosive industrial wars. Scarcely a year passed between 1894 and 1904 without WFM affiliates becoming involved in disputes with employers—disputes that often resulted in violence, loss of property and life, and military intervention.

These industrial conflicts molded Western labor's attitudes toward employers, society, and the state. Scarred and embittered by a decade of industrial warfare, many Western workers turned violently against the existing social order, found both an explanation and a remedy for their predicament in Marxist theory, and became in time the most radical and militant sector of the American labor movement.

During the ten years from 1894 to 1904, Western miners waged armed war with their capitalist adversaries. Miners' unions sometimes purchased and stocked rifles and ammunition, drilled in military fashion, and prepared if all else failed to achieve their objectives with rifle, torch, and dynamite stick. This resort to violence did not lack substantial reason, for mine operators proved equally martial, and usually less compromising, than their labor union foes. Businessmen also stored arms and ammunition; they, too, on occasion resorted to dynamite, hired Pinkerton men and agents provocateurs, and paid private armies to defend their properties when public authorities refused to provide such protection. Given the preparations and precautions undertaken by business and labor combatants, it is no wonder that contending armies clashed on the industrial battlefield at Cripple Creek in 1894, that mines were put to the torch at Leadville in 1896, or that armed miners seized a train and destroyed an ore concentrator in the Coeur d'Alenes in 1899.

When the mine owners had solidified their power locally as well as nationally, the workers' only alternative to submission became real class warfare. As the WFM waged one battle after another, it learned that the state was allied to capital, that Democrats were no better than Republicans, and that old friends could not be trusted. Only through internal organization and class solidarity could labor hope to find immediate security and ultimate salvation.

For a time, despite or possibly even because of the opposition's strength, the WFM thrived. The years between the unsuccessful 1899 struggle in the Coeur d'Alenes and the resumption of labor warfare in Colorado in 1903 were the union's golden age. In November 1901 the *Miners' Magazine* reported that the preceding six months had been the most prosperous in the union's life, with almost all of its affiliates increasing their membership and twenty new locals added. The WFM chartered another twenty locals the following year, and even considered the possibility of extending the organization across the border to Mexico. Early in 1903, on the eve of a brutal and decisive conflict in Colorado, the executive board reported that membership had increased by another one-third. At the same session the board recommended that the union's ritual and constitution be translated into Italian, Slavic, and Finnish to encourage solidarity among nationalities that had become increasingly important in the industry.

In the spring of 1903, then, the WFM's future seemed bright. Yet a year later the organization lay in a shambles. What happened in so short a time to turn success into failure, a glowing future into a despairing present?

The answer is not hard to find. As the WFM increased in strength and enjoyed continued success, Western employers became more anxious and hostile. Large nationwide corporations with Western interests particularly desired to weaken the miners' union before it became strong enough to demand a share of economic power in the industry. Consequently, business interests in Colorado decided to force the issue with the unions.

WFM leaders saw what was happening. They knew that in 1902 Colorado's mine owners had formed a statewide association to combat the miners' unions with money, propaganda, and Pinkertons. They also knew that larger corporate interests, through a combination of economic pressure and appeals to class loyalty, were enlisting local businessmen and professionals, previously allied to the miners, in a growing anti-union coalition. So it was hardly surprising when in February 1903 Charles Moyer, Boyce's successor as WFM president, complained, "We are being attacked on all sides by the Mill Trust and Mine Owners' Association."

Yet union officials reacted cautiously. Moyer emphasized that the WFM's purpose was to build, not to destroy: to avoid by all honorable means a war between employer and employee. At the same time, William D. Haywood probably described the union's position more accurately when he stated, "We are not opposed to employers, and it is our purpose and aim to work harmoniously and jointly with employers as best we can under this system, and we intend to change the system if we get sufficiently organized and well enough educated to do so."

WFM leaders clearly distinguished their long-term from their immediate goals. Whatever their ultimate objectives—and by 1902 they included a socialist society—their immediate demands hardly differed from those commonly sought by American Federation of Labor (AFL) affiliates.

But corporate interests in Colorado, like those elsewhere in America, disliked the short-term AFL goals as much as they detested the WFM's ultimate objectives. Corporations would not compromise with labor, in the short or the long run. Consequently, the delicately balanced modus vivendi between capital and labor collapsed in Colorado's mining districts and a miniature civil war erupted. It is well to examine why.

Secure in their control of most of Colorado's mining regions, in 1902–3 WFM leaders tried to carry organization a stage further by increasing union membership among the men who toiled in the state's mills and smelters. Compared to miners, millmen and smeltermen were poorly paid and overworked. By 1903 Colorado miners had had an eight-hour day for almost a decade; mill and smelter workers still labored up to ten or twelve hours daily. Miners maintained a $3.50 daily minimum wage; refinery workers' wages began at $1.80. Underground miners were well organized, mill workers barely organized.

The WFM chose as its new organizing target the reduction plants at Colorado City, where they chartered a smeltermen's local in August 1902. Colorado City was chosen because three major companies—Portland, Telluride, and Standard (the latter a subsidiary of United States Reduction and Refining)—refined ores shipped there from the Cripple Creek district. More important, as a working-class suburb of Colorado Springs it had a local power structure sympathetic to unionism.

As soon as the local union had been organized, however, the refining companies, led by Standard, counterattacked. Standard's general superintendent, J. D. Hawkins, immediately hired a Pinkerton agent who infiltrated the new local, reporting its activities and the names of its members to the company. As Hawkins learned the names of the employees who had joined the union, they were promptly fired.

It was to combat this anti-union tactic that Haywood himself came to Colorado City in October 1902 to demand Hawkins's permission to organize the mills. Haywood minced no words in expounding his union's position. He bluntly accused the superintendent of discharging workers solely on the basis of their union membership. Hawkins just as bluntly conceded the truth of Haywood's charges, emphasizing that the company would use its full powers to prevent union organization.

As rapidly as the union organized men, the company discharged them. Finally, in February 1903, matters came to a head. Standard, which until then had been firing union men one at a time, now removed twenty-three at once. The local union reacted immediately, on February 14 declaring a strike against all three Colorado City mills. The next day the smeltermen's local presented its demands to general manager Charles M. McNeill of Standard, allowing him ten days to reply. In retrospect, the union's manifesto seems exceedingly moderate: "We . . . desire the prosperity of the company and so far as our skill and labor go will do all we can to promote its interests. We cannot understand how any fair and reasonable company should discriminate against union labor."

But McNeill answered the union's moderation with recalcitrance and bitter hostility, and industrial conflict came to Colorado City. The Colorado City strike followed the pattern already well established in Western labor conflicts. When the workers walked out on February 14 they effectively closed down refining operations. Supported by the local community and its public officials, union pickets and deputy sheriffs patrolled the town and stopped strikebreakers from entering the area. But employers, also following the traditional script, outflanked labor, appealing for assistance to Republican governor James H. Peabody, from whom, on March 3, they obtained state troops. Three days after dispatching the militia for strike duty, Peabody explained to a mill official his unique brand of impartiality. "The placing of the troops at Colorado City," the governor wrote, was as much for the protection of workmen as the operators." Yet Peabody had ordered his militia officers to protect only the workers still in the mills, not those on strike; in fact, he had ordered the troops to curb most picketing.

Consequently, union leaders anxiously sought to settle the strike they had never wanted, asking only that the mills not discriminate against union men and that the workers already discharged for union membership be reinstated without prejudice. Even Governor Peabody agreed that these were reasonable demands, and he urged McNeill to accept the WFM's revised terms.

The governor eventually succeeded in arranging a conference between labor and management, which might have been productive had it not been for McNeill of Standard. After an all-day and all-evening session with Peabody on March 14, WFM officials and representatives of the Portland and Telluride mills agreed to settle the dispute on the basis of union proposals. More important, both companies consented to bargain with a union committee—in itself a major triumph for the principle of union recognition. But McNeill remained obdurate. Still insistent upon dictating to the union on a take-it-or-leave-it basis, McNeill absolutely refused to recognize any union committees.

In bringing the Portland and Telluride mills to terms with the union, Governor Peabody had been labor's friend. He seemed more so on March 19 when he withdrew the militia from Colorado City. But on that same day the governor described to a wealthy New York banker how he actually felt: "I feel sure that my action in enforcing law and order in Colorado, and notifying the lawless and law-violating element [i.e., WFM members] that they must obey the mandates of legal authority, has received the approval of the investing class of people, not only in Colorado, but throughout the country, and I can assure you . . . there will be no destruction to life and property if I can prevent it."

Moyer and Haywood, both well aware of the governor's basic antilabor attitude, realized they could not trust Peabody to bring McNeill closer to the WFM's bargaining position. So they warned the governor that unless McNeill negotiated with the union, Cripple Creek's miners might strike in sympathy with the millmen.

Cripple Creek's unions indeed had already threatened to strike mines that shipped ore to any of Standard's mills. But first they allowed district businessmen an opportunity to persuade McNeill to accept the WFM's terms. When he still refused to budge, Cripple Creek's mine owners were left with an unpalatable alternative: Either stop shipping ore to the Standard mill or be shut down by a sympathetic strike.

District businessmen who had lived peacefully with the miners' union for a decade saw no reason why McNeill could not do the same. They saw even less reason why an unnecessary labor conflict arising from the Standard manager's intransigence should cause mine owners to suffer hardship. Failing to persuade McNeill to negotiate with the union, Cripple Creek's businessmen next promised employment to any union member discharged by Standard. Meanwhile, they pleaded with Peabody to bring the Colorado City disputants together again for another attempt to settle the strike.

The governor decided upon one last effort to end the dispute. On March 19 he invited union leaders and company officials to appear before an advisory commission established to investigate the entire dispute. Both the union and the company, though less than enthusiastic about the idea, consented to appear before the governor's commission.

While powerless to enforce their findings, Peabody's commissioners hoped that open hearings might result in a mutually satisfactory understanding between the company and the WFM. But this could not be. The commissioners, in fact, soon found themselves investigating a labor dispute whose very existence was denied by the attorney for the United States Reduction Company. Claiming that the Standard "mill is full of men contented and anxious to remain in the employ of the company," the attorney denied that there were any issues about which to bargain. Moyer, however, continued to represent men who were discontented, who had been discharged for union membership, and who had struck but had never been reinstated. He again insisted that the company recognize the rights of the aggrieved workers and bargain with the union.

Unable to resolve these basic differences through public sessions, the advisory commission met privately on March 28–29 in Colorado Springs with union and company officials. At these closed sessions a settlement was finally hammered out that concentrated on two points: reinstatement of union members and strikers, and union recognition. McNeill finally consented to meet with Moyer and any union members in his employ, provided there was no reference to their union affiliation. In short, McNeill would meet with union officials but he would not negotiate with a trade union. Moyer, desperately eager to avert the full-scale labor war impending in the Cripple Creek district, accepted this compromise formula.

But after agreeing to reinstate discharged union men and to employ union members without discrimination, McNeill procrastinated. When Moyer and the WFM repeatedly protested delays in rehiring union men, McNeill insisted that productivity was too low to increase employment, and that the company could not remove loyal nonunion workers to make work for union members. It seems clear that the Standard official remained committed to his original intention of smashing the union.

Unable to weaken McNeill's resistance, WFM leaders now decided to throw their entire union's resources into the struggle for the right to organize and the principle of union recognition. This meant using union strength in Colorado's mining districts, most notably Cripple Creek.

The WFM mistakenly believed that in Cripple Creek it dealt from a strong hand, even a stacked deck. With some few exceptions, most notably the mayor of the town of Victor (himself a mine owner), the union controlled district public officials. Most local merchants, moreover, did a rousing business with the well-paid and free-spending miners. The local unions owned substantial buildings, had ample treasuries, and members who (as Haywood later remembered them) were "widely read men, and as of high a standard of intelligence, as could be found among workingmen anywhere."

But the employers now dealt from an even more carefully stacked deck. Through the spring of 1903 they had diligently been organizing a common businessmen's front to combat unionism and to win the assistance of the state government. In this they had been encouraged immeasurably by McNeill's successful resistance to the WFM. As their counterpart to the WFM, Colorado businessmen had on April 9, 1903, inaugurated the Citizens' Alliance movement. Soon nearly every mining community in the state had its Alliance; by October 25, 1903, when a statewide organization was born, the Alliance movement boasted a membership of over thirty thousand. To members of these new organizations, the "open shop" meant a company closed to union members, "proper" bargaining implied no negotiations with unions, and opposition to "class legislation" was applied to laws benefiting labor, never to measures favoring capital.

In whatever they did or proposed, the Alliances had the active encouragement of Colorado's governor. James H. Peabody possessed all the traits and ideas antilabor employers could possibly desire in the occupant of a statehouse. No governor in the United States more conscientiously fought labor. To Peabody, no welfare legislation ever seemed justified, no merely halfway restrictions upon trade unions satisfactory. He had worked himself up from shopkeeper to shop owner to bank president to governor; why could not Colorado's workers do the same for themselves without the aid of labor unions?

Publicly pledged to battle for his principles, Peabody cooperated with the Citizens' Alliance movement and even helped to organize an Alliance in his home town of Canyon City. In Colorado it became hard to determine whether the Republican party was a branch of the Alliance or vice versa. In the governor's mind there was no doubt: The two were identical! He advised Colorado Republicans to take as their slogan "the maintenance of law and order within our boundaries." His firm stance elicited admiring letters from all over the nation. "All the conservative interests in the country are deeply interested in your fight," one admirer assured him.

That Peabody meant precisely what he said soon became evident to WFM leaders. The governor had sent the militia when Colorado City mill managers had complained about largely nonexistent labor violence, but some months later, when WFM members were forcibly and brutally deported from Idaho Springs by the local mine owners' association, Peabody found the state's power unequal to the occasion. Apparently, Colorado could protect scabs' right to employment but not union members' right to dwell peaceably in their own community.

Under attack all over Colorado by a business-government alliance, the WFM decided to put its power to the test. On August 8, 1903, WFM members in the Cripple Creek district struck mines that had continued to ship ore to nonunion mills. That decision, not taken without grave misgivings, unleashed one of the most brutal class conflicts in American history.

The Cripple Creek strike at first appeared perfectly ordinary. Throughout August, although the mines remained shut and both sides held fast to their preconflict positions, peace prevailed. Strikers, supported by the sheriff, patrolled roads and depots, successfully keeping strikebreakers out of the district.

But Peabody and his conservative "law and order" backers could not allow labor to triumph. On September 2 Cripple Creek businessmen petitioned the governor for troops, and the following day Peabody dispatched an investigating committee to the district. Interviewing mine owners, businessmen, and the few anti-union politicians available (while studicusly avoiding union members and their sympathizers), Peabody's investigators on September 4 recommended that the governor send troops to Cripple Creek. That same day, despite the opposition of union officials, Teller County's commissioners, the county sheriff, and the Victor city council, all of whom denied any collapse in local law and order, Peabody dispatched the militia.

The officer in charge was General Sherman Bell, who promptly won a notorious place in American labor history. Bell's command preserved neither law nor order, nor did it apprehend criminals. Instead, when it served their purposes the troops violated the law, including the state and federal constitutions. Bell regularly appealed to "military necessity which recognizes no laws, either civil or social." Major McClelland, his junior officer, remarked, "To hell with the constitution, we aren't going by the constitution." Bell stated the purpose of his mission with terse brutality: "I came to do up this damned anarchistic federation."

And why shouldn't he "do it up"? Peabody had arranged with the Mine Owners' Association to pay the cost of placing the militia in the field. Colorado's troops clearly served private capital more than the public interest. To the governor, of course, the state and capitalism were synonymous.

Yet despite military repression, employers could not break the strike. Union benefits kept the miners contented while union cooperatives kept them fed and clothed. Some miners left the district and found union work elsewhere, and five hundred returned to work under a union contract at the Portland mine operated by James Burns, a local employer who retained his former sympathies. Only a few drifted back to work on a nonunion basis.

Meanwhile, halfway across the state in the isolated mountain mining region of Telluride, another conflict between the WFM and the Citizens' Alliance was getting under way. Here, where no sympathetic strike was involved, the union struggled to maintain the eight-hour day and the traditional minimum wage. Here capital was again the aggressor, as mine owners and local bankers, encouraged by Peabody, prepared to make war upon the WFM. Again the governor, who sympathized openly with Telluride's businessmen, intervened in a labor dispute, preparing to open a second front in his preventive class war.

Peabody conceived his own scheme for strikebreaking in Telluride. Advising his militia commanders to arrest all unemployed men (i.e., strikers) on vagrancy charges, the governor offered WFM members a simple choice: Return to work on the owners' terms, be punished for vagrancy, or leave the county. In addition, Peabody informed Major Zeph Hill that if the courts interfered with the new anti-union tactics the governor would declare the county under martial law, thus doing away with the right of habeas corpus.

Martial law and suspension of habeas corpus were also just what Peabody had been intending for Cripple Creek. Since the Colorado labor conflict had widened at Cripple Creek in August 1903, and even after its spread to Telluride, no appreciable violence had occurred in any strike area. Union members had been arrested on numerous charges, but none had been found guilty in court. This tranquility could not be expected to last, particularly if the governor planned to declare martial law. Prophetically, the *Miners' Magazine* reported on November 12, "It is very probable that the Mine Owners' Association at their next meeting will make arrangements to employ a few corporation dynamiters who will startle the different mining camps in the district by nocturnal explosions."

Two days later, someone tried to wreck a train carrying nonunion miners home from work. A week after that, on November 21, an explosion at the Vindicator Mine killed two men. The Mine Owners' Association then promptly issued a circular charging the WFM's "inner circle" with the two crimes and offering a $5,000 reward for apprehension of the criminals. The union, however, was probably correct about the Vindicator incident, remarking in effect that if there had been no strike it would have been dismissed as a routine mine disaster. Colorado's commissioner of mines verified the union's belief. The attempted train wreck, for which union members were later indicted, tried, and acquitted, turned out on the basis of evidence presented during the trial to have been an attempt by company detectives, acting as agents provocateurs, to implicate the union in violence, setting the stage for its final repression.

Nevertheless, these incidents supplied Peabody with a pretext for declaring martial law. On December 4, 1903, acting on a strained interpretation of the 1899 Coeur d'Alene precedent, he declared Teller County "in a state of insurrection and rebellion." Military rule thereupon supplanted civil authority, habeas corpus was suspended, and a general vagrancy order, similar to the one in effect at Telluride, was issued.

By December, then, Peabody was firmer than ever in his determination to crush the WFM. Nothing and no one would stand in his way. Of the Portland mine owner who continued to employ union men, the governor remarked, "I anticipate Mr. Burns will be permanently deposed, and I hope obliterated from that vicinity." In Peabody's world, what was good for capital was good for the worker. Throughout the protracted struggle the governor saw no difference between public power and private power, between the state of Colorado and corporate capitalism.

The WFM seemed doomed. From January through March 1904, affairs went from bad to worse for the union. More and more union men left the Cripple Creek district or returned to work there without their union cards as the mines resumed operations under military protection. Finally, on March 29, Cripple Creek employers announced the introduction of a permit system of employment intended to deny work to union members. At Telluride, meanwhile, union men continued to be "vagged" (arrested on charges of vagrancy) or deported. By March 10 that region was so placid that Peabody lifted martial law. Yet the governor simultaneously discarded all pretense that the militia was serving the community by appointing Bulkeley Wells, manager of Telluride's largest mine, as commander of a local militia unit composed entirely of area businessmen. Two weeks later Sherman Bell placed Telluride back under martial law, allowing Wells the opportunity to doff his mine manager's hat for a militia commander's cap. A few days later Bell and Wells arrested union president Moyer on a trumped-up charge of desecrating the American flag. In addition to being separated from their former local business and professional allies and denied due process of law, Colorado's striking miners were now isolated from their union president, who was kept in prison despite union efforts to secure his release through writs of habeas corpus.

With Moyer in prison, the union and its sympathetic strike both nearly crushed, and the 1904 WFM convention approaching, the union's executive board on May 20 resolved, "If the life of Charles H. Moyer be sacrificed to appease the wrath of corporate and commercial hate, then there will be forced upon the peaceful, law-abiding, and liberty-loving membership of our organization, the ancient words in the old, Mosaic law: 'An eye for an eye, and a tooth for a tooth.'" This somber rhetoric foreshadowed the worst incident of the entire Colorado conflict.

Early on the morning of June 6, as WFM delegates caroused in Denver's saloons and Governor Peabody rested quietly in a St. Louis hotel room (he was attending the World's Fair), a railroad train slowly moved into the Independence depot at Cripple Creek, where a large number of nonunion miners were waiting to board it. As the train approached the platform, a powerful bomb exploded. Arms, legs, and torsos scattered about the depot like windblown leaves; piercing cries shot from all directions through the still night air. Union men, local officials, militiamen, indeed, almost everyone in town rushed to the station to see what had happened. General Bell promptly wired Peabody: "14 men now dead, many more dying, and others wounded and mangled!"

As the governor mulled over the latest Colorado tragedy, his secretary informed him that the state supreme court had just sanctioned his earlier use of martial law as a preventive legal instrument, ruling, according to the governor's secretary, that "courts should not interfere with you [sic] that you have power to kill and imprison." From Peabody's point of view, the court could not have chosen a more opportune moment to define his authority.

Even before the damage at the Independence depot could be assessed, state officials and Citizens' Alliance members declared the WFM guilty. That same morning, local mine owners, assisted by the militia, took the law into their own hands. Because the county sheriff declined to arrest union men without evidence, employers organized a vigilante group that deposed the sheriff and then, joined by the troops, marched upon the union's headquarters in Victor. Armed union members briefly fought back, but, surrounded and outnumbered, they soon dropped their arms and surrendered to the businessmen's law.

Just after midnight, local justice was put into effect. Special kangaroo courts established for the occasion by the Citizens' Alliance deported union members, and the militia escorted them from the district. Only later was martial law reinstituted to give a thin legal veneer to obviously illegal actions in Cripple Creek.

The WFM had been soundly whipped in Colorado. On June 10 Bell issued a general deportation order, under which seventy-nine men were shipped to Kansas and others banished to desert regions in New Mexico and elsewhere. Stranded without funds or food, the deportees were warned never to return to Cripple Creek, even those who had wives and children there. Simultaneously, mobs ransacked the WFM's cooperative stores, the troops placed union sympathizers under tight surveillance, and the authorities hampered all efforts to aid the deportees. When national newspapers, which had treated the deportation story as front-page news, either criticized Peabody or demanded an explanation for the state's actions, the governor replied cavalierly that military necessity sometimes superseded legal right.

The WFM had nowhere to turn. The courts would not protect it against Peabody when the governor refused to execute legal decisions favorable to the union. President Roosevelt, having sent investigators to the scene, refused Moyer's demand that he intervene on the union's behalf. Without officially ending its strikes in Cripple Creek and Telluride, the WFM watched impotently as its local unions were destroyed.

From the ruins of Colorado's miners' unions, however, would arise an even more radical challenge to American capitalism and society: the IWW. As John Graham Brooks, one of Roosevelt's investigators of the Colorado struggle, wrote in his 1913 study of American syndicalism, "The I.W.W. was hammered out in the fires of that conflict."

It was the actions of their employers that convinced Western workers that labor and capital could never coexist peacefully. The betrayal of labor's cause by local businessmen and once-friendly politicians reinforced the miners' conviction that workers must trust to themselves and to their own power. The hostility of the state to labor and the disregard of popular mandates by Peabody and other officeholders convinced many workers that the ballot box was a fraud, and, indeed, that the only hope for improvement lay in economic organization and direct industrial action. In short, a decade of class war taught lessons not easily forgotten to many Western workers, among them men who founded, joined, and long remained loyal to the IWW. Ten years of industrial violence led such men to move from "pure and simple" unionism to industrial unionism to socialism and finally to syndicalism.

# 4

## From "Pure and Simple Unionism" to Revolutionary Radicalism

Of all the strains that went into the making of the IWW, none was more important than that represented by Western workers. Initially the Western miners gave the IWW the bulk of its membership and its finances. Later they contributed the IWW's two most famous leaders: Vincent St. John and William D. Haywood. Most important of all, the IWW's ideology and tactics owed more to the Western miners and their experiences in the mountain states than to any other source.

At first glance the Western Federation of Miners (WFM) appeared much like any other American trade union. Its original constitution, its bylaws, its objectives, its rhetoric were all quite ordinary. It waged strikes to protect wages, reduce hours, or gain union recognition—not, certainly, to make a revolution. Although the WFM originated as an industrial union, opening membership to all men who worked in and around the mines, it did not differ in any basic respect from the United Mine Workers of America, which organized all those laboring in and around the coal mines. Even so famous an American radical as Big Bill Haywood, during his early years as an official of the Silver City, Idaho, local of the WFM (1896–1900), concerned himself with enrolling all working miners in the union and not with revolution. Yet before it was five years old the WFM had easily become the nation's most militant labor organization, and before its tenth birthday it had become the most radical.

Having begun as an open, inclusive union, the WFM became even more so. This highly democratic labor organization devoted itself to the open union concept and the universal union card, accepting any member of a bona fide union without initiation fee upon presentation of his union card. The WFM never demanded a closed shop or an exclusive employment contract. It supported no apprenticeship rules, having no intention of restricting union membership. It wanted jobs for all, not merely for the organized few. As Boyce said in 1897, "Open our portals to every workingman, whether engineer, blacksmith, smelterman, or millman. . . . The mantle of fraternity is sufficient for all."

Three years later he expanded his concept of fraternity: "We will at all times and under all conditions espouse the cause of the producing masses, regardless of religion, nationality or race." Boyce's successor, Charles Moyer, urging better-paid and more skilled miners to support smelter and mill hands, warned that labor is only as strong as its weakest link. "The unskilled now constitute [the] weakest link in the chain of the labor movement. It is our duty and interest to strengthen it." He also put his argument in moral terms, strange perhaps to an American Federation of Labor (AFL) member but not to a former Knight or to a follower of Eugene Debs. Moyer insisted that the true trade unionist was his brother's keeper and that it was the obligation of the highly skilled to use their power to aid the less skilled.

The WFM's belief in solidarity and fraternity went deeper than platform oratory. The organization practiced it: Recall the Colorado labor war of 1903–4 and its origin in the WFM's decision to call out skilled miners in order to protect the mill hands' right to organize trade unions and bargain collectively. This commitment to industrial unionism and solidarity led the Western organization into conflict with the AFL. In 1896 the WFM had affiliated with the AFL; a year later it let its affiliation lapse. In the interval, during the unsuccessful WFM struggle at Leadville, Boyce had pleaded in vain with Gompers and the AFL for financial assistance. In company with another executive board member, Boyce even attended the 1896 AFL convention to carry the WFM's appeal for aid directly to the AFL's membership. But the convention proved a grave disappointment to the WFM delegates, who subsequently lost what little interest they had in the AFL.

By 1896–97, though Gompers and the AFL had won their battle against the Knights of Labor, they were not without labor critics outside of Western labor. Foremost among the opponents of the AFL within the labor movement was Eugene Victor Debs, the martyr of the 1894 Pullman strike, whose name was soon to become synonymous with American socialism. In 1896 Debs allied with Ed Boyce, and the two men worked closely during the final stages of the Leadville strike. Sometimes with Boyce, and sometimes on his own, Debs moved toward dual unionism, socialism, and finally to the creation of the IWW.

The son of Alsatian immigrant parents, Eugene Debs was born in 1855 and grew up in Terre Haute, Indiana, in respectable, if not affluent, circumstances. His should have been a typically nineteenth-century bourgeois life. Young Debs at first accomplished much within the American tradition of success. Although he left school at fourteen to work as a railroader, he rose rapidly in the esteem of fellow workers and his native townsmen. In 1875 Debs founded the first local lodge of the Brotherhood of Locomotive Firemen, but later, despite his activities as a "labor agitator," he was elected city clerk and then to the state legislature. Unsatisfied by his activities as a grocery clerk, city official, and Democratic legislator, Debs returned to the labor movement, becoming in 1880 grand secretary and treasurer of the Brotherhood of Locomotive Firemen as well as editor and manager of the *Firemen's Magazine* (both at a substantial salary).

Behind Debs's respectable American Victorian façade, a radical conscience rested uneasily. No man could serve the American labor movement in the 1870s and 1880s without a nagging concern over its future. Beginning in 1877 as a defender of the existing order and foe of that year's railroad strikers and rioters, over the succeeding fifteen years Debs became an opponent of unjust laws and the enemy of an iniquitous social order. Between 1877 and 1894 he discovered that the labor movement served only some workers, not all. He had witnessed members of the Railway Engineers break a strike waged by firemen; and then he had seen the firemen do the same, helping the Burlington Railroad break the 1888 engineers' strike. Deciding that divided unions could not combat united employers, Debs resigned his positions with the Locomotive Firemen and determined to establish a new labor organization that would open its doors to all railroad workers—operating and nonoperating, skilled and unskilled. Thus was born the American Railway Union (ARU), an industrial organization for all railway workers. Thus Eugene Debs took his first giant step on the road to radicalism.

Not only unskilled railroad workers flocked to the new union, but also many of the skilled, seeing in solidarity their best hope for betterment. In its first strike the ARU challenged and defeated James J. Hill's Great Northern Railway by compelling that corporation to rescind a recent wage cut. Success brought in more members from all over the nation, including the South.

But Debs had still to learn the lesson that Boyce and the Western miners were discovering: Unions fought not only employers but also the state. In the summer of 1894 the ARU found itself in a battle it had not sought: the Pullman strike. Debs knew his infant union should not strike in sympathy with Pullman employees who had recently affiliated with the ARU, and he advised against it. But Debs and fellow delegates at the ARU's 1894 Chicago convention could not close their hearts to the sufferings recounted by George M. Pullman's workers. So Debs and the ARU committed their total resources to the ensuing labor struggle. But Pullman had more resources to commit, including the support of the united Midwestern railroads and the power of the federal government. When president

Grover Cleveland intervened on behalf of the boycotted railroads, the end of the Pullman strike was no longer in doubt. The ARU was destroyed, and Debs spent six months in a Woodstock, Illinois, prison.

It has been said that "Debs entered Woodstock jail a labor unionist, and . . . came out a Socialist." Debs's own Social Democratic party, established in the summer of 1897, was anything but Marxist. Far from seeking to revolutionize American society, the Social Democrats proposed to go off into the wilderness (preferably to some unsettled Western territory) and establish the perfect society, thereby setting an example others would irresistibly follow. Still espousing the "utopian socialism" that Marx fifty years earlier had so savagely ridiculed, as a Socialist Debs still had much to learn.

But by 1897 he had come a long way as a radical, and was prepared to go much further. Debs had already moved from craft unionism to militant industrial unionism; now he was ready to move from utopian to Marxist socialism—which he did in 1901 when his Social Democrats united with Morris Hillquit's and Job Harriman's Socialist Labor party (SLP) insurgents to form the Socialist Party of America. (These insurgents were Socialists dissatisfied with Daniel DeLeon's dogmatic control of the SLP and his war with Gompers and the trade unions.)

For a quarter of a century Debs personified American socialism. Not because he was socialism's best theorist or most creative organizer; quite the contrary. Although a great orator and a stirring personality, Debs had a shallow intellect and proved a poor party organizer. Too often at Socialist party conventions, or when sectarianism threatened to split the party, Debs was at home, sick or drunk. But he had unusual credentials for an American Socialist. In a party dominated by German immigrants and Jewish lawyers and dentists, Debs was American born and, though a professed nonbeliever, a Christian almost by instinct. Debs Americanized and Christianized the Socialist movement. By doing so he made it acceptable, respectable, almost popular. For many followers who still retained traditional religious beliefs, Debs personified the essence of the Christ figure: the simple, humble carpenter who sacrifices himself to redeem a corrupt society. Standing on the speaker's platform, tall, gaunt, balding, slightly stooped, his eyes expressing years of suffering, his haunting voice piercing his audience's emotions, Debs played this role to the hilt.

Among those with whom Debs agitated for a better society were Ed Boyce and his associates in the WFM. Both Debs and Boyce had discarded the limitations of craft unionism for what they saw as the greater possibilities of industrial unionism; both also came to see that industrial unionism alone was not enough to bring a new society into existence. Sharing the experience of unhappy relations with Gompers and the AFL, Debs and Boyce decided to create a new federated labor organization.

Immediately after his disillusioning experience at the 1896 AFL convention, Boyce visited Debs in Terre Haute. Early the following January, Debs arrived in Leadville, and for the next three months he and Boyce spent a considerable amount of time together. From their discussions both labor leaders probably came away convinced that a new national labor organization was needed to accomplish what the AFL could not or would not do, and that this new labor organization must pledge itself to the destruction of American capitalism.

Boyce went to his own union's 1897 convention eager to put his increasing militancy into effect. First, he advised delegates that the WFM should purchase and operate its own mines because only then would miners achieve equality and freedom. Second, Boyce warned that if employers and the state continued to use military force to subjugate strikers, miners should assert their constitutional right to keep and bear arms. "I entreat you," he proclaimed, "to take action . . . so that in two years we can hear the inspiring music of the martial tread of twenty-five thousand armed men in the ranks of labor." Significantly, Boyce asserted that American workingmen would never regain their full rights through "trades unionism." "With this knowledge and the bitter experience of the past [Leadville, for example]," he concluded, "surely it is time for workingmen to see that trades unionism is a failure." The WFM delegates took their president's advice. Voting to stop per capita payments to the AFL, they laid plans for the creation of a Western labor organization.

By 1897, as we have seen, Western labor interests had merged with those of other radical reformers and labor leaders. Debs, for example, convened a national labor conference in Chicago in September 1897, whose participants included, along with Boyce, J. A. Ferguson, president of the Montana State Federation of Labor, and Daniel MacDonald, representing the Silver Bow Trades and Labor Assembly. The next month the Montana State Trades and Labor Council acted to bring Western trade unionists into a new coalition. And in December 1897 the WFM's executive board invited all Western unions to attend a meeting in Salt Lake City to found a new organization.

On May 10, 1898, Boyce watched labor union delegates from Montana, Idaho, and Colorado meet in Salt Lake City. The next day they voted to organize the Western Labor Union (WLU), and on May 12 they elected Dan MacDonald president of the new organization. A loyal AFL man in attendance described the new Western federation to Gompers as "only the Western Federation of Miners under another name. Boyce dominated everything. Boyce's influence with the miners is unquestionably strong. The majority believe him sincerely, and all of them fear to oppose him."

What manner of man was this Ed Boyce whom Western workers both respected and feared? As with so many other labor leaders, little beyond the barest facts is known about Boyce's life—and of these only a few details can be known with any certainty. He was born in Ireland in 1862, the youngest of four children whose father died at an early age. Educated in Ireland, Boyce arrived in Boston, the Irish immigrants' "Promised City," in 1882, but Boston attracted him only briefly. Less than a year later he went west, first to Wisconsin, and then to Colorado, where in 1883 he went to work for the Denver and Rio Grande Western Railroad. The railroad job brought him to Leadville, where he worked in the mines and first made contact with the labor movement; in 1884, he joined the local miners' union, then a Knights of Labor affiliate.

Like so many other Western workers, Boyce continued to drift from place to place and from job to job, seeking better conditions and greater opportunities, until in June 1887 he settled in the recently opened Coeur d'Alene mining district. There he became a local union leader and a key participant in the 1892 strike, a role that led to his arrest, imprisonment, and blacklisting. Released from prison early in 1893, Boyce attended the WFM's founding convention. By 1894 he was back at work in the Coeur d'Alenes, where he was the leading official of the Coeur d'Alene Executive Miners' Union as well as an influential figure in statewide Populist politics. Only two years later, still working in a local mine, Boyce was elected WFM president, an office he held until his voluntary retirement in 1902.

Under Boyce's aggressive leadership, the differences between Western labor and the AFL intensified. The WLU became more, not less, radical. Even the Western workers who retained sympathy for the AFL's position did so as missionaries for the Western point of view, not as true believers in Gompers's version of the labor movement. Although some Westerners realized that labor should unite in the face of united capital, they insisted that "we must try to teach our benighted brothers in the 'jungles of New York' and the East what we have learned here in the progressive, enterprising West." Underneath the whimsy lay a perfectly serious conviction.

Western workers were careful to spell out their points of difference with Gompers. Where the AFL emphasized skills and crafts, the Westerners demanded a policy "broad enough in principle and sufficiently humane in character to embrace every class of toil . . . in one great brotherhood." Where the AFL stressed the national craft union and complete union autonomy, the Westerners favored the industrial union, free transfer from union to union, and labor solidarity. Where the AFL sought to close America's gates to immigrants, the Westerners welcomed most newcomers, except Asians. Where the AFL preferred to seek betterment through the use of strikes, boycotts, and collective bargaining, the Westerners initially claimed that industrial technology and corporate concentration had made those tactics obsolete, leaving the working class but one recourse: "the free and intelligent use of the ballot."

Boyce's rhetoric, which his followers relished, neatly incorporated their view of American society. "There can be no harmony between organized capitalists and organized labor. . . . There can be no harmony between employer and employee—the former wants long hours and low wages; the latter wants short hours and high wages." Boyce told Butte's miners, whom he also reminded, "Our present wage system is slavery in its worst form. The corporations and trusts have monopolized the necessities of society and the means of life, that the laborer can have access to them only on the terms offered by the trust." He ended by proclaiming, "Let the rallying cry be: 'Labor, the producer of all wealth, is entitled to all he creates, the overthrow of the whole profit-making system, the extinction of monopolies, equality for all and the land for the people.'"

To achieve their better society, Western workers at first preferred political to economic action, the ballot and the statute to the strike and the boycott. As a Gibbsonsville, Idaho, miner wrote to the *Miners' Magazine*, "The majority of our members are beginning to realize . . . that strikes and lockouts are ineffectual weapons to use against capital. They are firm believers in political action. . . . Let labor break loose from the old parties and make itself a party of pure social democracy." A Declaration of Principles adopted at the WFM convention in 1900 proposed, among other items, public ownership of the means of production and distribution, abolition of the wage system, and the study of socialist political economy by union members. Agreeing with these principles, a union member in Granite, Montana, commented, "In government ownership we have a remedy for the trust which will minimize its evils and maximize its benefits; a remedy which will make the largest projects in the industrial world the most beneficial and will cause the inventive genius of the centuries to be applied for the benefit of all instead of for the benefit of the few."

Boyce's 1902 farewell address to the WFM convention summarized what by then had become the Western organization's guiding philosophy. Conceding that the major purpose of the union, like that of all labor organizations, was to raise wages and lower hours, Boyce nevertheless cautioned that permanent improvements would not come until miners recognized that pure and simple trade unionism would inevitably fail. The only answer to labor's predicament, he stressed, was "to abolish the wage system which is more destructive of human rights and liberty than any other slave system devised."

In keeping with Boyce's advice, the convention delegates voted to unite their organization with the Socialist Party of America. Early the following year the union's executive board under its new president, Charles Moyer, reaffirmed the WFM's radicalism by promising to make the union "an organization of class-conscious political workers that constitute the vanguard of the army that is destined to accomplish the economic freedom of the producers of all wealth."

The conflict between Western workers and the AFL was not primarily because of the Westerners' radicalism or socialism. Gompers and the AFL would have tolerated socialism in the West if it had been divorced from the labor movement, or if it had found a home within the AFL. What irked Gompers was the WFM's decision not only to go it alone but to establish a rival labor center in the West. At the WLU's birth in 1898 the AFL was still a fragile institution just over ten years old, a mere infant that Gompers desperately wanted to survive beyond childhood. If the WFM managed to live and thrive outside the AFL, other large national labor organizations, such as the United Mine Workers, might also choose to leave. It was to combat what he conceived to be dual unionism that Gompers fought Western labor's radicals.

After 1900, AFL organizers suddenly appeared in the previously neglected mountain states to compete with their WLU-WFM counterparts. Gompers's agents in the West attempted to convince workers that the future of the American labor movement was with the AFL, not the WLU. When AFL men failed thus to win over WLU locals, they tried to wreck them by organizing dual unions of their own, even offering employers inducements to deal with the AFL rather than the WLU.

Instead of dissolving the WLU and returning to Gompers's waiting arms, the WFM transformed the WLU into the American Labor Union (ALU) and embraced socialism more firmly than before. In part, this action was a tacit recognition that the WLU had never amounted to much, that, apart from locals among a handful of restaurant workers and other minor city trades, the organization had almost nothing to show for five years' effort. Conceding the failure of the WLU as a regional labor organization and letting it die an unmourned death, Western workers now decided to carry their challenge directly to the AFL by forming a national labor body—the ALU—that would compete with the AFL for members on a nationwide basis.

The ALU began where the WLU left off—but with one important difference. The ALU sent organizers east into traditional AFL territory and invited AFL affiliates, especially the Brewery Workers, to join the new national labor center. Although ALU leaders proclaimed their desire to live in peace with the AFL, they had every intention of weakening, if not destroying, the older national labor organization.

What did the ALU offer workers that could not be obtained through AFL membership? First, the ALU offered its members unswerving loyalty to socialist principles and to the Socialist party. Second, it offered members a constitutional structure more democratic than that of the AFL, one under which basic principles and policies would be established by membership referendum rather than by "irresponsible" officers. Third, it promised Western workers the assistance the AFL so often in the past had denied them. Most important, however, the ALU opened its membership to those neglected by the AFL: the semiskilled and the unskilled in America's basic industries, women, and immigrants ignored by the established labor unions.

Dan MacDonald, the ALU's president, argued the case for the unorganized, whose "position . . . is more exposed to the influence of unjust conditions and subject to greater impositions and greater burdens than the organized." Haywood emphasized that the AFL was merely a council of loosely affiliated trade unions representing a small minority of workers who, inculcated with the spirit of craft selfshness, continually engaged in jurisdictional warfare to monopolize union benefits for the favored few. In times of crisis, he said, the AFL had always proved impotent to aid its affiliates, usually sacrificing them on the "sacred alter of contract." To Gompers's impassioned defense of craft unionism, trade autonomy, and exclusive jurisdiction, Haywood retorted, "The diversity of labor is incapable of craft distinction; thus pure and simple trade unions become obsolete."

In keeping with its emphasis on industrial unionism, the ALU, though employing the rhetoric of political socialism, stressed the primacy of economic action, which the IWW would later label direct action. The ALU, for example, never required political conformity on the part of its members; in fact, it allowed each man to ride his favorite political hobby horse to exhaustion. Moreover, the organization's constitution barred any member from holding union office if he also held political office, regardless of party affiliation. "The A.L.U. is not a political organization. . . . With regard to its political character, it amounts to this: it simply recommends to the worker what to do and how to do it," claimed ALU officials, seeking to distinguish their organization from Daniel DeLeon's dual union, the Socialist Trades and Labor Alliance, which made membership in the SLP a requisite for membership. The ALU, its spokesmen maintained, would concentrate on the industrial field, leaving politics to other organizations.

From the first, the ALU cherished the two tenets most characteristic of the post-1908 IWW: the primacy of economic over political action and a belief in the syndicalist organization of the new society. As the ALU *Journal* expressed the organization's philosophy, "The economic organization of the proletariat is the heart and soul of the Socialist movement. . . . The purpose of industrial unionism is to organize the working class in approximately the same departments of production and distribution as those which will obtain in the cooperative commonwealth."

Western workers adopted still another principle later characteristic of the IWW: opposition to time contracts. Moyer, for example, informed WFM convention delegates in 1903, "It behooves us at all times to be free to take advantage of any opportunity to better our condition. Nothing affords the majority of corporations more satisfaction than to realize that they have placed you in a position where you are powerless to act for a period of years." The WFM and the ALU by 1903–4, like the IWW thereafter, believed that no agreement with employers was legally or morally binding and that workers could achieve their objectives only by remaining free to strike at will.

For all its radical rhetoric and militant principles, however, the ALU lacked substance. Like its predecessor, the WLU, its strength, funds, and membership came mainly from the WFM. In addition, its leading officials, Daniel Mac-Donald and Clarence Smith, were simply inherited from the WLU. Only in its grander ambitions and its more radical tone did the ALU differ.

Insubstantial as the ALU was, both the Socialist party and the AFL feared and even fought it. Although the ALU enlisted fervently, if not uncritically, in the socialist crusade, Socialist party members did not always respond in kind. After all, in its publications and propaganda the ALU emphasized that union interests would always take precedence over party considerations, victory in the shop precedence over victory at the ballot box. To some American Socialists—among them such Socialist party leaders as Victor Berger, Morris Hillquit, and Max Hayes—the ALU seemed uncomfortably radical and revolutionary. These Socialists naturally welcomed the ALU's endorsement of their party, but they deprecated Western labor's war with the AFL, compared the ALU to DeLeon's infamous Socialist Trades and Labor Alliance, and refused to sanction the ALU's existence as a national organization.

Socialist party leaders were in fact gambling their party's future upon an alliance with the AFL, the trade unions, and the skilled workers. The party's dominant faction believed that its best hope lay in capturing the AFL and its affiliates from within; thus anything that weakened that strategy by vitiating Socialist strength inside the AFL had perforce to be condemned. In terms of party strategy, they believed, Socialists best served the cause by staying in Gompers's organization, not by deserting it to join the ALU. So many American Socialists, following Gompers's lead, fought the ALU. This Socialist strategy proved wrong; the AFL was beyond capture, but American Socialists could not foresee in 1904 what today seems to have been so inevitable.

Despite opposition, the WFM tried to build a substantial, independent radical labor organization devoted to industrial unionism. Recognizing the failure of the WLU and regional radicalism, the WFM had created the ALU. But only a year after the ALU's birth—perhaps stillbirth would be a more accurate description—the WFM had to concede another failure. For just when the WFM became involved in the most serious crisis of its existence—the 1903–4 Colorado labor war described earlier—the ALU proved incapable of saving the WFM from utter defeat. The defeat in Colorado convinced WFM leaders of their absolute need for a radical new national labor organization, one that could truly revolutionize American society. The WFM in 1904 initiated conferences that led the following year to the founding of the IWW.

The WFM's twelfth annual convention, meeting in Denver in June 1904 as the Colorado labor conflict moved toward its violent climax, instructed its executive board to plan "for the amalgamation of the entire working class into one general organization." Soon thereafter Haywood and Moyer met informally with Dan MacDonald of the ALU and George Estes of the United Railway Workers, which represented the scattered remnants of Debs's American Railway Union. That November six men conferred secretly in Chicago to discuss a general reformation of the American labor movement. The six included Clarence Smith, secretary of the ALU; Thomas Hagerty, editor of *The Voice of Labor,* then the ALU's official journal; George Estes and W. L. Hall, representing the United Railway Workers; Isaac Cowen of the Amalgamated Society of Engineers;* and William E. Trautmann, recently deposed editor of the *Bräuer Zeitung,* official organ of the Brewery Workers. Invited but unable to attend were Eugene Debs and Charles O. Sherman.

The six conferees immediately agreed, as Clarence Smith later remembered it, that America must have "a labor organization that would correspond to modern industrial conditions." On November 29, 1904, they addressed a letter to some thirty individuals known to favor industrial unionism, socialism, and a reformation of the labor movement. The addressees included members of the Socialist party and the SLP, industrial unionists and craft unionists, non-

* An American branch of the English organization of the same name, then engaged in a jurisdictional dispute with the American International Association of Machinists as well as with Gompers and the AFL.

AFL members and AFL members, as well as men who can only be labeled fellow travelers in the cause of radicalism and unionism. The letter concluded by inviting the addressees "to meet with us in Chicago, Monday, January 2, 1905, in secret conference to discuss ways and means of uniting the working people of America on correct revolutionary principles . . . as will insure its [labor's] integrity as a real protector of the interests of the workers."

Most of those invited—twenty-two, to be exact—did attend the January conference. Twelve others who endorsed the conference's purposes begged off for various reasons. Among the latter were Debs, who pleaded poor health, D. C. Coates, and Ed Boyce. As for Debs, Hagerty and Trautmann reported that they had met privately with him in Terre Haute, and that he enthusiastically supported the conference's purpose. Daniel DeLeon, soon to become the most contentious personality in the early IWW, was not even invited to the January session.

Two men refused to attend, and their refusal carried great significance. They were Victor Berger and Max Hayes, both influential in the Socialist party. Berger did not even reply, while Hayes's response reflected prevailing Socialist party attitudes. Most Socialists, it was obvious, still pinned their hopes on winning over the AFL and its skilled working-class membership. Hayes, himself a craft unionist and also an AFL member, proved no exception. "If I am correct," he wrote to W. L. Hall concerning the proposed labor conference, "it means another running fight between Socialists . . . and all other partisans. Let me say frankly that under no circumstances will I permit myself to be dragged into any more secession movements or fratricidal war between factions of workers."

Without Berger, Hayes, or the blessings of the Socialist party, twenty-one men and one woman—the famous Mother Jones*—met secretly at 122 Lake Street, Chicago, on January 2, 1905. The only significant union group present came from the American West: the WFM sent Haywood Moyer, and John O'Neill, while MacDonald, Smith, and Hagerty represented the ALU (which was in fact only a WFM subsidiary). The others in attendance spoke only for themselves or for fractional, insignificant labor groups. Trautmann, one of the most influential men at the meeting, had just been deposed as editor of the *Bräuer Zeitung* because of his acidulous anti-AFL editorials. Like most of the conferees, he was more a propagandist than a labor leader or union organizer.

For three days this motley assortment of radicals thrashed out their differences, at last agreeing upon eleven principles for reforming the labor move-

* Mother Jones had won her fame in the labor movement as the grandmotherly organizer of coal miners and flaming advocate of their rights during tempestuous coal strikes, in which she had taken a leading role.

ment. Of these the following were the most significant: (1) creation of a general industrial union embracing all industries, (2) the new organization to be founded on recognition of the class struggle and administered on the basis of an irrepressible conflict between capital and labor, (3) all power to reside in the collective membership, (4) universal free transfer of union cards, and (5) a call for a general convention to form a national labor organization in accordance with the conference's basic principles.

Considerable confusion remained hidden within the eleven principles. The proposed organization ostensibly devoted to industrial unionism, for example, was also dedicated in advance to "craft autonomy locally; industrial autonomy internationally; working class unity, generally." Just how the conferees expected to retain craft autonomy and industrial unionism, industrial autonomy and working-class solidarity, went unexplained. Nor did the conferees reach a consensus about the proper political role for their proposed organization. Socialists saw it essentially as a branch of the party (the SLP, if they were DeLeonites), yet the Westerners, while claiming to be Socialists, remained suspicious of politics, politicians, and the state. Representing the Western influence predominant at the January sessions, Hagerty pushed through the following resolution: "That this Union be established as the economic organization of the working class without affiliation with any political party." Hardly a position to excite Socialist party politicians!

But uncertainties and conflicts dissolved in the euphoric atmosphere of the Chicago conference, which, at its end, adopted the Industrial Union Manifesto. The manifesto asked all true believers in industrial unionism to meet in Chicago on June 27, 1905, to establish a new national labor organization based upon the Marxist concept of the class struggle and committed to the construction of the cooperative commonwealth. This invitation was sent to American radicals and trade unionists, and to European labor organizations, among whom it engendered especially acute interest and heated debate. Max Hayes continued to criticize these proposals and to deny that Socialists had formulated them. (On the last point he was more than half right.) Even Samuel Gompers joined the debate, devoting three issues of the *American Federationist* to an attack upon the so-called industrial unionists, whom he labeled "union smashers." Algie Simons and Frank Bohn, both participants in the January conference, debated the significance of the manifesto in the *International Socialist Review*. Conceding the importance of the approaching industrial union convention, as well as the failure of the AFL to adjust to contemporary economic life, Simons yet wondered, "Is the present the proper time for such a change to come? If it is not, then this organization will be a thing born out of due time, a cause of disorder, confusion, and injury." For a time, Simons surmounted his doubts and favored the new challenge to the AFL. His reservations nevertheless illustrate just how tenuous indeed was the connection between the Socialist party's anti-AFL faction and the birth of the IWW. Frank Bohn, then an SLP member, answered Simons's questions and in so doing demonstrated why his party, rather than the Socialist party, linked itself tightly to the IWW. Denying the possibility of capturing the old unions by boring from within, Bohn considered the occasion ripe for industrial unionism. Hence he called upon his friends within the SLP and also within the craft unions to enter the proposed new labor organization, scuttle trade unionism, and adopt class-conscious industrial unionism.

On the hot early-summer day of June 27, 1905, in a stuffy, overcrowded, smoke-filled, boisterous auditorium in Brand's Hall on Chicago's near north side, Bill Haywood called to order "the Continental Congress of the Working Class." As the 203 delegates listened intently, Haywood proclaimed,

> We are here to confederate the workers of this country into a working class movement that shall have for its purpose the emancipation of the working class from the slave bondage of capitalism. . . . The aims and objects of this organization should be to put the working class in possession of the economic power, the means of life, in control of the machinery of production and distribution, without regard to capitalist masters. . . . This organization will be formed, based and founded on the class struggle, having in view no compromise and no surrender, and but one object and one purpose and that is to bring the workers of this country into the possession of the full value of the product of their toil.

The delegates delighted in Haywood's every phrase, for who could better voice their common detestation of the AFL and their ultimate desire for a better world? But on few other matters were they agreed. What else could be expected? Sixty-one delegates represented nobody but themselves. Seventy-two belonged to labor unions with a collective membership of more than ninety thousand, but they did not represent those trade unions, and in effect also spoke only for themselves. Seventy delegates represented slightly over fifty thousand union members, but of these seventy, only Moyer and Haywood, representing the forty thousand members of the WFM and the ALU, spoke for any significant number of union members. The two Westerners outvoted all other convention delegates by ten to one. (The ALU claimed 16,750 members, but many of these were fictional, or only WFM members counted twice.) Only five tiny AFL locals came to Chicago prepared to affiliate with the new organization; indeed, most AFL men at the convention represented themselves, not their unions. Under these circumstances, headstrong or exceptional men such as Debs, Haywood, Hagerty, Trautmann, and even Daniel DeLeon (though his role has been repeatedly exaggerated) exerted a disproportionate influence.

Most students of the IWW's history have on one occasion or another tried their hands at distinguishing the various factions and ideologies represented at the founding convention, usually emphasizing the alleged role of a so-called syndicalist component. Probably the most accurate analysis of the factions, however, is that produced by a nonacademic analyst, Ben H. Williams, editor of *Solidarity* from 1909 to 1916, who was also perhaps the most astute IWW theoretician. In his memoirs Williams distinguishes three groups present at the founding convention. First were the WFM and other union veterans. This group was earnest in its desire to create an industrial union initially unattached to any political party that could in due time develop its own "political reflex." (This faction in time became the syndicalist component, but it had not yet reached that ideological point.) Second were the DeLeonites, who aimed to place the new organization under the tutelage of the SLP. Third, the Socialist party politicians prepared to bypass the new organization if it failed to follow their vote-getting program. Williams also describes a fourth faction: the "also-rans," would-be craft union leaders ambitious to get back in the labor game for possible personal gain. Unfortunately, it was from this last faction that the IWW selected its first and only president, Charles O. Sherman.

It is noteworthy that Williams's spectrum of factions includes neither anarchists (though Lucy Parsons, wife of Haymarket martyr Albert Parsons, was an honored guest) nor syndicalists. Almost all the delegates, as Williams himself knew from firsthand experience, were in 1905 committed to some form of Socialist politics. The seeds of syndicalism, as we have already seen, were sown well before 1905, but they did not flower until several years after.

On the surface, despite the presence of so many factions known for their disputatious character, unity seemed to prevail at the convention. At first, SLP members, Socialist party members, and trade unionists buried their differences in fevered anti-AFL, anti–Sam Gompers oratory. Trautmann began this type of speechmaking by indicting the AFL for its class collaboration and its leaders (the "labor lieutenants of capitalism") for joining with the captains of industry to exploit the unskilled, be they women, children, or immigrants. Debs, DeLeon, and Hagerty followed Trautmann to the rostrum, each adding his own scathing comments about the AFL's "labor fakirs." Debs and DeLeon, sectarian enemies of long and bitter standing, even complimented each other's sudden conversion to good sense.

This kind of harmony, abundant during the convention's first five days, fled the hall on the sixth. As the temperature rose and tempers flared, delegates began to discuss just what their new organization was to do and how it would do it.

Two questions—decisive ones having to do with the new organization's politics and structure—particularly divided the convention as it went about the business of drawing up a constitution. Some Socialists had assumed, naturally though unwisely, that the delegates would endorse the Socialist party. Union delegates from the West, given their immense voting power, could easily have eliminated all reference to politics from the new organization's constitution. Instead, as a concession to Socialists from both parties, whom they desired to keep in the fold, the Westerners approved the second, or political, paragraph of the IWW constitution preamble, which read, "Between these two classes a struggle must go on until all the toilers come together on the political, as well as the industrial field, and take hold of that which they produce by their labor through an economic organization of the working class, without affiliation with any political party." One convention delegate found this clause beyond comprehension. Obscurity was, of course, the precise purpose of the political clause, so as to make it acceptable simultaneously to incipient syndicalists, Socialist party advocates, and SLP members.

Equally controversial was Hagerty's plan for the structure of the organization, the so-called "Wheel of Fortune" involving a "general administration" at the hub, five departments at the circumference, and thirteen industrial divisions in between. None of the delegates really knew what the Wheel meant or how Hagerty proposed to effect it.

Debate waxed hot and heavy on Hagerty's proposal. Although many delegates felt that adoption of the Wheel would result in the kind of organizational chaos that had destroyed the Knights of Labor, the convention finally endorsed Hagerty's organizational scheme. Why delegates voted as they did is not clear; perhaps they did so partly because the Wheel, like the political clause, could be interpreted differently to every individual's own satisfaction, perhaps because they perceived that it would always remain only a confusing diagram, never a fact of organization life.

Considerably less trouble and debate went into selecting the new organization's name and its general officers. Without dissent, delegates agreed to call their creation the Industrial Workers of the World. Then, possibly to deflate the overwhelming numerical preponderance of Western workers, but more likely because Moyer and Haywood felt unable to serve two organizations simultaneously and chose to remain in executive office with the WFM, the delegates chose two Easterners, Charles O. Sherman and William Trautmann, as president and secretary-treasurer, respectively. (The IWW's first executive board more accurately reflected Western influence and power.)

The convention had sought to achieve what Haywood had defined as its primary objective: "We are here for the purpose of organizing a *Labor Organization,* an organization broad enough to take in all the working class. What I want to see from this organization is an uplifting of the fellow that is down in the gutter . . . *realizing that society can be no better than its most miserable*" (italics added). In order to carry out Haywood's recommendation, the IWW's constitution opened membership to all workers, skilled and unskilled, native and immigrant, child and adult, male and female, black, white, and even Asian. It provided for low, uniform initiation fees, still lower dues, and free universal transfer of union cards. Although it vested in the executive board sole authority to declare strikes, the constitution, by making convention decisions subject to open membership referenda, placed ultimate power in the membership.

Having adopted a name, endorsed an organizational Wheel, and written a constitution, on the afternoon of July 8 the convention adjourned *sine die*. Algie Simons, writing soon afterward, claimed that the sessions had marked "a decisive turning point in American working class history."

# 5

## The IWW under Attack, 1905–7

Initially it appeared that the history of the IWW would be synonymous with the life of Father Thomas J. Hagerty, one of the most unusual and colorful figures behind its creation. Hagerty had been the principal author of the January 1905 manifesto, the preamble to the IWW constitution, and the creator of the "Wheel of Fortune." After 1905 he vanished from the radical scene.

Hagerty's connection with the IWW seems at first glance inexplicable. Only three years before the IWW's founding convention, Thomas J. Hagerty quietly pursued his vocation as a Roman Catholic priest (assistant to the rector of Our Lady of Sorrows Catholic Church in Las Vegas, New Mexico), saying Mass, hearing confessions, and baptizing infants. Having finished seminary training in 1895, he had served briefly at a Chicago parish, and at two parishes in Texas, before moving to Las Vegas.

That Hagerty was an unusual priest soon became clear. At one Texas parish he championed exploited Mexican railroad workers. When railroad managers complained of his agitation, Hagerty is said to have replied, "Tell the people who sent you here that I have a brace of Colts and can hit a dime at twenty paces." Shortly after this incident Hagerty was transferred to the Archdiocese of Santa Fe, where his activities became even more peculiar. After only a few months at his new assignment, Hagerty attended the 1902 joint convention of the Western Federation of Miners (WFM) and the Western Labor Union (WLU), urging delegates to endorse the Socialist party. Then, instead of returning to his parish duties, he toured Colorado's mining camps to propagandize for the American Labor Union (ALU) and socialism.

While absent from New Mexico, Hagerty had been suspended from his priestly duties, for when word of his stand reached church superiors, the archbishop disowned his radical priest. Hagerty, insisting that Marxism and Catholicism were compatible, settled in Van Buren, Arkansas, still claiming to be a priest in good standing. As he put it to an Indiana audience "I am a Catholic priest, as much a Catholic as the Pope himself."

But the Socialist party soon became too tame for Hagerty. Impatient with parliamentary reform Socialists, whom he labeled "slowcialists," Hagerty began to advise audiences, "We must have revolution, peaceable if possible, but, to tell the truth, we care not how we get it." These more radical views brought Hagerty the editorship of the ALU's monthly, *The Voice of Labor*. At the first IWW convention, Hagerty joined the more radical delegates who belittled ballot box reform.

After his triumph at the June 1905 convention, Hagerty disappeared from sight. Hagerty never accounted for his separation from American radicalism; indeed, never again did he speak or write publicly. None of his old radical acquaintances even saw him until 1917, when Ralph Chaplin, editor of *Solidarity*, found a man resembling Hagerty living in Chicago under the name Ricardo Moreno, eking out a bare existence by teaching Spanish. By 1920 Moreno, *né* Hagerty, had joined the multitude of derelicts filling Chicago's skid row on West Madison Street, outcasts whom even the IWW ignored.

What happened to Father Hagerty after 1905 was a portent for the organization he helped found. The ex-priest's radicalism failed to survive the June convention. The product of that convention, the IWW, beset by enemies without and within, scarcely survived its first two years.

The IWW expected opposition from the American Federation of Labor (AFL) and Gompers, and received it. Gompers had employed a special agent to attend the June 1905 convention and to keep him informed of developments in Chicago. Afterward, Gompers's informant remained in contact with the IWW leaders and reported regularly to his employer.

Luke Grant, Gompers's agent, sent reports detailing the chaotic state of the IWW. Its very chaos, he claimed, largely accounted for his delays in providing the information Gompers desired. Apparently on the best terms with president-elect Sherman and secretary-treasurer-elect Trautmann, who provided him with essential IWW data, Grant did his best to reassure an obviously troubled Gompers that the IWW was not a threat to the AFL. No one in Chicago, he reported, neither trade unionists nor socialists, endorsed the industrial union scheme, which seemed destined for an early demise. Grant also informed Gompers of divisions in the new organization between Socialist party and Socialist Labor party (SLP) men and between ALU members and followers of DeLeon's Socialist Trades and Labor Alliance.

But these reports did not put Gompers's mind to rest. To Gompers, the IWW was nothing less than a creation of American Socialists intended to replace the AFL. Consequently, Gompers and his executive council warned all AFL affiliates to guard against IWW infiltration and to refuse to cooperate with members of the new organization. AFL members were told not to support IWW strikes; they were also absolved from the sin of crossing IWW picket lines. In Montana the State Federation of Labor and the Silver Bow Trades and Labor Council purged WFM locals because of their affiliation with the IWW. Gompers personally delivered a blistering attack upon the WFM at the AFL convention in 1905. With scarcely a murmur of dissent, the AFL convention voted to discontinue defense aid to the WFM.

Less expected by the IWW's founders was opposition from the Socialist party. After all, the leading socialist personality, Eugene Debs, and a prominent party theoretician, Algie Simons, had attended the 1905 convention. Moreover, the IWW had succeeded by the Debs-DeLeon axis in uniting the divided American socialist movement and promised to add new strength to the radical cause.

But most Socialists suspected the new labor organization on two grounds. First, they could not quiet their suspicions of DeLeon and his motives. They were convinced that DeLeon would once again split the socialist movement, as he had done in 1897. Second, most Socialists still dreamed of capturing the AFL from within and viewed those comrades who deserted to the IWW as weakening left-wing strength within the AFL. As a result, the Socialist party and press, dominated by among others Victor Berger, Max Hayes, and Morris Hillquit, fought to avoid any connection between the Socialist party and the IWW.

Left-wing Socialists like Simons and Debs tried to defend the IWW. Simons claimed that the IWW had no wish to involve the party in internecine labor strife, though every IWW official was a Socialist party member. If trouble should come, he warned, "it will be because of those who are so anxious to gain the favor of the A.F. of L. officials that they must heap their abuse on every one who does not kow-tow to their pure and simple god." To Simons, Socialist chances of capturing the AFL then seemed slim; Gompers's machine of 1905–6 was simply too well entrenched to be overthrown. Debs agreed. He could not understand how Socialists could remain in the pro-capitalist AFL.

Despite the arguments of Debs and Simons, most Socialists preferred to remain within and support the AFL. Soon Simons himself would leave the IWW, and a short time later Debs would follow suit. Both learned in somewhat rude fashion that while the IWW's leaders endorsed socialism, they were unwilling to subject the new labor organization to Socialist party discipline or to accept unquestioningly socialist programs and ideology. Thus the IWW and the Socialist party maintained an uneasy, tenuous relationship—sometimes fighting, sometimes cooperating, but seldom understanding each other.

Under attack by trade unionists and by many Socialists, the IWW suddenly confronted hostile government authorities and public opinion. Events in Idaho, which had little to do with the IWW, nevertheless deeply affected the Wobblies and their cause.

Ice covered the streets of Caldwell, Idaho, the hometown of former governor Frank Steunenberg, on the afternoon of Saturday, December 30, 1905. Before strolling his daily mile from Caldwell's business district to his home, Steunenberg paused as always in the lobby of the Saratoga Hotel, rocking for a while in his favorite chair, reading the newspapers, and talking to admiring friends. Financially secure thanks to business contacts he had made during his term as governor (1897–1901), Steunenberg was Caldwell's leading citizen. No longer was he the stern governor who had fought the WFM in the Coeur d'Alenes, driven its members out of the mines, and sent one of its officers to prison. Almost everyone had forgotten his role as strikebreaker in 1899; those in Caldwell who did remember applauded his decision at the time to repress "lawless, unamerican" labor. But on that cold December day the Coeur d'Alenes became more than a distant memory. As Steunenberg read and rocked, a furtive stranger watched intently. Unbeknownst to all, that stranger, a drifter known as Harry Orchard, had for several weeks been observing the movements and habits of the ex-governor. When Steunenberg entered the hotel lobby on December 30, Orchard hastened to the ex-governor's home, where he planted a bomb rigged to explode upon the opening of the front gate. Even before the stranger had returned to his room in the Saratoga, Steunenberg had opened his front gate, triggering an explosion. A few moments later, he died without regaining consciousness.

The assassination stunned Caldwell. Immediately public officials acted. Municipal authorities forbade anyone to leave town, while governor Frank Gooding and other state officials rushed to Caldwell. By then the sheriff had arrested some of the more promising local suspects, among them Harry Orchard.

Orchard had courted arrest. He had lived at the Saratoga for several months without visible means of support. Supposedly a sheep buyer, he bought no sheep. After the murder he made no attempt to escape. Indeed, he made himself more conspicuous. When local police arrested him on January 1, 1906, they easily discovered in his room the ingredients used in the lethal bomb. Such behavior was puzzling, if not inexplicable. Perhaps a psychotic personality disorder led Orchard into a life of violence, and perhaps that same disorder eventually caused him to seek penance for his (mis)deeds.

Idaho officials professed little difficulty in discovering the alleged assassin's motives. Ever since the 1899 Coeur d'Alene conflict they had been convinced that an "inner circle" controlled the WFM, and that this "inner circle" plotted the destruction of property as well as the assassination of capitalists and public officials opposed to the union. Had not Frank Steunenberg been just such an opponent? So reasoned Idaho's officials. The state's problem, then, was not to find a motive for Orchard's deed; rather it was to connect the "hired" assassin to his employers, the "inner circle" of the WFM. To this problem Governor Gooding turned his attention.

Precedent guided Gooding. Thirty years earlier Pennsylvania had destroyed a similar "inner circle," that of the notorious Molly Maguires. The man responsible for the apprehension and execution of nineteen Mollies, James McParland, was near at hand in 1906. McParland's success in Pennsylvania had transformed the Pinkerton National Detective Agency, for which he worked, into the principal institution to which private employers and public officials turned for discreet and effective antilabor espionage. McParland, in fact, now managed Pinkerton's Denver office, which Governor Gooding contacted on January 8, asking McParland to direct Idaho's investigation with the purpose of linking Orchard to the WFM's "inner circle." Almost simultaneously, Gooding also appointed James H. Hawley and William Borah—the men who had prosecuted the WFM in 1899—to prosecute the union once again. Thus, even before Orchard confessed, state officials knew whom they were after: Charles Moyer and William D. Haywood.

Once on the job, McParland ingratiated himself with Orchard. The Pinkerton official intimated that even a multiple murderer like Orchard could receive both the grace of God and the clemency of the state. Advised by McParland that if he cooperated with the authorities "the sentiment that now existed would be reversed, that instead of looking upon him as a notorious murderer they [the public] would look upon him as a saver, not only of the State of Idaho, but of all States where the blight of the Inner Circle of the Western Federation of Miners had struck," the frightened Orchard agreed to make a full confession in the hope of escaping the gallows.

Day and night for the next month, McParland and Orchard labored over the details of the confession. Together they made certain that almost every unsolved crime associated with labor conflict in the mountain West was laid at the door of the WFM. As sleuth and slayer constructed this curious "confession" (in which fact and fiction were strangely bound), the states of Colorado and Idaho plotted still more unorthodox actions.

None of the WFM's "inner circle"—neither Moyer, Haywood, George A. Pettibone (a former union member, now a small Denver retailer and good friend of union officials), nor L. J. Simpkins (a member of the WFM general executive board representing Idaho miners)—had been in Idaho at the time of Steunenberg's murder. This was known to Idaho officials, who also knew that under the laws of Colorado and the United States, though not those of Idaho, Moyer, Haywood, and Pettibone could not be extradited. The law notwithstanding, Idaho and Colorado officials hatched a scheme to extradite the three suspects (all then Denver residents) by abduction. Working together under McParland's guidance, the governors of Idaho and Colorado executed their scheme. On February 15 Colorado Governor MacDonald honored extradition papers, authorizing the union leaders' immediate arrest. In order to prevent the accused from instituting habeas corpus proceedings, authorities delayed until Saturday evening, February 17, before making arrests. That night Moyer was seized at a Denver railroad station and Pettibone at home; Haywood, in a bizarre twist, was apprehended in a brothel. At dawn the next day, Denver police brought the three manacled prisoners unobtrusively to the railroad depot, where they were placed on a specially made-up train that sped them to the Boise prison and a date with the hangman. After their dubious extradition and forcible abduction they had not been allowed to communicate with friends, families, or attorneys.

Union attorneys finally learned of their clients' abduction on February 22. They filed for habeas corpus writs in state and federal courts. But all courts, including the United States Supreme Court, refused relief. The various appeals courts ruled that Idaho's loosely drawn extradition statutes provided a legal basis for the abductions of Haywood, Moyer, and Pettibone. The Supreme Court majority argued, moreover, that the method of extradition, even if illegal, was immaterial to the issue at hand: the presence within Idaho's jurisdiction of three defendants properly indicted on charges of conspiracy to commit murder. Only one Supreme Court dissenting justice, Joseph McKenna, condemned the extradition methods. Despite protests from organized labor, respected liberals, notable radicals, and most socialists (Debs even threatened armed revolution if Haywood were convicted), the prisoners were indicted for Steunenberg's murder on March 6 and remanded to jail to await their fate.

For the next year they languished in prison while McParland desperately sought evidence and witnesses to corroborate Orchard's confession. Under Idaho law, without corroboration, Orchard's testimony would by itself be insufficient to prove conspiracy. McParland proceeded in two ways. First, he tried the tactics that had already drawn a confession from Orchard. When a purported accomplice in the Steunenberg assassination, one Steve Adams, was arrested on February 20, 1906, McParland threatened him with execution unless he corroborated Orchard's confession. Like Orchard, the new prisoner confessed and received the benevolence of the state, including a private bungalow and friendly visits from Gooding, Hawley, and Borah. McParland, still uncertain of his case, next decided that the best policy would be to obtain a confession from a member of the "inner circle" itself. He looked to Charles Moyer as his man. McParland had heard rumors about a rift between Moyer and Haywood, and even gossip of an unsuccessful plot by Haywood and Pettibone to assassinate the WFM president. But much as he worked on Moyer, McParland failed to win a third convert.

Meanwhile, much to McParland's chagrin, Steve Adams retracted his corroborating confession. Soon after Adams's arrest, Clarence Darrow, the famed Chicago lawyer, had been appointed chief defense attorney. Knowing how McParland had inveigled Adams's confession, Darrow assured the prisoner that if he retracted, Idaho would be unable to convict him of murder. Won over by Darrow's impressive arguments, Adams repudiated his confession. He was then rearrested for the murder of two missing claim-jumpers, and his trial was set for February 1907 in Wallace, Idaho—in the Coeur d'Alenes, where the whole bloody business had begun fifteen years earlier.

The first Adams trial previewed the subsequent Haywood case. James H. Hawley prosecuted and Darrow and Edmund Richardson, the WFM's Denver attorney, defended—the identical legal lineup that would meet again during the Haywood trial. When the defense's case unfolded, McParland perceived immediately what was happening. "You can see from the whole course of Richardson's and Darrow's arguments that they are simply trying the Moyer, Haywood, and Pettibone cases," he reported, "and all they fear is that Adams will be convicted, taken down to the penitentiary, where no doubt . . . he would return to his original statements." The defense won a technical victory in Wallace, the jury dividing evenly. But even with its corroborating witness now lost, Idaho decided to prosecute Haywood and the others.

America impatiently awaited the trial, which was finally scheduled to open in Boise on May 9, 1907. Correspondents and freelancers jammed the courtroom to hear the confession of Harry Orchard, converted by the grace of God and the wit of McParland, and to observe the response of William D. Haywood. Haywood was chosen by the state to be prosecuted first because he seemed more irascible and more fearsome than the other two defendants and thus less likely to elicit sympathy from a jury. The journalists also came to observe one of the most impressive arrays of legal talent ever assembled in a Western courtroom: Hawley, the dean of Idaho lawyers, and Borah, a rising young star in the Republican party, for the prosecution; Richardson, perhaps Denver's outstanding attorney, and Darrow, just then approaching the acme of his career, for the defense.

Even before the trial opened, both defense and prosecution perceived conspiracies everywhere. While attorneys examined prospective jurors in court,
Pinkerton men and agents for the defense investigated them outside. Both sides
skirted the edges of legality in approaching and examining veniremen. But
defense and prosecution finally overcame their suspicions sufficiently to settle on a jury of twelve elderly men—all farmers over fifty, none of whom had
ever been a WFM member or worked in a mine. Meanwhile, the prosecution
uncovered further "conspiracies"; nothing, it seemed, was beyond the WFM's
power. Borah had just been indicted on a federal land fraud charge, leading
Hawley to conclude that the United States Justice Department had acted in
collusion with Haywood's friends!

While the prosecution fantasized nonexistent WFM conspiracies, it continued to hatch quite genuine plots of its own. Still hopeful that he could break
Moyer, McParland indirectly approached the union president. He sent Moyer
fine cigars, together with daily newspaper reports of Orchard's unshakable
testimony. A prison guard suggested to the WFM president, "I know . . . you
love your wife, and you are still a comparatively young man and if I were in
your place I would make at least an effort to save myself not caring what the
world might say." McParland believed he could convert Moyer partly because
of Orchard's claim that Moyer opposed Haywood, partly because the union
president's wife hated Big Bill, and partly because he suspected that Moyer
harbored ambitions to become a conservative and "respected" labor leader,
much on the order of John Mitchell of the United Mine Workers. But Moyer
refused to talk. He would not see McParland, and his estrangement from Haywood, which was later to have major repercussions, for the moment remained
private and muted.

Thus the prosecution based its entire case on Orchard's testimony, which,
in the event, proved too good by half. The eager Orchard confessed to crimes
the defense easily established he could never have committed. Described by a
sympathetic journalist as like nothing so much as the neighborhood milkman,
the defendant was revealed during defense attorney Richardson's brilliant
cross-examination to be not only a thief and a murderer but also a perjurer, a
bigamist, and an agent provocateur.

On July 27, after more than two months of testimony and cross-examination, the jury finally retired to consider a verdict. The prosecution appeared
optimistic, the defense pessimistic. But when the jury returned its verdict in
the early morning of July 28 Haywood was found not guilty! In fact, as a juror
later remarked to a reporter, most of the jury considered Haywood innocent

throughout the trial, feeling "that there was nothing against the accused but inference and suspicion."

But Hawley, McParland, and the state remained convinced of the WFM's guilt. Rather than dismiss the charges still pending against Moyer and Pettibone, they decided to try Pettibone next, after again inveigling corroborating evidence from a muddled Steve Adams. But once again Adams repudiated a confession and eluded the toils of "justice," beating old murder charges in Idaho as well as new ones in Colorado. Without Adams's testimony, Idaho failed to convict Pettibone, whom a jury acquitted in January 1908.

Instead of suggesting to Hawley the weaknesses of the state's case, the acquittals merely confirmed in his mind the true extent of the WFM "conspiracy." The WFM, according to the Idaho prosecutor, not only assassinated its enemies, it also corrupted and terrorized juries. Losing all faith in the perspicacity of twelve honest men, Hawley now claimed that Idaho juries consisted of Socialists, "people who are afraid, those who are bought up, and the criminal element." This being the case, the prosecution reluctantly decided to drop its charges against Moyer, thus terminating the great Idaho labor conspiracy trials.

Haywood, Moyer, and Pettibone had been exonerated, and the $140,000 raised for their defense was well spent. Although failing to achieve its immediate objectives, the prosecution effort was not without effect. The months of newspaper publicity, the testimony of Orchard, and the knowledge that labor violence and murders had occurred regularly during Western industrial disputes fixed in the public mind an image of the WFM and the IWW as violent, antisocial organizations synonymous with anarchism and bloody revolution. The trials also transformed small fissures within the WFM and the IWW into gaping holes. The incarceration of Moyer and Haywood removed just when they were most needed the IWW's most experienced, capable, and popular leaders. Their long imprisonment also deeply affected the two men, though in quite different ways. It impelled Haywood further in the direction of radicalism, while it led Moyer toward a more conservative position. This was the change McParland had perceived and tried to exploit. With Haywood in jail, the more conservative influences within the WFM, those to whom Moyer was being drawn and who wanted to make both the WFM and the IWW more "respectable" and less revolutionary, gained control. The eventual result of the conservatives' rise to power was civil war within the WFM and its departure from the IWW.

At the birth of the IWW in June 1905, the organization appeared to be powerful, including three major departments (mining, metals and machinery, and transportation), numerous scattered locals and industrial councils, recruiting unions attached directly to general headquarters, and the remnants of the ALU. As to membership, General President Sherman and Secretary-Treasurer Trautmann agreed that in June 1906, despite some setbacks, it stood at sixty thousand, counting all departments and directly affiliated locals. Beneath this impressive façade, however, glaring weaknesses would soon be revealed.

In fact, the IWW was so poor at birth that it operated initially with books, furniture, and office methods inherited from the defunct ALU. Of the three departments ostensibly a part of the organization, two scarcely existed. The transportation department never had the three thousand paid-up members required for departmental status (let alone one thousand actual members), and the 1906 convention would refuse to recognize that department's existence. The metal and machinery department began life with somewhat brighter promise. Almost immediately, however, one of its major components seceded; Isaac Cowen, leader and founder of the American branch of the Amalgamated Society of Engineers, having led his men into the IWW, soon led them back out again. With Cowen's secession, the metals and machinery department lacked sufficient numbers for legal existence as a department, and it, too, was denied departmental status by the 1906 convention. Only the WFM, with 27,000 paid-up members, constituted a valid department (mining), and after the 1906 convention it also would secede, leaving the IWW, only a year after its creation, close to death. Vincent St. John's 1911 estimate of the IWW's paid-up membership in 1905–6 as 14,000 (including the WFM) was probably not far off.

Weak though the IWW was, it did not shrink, as we have already seen, from combating either the AFL or the Socialist party. It engaged in countless unnecessary strikes as Trautmann led the IWW in repeated attempts to capture AFL affiliates, particularly among coal miners and brewery workers. By January 1906 the IWW had become so aggressive in its incursions upon AFL affiliates that Max Hayes feared the imminent outbreak of civil war within the labor movement.

Much, if not all, of the IWW's impotence and failure, however, resulted from incompetent leadership. Neither Sherman nor Trautmann was qualified to administer a large labor organization.

Little is known about the life or career of Charles O. Sherman. What is known reflects slight credit on the man. According to Samuel Gompers, Sherman had been a blacklist victim of the 1894 Pullman strike, and Gompers, feeling sympathy for a victimized trade unionist and upon the recommendation of friends, had commissioned Sherman as an AFL organizer in 1902 or 1903. Sherman promptly created a paper union—the United Metal Workers International Union—which, upon receiving an AFL charter, turned upon its benefactor, declaring jurisdictional war on other AFL international unions. Sherman and his paper organization refused to abide by AFL executive council decisions, Sherman claiming that through oversight he had failed to inform Gompers that the United Metal Workers had withdrawn from the AFL.

But Sherman was hardly neglectful or forgetful. *Duplicity* seems a better word to describe what he had been up to. From November 1904 he participated in the conferences that led to the formation of the IWW, yet on December 27, 1904, he informed Gompers that the United Metal Workers was still a legal AFL affiliate. A week later, he signed the Industrial Union Manifesto. Unable to build his union empire within the AFL, Sherman entered the IWW to become that organization's first and only president. His record as IWW president was in keeping with his efforts as an AFL organizer. Once again he used a union position to increase his power and line his own pockets. He personally selected all IWW organizers, most of whom proved more notable for the expenses they accumulated than for the number of their recruits. He also contracted with a firm in which he had a direct financial interest for union labels and IWW insignia.

More revolutionary, perhaps more principled than Sherman, Trautmann was hardly a more capable administrator. He may have been an effective editor, essayist, and polemicist, but he was no executive. Born of German-American parents in New Zealand in 1869 (the same year as Haywood), he participated in the labor and socialist movements of Russia and Germany (from which he was expelled under Bismarck's antisocialist laws) before coming to the United States. Here he organized for the Brewery Workers' Union in Massachusetts, edited the *Bräuer Zeitung,* translated Marx into English, wrote industrial union propaganda tracts, and participated in the founding of the IWW. As secretary-treasurer of the IWW, Trautmann failed to maintain accurate membership records of either individuals or local unions, and his financial accounts were in even worse shape. At the 1906 convention he could not even produce a financial report. A year later, as the IWW's first general organizer, he organized no one. By 1913, having already figured in two IWW purges, Trautmann himself left the IWW to become a full-time propagandist for Daniel DeLeon's schismatic, paper IWW.

Under such leadership it is small wonder that the IWW made no progress its first year and began its second year with its only significant affiliate, the WFM, alienated. Even capable leaders would have had difficulty holding together an infant organization under attack by the AFL, the bulk of the Socialist party, and the state of Idaho. Sherman and Trautmann were certainly not the men to do it.

As early as January 1906, Max Hayes reported that an internal battle loomed within the IWW, with industrialists and Socialists on one side and DeLeonists and anarchists on the other. Rumors abounded that Sherman and the WFM had soured on DeLeon, Trautmann, and their adherents. Hayes quoted an IWW member as saying, "If a convention were held next month . . . I predict the academic vagaries forced upon us by the DeLeon-Anarchist combine will be dropped for a plain fighting program that everybody can understand and conjure with." Part of Hayes's report represented the wishful thinking of an anti-DeLeon, anti-IWW Socialist, but a substantial portion reflected reality.

Indeed, by midsummer 1906 the predicted conflict had erupted. In July an IWW member suggested in the *Industrial Worker* that the organization had no need of a president, nor even of department heads. About the same time a Chicago-based group spearheaded an effort to revise drastically the IWW's constitution and structure. On August 14, sixteen locals, representing the metals and machinery department, the transportation department, bookbinders, printers, and cigarmakers, met in Chicago and resolved unanimously to seek to abolish the office of president.

Simultaneously, other divisive issues emerged. Debs and DeLeon may have shaken hands across the bloody chasm of the past, but their respective followers clearly had not. Within the IWW, SLP members and Socialist party members began to fight with sectarian virulence.

Thus, as the IWW prepared for its second convention, one faction linked to the WFM and the Socialist party rallied around President Sherman in opposition to DeLeon's influence and the demands of the so-called revolutionaries. A second faction, tied to the SLP and including prominent WFM members, schemed to remove Sherman, abolish his office, and purge the IWW of all "antirevolutionary" sentiments—whatever precisely was meant by that. The convention would determine which faction was to predominate. Would the IWW remain united, or was it indeed, as later described by Ben Williams, a house built with unsuitable materials "and without first excavating and laying the foundation"?

On Monday morning, September 17, President Charles O. Sherman called to order in Chicago the second annual convention of the IWW. The four-man WFM delegation again controlled the largest number of convention votes (436); Daniel DeLeon once more led the ideologues who were in attendance. Notably absent were Moyer, Haywood, Father Hagerty, Eugene Debs, and Algie Simons. Not a single delegate among the thirty-two purported Socialist party members ranked high in the party hierarchy. But the thirty delegates who belonged to the SLP included the party tyrant, DeLeon, and many of his lieutenants. Whereas a spirit of unity had marked the founding convention, the second session was rent by dissension.

For the next five days pro- and anti-Sherman factions waged war. Led by DeLeon, who served as their parliamentary tactician, the insurgents succeeded in denying convention seats to disputed pro-Sherman delegates representing the metals and machinery and transportation departments. Instead the insurgents awarded seats to delegates representing locals in those two departments hostile to Sherman. This, in effect, gave the insurgents a solid convention majority.

Unexpectedly triumphant, many so-called revolutionary delegates now found themselves the victims of economic retribution. Representing only themselves or weak unions, they were given, at best, a meager mileage allowance; at worst, no allowance at all. The pro-Sherman delegates, by contrast, received a generous expense allowance, much of it drawn from the organization's treasury. The Shermanites now struggled to delay convention proceedings in order to weaken their opponents, many of whom might soon be forced by lack of funds to leave Chicago for home. To avert just such a contingency, one of the "revolutionary" delegates proposed that he and his needy brethren receive $1.50 a day from the IWW's treasury.

As this proposal approached a vote, the IWW's chief executives, Sherman and Trautmann, joined the verbal war. The president took the floor to appeal for moderation and reason while the secretary-treasurer sounded the tocsin for revolution. Trautmann demanded that the convention purge forthwith the "conservative" Sherman and his "reactionary" followers in order to transform the IWW into a pristine revolutionary organization. Responding to Trautmann's call, the convention majority rammed through the proposal to pay a per diem to needy (read: anti-Sherman) delegates. In the face of powerful opposition from more conservative, anti-Socialist WFM delegates led by Butte's John McMullen, DeLeon rallied the "revolutionary" forces behind his leadership to vote for a suspension of the IWW constitution.

This vote made the convention schism irrevocable. Charles Mahoney, acting president of the WFM and also acting convention chairman, after being regularly thwarted in rulings by what he thought to be deluded and dangerous DeLeonites, confided to John O'Neill, editor of the *Miners' Magazine,* that the convention majority's arrogance would result either in the immediate withdrawal of the WFM from the IWW or in the disruption of the entire organization.

Mahoney's critics thought they detected a scheme by WFM conservatives to tear down the IWW. To avoid that possibility the "revolutionaries" abolished the office of IWW president. When Mahoney, asserting his authority as convention chairman, declared the vote to abolish Sherman's office out of order, an SLP member retorted, "It is a revolution." To which John McMullen angrily remarked, "All right, if you want a revolution, have it." And a revolution the delegates had, overruling Mahoney by a vote of 342 to 276.

So ended the façade of IWW unity. McMullen, speaking for the "conservative" WFM faction, criticized the proceedings as unconstitutional. He insisted that he and his supporters could not and would not remain any longer in Chicago. Fred Heslewood, a WFM alternate delegate, rose to answer McMullen: "If he means the reactionists are going to leave this convention I hope to God they do, and I wish they had never come." At this juncture Sherman spoke a bitter farewell to the organization he had led for only a year. Denouncing the "conspiracy" that had surrendered the IWW to DeLeon, the deposed president pronounced burial rites, declaiming, as much in sadness as in anger, that the IWW is "today a corpse . . . ready for the funeral."

The final crisis came on the morning of October 2, when the convention majority declared all constitutional amendments in force and proceeded to elect new officials. Overruled once again, Mahoney bolted the convention and took several WFM men out with him. Unable to win their battle within the convention, these men carried their fight to the WFM, where their chances for victory were distinctly better. For the next year and a half, the struggle that had raged on the floor of Brand's Hall would be repeated within the ranks of the WFM.

With Sherman deposed and his office now abolished, Trautmann became the official leader of the IWW with the title of general organizer. DeLeon, who had dominated the convention debates, retired to the background, assuming no official position in the organization, though several of his followers were elected to the new executive board, along with Heslewood and Vincent St. John of the WFM.

The victory of the "revolutionaries" at first seemed Pyrrhic, for not only did it splinter the IWW's largest affiliate, with the bulk of the organization's paid-up membership, but the Sherman faction simply refused to accept defeat. Indeed, for a time the deposed Sherman operated his own IWW! Backed by Mahoney and the WFM executive board, Sherman called his preconvention executive board into session, expelled Trautmann from office, ruled the 1906 convention's action null and void, declared the unamended 1905 constitution still in force, and asked that all per capita payments be sent to his "legal" IWW. Sherman and his cohorts also seized physical control of IWW headquarters and books while awaiting the funds that would enable them to fight their opponents in court.

When St. John, Heslewood, and W. I. Fisher, representing the executive board elected at the 1906 convention, went to IWW headquarters at 148 West Madison Street on the morning of October 4, they found a strange sight. Inside the offices were their organizational enemies, claiming to be in legal possession of IWW properties; outside were private detectives entrusted with protecting the office from the anti-Sherman faction.

The next step in the factional feud involved an unusual bit of historical irony. The contending IWW factions, both purportedly hating capitalism, resorted to capitalist courts to press their respective legal claims. Sherman's group, represented by Seymour Stedman, a Socialist party lawyer, asked the judiciary to validate its possession of IWW properties, including furnishings, books, ledgers, membership lists, and the official journal. Trautmann's faction, finding itself without so much as a postage stamp, asked the courts to declare the 1906 convention decisions binding and to order Sherman to turn all IWW properties over to the officers elected and installed at the second convention. The courts eventually ruled in Trautmann's favor, capitalist justice thus giving "revolutionary wage slaves" at least one victory.

Forced by the courts to relinquish his claims to the presidency and to the physical assets of the organization, Sherman took his case to the WFM, hoping it would endorse a reestablished IWW. To present his claims fully, for a time Sherman published the *Industrial Worker* at Joliet, Illinois, carrying on the sheet's masthead the magic names of Eugene Debs, Algie Simons, John O'Neill, Jack London, and William D. Haywood, among others. In retaliation, Trautmann issued a series of special IWW bulletins. The rivals also carried on their quarrel in the columns of the *Miners' Magazine,* striving desperately to elicit endorsement from the imprisoned Moyer and Haywood as well as from 27,000 loyal WFM members.

Just after the 1906 convention adjourned, the Trautmann faction plainly asked WFM members, "Which do you want? Pure and simple unionism, more corrupt and rotten than in the American Federation of Labor, or straight revolutionary workingclass solidarity as proclaimed in the Manifesto and Preamble of the I.W.W.?" Most WFM members were probably uncertain what they wanted. A minority, led by McMullen, undoubtedly desired pure-and-simple industrial unionism; pork chops, in other words, without revolution. Another minority group, this one led by St. John, Heslewood, and Al Ryan, unabashedly chose revolution.

The rift in the IWW and WFM also caused dissension behind prison walls. In the Ada County jail, Moyer and Haywood reacted quite differently to the events of September and October 1906. As we have already seen, an estrangement had developed between the two. On October 2, the day Mahoney and McMullen walked out of the IWW convention, Moyer wrote WFM acting secretary James Kirwan, "I want to serve notice on those calling themselves revolutionists that their program will never receive my endorsement, nor that of the Western Federation of Miners, if in my power to prevent it. By the gods, I have suffered too much, worked too hard to ever tamely submit to the Western Federation of Miners being turned over tamely to Mr. Daniel DeLeon." Hence Moyer castigated the Trautmann faction, intimated endorsement of Sherman's position, and demanded a membership referendum on the IWW convention's actions.

Haywood, unlike Moyer, preferred to withhold final judgment about the IWW controversy until he had more substantial information, though he did advise the WFM to remain within the IWW. Before long he made his opinion in the controversy known, condemning the Sherman faction without condoning the 1906 IWW majority, which, in his words, was "entirely too harsh. . . . The Gordian, presidential and other knots that you cut with a broad axe, were only slipknots that could have been easily untied." Above all, Haywood wanted to avoid personalities and to make sacrifices for labor unity. Believing that Trautmann and St. John were in the right, he nevertheless implied that the insurgents could have accomplished their objectives without dividing the IWW and the WFM. Yet Haywood had to confess, "I have been unable to devise any means of effecting a reconciliation."

But with Moyer and Haywood in prison, the anti-IWW faction dominated the WFM. Mahoney and Kirwan notified all union locals in November 1906 not to participate in a referendum on the 1906 convention being conducted by Trautmann. The following month the WFM executive board declined to pay per capita dues to either IWW faction and announced that a membership referendum had overwhelmingly declared the 1906 IWW convention invalid.

In response, the Trautmann IWW on January 15, 1907, suspended the mining department (WFM), at the same time announcing the results of its own referendum vote, which overwhelmingly (3,812 to 154) endorsed the 1906 convention and the new IWW officials. Trautmann demonstrated, moreover, that when the votes in the IWW referendum were combined with those in the WFM election, a majority of the total endorsed the 1906 convention (5,712 in favor, 2,912 opposed).

Meanwhile, an increasingly moderate WFM leadership had to contend with its critics. Before the 1907 national convention of the union, rumors of compromise spread. In March, Haywood wrote to St. John, "I fear more than anything else a repetition of the useless and meaningless wrangle at the coming convention. . . . It must be prevented. It is just to demand the retirement of the officers of both factions of the Industrial Workers of the World, if by so doing, an amalgamation of the rank and file can be brought around." But Trautmann's supporters would not compromise, and they brought their case before the 1907 WFM convention, the bitterest in the organization's history.

For almost a month delegates debated the IWW question. St. John, Heslewood, Ryan, Percy Rawlings, and Frank Little (who would later figure prominently in IWW history) led the convention radicals; Mahoney, O'Neill, Kirwan, and McMullen guided the moderates. When Acting President Mahoney and a majority of the resolutions committee opposed affiliation with either IWW faction, the radicals vowed to continue their struggle within the WFM until they prevailed.

The moderates won by an overwhelming majority—more than two to one on important issues (239½ to 114). So ended, with a whimper, the WFM's flirtation with revolutionary unionism.

The IWW now appeared doomed. With its largest affiliate gone and no replacement in sight, what remained? Even Haywood announced publicly, "As to the reconstruction of the I.W.W. nothing will be done until the time is ripe for it, and that will not be until organized labor in general offers less opposition to the movement." O'Neill, always less reserved, proclaimed, "The I.W.W. is but a reminiscence. It is dead, and the sooner we forget the stench the better."

But Trautmann and his supporters vowed to demonstrate that the IWW was a very lively corpse, willing and able to resist those who wished to bury it. Whether Trautmann or O'Neill was the better prophet, only the subsequent history of the IWW would determine.

William Dudley "Big Bill" Haywood, the most famous of all Wobblies, in a soapbox pose.

Vincent St. John, the IWW's secretary-treasurer.

IWW members parade their views in Pittsburgh, Pennsylvania.

The staff of *Solidarity* was jailed in 1910. Editor Ben Williams is the third man from the left.

Joseph Ettor, the IWW's charismatic chief organizer, with fellow workers.

The "Rebel Girl," Elizabeth Gurley Flynn, with Big Bill Haywood and the children of Paterson's silk workers, 1913.

Joe Hill, Wobbly bard and martyr.

Wobblies protest the policies of the Oliver Steel Company, 1913.

Frank Little, the itinerant
IWW agitator who was
lynched by vigilantes in Butte,
Montana, in August 1917.

Rifle-toting Arizona vigilantes load suspected Wobblies onto a cattle car, July 12, 1917.

A typical IWW hall in the Washington State timber region, 1917.

# 6

## The IWW in Action, 1906–8

From 1906 to 1908 the IWW, though often interred by its enemies, never took to the grave. Despite manifold weaknesses, it waged industrial conflicts in cities as far removed as Skowhegan, Maine, and Portland, Oregon; Bridgeport, Connecticut, and Goldfield, Nevada. It organized workers in textiles, lumber, mining, and other trades. It survived lost strikes, withstood the economic panic and ensuing recession of 1907–8, and endured a second internal split. By the end of 1908 the IWW had assumed what thereafter remained its basic characteristics and purposes. During these formative years the IWW also created enduring myths about itself and committed mistakes that it never overcame.

One of the most enduring IWW myths is of an alleged Golden Age associated with organizational success in the isolated Nevada mining camp of Goldfield, where, within a year of its founding, the IWW had organized all the workers in the community except for a handful of American Federation of Labor (AFL) building tradesmen. Newsboys, waiters, bartenders, cooks, clerks, maids, hard-rock miners, reporters—John Dos Passos's Mac in *The 42nd Parallel* first gives his loyalty to the IWW in Goldfield—all carried the red IWW card. No more complete amalgamation of workers had ever existed in the American labor movement.

Yet Goldfield could better be called the IWW's Gilded Age. Never achieving anything approaching complete success, the IWW left Goldfield in total defeat. With only minor variations, the Goldfield story repeated the theme of class warfare earlier played out in similar Idaho and Colorado mining towns. Miners early joined the Western Federation of Miners (WFM), which quickly established the upper hand in employer-employee relationships. For a time, unionism flourished as workers maintained an unusual degree of job security.

After the founding of the IWW in 1905 and the affiliation of the WFM as its mining department, the Wobblies invaded the camp. Goldfield's WFM Local 220 already included some of that union's most radical members, many of them refugees from the bitter 1903–4 Cripple Creek and Telluride conflicts. The creation of the IWW enabled these "radicals" to extend their organizational hold over the community. The IWW captured a local town workers' federal union formerly affiliated with the AFL. Renamed Local 77, IWW, it claimed to represent all Goldfield's town workers and also those in the neighboring mining community of Tonopah.

Events in Goldfield stimulated local Wobblies to further successes. On September 10, 1906, at a time when the national leaderships of the IWW and the WFM were drawing apart, both organizations' Goldfield affiliates amalgamated, the town workers and the miners merging into an enlarged WFM-IWW Local 220. Even after the WFM seceded from the IWW in January 1907, Goldfield's workers remained united in a Wobbly-dominated coalition. The allies functioned aggressively. On December 20, 1906, they struck local mines to obtain higher wages and shorter hours, and within three weeks the miners gained their major objectives as well as added fringe benefits. By March 1907 the amalgamated union claimed three thousand dues-paying members, and it felt secure enough to order all local businesses to go on the eight-hour day— a request promptly accepted. Not satisfied with domination of the mines and local businesses, Local 220 waged war with an AFL carpenters' local, demanding that all carpenters take out red cards or be denied employment in and around the mines. This attack against the AFL carpenters marked the farthest penetration of the IWW-WFM coalition in Goldfield.

Shortly thereafter, a unique concatenation of circumstances drove a wedge between the town workers and the miners, thereby destroying unionism in Goldfield. In the spring of 1907, with Haywood coming to trial, Goldfield opponents of the WFM and IWW asserted that they now had evidence to prove that they were combating not a labor union but a criminal conspiracy. Simultaneously, internecine conflict immobilized the WFM as a result of its secession from the IWW. Moreover, the AFL chose this moment to attack the WFM-IWW axis in Goldfield, and Gompers dispatched a special organizer to the area to join with mine owners and conservative WFM members in fighting the IWW and reasserting AFL hegemony. Soon economic panic and recession would make this bad union scene even worse.

The counterattack by mine owners and local businessmen, well aware that Local 220's conservatives and radicals were bitterly fighting among themselves, came in March 1907. Forming a Businessmen's and Mine Owners' Association, they refused to employ IWW members. On March 15, supported by the AFL, they closed all local places of business, then reopened them three days later without IWW employees. Throughout March and most of April, local mines remained closed as owners and WFM moderates sought to purge Wobblies from the miners' union.

At this stage Goldfield's class lines had become hopelessly confused. Only one thing was certain: Goldfield was no longer an IWW utopia. On one side, local businessmen and mine owners stood with AFL members and conservative miners; on the other, radical town workers and miners sympathetic to the IWW held fast to their position. Both sides went armed.

A majority of the miners and employers, rather than risk open warfare in such a confused situation, came to terms on April 22, 1907. The miners' union protected its prevailing rate of wages and won jurisdiction over all employees working in and around the mines. Employers in return gained a promise that town labor disputes would not be allowed to interfere with mine operations. The agreement, intended to last for two years, brought labor peace through the summer and early fall of 1907.

With the IWW apparently beaten, the mine owners became more aggressive. Goldfield businessmen professed to have fought the IWW partly because Wobblies were "subversive radicals" and partly because they were alleged criminal conspirators. But in fact it was organized labor per se, not criminal conspirators, the employers were seeking to combat. They cooperated with the AFL only because that group had never organized local miners or town workers and therefore posed no threat to employers' economic power.

Goldfield's mine owners publicly revealed their anti-union attitude in November 1907, when they broke their April agreement with the miners' union. Using the panic of that year and the subsequent monetary stringency as a pretext, the owners announced they would stop cash payments to their workers. Rejecting union compromise offers, they declared war against organized labor.

At this juncture, Nevada's public authorities were in no position to aid Goldfield's employers: The state lacked either militia or police for the job. Goldfield's businessmen also realized that town and county officials could not be relied upon to combat labor. Thus, employers devised a scheme with governor John Sparks to bring in federal troops. In a secret meeting on December 2, 1907, the mine owners and the governor agreed that Sparks, upon receipt of a coded wire, would request federal troops. No Goldfield town or county officials were informed of these arrangements. Immediately upon their return to Goldfield, mine owners dispatched the prearranged code message to Sparks, who on December 3 asked President Roosevelt for troops. After a brief legal contretemps between the governor and the president, Roosevelt ordered the soldiers to Goldfield two days later. On December 6 federal troops arrived in what to all appearances was an orderly, peaceful community. Only two weeks later, on December 20, agents sent by Roosevelt to investigate the situation wired the president, "Our investigation so far completely has failed to sustain the general and sweeping allegations by the governor in calling for troops.' But the federal agents soon discovered why mine owners and the governor wanted federal troops. The mine owners, they learned, had determined to reduce wages and also to refuse to employ WFM members—steps they feared to take without military protection.

Aware of all this, Roosevelt nevertheless maintained the federal presence in Goldfield. The troops had been dispatched when there was no need for them, but the mine owners soon created that need, for the president's investigators went on to report that a wage reduction and new "yellow-dog" contracts, posted December 12, would cause the miners' union to resort to violence if the troops were withdrawn. Roosevelt, convinced that Haywood and the WFM "inner circle" were murderers, thought the worst of Goldfield's miners. Federal troops thus remained on duty to preserve Goldfield's peace until March 1908, when state police, recently provided for by a special session of the Nevada legislature, replaced them.

The miners' union was by now a shambles. On April 3, when it finally voted to end its strike, only 115 men cast ballots, the remainder having left the union or the area.

So ended the IWW's Golden Age—and with it the dreams of quick and easy organization of American workers into One Big Union powerful enough to dictate to employers. The Wobblies now knew what to expect in the future. Both the AFL and the WFM would fight them, and its members would scab on them, employers would take advantage of labor's internal divisions, and public authorities would be hostile and repressive. Most important, it became obvious that the more successful the IWW was in achieving its economic goals, the more it would meet employer and public opposition. Radicalism and revolutionary rhetoric were tolerable as long as they were not translated into actual economic power.

The defeat in Nevada notwithstanding, Wobblies liked to look back upon the Goldfield experience as a time when they had demonstrated, temporarily at least, that the One Big Union idea really worked, that laborers from many different occupations could be united into one organization, that an injury to one could be made the concern of all. A romanticized version of Goldfield became the ideal to be realized. This ideal kept the IWW alive from 1906 to 1908, as it tried to organize workers hitherto thought unorganizable.

Yet the Goldfield debacle convinced some Wobblies that the organization should concentrate upon recruiting members in the urban industrial East. Ben

H. Williams, a member of the general executive board, maintained that Eastern workers, though less imbued than their Western brothers with the spirit of revolutionary industrial unionism, were less mobile and hence superior material for organization.

Williams's observation did not pass unheeded. In 1907–8, articles in the *Industrial Union Bulletin* described IWW-led industrial conflicts in Bridgeport, Connecticut, in Skowhegan, Maine, and in Schenectady, New York. The Bridgeport and Schenectady strikes are particularly important for what they reveal about IWW methods and principles. In Bridgeport the Wobblies welded together unskilled Hungarian immigrants and skilled native-born Americans in a united front that in August 1907 won important concessions from the American Tube and Stamping Company. Even the AFL organizer sent to Bridgeport to keep the International Association of Machinists from supporting the dual union's strike was impressed by the IWW's hold on the Hungarians. "The devotion of these Hunks to the dual union is pathetic," he informed Gompers. "They sit at strike meetings listening to speakers whose speeches they cannot understand and join in the applause at the end louder than any of the others." At the General Electric works in Schenectady, the IWW demonstrated direct industrial action. On December 10, 1906, when the company refused to reinstate three discharged Wobblies, three thousand union members sat down inside the plant. As a local paper reported, "They did not walk out but remained at their places, simply stopping production." Wobblies thus initiated the first recorded sitdown strike in American history.

These two conflicts foreshadowed the IWW's future course. They demonstrated that the primary aim of industrial action was immediate improvements in wages and working conditions and the redress of specific grievances. For most Wobblies the revolution was in the future—the empty belly was today's concern. Bridgeport and Schenectady also revealed the IWW's ability to do the unexpected and dramatic, as well as to attract previously neglected, unskilled immigrants into the same organization with skilled native-born Americans.

The IWW made its deepest Eastern inroads among textile workers. In Paterson, New Jersey, by March 1907 the Silk Workers' Industrial Union No. 152 had over one thousand members whose job classifications cut across craft lines. At the year's end, General Organizer Trautmann informed an executive board session that the IWW had organized about 5,000 textile workers: 3,500 in Paterson, 700 in New Bedford, 50 in Lawrence, and the remainder scattered among Providence, Woonsocket, Fall River, Hoboken, and Lancaster. Acting upon Trautmann's suggestion, the general executive board issued a call (published in English, French, German, and Italian) for a convention to be held on May

Day 1908 in Paterson's IWW Hall to establish a National Industrial Union of Textile Workers (NIUTW).

Twenty-two delegates, representing textile workers from Paterson, Providence, Woonsocket, New Bedford, Lawrence, and Lowell, attended this convention. Three days of discussion and debate produced the NIUTW, the first such national industrial organization established within the IWW structure. Although the NIUTW opened membership to wage workers in every branch of textile production, its constitution allowed for union subdivisions based upon either language or production unit. The constitution also recognized the NIUTW's subordination to the IWW's general executive board on all vital issues. In later years, this organization would wage several of the IWW's most notable struggles.

Concentration upon Eastern workers did not cause the IWW to neglect the Westerners responsible for the organization's birth. Quite the contrary. Appeals and demands for the organization of migratory farm workers filled the IWW press. Correspondents also urged the IWW to recruit among West Coast Asian workers. Unlike the AFL (or for that matter all other American labor organizations), which refused to organize Asians and sought through legislation to exclude them from the country, the IWW opposed exclusion laws and actively sought Asian recruits. J. H. Walsh, a West Coast organizer, reported that the Japanese-American newspaper *The Revolution* had opened its columns to the IWW and that he, Walsh, was hot on the trail of two Chinese Socialists. Meanwhile, the Wobblies' journal, the *Industrial Union Bulletin (IUB)*, editorially welcomed Japanese laborers to America, commenting, "Japanese workmen already hold cards in the I.W.W. and more are coming. They are welcome."

The Western work first brought to notice Elizabeth Gurley Flynn, destined as "the rebel girl" to become the most publicized of all IWW personalities. In 1907, though still only a teenager, Flynn carried the industrial union message west to Duluth and up and down the Mesabi Iron Range. A Duluth paper described her platform manner as follows: "Socialistic fervor seems to emanate from her expressive eyes, and even from her red dress. She is a girl with a 'mission.'" Encountering timidity and fear on the part of the miners, Flynn promised to make a second speaking tour in order to keep alive the interest in the IWW aroused by her messianic speeches.

But in these early years, as also in its later life, the IWW proved most successful in reaching the lumber workers of the far West. These loggers, commonly referred to as "timber beasts" in the IWW press, worked in an anarchic industry. The physical hardships and deprivations associated with the lumber industry—particularly the isolation deep within the rain forests, miles from cities and the amenities of civilized life—made working conditions an even more miserable burden than low wages.

This the IWW sought to alter by transforming the "timber beast" into a man. But the lumber industry proved tough to organize. Employer attitudes toward labor were as primitive as the working conditions and as aggressive as the competition between companies. No union could be permitted to stand between an employer and his "right to employ whoever he sees fit."

Yet loggers were perfect IWW recruits. Mostly native-born Americans or northern Europeans, they spoke English, lived together, drank together, slept together, whored together, and fought together. Isolated in the woods or in primitive mill towns, they were bound by ties much stronger than their separate skill or job classifications. Whether skilled or unskilled, they wanted room to dry their clothes, clean bunks, decent bedding, and good food. They were tired of carrying bindles* on their backs as they moved from job to job and camp to camp. The IWW promised loggers bindle-burning parties and decent working conditions to be won through industrial solidarity. Within a year of its founding, the IWW local in Seattle had over eight hundred members and by March 1907 had established new locals in the mill and lumber port towns of Portland Tacoma, Aberdeen, Hoquiam, Ballard, North Bend, Astoria, and Vancouver. The union idea was becoming contagious.

Employers, of course, were aware of the IWW's penetration into the lumber industry, but the public was not—that is, until March 1, 1907, when the IWW took command of a spontaneous walkout by Portland's mill workers. The IWW appeared on the Portland scene after a few mill hands had walked out following an unanswered call for higher wages and shorter hours. Organizers Fred Heslewood and Joseph Ettor soon went to work. Within a week they closed almost every mill in town and had over two thousand men out on strike. Claiming over eighteen hundred members, the IWW's Portland local (No. 319) formulated demands for a nine-hour day and a $2.50 minimum daily wage.

Like all the early IWW strikes, this one had immediate objectives. Ettor and Heslewood educated the strikers to the realities of the class struggle but persistently urged their followers to be orderly and restrained. The two agitators mentioned revolution only as a future possibility, never as an imminent prospect.

Yet even the struggle over present realities intensely disturbed employers. Again, what vexed them more than questions of wages and working conditions was the issue of power. Washington's employers fervently hoped that the IWW

* The bindle consisted of the bedding the logger was required to provide wherever he worked, giving rise to the nickname *bindlestiff*.

offensive could be confined to the Portland area, but whatever happened, lumbermen intended to present a united front against the IWW.

The cards in this instance were stacked in favor of management. The Portland mills maintained their unity and, with support from lumber firms to the north, held fast against the strikers. Local AFL affiliates refused to cooperate with the strikers; indeed, the AFL Central Labor Council and the Portland building trade unions cooperated with employers to fight the IWW. In fact, the Portland mills, with local AFL approval, successfully recruited nonunion workers, and by March 18 one employer concluded, "The strike forces have disintegrated." The next day Portland's mills reopened, and ten days later the strike had been completely crushed.

IWW organizers attempted to minimize their defeat. Heslewood claimed the conflict had resulted in improved working conditions for the strikers and had given IWW agitators forty days in which to educate workers to the necessity of revolutionary industrial unionism. He had a point. The IWW may have lost the immediate conflict, but the strikers and most other workers in the lumber industry did benefit from the Portland struggle. In the aftermath of the strike the Puget Mill Company decided that it would "be well for the company to do everything in its power to have things pleasant for the men." In the future, Western loggers would remember that it was the IWW, not the AFL, that had improved the conditions of their work.

Despite its coast-to-coast industrial activities, the IWW had painfully little in the way of organizational results to show for its efforts of 1907 and 1908. At the uneventful 1907 convention, Trautmann reported that the organization had 31,000 members. But of that number, at most only 10,000 paid monthly dues, and half the membership regularly moved in and out of the organization, leading to considerable double counting. A year later, Trautmann reported that the IWW, despite its well-conducted strikes at Bridgeport and Skowhegan, had lost not only all its members in those cities but also its prestige as an organization. Vincent St. John offered the 1908 convention equally disquieting news, for he estimated that since the 1907 convention the IWW had organized seventy-six locals and three district councils, but over the same period sixty-three locals had disbanded.

The IWW's failure to progress was scarcely alleviated by the 1907 panic. Economic decline aggravated an already grievous organizational collapse. In December 1907, Trautmann reported that organization revenues had fallen by half. Appeal after appeal to delinquent locals and members to pay indebtedness brought no answer. The general executive board levied a special assessment but could not collect it. Printing and office bills grew, receipts dropped—

still no relief was forthcoming. The general executive board finally curtailed all administrative expenses, including organizing activity, in order to preserve publication of the *IUB*, which, the board told itself, could spread the gospel of industrial unionism better than organizers. Even so, financial stringency compelled the board to reduce the publication of its journal from a weekly to a biweekly.

Economic conditions certainly did not help matters any, but a large share of the IWW's failure must be laid directly at the organization's doorstep. Even before the economic downturn of 1907–8, the IWW had proved unwilling to correct internal deficiencies. The minutes of a September 1907 executive board meeting revealed that the IWW could not, or at any rate would not, finance its organizers. Organizers were expected to support themselves through commissions earned on the sale of IWW literature. Only those who could sustain themselves were allowed to remain in the field. That left five men—Walsh, Ettor, Williams, Heslewood, and James P. Thompson—to organize workers from Maine to California. Furthermore, IWW locals and members refused to pay their dues to general headquarters.

Organizational chaos worsened the financial problems. At a general executive board meeting in December 1907, James Thompson, then organizing in New England, explained the difficulties he faced because the IWW constitution lacked provision for national industrial unions. Then and there, without recorded discussion or debate, the general executive board resolved that three thousand members engaged in the same industry but organized in not less than seven different localities constituted a national industrial union. But most IWW members, unaffected by such grandiose paper schemes, remained in mixed locals that disbanded regularly because of barren treasuries, incompetent leaders, or both. Other aspects of the IWW's internal organization were open to criticism. Ettor, for example, found Wobblies prone to ridicule all union officials as tin gods, and he witnessed IWW locals practicing unrestrained rotation in office: Each weekly meeting would elect a new set of officials. Untempered democracy, Ettor concluded, resulted in poorly administered locals, impulsive and ill-planned strikes, and the consequent disillusionment of the workers whom the IWW wished to reach.

St. John was convinced that the IWW could produce no results until it obtained the funds necessary to saturate an industry with organizers as well as the power to protect IWW members against hostile employers. He confessed his own inability to break the vicious circle plaguing the IWW. No funds meant no organizers meant no members; no members meant no funds meant no organizers.

Although leaders like St. John, Trautmann, and Williams perceived their organization's basic weaknesses, they could not quite bring themselves to admit that these weaknesses were the result of chronic internal ailments; instead, they sought scapegoats. They found their devil in Daniel DeLeon.

DeLeon was never an easy man to get along with. Desiring to be an American Lenin, he compelled uniformity among his disciples. He shared Lenin's iron will as well as his intense desire to command men and to make history. But DeLeon sought to make his revolution in a distinctly nonrevolutionary society. Claiming to have been born in Curaçao in December 1852, the son of a Dutch Jewish colonial family, DeLeon was apparently American born. So fully and relentlessly did he distort the circumstances of his birth and early life that little that is historically sound is known about DeLeon's youth. What passes for biography is largely a composite of his own peculiar fictions, the product of what one scholar has characterized as the mind of a pathological liar. DeLeon apparently obtained a law degree from Columbia University in 1878, lectured there in Latin American history in 1883, participated in reformer Henry George's 1886 New York City mayoralty campaign, and then flirted with the Knights of Labor and Edward Bellamy's Nationalist movement. This checkered course ultimately brought him to the Socialist Labor party (SLP), whose high priest he became in 1892, as editor of *The People,* the party's journal. As Marxist socialism's principal advocate in America, DeLeon would make more heretics than converts. Once in firm control of the SLP, DeLeon sought to capture the remnants of the dying Knights of Labor. Failing in this, he modestly decided to seize the AFL. Again he was repelled, this time more swiftly. He never took defeat lightly. Unable to control the AFL, he determined to destroy it. In order to do so, DeLeon established the Socialist Trades and Labor Alliance in 1895.

At this stage in his life, DeLeon maintained that his revolution must come through political action, that the economic organization (that is, the trade union) must be subordinate to the political party. When members of the SLP disagreed with DeLeon's dogmatism on the trade union issue and still tried to bore within the AFL, they were promptly expelled. Tolerating no dissent, DeLeon was beset by enemies on all sides. Gompers was a bitter, vindictive critic; Debs, Berger, and most Midwestern Socialists wanted no part of New York's "Red Pope of Revolution." By 1900 he was left with a declining SLP and a moribund Trades and Labor Alliance.

Despite adversity, DeLeon refused to change his ideology or his tactics—that is, until the founding of the IWW in 1905 offered him a new opportunity. DeLeon now suddenly discovered that economic action was more important than political action and that the industrial union, not the political party, was the instrument of revolution. With his followers, he joined the IWW.

DeLeon went only where he could lead; he wanted disciples, not allies, sycophants, not comrades. Hence, DeLeon and his lieutenants at once set about to transform the IWW into an adjunct of the SLP. SLP men promoted the propaganda of politics at the expense of industrial unionism; they recruited for the party, not for the union; and wherever DeLeonites were active, factionalism and political argumentation weakened IWW locals.

Most Wobblies, indeed, had little in common with DeLeon or his party. Western workers, still a major influence in the organization, had shed none of their deeply ingrained suspicions about the efficacy of political action. From their own experiences, they were convinced that the state was usually their enemy and that politics more often than not had brought them no relief. "If you ignore the ballot box and put your efforts into the building up of the Industrial Workers of the World," an Arizona miner informed the 1907 WFM convention, "you can get all the good things of life."

But DeLeon and his SLP disciples gave only lip service to industrial unionism. When they spoke at IWW meetings or circulated literature during strikes, they concentrated upon criticizing the Socialist party. Not unexpectedly, the IWW general executive board warned all IWW representatives in June 1907 against introducing political fights into union affairs.

The fight with DeLeon finally erupted openly in December 1907. James Connolly, later to become a martyr in the 1916 Dublin Easter Rising, was an IWW organizer in New York City in 1907, when he asked for an emergency general executive board meeting to discuss the possibility of recruiting large numbers of New York workers. But before the session could be held, DeLeon demanded a secret conference on "a matter of importance." His "important matter" turned out to be a warning that Connolly was an unreliable maverick hostile to the SLP. At the special secret meeting, DeLeon delivered an invective-filled tirade, which became so bitter that Ben Williams, chairing the session, declared DeLeon out of order.

The internal struggle was now in earnest. Speaking before a New York SLP audience in March 1908, Williams angrily declared that experience had taught him that the IWW received a hearing and a response from workers only in proportion to its ability to avoid political entanglements. Insisting that the political party was but a reflex of the industrial union, Williams concluded, "We say to those who cannot adjust themselves to the I.W.W. position, 'Hands Off!' whether such individuals belong to one or the other of the two Socialist Parties."

As the 1908 convention approached, the DeLeonites made one last effort to dominate the IWW. Paying up their back dues by the hundreds, they packed the IWW mixed local in New York and selected DeLeon and his adherents as the city's convention delegation. But the DeLeonites failed to take into account rank-and-file hostility to them and their plans.

Two thousand miles from the convention city of Chicago, in Portland, Oregon, IWW organizer John H. Walsh started a movement that ensured DeLeon's defeat. Walsh described his tactics in dispatches to the *IUB*. On September 1, 1908, nineteen men gathered in the Portland railroad yards, he wrote, "all dressed in black overalls and jumpers, black shirts and red ties, with an I.W.W. book in his [*sic*] pocket and an I.W.W. button on his [*sic*] coat." Seizing a cattle car, they started on their side-door coach journey east to Chicago. Northward went the Overalls Brigade as their "Red Special" took them first to Centralia, Washington, and then to an unexpected overnight stay in Seattle's jail. Undeterred by imprisonment, they hopped a second freight which carried them through Spokane; Sand Point, Idaho; Missoula, Montana, and points east. All along the route Walsh held propaganda meetings and sold literature to keep his brigade fed.

These Westerners sang their way across Montana, eating in the "jungles," preaching revolution in the prairie towns they besieged, and singing constantly. In five weeks of riding the rails the Overalls Brigade and its singing platoon traveled over 2,500 miles, held thirty-one meetings, and sold more than $175 worth of literature and about $200 in song sheets (the parent of the now famous *Little Red Song Book*).

Other anti-DeLeonites converged upon Chicago from the east. Ben Williams arrived in town to find Vincent St. John fearful of bringing the DeLeon-SLP issue before the convention. Williams argued that confining the issue to New York, as St. John hoped to do, was impossible, for the future of the entire IWW hinged upon the relationship between the concept of industrial unionism, the ideology of the SLP, and the role of politics in bringing about the revolution. Hence he demanded that the entire New York controversy be laid before the convention. After much hesitation, St. John finally agreed.

The fourth IWW convention differed considerably from its three predecessors. For the first time since the organization's founding, the West Coast was well represented, having sent delegates from Seattle, Portland, and Los Angeles. Notable by their absence were Socialist party members and intellectual fellow travelers. The stage was now set for the great struggle over DeLeon's role in the IWW. Williams and the Eastern intellectuals would provide anti-DeLeon ideological ammunition; Walsh's Western Brigade would provide votes and militancy.

The convention opened on September 21, with chairman St. John calling upon Walsh's Overalls Brigade to sing "The Marseillaise." The martial spirit aroused, the delegates heard Trautmann ask them to march to war against DeLeon and the SLP, as he defined the central issue confronting the convention: Would the IWW become a tail to a political kite, or would it be left free to organize workers into industrial unions?

Not until its fourth day did the convention come to grips with this central issue. On that day, September 24, the credentials committee recommended by a vote of three to one that DeLeon not be seated because he belonged to the wrong local. DeLeon was given an opportunity to argue his case before the delegates. Resorting to personal invective as usual, DeLeon claimed that his enemies were the men who had retarded the industrial union movement, and that the convention, instead of "sticking the knife into me should stick it into Trautmann and Williams." But the delegates proceeded to stab DeLeon, voting forty to twenty-one to adopt the credentials committee recommendation.

With DeLeon ousted, the delegates quarreled cantankerously over their organization's political role. Ideological lines became more confused than ever. A clear majority had removed DeLeon because of his ideological stress on political action, yet the constitution committee voted to recommend that the IWW preamble be left untouched, overruling a minority that had insisted that it be amended to remove all reference to political action. The final vote on the question was as close and as confused as the heated debate preceding it. At least twelve delegates who had voted against DeLeon balloted in favor of retaining the IWW preamble as it stood. A bare three-vote majority (thirty-five to thirty-two) deleted political action from the preamble.

The convention's decision to drop all reference to politics from the preamble did open the IWW to the criticism that it was simply an anarchist organization composed of dynamiters. DeLeon was among the first to attack the "new" IWW on just those grounds, calling Wobblies "bums, anarchists, and physical force destroyers." He even formed his own IWW,* ostentatiously dedicated to orderly, peaceful action through political and parliamentary tactics.

But DeLeon and others who accepted his critique of the post-1908 IWW misunderstood what the convention had done. The delegates had simply put the IWW where the AFL had been since 1895. Both labor organizations now refused direct endorsement of, or alliance with, any political party. Moreover, the IWW, like the AFL, did not and could not determine rank-and-file attitudes or actions on political issues. Delegates to the 1908 convention recognized, as Gompers had over a decade earlier, that political debates between

* The so-called Detroit IWW existed largely on paper.

socialist factions wrecked union locals and undermined labor's morale. Hence, the Wobblies decided to keep political debate within the party, where it belonged, and to promote industrial action within the IWW, whereby workers could improve their lives.

Other equally erroneous misconceptions about the IWW arose as a result of the 1908 convention. Critics of the IWW, especially DeLeon, emphasized the role of the Overalls Brigade, or "Proletarian Rabble and Bummers." Charging that the "slum proletariat" and the "bum brigade" had taken over the organization, DeLeon asserted that because of this the IWW would never achieve stability, since "hoboes" would neither pay adequate dues nor tolerate competent officials. Yet the "hobo" delegates at the 1908 convention, quite unlike those imagined by DeLeon, opposed dues reduction and urged instead that they be raised. Walsh reported that the Western rank and file considered dues reduction a cheap proposition and wondered how an organization could exist without adequate funds. Western Wobblies themselves never doubted that an organization needed funds and effective leaders to survive and grow.

Unfortunately, neither Westerners nor Easterners, neither rank and file nor leaders, could do anything about industrial depression, unemployment, and delinquent dues payment. The 1908 convention thus sanctioned the established practice of using only organizers who sustained themselves through the sale of literature and buttons.

The reconstituted IWW thus began its life inauspiciously. When St. John assumed office as general organizer (Trautmann was demoted to secretary-treasurer), he found the IWW practically without income and deeply in debt. The membership consisted of a few mixed foreign-language locals in the East and a few hundred seasonal workers in the West. The WFM, the AFL, and both Socialist parties assailed the IWW as an aggregation of "anarchists and bums." Eugene Debs quietly allowed his IWW membership to lapse. When St. John suspended publication of the *IUB* in March 1909, he could not even hint at a possible date for resumption of publication. Even limited organizing activity ground to a complete halt. Yet it was this post-1908 organization that was able to contribute something new to the labor movement.

During most of those years the IWW's fortunes were guided by Vincent St. John as general organizer (1908–15), and its philosophy and approach were expounded by Ben Williams, editor of *Solidarity*, the official IWW journal, from 1909 until his retirement in March 1917. To these two men, about whom Americans know so little, the IWW owed much of its success and influence in the years before World War I.

Vincent St. John, better known to his friends and associates as the Saint, commanded the total respect and allegiance of the young rebels who flocked to the IWW. Elizabeth Gurley Flynn later wrote of him, "I never met a man I admired more."

Born in Newport, Kentucky, on July 16, 1876, of Irish-Dutch ancestry, St. John had an unsettled home life. Between 1880 and 1895 he moved with his family to New Jersey, Colorado, Washington State, and California. At nineteen Vincent returned alone to Colorado to begin a tempestuous life as a miner, prospector, and union organizer. As president of the Telluride Miners' Union, he managed the successful 1901 strike; shortly after this, he became a local hero by risking his life in a mining disaster to save others. But he was no hero to local mine managers, who accused him of assassinating the manager of the Smuggler Union mine. For two years (1902–3) local and state authorities hounded St. John. Lacking evidence, public officials could not prosecute him, but private employers could and did blacklist him throughout Colorado. As a WFM hero and a close associate of the union's national officers, he was implicated in the Steunenberg case; McParland included St. John among the members of the "inner circle" and even provided Colorado authorities with loose circumstantial evidence sufficient to bring St. John to trial for murder. He moved from one scrape with the law to another. A leader in the anti-Sherman IWW factional fight of 1906, he battled with private detectives and city police. A strong advocate of the IWW, unlike some other WFM leaders, St. John went to Goldfield in 1906 to lead the IWW town workers and their WFM allies, only to be shot in the right hand, which as a result became permanently crippled. Finally, in 1917, though no longer associated with the IWW in an official capacity, St. John, with other IWW officials, was arrested, indicted, tried, and convicted by federal authorities.

Vincent St. John's bitter experiences as a worker and as a union official, and not books or theories, shaped his thoughts and actions. Blessed with an unusual ability to act immediately and effectively without undue philosophizing or procrastinating, he obtained the best from his subordinates, in whom he instilled his own ability to act under fire. Decisiveness suited St. John. Under his direction the IWW became noted for its tactics of direct action and its avoidance of political action, though St. John had once been a Socialist party member and even a party candidate for public office. Experience, not European syndicalist ideas, convinced him that political activities disrupted union organization and that labor's betterment lay in militant industrial unionism. Hence, he struggled to save the IWW from Daniel DeLeon on one hand and from the "anarchist freaks" on the other.

St. John's physique and manner scarcely accorded with the life of the man of action he was. Short and slight, he moved quickly and gracefully. Always in conflict with union opponents, employers, and the law, he was nevertheless quiet, self-contained, and modest.

Ben H. Williams, the second influential figure during the IWW's early years, led a similarly nomadic life. Williams, like St. John, traveled extensively and had a firsthand experience of a broad spectrum of American life. But while St. John derived his ideas largely from personal experience, Williams's ideas originated as much in reading and reasoning. While the Saint's life tended toward action, Williams more and more turned to a life of thought and theory. While St. John administered general headquarters, Williams edited the official journal, providing the IWW with whatever formal ideological structure it had.

Like St. John, Williams was American to the core. Born in the slate quarry town of Monson, Maine, in 1877, he was named Benjamin Hayes in honor of the recently elected Republican president. When his father deserted the family in 1888, young Williams moved with his mother to Bertrand, Nebraska, where a half-brother ran a small print shop. Here his kinsman introduced him to the realities of exploitation, driving the young apprentice to exhaustion. Here Williams introduced himself to radicalism, later recalling about those Nebraska days, "The Western farmers' revolt was in full swing with the Farmers' Alliance. . . . Before my twelfth year, I was introduced to all the social philosophies—anarchism, socialism, communism, direct legislation, and Alliance programs—absorbing the ideas of a New America and a better world." From this Williams moved on to a reading of Bellamy, Marx, and Thomas Henry Huxley, linking together Bellamy's utopianism, Marx's materialistic revolutionary credo, and Huxley's evolutionary schema. Williams even managed a formal education at Tabor College in Iowa in the late 1890s.

Learning led Williams to seek action in the world. In 1898 he interested himself in DeLeon's SLP and its effort to organize workers through the Socialist Trades and Labor Alliance. A little later he met Frank Bohn and Father Hagerty, who further influenced him to devote his life to working-class organization. By 1904 he was lecturing and organizing for the SLP, and he naturally followed his party into the IWW in 1905. As a Wobbly, Williams organized unions in the redwood forests around Eureka, California, all the time growing increasingly disillusioned with the SLP's emphasis on political action and its neglect of union organization. Elected to the general executive board at the 1907 convention, he became its unofficial chairman. As an opponent of DeLeon he led the 1908 struggle that culminated in DeLeon's ouster. When his term on the board ended in 1909, Williams hoboed to New Castle, Pennsylvania, where he became editor of *Solidarity,* the job he held until he left the IWW in 1917.

Williams arrived in New Castle looking every bit the radical intellectual. Short and slight, he had narrow, sloping shoulders and a sensitive face more suited for life in the study than in the mine pit or on the picket line. With clear, piercing eyes topped by thin eyebrows, a fine, straight nose, well-formed, thin lips, a clear complexion, and a well-trimmed Van Dyke, he looked like a soft-grained American version of Lenin and other Bolshevik revolutionaries.

# 7

# Ideology and Utopia: The Syndicalism of the IWW

From 1909 to 1919 a legend enveloped the IWW. Many Americans, especially during World War I and the postwar Red Scare, became convinced that the Wobblies were "bolshevik desperadoes." The hobo Wobbly had replaced the bearded, bomb-carrying anarchist as a bogeyman in the middle-class American's fevered imagination. This version of the Wobbly died hard.

With the IWW, as with other radical organizations that have been romanticized and mythologized, the legend is several removes from reality. Wobblies did not carry bombs, nor burn harvest fields, nor destroy timber, nor depend upon "the machine that works with a trigger." Instead they tried in their own ways to comprehend the nature and dynamics of capitalist society and through increased knowledge, as well as through revolutionary activism, to develop a better system for the organization and functioning of the American economy.

IWW beliefs must be understood in terms of those whom the organization tried to organize. After the defection of the Western Federation of Miners in 1907, Wobblies concentrated upon the workers neglected by the mainstream of the labor movement: timber beasts, hobo harvesters, itinerant construction workers, exploited eastern and southern European immigrants, racially excluded African Americans, Mexicans, and Asian Americans.

The men who associated with the IWW in its heyday were largely first-generation citizens of an industrial society. As is frequently noted, immigrants from the south and east of Europe often first experienced urban industrial life upon their arrival in the New World. But dispossessed native-born Americans were equally newcomers to industrial society who also made the frightening journey from a preindustrial to an industrial society. Caught between two systems and two modes of existence, these immigrants—internal and external—were indeed uprooted. Torn from an old, ordered, and comprehensible way of life, they found themselves unable to replace it with an integrated and meaningful mode of existence and soon became the human flotsam and jetsam of early industrial capitalism's frequent shipwrecks.

Feeling impotent and alienated, these workers harbored deep grievances against the essential institutions of the ruling classes: police, government, and church. Hence, Wobblies exhibited a high susceptibility to unrest and to radical movements aimed at destroying the established social order.

This is what IWW leaders sensed. The leadership consisted largely of two types: skilled workers and formerly successful trade union officials such as Haywood, St. John, Joseph Ettor, and Frank Little; and restless intellectuals such as Ben Williams, Justus Ebert, and the Swedish immigrant syndicalist John Sandgren. These men shared a common desire to effect a nonpolitical revolution in America and a common alienation from the American Federation of Labor (AFL) and from reformist American socialists. Eager to make a revolution that would destroy the existing system root and branch, they naturally turned to those most alienated from the American dream—and located them in the lower strata of a rapidly changing society.

The IWW clearly shaped its doctrines and its tactics to attract such recruits. That is why it maintained low initiation fees and still lower dues, why it allowed universal transfer of union cards, why it belittled union leaders as the labor lieutenants of capitalism, and why, finally, it derogated business unionism as porkchop unionism and trade union welfare systems as coffin benefits. IWW members simply could not afford the initiation fees and dues required to sustain business unionism; partly because of their feelings of impotence and partly because they moved from industry to industry, Wobblies also needed self-leadership and self-discipline more than the counsel of professional, bureaucratic union officials. Thus, only by implementing policies sure to keep its treasury bare and its bureaucracy immobilized could the IWW attract the followers it sought.

Basically, the IWW did what other American unions refused to do. It opened its doors to all: black and Asian, Jew and Catholic, immigrant and native. Wobbly locals had no closed membership rolls, no apprenticeship regulations. As West Coast organizer George Speed put it, "One man is as good as another to me; I don't care whether he is black, blue, green, or yellow, as long as he acts the man and acts true to his economic interests as a worker."

The disinherited joined the IWW by the thousands because it offered them "a ready made dream of a new world where there is a new touch with sweetness and light and where for a while they can escape the torture of forever being indecently kicked about." Or, as Carleton Parker discovered of his wandering rank and file, the IWW offered "the only social break in the harsh search for work that they have ever had; its headquarters the only competitor of the saloon in which they are welcome. They listen stolidly to their frequent lecturers with an obvious and sustained interest. . . . The concrete details of industrial renovation find eager interest."

But, as Rexford Tugwell perceptively noted in 1920, the revolutionary potential of the poor in America is limited. "No world regenerating philosophy comes out of them and they are not going to inherit the earth." When Tugwell wrote those lines, the IWW had been fatally weakened by federal and state repression. Yet for a time, from 1909 to 1917, the IWW seemed well on the way to organizing the revolutionary potential of the poor.

The IWW, it is true, produced no intellectual giants. It did not spawn a Karl Marx or a Georges Sorel, a Lenin or a Jean Jaures, or even an Edward Bellamy or a Henry George. It offered no genuinely original ideas, no sweeping explanations of social change, no fundamental theories of revolution. Wobblies instead took their basic concepts from others: from Marx the concepts of labor value, commodity value, surplus value, and class struggle; from Darwin the idea of organic evolution and the struggle for survival as a paradigm for social evolution and the survival of the fittest class; from Bakunin and the anarchists the "propaganda of the deed" and the idea of direct action; and from Sorel the notion of the "militant minority." Hence, IWW beliefs became a peculiar amalgam of Marxism and Darwinism, anarchism and syndicalism—all overlaid with a singularly American patina.

As early as 1912 William E. Bohn, an astute journalist and observer of the American scene, could declare that the IWW "did not come into being as the result of any foreign influence. It is distinctly an American product." Ben Williams agreed. For seven years, as editor of *Solidarity,* he vigorously criticized those who associated the IWW with foreign ideologies. "Whatever it may have in common with European labor movements,' he insisted, the IWW "is a distinct product of America and American conditions." IWW ideologues did turn to the writings of Marx and Darwin for social theory. Yet they also drew upon an older American tradition, dating back to the era of Jefferson and Jackson, which divided society into producers and nonproducers, productive classes and parasites.

Wobblies never questioned the labor theory of value or the other basic tenets of Marxian economics. Indeed, since labor created all value, the worker was robbed when (as under capitalism) he did not receive the money equivalent of his full product. Capitalism and thievery were thus synonymous: Profits represented the capitalist's seizure of his worker's surplus value. This robbery could end only with the abolition of capitalism.

Like Marx, the Wobblies also believed that the working class, or proletariat, would rise up in wrath and destroy the capitalists. Like Marx, they asserted that capitalism carried the seeds of its own destruction and that workers would create "the new society within the shell of the old." Like Marx, again, they saw in the class struggle "the relentless logic of history," which would roll on until, as the IWW proclaimed in its preamble, the workers of the world organize as a class, take possession of the earth and the machinery of production and abolish the wage system."

The IWW was never precise in its definition of class. Sometimes Wobblies divided society into two classes, capitalists and workers; sometimes they perceived distinct and separate subclasses within the two major categories; and sometimes they followed Haywood's example of dividing "all the world into three parts: the capitalists, who are the employing class that makes money out of money; the skilled laborers; and the masses." The IWW, of course, represented the masses who would act as the agents of the new and better social order.

Wobblies also reversed common American assumptions about the applicability of Darwinian evolution to social change. In the IWW's amalgam of Marxism and Darwinism, capitalism was the stage preceding the establishment of the workers' paradise. In the IWW's view, since the working class was most fit, its mode of organization would be superior to that of the capitalists, and thus would enable the IWW to build its new order within the shell of the old. Thus was social Darwinism stood on its head; thus would the beaten become the fit; thus would the slaves become the masters.

Wobblies glorified themselves as the saviors of society. The IWW perceived in America's disinherited the raw material for the transformation of a basically sick society. Writing to the *Industrial Worker* from a Louisiana jail, the organizer E. F. Doree was moved to poetry: "Arise like lions after slumber / In unvanquishable number. / Shake your chains to earth like dew / Which in sleep have fallen on You. / Ye are many, they are few." "We are many," proclaimed *Solidarity*. "We are resourceful; we are animated by the most glorious vision of the ages; we cannot be conquered, and we shall conquer the world for the working class." Listen to our song, urged the paper, printing the IWW's own version of the "Internationale":

Arise, ye prisoners of starvation!
Arise, ye wretched of the earth!
For justice thunders condemnation.
A better world's in birth.

No more tradition's chains shall bind us;
Arise, ye slaves! No more in thrall!

The earth shall stand on new foundations;
We have been naught—We shall be All!

'Tis the final conflict!
Let each stand in his place.
The Industrial Union
Shall be the Human Race.

The song epitomizes the IWW's ultimate objectives: a combination of primitive millenarianism and modern revolutionary goals. It seems clear that the IWW shared with primitive millenarians an instinctive distaste for the world as it was, as well as hope for the creation of a completely new world, a Judgment Day when the exploiters would be turned out and the banner of industrial freedom raised over the workshops of the world "in a free society of men and women."

Notwithstanding this belief in ultimate revolution, the IWW constantly sought opportunities to improve the immediate circumstances of its members. Speakers and publications emphasized a twofold purpose: "First, to improve conditions for the working class day by day. Second, to build up an organization that can take possession of the industries and run them for the benefit of the workers when capitalism shall have been overthrown." A Wobbly organizer said simply, "The final aim . . . is revolution. But for the present let's see if we can get a bed to sleep in, water enough to take a bath and decent food to eat."

But utopia and revolution always lurked just beneath the surface. To the convinced Wobbly, each battle, whether for higher wages or shorter hours, better food or better bedding, prepared the participant for the final struggle with the master class. Only by daily fights with the employer could a strong revolutionary organization be formed. "The very fights themselves, like the drill of an army, prepare the workers for ever greater tasks and victories."

IWW leaders made no bones about their quarrel with other labor leaders who contented themselves with wringing short-term concessions from employers. Joe Ettor proudly proclaimed the IWW's unwillingness to subvert its ideas, make peace with employers, or sign protocols and contracts. Like Marx, he said, "we disdain to conceal our views, we openly declare that our ends can be attained only by the forcible overthrow of all existing conditions."

Unlike primitive millenarians, Wobblies did not expect their revolution to come about through "a divine revelation . . . an announcement from on high [or] . . . a miracle." Furthermore, they expected neither the inevitable Marxist class struggle nor the ineluctable Darwinian evolution of society alone to make their revolution. Inevitable it was, but they could assist the course of history. "Our organization is not content with merely making the prophecy," asserted *Solidarity*, "but acts upon industrial and social conditions with a view to shaping them in accord with the general tendency."

The Wobblies believed they could best make history by seizing power. He who held power ruled society. The IWW proposed to transfer power from the capitalists, who used it for antisocial purposes, to the proletariat, who, they fondly believed, would exercise it for the benefit of humanity.

The IWW's gospelers with their doctrine of power made a great deal of sense to men in the social jungle who saw naked force—by employers, police, and courts—constantly used against them. When an IWW pamphlet proclaimed, "It is the law of nature that the strong rule and the weak are enslaved," Wobblies simply recognized the reality of their own lives writ large. George Speed, an admired IWW organizer, expressed their emotions tersely. "Power," he said, "is the thing that determines everything today. . . . It stands to reason that the fellow that has got the big club swings it over the balance. That is life as it exists today."

The IWW's antipathy toward political action also made sense to its members. Migratory workers moved too often to establish legal voting residences. Millions of immigrants lacked the franchise, as did the blacks, women, and child workers to whom the IWW appealed. Even the immigrants and natives in the IWW ranks who had the right to vote nourished a deep suspicion of government. To them the policeman's club and the magistrate's edict symbolized the state's alliance with entrenched privilege. Who knew the injustices of the state better than a Wobbly imprisoned for exercising the right of free speech or clubbed by bullying policemen while picketing peacefully for higher wages? Daily experience demonstrated the truth of Elizabeth Gurley Flynn's comment that the state was simply the slugging agency of the capitalists. Hence, Wobblies refused to believe that stuffing pieces of paper—even socialist ones—into a box would transform the basically repressive institution of the state into a humane one.

Representing workers who could not conceive of political power as a means to alter the rules of the game, Wobblies had to offer an alternative. This they discovered in economic power. Naively believing themselves better Marxists than their socialist critics, Wobblies insisted that political power was but a reflex of economic power, and that without economic organization behind it, labor politics was "like a house without a foundation or a dream without substance." IWW leaders concentrated on teaching their followers how to obtain economic power. To quote some of their favorite aphorisms, "Get it through industrial organization," "Organize the workers to control the use of their labor power," "The secret of power is organization," and "The only force that can break . . . tyrannical rule . . . is the one big union of all the workers."

From the IWW point of view, direct action was the essential means for bringing its new society into existence. As defined by Wobblies, direct action included any step taken by workers at the point of production that improved wages, reduced hours, and bettered conditions. It encompassed conventional strikes, intermittent strikes, silent strikes, passive resistance, sabotage, and the ultimate direct action measure: the general strike, which would displace the capitalists from power and place the means of production in working-class hands. Direct action, according to Haywood, would eventually reach the point at which workers would be strong enough to say, "Here, Mr. Stockholder, we won't work for you any longer. You have drawn dividends out of our hides long enough; we propose that you shall go to work now and under the same opportunities that we have had."

The emphasis on direct action in preference to parliamentary politics or socialist dialectics represented a profound insight by IWW leaders into the minds of industrial workers. Abstract doctrine meant nothing to the disinherited; specific grievances meant everything! Justus Ebert expressed this idea for the IWW: "Workingmen on the job don't care . . . about the co-operative commonwealth; they want practical organization first, all else after."

The Philadelphia Longshoremen, an IWW affiliate that successfully used direct action and actually controlled job conditions, urged, "We have work to do. We function as a job organization and have no time to split hairs. Job control is the thing." How much like the AFL!

But while the IWW's emphasis on direct action, job control, and economic power resembled the AFL's line, the Wobblies' rhetoric was of an entirely different order. Restrained in action, Wobblies were considerably less restrained in utterance. Where the AFL spoke cautiously of law and order, the IWW exuberantly discussed the law of the jungle. Where the AFL pleaded for contracts and protocols, the IWW hymned clubs and brute force. Where the AFL sought industrial harmony, the IWW praised perpetual industrial war.

Consequently, it became easy for critics of the IWW, whether on the right or the left, to listen to Wobbly speakers, to read Wobbly propaganda, and to conclude that the IWW actually preferred bullets to ballots, dynamite to mediation. After all, Wobblies constantly announced that their organization respected neither the property rights of capitalists nor the laws they made. "I despise the law," Haywood defiantly informed a Socialist party audience, "and I am not a law-abiding citizen. And more than that, no Socialist can be a law-abiding citizen." He warned Socialist party members fearful of breaking the law and going to prison. "Those of us who are in jail—those of us who have been in jail—all of us who are willing to go to jail care not what you say or what you do! We despise your hypocrisy. . . . We are the Revolution!"

Wobblies even enjoyed comparing themselves to antebellum abolitionists, who also had defied laws that sanctioned human bondage and who had publicly burned the Constitution. As James Thompson boasted, "We are the modern abolitionists fighting against wage slavery." Some Wobblies may indeed have considered unsheathing the Lord's terrible swift sword. St. John, for one, admitted under questioning that he would counsel destruction of property and violence against persons if it accomplished improvement for the workers and brought the revolution closer. Other IWW leaders conceded they would be willing to dynamite factories and mills in order to win a strike. All of them hurled their defiance at "bushwa" law.

Such talk led most Americans to conclude, as did Harris Weinstock of the Federal Commission on Industrial Relations, that "it is the organized and deliberate purpose of the I.W.W. to teach and preach and to burn into the hearts and minds of its followers that they are justified in lying; that they are justified in stealing and in trampling under foot their own agreements and in confiscating the property of others."

Having created this image of itself, the IWW simultaneously tried to dispel it. To the convinced Wobbly, Weinstock's words better described the practices and attitudes of the American capitalist. Although the IWW employed the vocabulary of violence, more often than not it practiced passive resistance, and was itself the victim of violence instigated by law enforcement officials and condoned by the law-abiding. In fact, even the Wobblies' vocabulary was ambivalent, the language of nonviolence being employed at least as frequently as that of violence. Big Bill Haywood, for example, told a reporter during the 1912 Lawrence textile strike, "I should never think of conducting a strike in the old way. . . . I, for one, have turned my back on violence. It wins nothing. When we strike now, we strike with our hands in our pockets. We have a new kind of violence—the havoc we raise with money by laying down our tools. Pure strength lies in the overwhelming power of numbers."

Any careful investigator of the IWW soon becomes aware that the organization regularly proclaimed the superiority of passive resistance over the use of dynamite or guns. Vincent St. John, while conceding the possible usefulness of violence under certain circumstances, nevertheless insisted, "We do not . . . want to be understood as saying that we expect to achieve our aims through violence and through the destruction of human life, because in my judgment, that is impossible."

*Solidarity*, the *Industrial Worker*, and IWW pamphlets all preached the same nonviolent message. "Our dynamite is mental and our force is in organization at the point of production." Again and again IWW publications advised members, "We do not advocate violence; it is to be discouraged."

In actuality, Wobblies looked to nonviolent tactics in order to throw into sharper relief the brutality of their enemy and to win sympathy for their sufferings. Passive resistance, *Solidarity* editorialized, "has a tremendous moral effect; it puts the enemy on record; it exposes the police and city authorities as a bunch of law breakers; it drives the masters to the last ditch of resistance. 'Passive resistance' by the workers results in laying bare the inner workings and purposes of the capitalist mind. It also reveals the self-control, the fortitude, the courage, the inherent sense of order, of the workers' mind. As such, 'passive resistance' is of immense educational value."

But IWW passive resistance should not be confused with pacifism. Nonviolence was only a means, never an end. If passive resistance resulted only in beatings and deaths, then the IWW threatened to respond in kind. Arturo Giovannitti, sometime poet and Wobbly, put the IWW's position bluntly: "The generally accepted notion seems to be that to kill is a great crime, but to be killed is the greatest."

In most cases the IWW hoped to gain its ends through nonviolent measures, through what it described as "Force of education, force of organization, force of a growing class-consciousness and force of working class aspirations for freedom." One forceful method explicitly advocated by the Wobblies—indeed, the tactic with which they are most indelibly associated—was sabotage. To most Americans, sabotage implied the needless destruction of property, the senseless adulteration of products, and, possibly, the inexcusable injuring of persons. Wobblies did not always dispel such images. The *Industrial Worker* suggested to harvest hands in 1910, "Grain sacks come loose and rip, nuts come off wagon wheels and loads are dumped on the way to the barn, machinery breaks down, nobody to blame, everybody innocent . . . boss decides to furnish a little inspiration in the shape of more money and shorter hours . . . just try a little sabotage on the kind hearted, benevolent boss . . . and see how it works." For the next three years the paper continued to urge this method upon its readers, telling them, "Sabotage is an awakening of labor. It is the spirit of revolt." This campaign culminated in 1913 with a series of twelve editorials fully explaining the methods of sabotage and when they should be used.

To help Wobblies find out what sabotage meant, Elizabeth Gurley Flynn prepared a new translation of Emile Pouget's classic, *Sabotage*, which the IWW published and distributed in 1915. Even Ben Williams, generally unenthusiastic about the effectiveness of sabotage, felt constrained to recommend its use. "Sabotage has great possibilities as a means of defense and aggression," he explained. "It is useless to try to argue it out of existence. We need not 'advocate it,' we need only explain it. The organized workers will do the acting."

What was actually meant by all this talk? Some Wobblies might have agreed with James Thompson, who said, "I not only believe in destruction of property, but I believe in the destruction of human life if it will save human life." But most stressed sabotage's nonviolent characteristics. Repeatedly, IWW speakers asserted that sabotage simply implied soldiering on the job, playing dumb, tampering with machines without destroying them—in short, simply harassing the employer to the point of granting his workers' demands. Sometimes, it was claimed, the workers could even effect sabotage through exceptional obedience: Williams and Haywood were fond of noting that Italian and French workers had on occasion tied up the national railroads simply by observing every operating rule in their work regulations.

Yet, hard as they tried, state and federal authorities could never establish legal proof of IWW-instigated sabotage. Rudolph Katz, a DeLeonite who had followed his leader out of the St. John IWW in 1908, was perhaps close to the truth when he informed federal investigators, "The American Federation of Labor does not preach sabotage, but it practices sabotage; and the I.W.W. preaches sabotage, but does not practice it."

Until the IWW succeeded in organizing all workers into industrial unions, which combined to form the celebrated One Big Union that would eventually seize control of industry, it had to employ practices and tactics much like those of any labor union. Accordingly, the IWW encouraged strikes to win immediate improvements in working conditions, for such strikes served a dual purpose: They offered the men involved valuable experience in the class struggle and developed their sense of power, and they weakened the capitalist's power. When conventional strikes failed, the IWW recommended the on-the-job strike—essentially a form of nonviolent sabotage—and the intermittent or short strike begun when the boss least expected it and ended before the strikers could be starved or beaten.

The IWW never lost its vision of the ultimate revolution. Thus, many demands associated with AFL industrial conflicts were absent from those of the IWW. With improvements in working conditions, the AFL unions demanded recognition and ironclad contracts. The IWW spurned both. It would achieve its closed shop "by having an 'open union' for everybody who toils." In other words, collective action and voluntary cooperation by the exploited, not capitalist concessions, would bring the true closed shop. Wobblies were convinced that employer benevolence only lessened working-class solidarity. For somewhat similar reasons, the IWW refused to sign contracts that restricted the right to strike for stated periods of time. All workers had to retain the right to strike simultaneously, the IWW reasoned, or employers could play one group of workers off against another. Workers, moreover, had to be free to strike when employers were weakest, but time contracts provided employers with the option to choose the moment of conflict and to prepare for it in advance. Finally, without the unreserved right to strike, the IWW could not wage the class war, and without the ongoing class struggle there could be no revolution and no cooperative commonwealth.

The organization's refusal to sign contracts raised problems that the IWW never resolved. American employers were never particularly happy dealing with labor unions, and certainly under no circumstances would they negotiate with a labor organization that refused to sign contracts and insisted that capitalists had no rights worthy of respect. Hence, employers constantly used the IWW's no-contract principle to rationalize their own resistance to any form of collective bargaining. If the IWW could not negotiate with employers, how could it raise wages or improve working conditions? If it could offer its members nothing but perpetual industrial warfare, how could it maintain its membership, let alone increase its ranks? On the other hand, if the IWW did sanction contracts, win recognition, and improve its members' lives, what would keep them from forsaking revolutionary goals and adhering to the well-established AFL pattern? If the IWW began to declare truces in the class war, how could it bring about the ultimate revolution? In the end, IWW leaders usually subordinated reform opportunities to revolutionary necessities, while the rank and file, when it could, took the reforms and neglected the revolution.

Even for Wobblies who cherished the hope of revolution, the means of achieving their dream remained vague. Politics or working-class violence would not accomplish it. What, then, remained? "In a word," wrote Haywood and Ettor, "the general strike is the measure by which the capitalistic system will be overthrown."

Neither Haywood nor any other Wobbly ever precisely defined the general strike. Haywood described it as the stoppage of all work and the destruction of the capitalists through a peaceful paralysis of industry. Ben Williams insisted that it was not a strike at all, simply "a 'general lockout of the employing class' leaving the workers in possession of the machinery of distribution and production." Whatever the exact definition of the general strike, Haywood wrote, when its day comes "control of industry will pass from the capitalists to the masses and capitalists will vanish from the face of the earth."

The precise date of the general strike that would usher in the arrival of the IWW's utopia remained as vague for Wobblies as the millennium, or Judgment Day, does for Christians. But the *prospect* of such a Judgment Day was intended to stir among the toiling masses the same ecstatic belief and fanaticism that anticipation of the Second Coming arouses among evangelical Christians. Only with such true believers could the IWW build its One Big Union that would, when fully organized, ring the death knell for American capitalism. In other words, in IWW ideology workers represented a chosen people who through faith and works—faith in the One Big Union and such works as peaceful sabotage—would attain salvation and enter the Kingdom of Heaven here on earth.

Wobblies never quite explained how their terrestrial paradise would be governed. They did agree that the state, as most Americans knew it, would be nonexistent. "There will be no such thing as the State or States," Haywood said. "The industries will take the place of what are now existing States." "Whenever the workers are organized in the industry, whenever they have a sufficient organization in the industry," added St. John, "they will have all the government they need right there." Somehow each industrial union would possess and manage its own industry. Union members would elect superintendents, foremen, secretaries, and all the managers of modern industry. The separate industrial unions would also meet jointly to plan for the welfare of the entire society. This system, "in which each worker will have a share in the ownership and a voice in the control of industry, and in which each shall receive the full product of his labor," was variously called the Cooperative Commonwealth, the Workers' Commonwealth, the Industrial Commonwealth, Industrial Democracy, and Industrial Communism.

It was in their views about the general strike and the governance of utopia that Wobblies diverged farthest from the modern revolutionary spirit, for these two vital matters were indeed left as vague as the primitive millenarians' eschatology. How the IWW expected to displace capitalism from power peaceably, when the masters of the "Iron Heel" couched their answer in "roar of shell and whine of machine-guns," advocates of the general strike failed to explain. Like primitive millenarians, but unlike modern revolutionaries, Wobblies almost expected their revolution to make itself, if not by divine revelation, at least by a miracle (secular, of course). Some Wobblies even saw the roots of their doctrine in the works of the "Hobo Carpenter from Nazareth," whose call, "stripped of the mystical and mythical veil of Constantine and his successors, and clothed in the original garb of communism and brotherhood, continues to sound intermittently across the ages."

While IWW ideology derived much of its spirit from Socialist party doctrine, the two maintained only an uneasy harmony. Both Wobblies and Socialists drew their inspiration from similar ideological sources, both opposed the
capitalist order, and both demanded the establishment of a just and egalitar-
ian new order. Beyond that, they conflicted more often than they agreed.

Industrial unionism, Haywood once said, was socialism with its working
clothes on. But after 1913, when Haywood was recalled from the Socialist party's national executive committee, IWW industrial unionists and American
Socialists had little in common. American Socialists, optimistic about their
future prospects and eager to widen the popular base of their party, subordinated revolutionary fervor to the cause of immediate reform and popular ac-
ceptance. Wobblies, more pessimistic about the future and more respectful of
capitalism's staying power, tried to instill revolutionary fervor in their adherents. The Socialist party, unlike the IWW, had no room for men who counseled defiance of the law, neglect of the ballot box, and "real" revolution.

Despite the fuzzy-mindedness of some Wobbly thinkers, there was absolutely
no incompatibility between industrial unionism and syndicalism. The IWW
took over George Sorel's syndicalist concept of the militant minority, claiming in the words of the *Industrial Worker,* "Our task is to develop the conscious,
intelligent minority to the point where they will be capable of carrying out the
imperfectly expressed desires of the toiling millions," who were still "hopelessly
stupid and stupidly hopeless." Whenever some Wobblies attempted to dispute
their organization's syndicalist tendencies, other more perceptive members
stressed the IWW's basic similarity to European syndicalism. John Sandgren,
a Swedish immigrant and IWW theorist who maintained close contact with
the labor movement of his native land, tried to impress upon Wobblies their
obvious likeness to Scandinavian syndicalists. The Socialist Robert Rives La-
Monte, while acknowledging that "because Revolutionary Unionism is the
child of economic and political conditions, it differs in different countries,"
nevertheless firmly asserted, "In spite of superficial differences this living spirit
of revolutionary purpose unifies French and British syndicalism and American Industrial Unionism. To forget or even make light of this underlying iden-
tity can but substitute muddle-headed confusion for clear thinking." Finally,
John Spargo's 1913 definition of syndicalism clearly encompasses the IWW's
mode of operation. Syndicalism, he wrote, "is a form of labor unionism which
aims at the abolition of the capitalist system. . . . The distinctive feature of its
ideal is that in the new social order the political state will not exist, the only
form of government being the administration of industry directly by the workers themselves."

In the final analysis, ideological disputation remained a form of academic nitpicking to most Wobblies, for the organization always appealed to the activist rather than the intellectual. It sought to motivate the disinherited, not to satisfy the ideologue. As an IWW member noted, "It is not the Sorels . . . La-Montes and such figures who count the most—it is the obscure Bill Jones on the firing line, with stink in his clothes, rebellion in his brain, hope in his heart, determination in his eye and direct action in his gnarled fist." To such as "Bill Jones" the IWW carried its gospel from 1909 to 1917.

# 8

## The Fight for Free Speech, 1909–12

"Quit your job. Go to Missoula. Fight with the Lumber Jacks for Free Speech," the *Industrial Worker* encouraged its readers on September 30, 1909. "Are you game? Are you afraid? Do you love the police? Have you been robbed, skinned, grafted on? If so, then go to Missoula, and defy the police, the courts and the people who live off the wages of prostitution." Thus did the IWW proclaim the first of its many fights for free speech.

Many years after the IWW's free-speech fights had faded from public memory, Roger Baldwin, founding father of the American Civil Liberties Union (ACLU), recalled that the Wobblies "wrote a chapter in the history of American liberties like that of the struggle of the Quakers for freedom to meet and worship, of the militant suffragists to carry their propaganda to the seats of government, and of the Abolitionists to be heard. . . . The little minority of the working class represented in the I.W.W. blazed the trail in those ten years of fighting for free speech [1908–18] which the entire American working class must in some fashion follow."

For Wobblies free-speech fights involved nothing so abstract as defending the Constitution, preserving the Bill of Rights, or protecting the civil liberties of American citizens. They were instigated primarily to overcome resistance to IWW organizing tactics and also to demonstrate that America's dispossessed could, through direct action, challenge established authority. To workers dubious about the results achieved by legal action and the reforms won through political action, the IWW taught the effectiveness of victories gained through a strategy of open yet nonviolent confrontations with public officials.

The IWW and its members did challenge the law and endure violence and imprisonment to win free speech—that is, the right for their soapboxers to stand on street corners or in front of employment offices and harangue working-class crowds about the iniquities of capitalism and the decay of American society. But behind the right to speak freely lay more important IWW goals. Many Wobblies considered street speaking the most effective means of carrying their gospel to Western workers. Many an IWW recruit—among them Richard Brazier, who later became a leader in the Northwest and also a member of the general executive board—testified to how urban soapboxers such as Joe Ettor aroused his initial interest in the IWW. The IWW and the Western workers also had a common enemy in the city: the employment agent or "shark." These "sharks," against whom the IWW directed most of its street-corner harangues, controlled employment in agriculture and lumber. With anti-union employers they maintained the heavy labor turnover among the unskilled workers that kept labor organization out of the fields and forests, wages low, and working conditions primitive. If the IWW could break the links connecting the "shark," the employer, and the transient laborer, it could loosen the heavy chain of economic circumstances that kept the Western worker in semi-bondage.

Breaking the hold of the employment agencies on the job market would be the initial step in improving working conditions and raising wages, results that would themselves ensure a sharp rise in IWW membership. Here is the primary reason the IWW demanded free speech in Spokane, Fresno, Missoula, Aberdeen, Minot, Kansas City, and scores of other Western cities where migratories laid over between jobs or patronized employment agencies to find new jobs. Three of these many free speech struggles reveal the pattern of IWW confrontations and their role in the history and development of the organization: Spokane, 1909–10; Fresno, 1910–11; and San Diego, 1912.

The first significant IWW struggle for free speech erupted in Spokane, Washington, the hub of the Inland Empire's agricultural, mining, and lumber industries and the central metropolis for all of eastern Washington, eastern Oregon, and northern Idaho. Here employers came to find labor for the mines of the Coeur d'Alenes, the woods of the interior, and the farms of the Palouse and other inland valleys.

What the IWW accomplished in Spokane was in some respects truly remarkable. Recruiting largely among workers whose lives were often brutal and violent, the IWW channeled working-class hostility toward employment agencies into constructive courses. Soapboxers warned angry workers that broken heads and shattered windows would not put the "sharks out of business." No! they thundered. "There is only one way you can get out of their hold. That is by joining the I.W.W. and refusing to go to them for jobs."

The IWW's message was heard. Overalls Brigade "General" J. H. Walsh had come to Spokane after the 1908 convention and within six months rejuvenated a previously moribund IWW local. The revitalized union leased new headquarters, which included a large library and reading room, ample office space, and an assembly hall seating several hundred. It held inside propaganda meetings four nights a week, operated its own cigar shop and newsstand, and even featured regular movies. When local authorities restricted street speaking, the Spokane local published its own newspaper, the *Industrial Worker,* which reached a wide local working-class audience. Walsh's local even retained a Spokane law firm on a yearly retainer, as well as maintaining a voluntary hospital plan for members. All this was supported by the dues of twelve hundred to fifteen hundred members in good standing and twice that number on the local's books. For the first time, or so it seemed, a labor organization had succeeded in reaching the Inland Empire's migratory workers.

IWW growth brought an immediate and inevitable reaction from Spokane's employers, "sharks," and officials. In March 1909 the city council, acting on complaints from the chamber of commerce, prohibited street-corner orations by closing Spokane's streets to Wobblies and all other "revolutionists." It did so partly because the soapboxers castigated organized religion and partly because IWW oratory had a greater effect than "respectable" citizens realized on "the army of the unemployed and poorly paid workers." Christianity and patriotism became the employment agents' first line of defense against the IWW onslaught. Thus, Spokane's initial street-speaking ordinance allowed religious groups, most notably the Salvation Army, the IWW's major competitor, the right to speak on the city's streets.

The IWW maintained that its organizers would continue speaking until the ordinance was repealed or made binding on all organizations. On March 4 the city council placed religious groups under the ban, but the IWW remained unsatisfied. That very day J. H. Walsh himself mounted a soapbox and addressed his "fellow workers and friends," only to be hauled off to jail by local police. Later he was tried, convicted, and fined for violating the local street-speaking ordinance. For the next several days, as Walsh's legal appeals moved through the various courts, Wobblies spoke on Spokane's streets—and were promptly arrested and jailed. As the number of those arrested rose, so did the fines and the length of imprisonment. In March 1909 Spokane's jail filled with Wobblies, ten to twelve men crammed in cells built to accommodate only four.

But the Wobblies refused to give up the struggle. Instead, they sang revolutionary songs, refused to work on the jail rock pile, held daily business meetings, made speeches, and preserved their militancy even within the prison walls. Those who passed by Spokane's jail during those March days must have thought it an odd prison when they heard the words of the "Red Flag" or the "Marseillaise" filtering out from behind the bars.

As spring approached, the migratories began to leave Spokane for the countryside. Under these circumstances, city authorities released the imprisoned Wobblies, while state courts considered the constitutionality of Spokane's street-speaking ordinance. Spring and summer were not the time for the IWW to contend for free speech: It had to wait for its members to return for another winter in the city.

With the bulk of the migratories temporarily away, Spokane's officials acted to avert another winter of discontent. On August 10 the city council enacted a revised law that allowed religious groups to hold street meetings but required all other organizations to obtain permits before doing so. The *Industrial Worker* promptly warned the city fathers that the IWW would not ask permission to speak on the streets its members had built.

Summer ended, the migratories returned to Spokane, and IWW soapboxers again took to the streets. The inevitable followed. On Monday, October 25, the police arrested Jim Thompson for street speaking without a permit. The IWW promptly demanded the inalienable right of free speech and also declared that it would send as many men to Spokane as were needed to win its struggle. Despite the IWW's threat and a legal ruling declaring the revised street-speaking ordinance discriminatory and unconstitutional, the battle continued to rage. On November 1, the day of the legal decision ruling the ban on speaking unconstitutional, the IWW initiated round-the-clock street meetings. Spokane's police promptly arrested each speaker who mounted a soapbox. Before long the city jail held every local IWW leader: Walter Nef, Jim Thompson, James Wilson, C. L. Filigno, and A. C. Cousins. Passive resistance and confrontation tactics as a form of direct action were being put to the test in Spokane.

The city fathers used every instrument of power they controlled to thwart the IWW. Before the battle ended almost four hundred Wobblies had been jailed. For a time, public officials reasoned that if they could incapacitate the IWW's leaders, the fight would dissipate. Such reasoning lay behind the city's decision to raid IWW headquarters on November 3 and to arrest local Wobblies on criminal conspiracy charges; it was also behind the move to arrest the editors of the *Industrial Worker.* None of this decisively stifled the Wobblies, however, for as one policeman remarked, "Hell! we got the leaders, but damned if it don't look like they are all leaders."

After their arrest Wobblies received a further taste of Spokane justice. When Frank Little appeared in court, the presiding magistrate asked him what he had been doing at the time of his arrest. "Reading the Declaration of Independence," Little answered. "Thirty days," said the magistrate.

Arresting police officers used their clubs liberally. Jail life proved even worse: twenty-eight to thirty Wobblies were tossed into an eight- by six-foot sweat-box, where they steamed for a full day while staring at bloodstained walls. After that they were moved into an ice-cold cell without cots or blankets. Those who did not weaken from the heat of the first cell often collapsed from the chill of the second. Because Spokane's regular jails could not accommodate the hordes of IWW prisoners, the city converted an unheated, abandoned schoolhouse into a temporary prison. There, in mid-winter, jailers offered scantily clad prisoners two ounces of bread daily, soft pine for a pillow, and hardwood for a bed. Once a week jailers marched the prisoners out in order to have them bathe for allegedly sanitary reasons. Taken to the city jail, the Wobblies were stripped, thrust under an ice-cold shower, and then, often in frigid weather, marched back to their unheated prison.

The IWW estimated that as a result of this treatment, 334 of the 400 men in prison for 110 days (from November through March) were treated in the emergency hospital a total of 1,600 times. Many left prison with permanent scars and missing teeth; the more fortunate walked away with weakened constitutions. When police repression and prison brutality failed to weaken the Wobblies' resistance, the authorities resorted to different tactics. After raiding and closing IWW headquarters, they denied every hall in Spokane, except Turner Hall, to the Wobblies. Police seized copies of the *Industrial Worker* and arrested the men—even the boys—who peddled the paper. Unable to function in Spokane, the IWW moved its headquarters and all its defense activities to Coeur d'Alene City under the direction of Fred Heslewood and published the *Industrial Worker* in Seattle.

The IWW ultimately triumphed because of the spirit and determination of its members. When IWW headquarters pleaded for volunteers to fight for free speech, scores of Wobblies descended upon Spokane. One Wobbly left Minneapolis on November 10, traveling across North Dakota and Montana atop a Pullman car despite subzero temperatures. Arriving in Spokane on November 21, somewhat chilled but ready to fight, he was arrested by police two days later. He was not alone: Hundreds like him came to Spokane, and hundreds more were ready to come. All intended to make the free-speech fight an expensive and difficult proposition for Spokane's taxpayers.

No one better exemplified this IWW spirit than the "Rebel Girl," Elizabeth Gurley Flynn. Only nineteen years old and recently released from a Missoula jail (where another free-speech battle had ended), she was several months pregnant when she arrived in Spokane in November 1909. Local papers described her at that time as a "frail, slender girl, pretty and graceful, with a resonant voice and a fiery eloquence that attracted huge crowds."

Flynn was all agitator. Daughter of immigrant Irish parents, at fifteen or sixteen she made her first speech as a "materialistic socialist" before her father's radical club in Harlem, at seventeen she had been arrested for street speaking in New York, and at nineteen she was jailed, first in Missoula, then in Spokane. So adept an agitator was she that the Spokane authorities considered her the most dangerous and effective of Wobbly soapboxers. When a young attorney suggested to the city fathers that she not be tried along with the men on charges of criminal conspiracy, the local officials responded, "Hell, no! You just don't understand. She's the one we are after. She makes all the trouble. She puts fight into the men, gets them the publicity they enjoy. As it is, they're having the time of their lives."

Spokane brought Flynn to trial on charges of criminal conspiracy with a young Italian Wobbly named Charley Filigno. Not unexpectedly, the jury declared on February 24, 1910: "Filigno, guilty. Elizabeth Gurley Flynn, not guilty." An enraged prosecutor demanded of the jury foreman, "What in hell do you fellows mean by acquitting the most guilty, and convicting the man, far less guilty." To which the foreman calmly replied, "She ain't a criminal, Fred, an' you know it! If you think this jury, or any jury, is goin' to send that pretty Irish girl to jail merely for bein' bighearted and idealistic, to mix with all those whores and crooks down at the pen, you've got another guess comin'."

But looks can be deceiving, and in Flynn's case they certainly were. After the fight in Spokane she proceeded to bigger and better battles. She was with the IWW at Lawrence, Paterson, and Everett. Still later, with Roger Baldwin, she helped found the American Civil Liberties Union (ACLU) and fought to defend the rights of the poor and the exploited. Her vision of democracy took her from the Socialist party to the IWW to the ACLU and ultimately in the 1930s to the Communist party. From her first speech before the Harlem Socialist Club as a teenager to her last talk as a Communist, Flynn remained true to what she allegedly told theatrical producer David Belasco, upon turning down a part in a Broadway play: "I don't want to be an actress! I'm in the labor movement and I speak my own piece." The piece she spoke in Spokane in the winter of 1909–10 aided the IWW immeasurably. She won national attention and sympathy that no male agitator could.

The Spokane struggle continued through the winter of 1910, as public officials resorted to further repressive measures. On February 22 Spokane officials crossed the state line into Idaho, raided IWW defense headquarters in Coeur d'Alene City, and arrested Fred Heslewood on a fugitive warrant. In response the IWW advised its members, "Let us go to Spokane, fill their jails and overthrow the whole tottering edifice of corruption misnamed the Spokane City Government."

Faced with this unrelenting nonviolent resistance, city officials finally weakened. From the IWW's point of view, Spokane's authorities chose a propitious moment for compromise, for by the end of February the Wobblies also were weakening in their resolve. St. John and other IWW officials found it harder and harder to recruit volunteers for the Spokane fight. When spring came it would be even more difficult. Acting the part of realists, not visionary revolutionaries, a three-man IWW committee, including William Z. Foster, a new member, approached Spokane's mayor to discuss peace terms. In truth, neither side had much stomach for continued warfare. For one thing, the city could not stand the expense of several hundred individual legal trials, including the ensuing appeals; for another, the IWW had exhausted campaigners and it lacked new recruits to take up the slack. Thus, on March 3, 1910, after a series of conferences between IWW representatives and various city officials, peace came to Spokane.

The IWW won its major demands. Indoor meeting places would no longer be denied to the organization, and it could also hold peaceful outdoor meetings without police interference. Spokane agreed to respect the IWW's right to publish the *Industrial Worker* and to sell it on the city's streets. Complicated terms were also devised to secure the release of the Wobblies still in prison. Significantly, the authorities assured the IWW that free speech would be allowed on city streets in the near future.

Wobblies also won the secondary demands that had undergirded their fight for free speech. In the midst of the battle, Spokane officials had initiated reforms in the employment agency system, rescinding the licenses of the worst of the "sharks." After the battle, public officials throughout the Northwest attempted to regulate private employment agencies more closely.

As viewed by the Wobblies, the Spokane free-speech fight had been an impressive triumph for the twin principles of direct action and passive resistance. The discipline maintained by the free-speech fighters and the passivity with which they endured brutalities won the respect of many parties usually critical of or hostile to the IWW. During the struggle local socialists, Spokane's AFL members, and WFM members in the Coeur d'Alenes, as well as "respectable" townspeople, contributed money, food, or just plain sympathy to the Wobbly cause. Passive resistance also showed what migratory workers who lacked the franchise might accomplish by more direct means. *Solidarity* grasped the les-

son of Spokane when it observed, "By use of its weakest weapon—passive resistance—labor forced civic authorities to recognize a power equal to the state."
If labor can gain so much through its crudest weapon, it asked, "what will the
result be when an industrially organized working class stands forth prepared
to seize, operate, and control the machinery of production and distribution?"

But free speech on the streets of Spokane did not guarantee successful labor organization among the workers of the fields, woods, and construction
camps of the Inland Empire. In 1910 the IWW had only learned how to attract
migratory workers during their winter layovers in town; it had not yet hit upon
the secret of maintaining an everyday, effective labor organization out on the
job among workers who moved freely. It had not yet discovered how to survive when employers set armed gunmen upon "labor agitators" and summarily
discharged union members. However, victory in Spokane did inspire the soapboxers and organizer-agitators so prominent within the IWW to carry their
campaigns for free speech to other Western cities where migratories gathered
to rest or to seek employment.

One such city was Fresno, California, where ranchers from the lush San
Joaquin Valley came to acquire labor for their vegetable and fruit farms. Fresno had become the most active IWW center in California, and no other local
in the state could compare to Fresno Local 66 in size of membership or militancy of spirit. Late in 1909 and early the following year, Local 66 had unexpected success in organizing Mexican-American railroad laborers and migratory farm hands—a development not at all to the liking of city officials, the
management of the Santa Fe Railroad, or the ranchers. As Wobblies continued to hold open street meetings and to win more recruits for their organization, minor skirmishes with the police rose in number—so much so that by
May 1910 the local IWW forecast a full-scale free-speech fight. Fresno was ready
for the challenge. Its police chief had revoked the IWW's permit to hold street
meetings and had threatened to jail on vagrancy charges any man without a
job (serving as an IWW official was not considered employment). This led
Frank Little, the leading local Wobbly, to predict that when the summer harvest ended, Wobblies would invade Fresno to battle for free speech.

That fall a struggle similar in all basic respects to the one recently terminated in Spokane erupted in Fresno. In this case no money would be wasted on
lawyers and defense funds; whatever funds the Fresno local obtained would
be used to keep Wobblies on the streets, the local court docket crowded, and
Fresno's pocketbook empty. "All aboard for Fresno," announced the *Industrial Worker* on September 10, "Free Speech Fight On."

Fresno's town fathers responded to the IWW invasion just as their civic neighbors to the north had done. First, they closed every hall in the city to the Wobblies, who were thus compelled to reestablish headquarters in a large rented tent outside the city limits. Fresno police followed up with a series of wholesale arrests that, by mid-November, temporarily broke IWW resistance. By the end of the month, though, the Wobblies were back on the streets in increasing numbers, and the more men Fresno arrested, the more Wobblies seemed to materialize. Fresno learned the hard way that arrests did not subdue militant Wobblies. Worse yet, the city discovered that it had no statute forbidding street speaking, thus invalidating the charges on which the bulk of the arrests had been made. With the city thus deterred from legal action, mob action resulted. On the evening of December 9 a large mob gathered outside the city jail, where it severely beat a number of Wobblies who had come to visit imprisoned fellow workers. Its martial spirit duly aroused, the mob promptly marched out to the IWW's tent camp and put it to the torch. That evening, St. John wired Fresno's mayor: "Action of 'respectable mob' will not deter this organization. . . . Free speech will be established in Fresno if it takes twenty years."

Met by mob violence, the IWW counseled passive resistance. Despite legal and extralegal repression (Fresno on December 20 had enacted an ordinance banning street speaking), Wobblies continued to arrive in town in increasing numbers. Moving in and out of Fresno, and also in and out of jail, they encountered repression and brutality. What kept them coming and going was the same spirit and determination that motivated their leader in Fresno, Frank H. Little.

If Elizabeth Gurley Flynn was the "Rebel Girl," Frank Little was the "hobo agitator." More than any other individual he personified the IWW's rebelliousness and its strange compound of violent rhetoric, pride in physical courage, and seemingly contradictory resort to nonviolent resistance. Part Native American, part hard-rock miner, part hobo, he was all Wobbly. A tall, spare, muscular man with a weatherbeaten yet ruggedly handsome face, Little looked the complete proletarian rebel. As James P. Cannon, an old friend who fought with Little in Peoria and Duluth, remembered him, "He was always for the revolt, for the struggle, for the fight. . . . He was a blood brother to all insurgents . . . the world over."

This one-eyed rebel never occupied a comfortable union office or kept books like his close associates, St. John and Haywood; instead, he always went where the action was. From 1900 to 1905 he fought in the major WFM industrial conflicts, joining with that union's militants and following them into the IWW, where he remained when the WFM withdrew. In 1909 he was in Spokane, the following year in Fresno. In later years Little would turn up in San Diego, Duluth, Butte—anywhere Wobblies fought for a better world. Whenever miners, harvesters, or construction workers needed a leader, Little was available. When fear immobilized workers, he set an example for others to follow. His utter fearlessness brought him to Butte in 1917 to aid rebellious copper miners. By this time he was an ailing rheumatic, bearing the vestiges of too many beatings and too many jailings, and hobbling about on crutches as the result of a recently broken leg. Yet Little remained the active agitator—an agitator apparently so terrifying to the "respectable" that on August 1, 1917, Montana vigilantes lynched him and left his body dangling from a railroad trestle on Butte's outskirts.

In 1910–11 Little was still a reasonably healthy man. He demonstrated in Fresno how a man unafraid—a man whose life had already taken him, and would later take him again, from one violent incident to another—could also lead a struggle based entirely on the moral suasion of passive resistance.

Frank Little instilled his own rebelliousness in those who fought for free speech in Fresno. In jail Wobblies sang rebel songs, held propaganda meetings, and transacted the somewhat irregular business of Local 66. They talked so cantankerously and sang so loudly that their jailers took unusual steps to silence the noisy ones. A guard gagged one Wobbly with his own sock. Wobblies responded to repression within the jail by mounting what they labeled a "battleship," which meant continuous yelling, jeering, and pounding on cell bars and floors until the guards felt compelled to use more forceful measures.

The sheriff thus denied his prisoners adequate sleeping gear, tobacco, reading materials, and decent food. When this failed to still the tumult, he resorted to physical force. Firemen appeared at the city jail with a 150-pound pressure hose, which was turned on the cell holding the Wobblies. Prisoners tried to protect themselves by erecting a barricade of mattresses. But the pressure of the water swept the mattresses away and drove the Wobblies against the cell wall. Some Wobblies sought refuge by lying flat on the floor, but the hose was aimed down upon them, the stream of water then thrusting them up into the air like toothpicks. Even the most rebellious soon had enough of this treatment. Yet the firemen maintained the water pressure for fully a half-hour, and before they left almost every prisoner found his clothes in shreds and his body black and blue. The Wobblies spent the remainder of that chill December night up to their knees in water.

Some Wobblies broke under these tactics, promising to leave town if released. But most refused to compromise. They served out their time and then returned to Fresno's streets to soapbox.

The IWW's refusal to terminate its struggle had the same effect in Fresno as it had had earlier in Spokane. Each prisoner demanded a jury trial, managed his own defense, and challenged as many prospective jurors as possible. Wobblies used every delaying tactic their limited legal knowledge made available. On a good day Fresno's courts might try two or three men; however many Wobblies they sentenced, it seemed more were always on the docket. To make matters worse, still more Wobblies were always on the road to Fresno. This eventually became too great a burden for the city's taxpayers, judges, and businessmen.

Fresno's officials finally weakened in their resolve to repress their antagonists. Again, IWW leaders proved realistic and able negotiators. Well aware that local authorities hated to compromise while under pressure, the Wobblies allowed secret and informal talks to proceed. These conferences began on February 25 when a local citizens' committee visited the Fresno jail in order to ascertain the IWW's truce terms. In less than two weeks the citizens' committee and city officials consented to the release of all IWW prisoners and to a guarantee of the organization's right to speak on Fresno's streets. Finally, on March 6 Local 66 wired IWW headquarters, "The Free Speech Fight is over, and won. . . . Complete victory."

What the IWW won in Fresno was not precisely clear. No public settlement terms were announced, either by the local IWW or by Fresno's citizens' committee. Moreover, for the next several years Local 66 and Fresno disappeared from mention in the IWW press; Frank Little left the area to fight IWW wars elsewhere, and the San Joaquin Valley's fruit pickers remained unorganized, overworked, and underpaid—in brief, an inglorious and inconclusive climax. In Fresno as in Spokane, the IWW had learned how to contact the migratories in town but not how to organize them on the job.

As propaganda, however, the IWW may have gained something from the Fresno struggle. It demonstrated once again that the most exploited and dependent groups in American society could act for themselves—and act peaceably at that—and that they also had the power—nonpolitical power, of course—to alter the prevailing arrangements of the local community. Yet the Fresno fight left behind no effective labor organization to capitalize on the IWW's apparent "victory," and no immediate membership growth followed this new triumph for free speech.

The Spokane and Fresno victories led Wobblies to contend for free speech elsewhere, though with uneven success. Almost always these fights were associated with efforts to organize lumber workers and migratory harvesters. In one tragic case the IWW's campaign for free speech was entirely unrelated to the objectives of labor organization. In San Diego in 1912 the IWW learned the limits of passive resistance, as well as the folly of concentrating its limited power on tangential causes.

In 1912 San Diego was a comfortable city of fifty thousand, mostly well-to-do devotees of the area's ideal climate. It had a small and contented working class and no important or large industries threatened by labor difficulties. No migratories drifted into town en masse to spend the winter, and no ground seemed less fertile for IWW efforts. Indeed, never did the number of Wobblies in San Diego exceed a few hundred. Yet those few, as a contemporary journalist commented, "goaded the authorities and the populace into a hysterical frenzy, into an epidemic of unreasoning fear and brutal rage, into a condition of lawlessness."

For years E Street between Fifth and Sixth Avenues in the heart of downtown San Diego had served as a sort of Hyde Park Speakers' Corner. Every evening Socialists and anarchists, savers and atheists, suffragists and Wobblies harangued the faithful from their accustomed spots on the corner. But in December 1911 San Diego's city council closed the downtown area to street meetings. In response, Wobblies, Socialists, single-taxers, and even the local AFL men created a broad coalition called the Free Speech League. From the day the anti-street-speaking ordinance took effect, February 8, 1912, police and league members clashed over the right of free speech. By February 12, ninety men and women had been arrested, and by February 15, 150 prisoners languished in city and county jails. Day and night for the next several weeks, the league held free-speech meetings and the police arrested speakers, until the county and city jails were crowded beyond normal capacity.

Before long, what began as a common struggle by a broad coalition of anti-establishment organizations became a largely IWW-led struggle. Although the non-Wobbly groups continued to participate in the San Diego struggle, the public, locally and nationally, associated the conflict with the IWW. The battle did, in fact, feature the tactics the IWW had tested successfully in Spokane and Fresno.

Although San Diego had less to fear from the Wobblies than either Spokane or Fresno, it nevertheless acted more savagely to repress free speech. No brutality proved beyond the imagination of San Diego's "good" citizens. What the police could not accomplish by stretching the local law's elastic fabric, private citizens, acting as vigilantes, did.

San Diego's brand of vigilante justice has been described best by some of the Wobblies who experienced it. On the night of April 4 or 5, 1912, Albert Tucker and 140 other men, half of whom were under twenty-one years of age, hopped a freight train out of Los Angeles bound for San Diego. About one o'clock that morning the train slowed down and Tucker noticed on either side of the freight cars about four hundred men armed with rifles, pistols, and clubs of every variety. Tucker has vividly portrayed what ensued.

> We were ordered to unload and we refused. Then they closed in around the flat car which we were on and began clubbing and knocking and pulling men off by their heels, so inside of a half hour they had us all off the train and then bruised and bleeding we were lined up and marched into [a] cattle corral. . . . They marched us several times, now and then picking out a man they thought was a leader and giving him an extra beating. Several men were carried out unconscious . . . afterwards there was a lot of our men unaccounted for and never have been heard from since. . . . In the morning they took us out four or five at a time and marched us up the track to the county line . . . where we were forced to kiss the flag and then run a gauntlet of 106 men, every one of which was striking at us as hard as they could with their pick axe handles.

"Thus did San Diego," in the words of anti-IWW journalist Walter Woehlke, "teach patriotism and reverence for the law."

That all of this vigilante violence had occurred with the connivance of local public officials soon became known to the entire nation. Governor Hiram Johnson, Progressive politician extraordinary, under pressure from the AFL, the Socialist party, the IWW, and many influential Californians, some of whom had played a prominent role in his election, dispatched special investigator Harris Weinstock to San Diego. Weinstock's investigation corroborated all the Free Speech League's charges of police and vigilante brutality. A thoroughly outraged Weinstock compared San Diego's behavior to the worst excesses of the tsarist Russian regime.

This public condemnation notwithstanding, San Diego vigilantes continued their previous activities. Early in May 1912 police fatally wounded an IWW member. On May 15 anarchist Emma Goldman and her manager-lover, Ben Reitman, arrived in town to lend their voices to the struggle. When they debarked at the railroad station they found a howling mob, including many women, screaming, "Give us that anarchist; we will strip her naked; we will tear out her guts." That evening vigilantes abducted Reitman from his hotel room. Placing him in the back seat of an auto, they tortured him as they sped out of town. About twenty miles beyond San Diego's limits the vigilantes stopped the car, got out, and proceeded to a second round of torture. As later described by Reitman, this is what happened: "With tar taken from a can [they] traced I.W.W. on my back and a doctor burned the letters in with a lighted cigar."

In 1912 San Diego's public officials turned to the federal Justice Department for support. Early in May city police superintendent John Sehon asked attorney general George Wickersham for federal assistance in local efforts to repress the subversive, un-American IWW. Well before that date Sehon had been cooperating with the federal attorney for southern California (John McCormick) and with private detectives appointed by a citizens' committee controlled by sugar king John Spreckels and anti-union Los Angeles newspaper magnate Harrison Gray Otis. Sehon, the federal attorney, and the private detectives searched for evidence linking the IWW to an alleged plot to overthrow the constituted authorities in San Diego and Washington, D.C., and also to join the Mexican Revolution, the aim here being to capture lower California for the IWW. Where these diligent investigators could not find evidence, they manufactured it. On May 4 Sehon informed the Justice Department that Wobblies were preparing "to overthrow the Government and take possession of all things." Armed with guns and dynamite and led personally by St. John and Haywood, the Wobblies, according to Sehon and United States Attorney McCormick, had organized "a criminally treasonous" conspiracy that had to be nipped in the bud by federal authorities.

Fortunately, Attorney General Wickersham remained calm and collected. Despite strong pressure from one of California's senators and from San Diego's congressman, Wickersham realized that the IWW posed no threat to American stability or security. But as a Republican politician with a presidential election upcoming, Wickersham mollified southern California Republicans by allowing McCormick to continue his federal investigation for evidence of IWW subversion.

Throughout the summer of 1912, San Diego officials tried unsuccessfully to involve the Justice Department in the local conflict. McCormick even impaneled a Los Angeles grand jury to take evidence in an attempt to indict Wobblies for criminal conspiracy. In the opinion of a Justice Department official in Washington, McCormick's grand jury proved no more than that Wobblies "are apparently self-confessed liars and law-breakers, but there is nothing indicating a specific attack upon the Government of the United States." After having allowed McCormick and his Republican supporters to have their fun, Wickersham ordered federal proceedings against the IWW dropped.

At this juncture southern California's "reactionary" Republicans went over the attorney general's head, carrying their case for federal repression of the IWW directly to president William Howard Taft. F. W. Estabrook, a prominent member of the Republican National Committee and an industrialist whose own factory had earlier been struck by the IWW, suggested to the president "that this matter [the San Diego conflict] is of the greatest importance, not only in a political way . . . but . . . it is time that vigorous action, whenever opportunity occurs, should be taken to stamp out the revolutionary methods of this anarchistic organization." More to the point, Estabrook assured Charles Hilles, Taft's secretary, that vigorous anti-IWW action would guarantee California's votes for Taft in the November election; furthermore, he added, such action would weaken the cause of the Hiram Johnson Progressive Republicans, who supported Theodore Roosevelt and the Progressive party in 1912.

Taft was receptive to Estabrook's suggestions. Political intrigue and his desire to be reelected apparently clouded his usually clear mind, for Taft wrote as follows to Wickersham on September 7: "There is not any doubt that that corner of the country is a basis for most of the anarchists and the industrial world workers [sic]. . . . We ought to take decided action." In other words, Taft expected repression of the IWW to win California's electoral votes.

Lacking presidential ambitions himself, Wickersham remained calm. Acceding to Taft's desire to investigate IWW subversion, the attorney general nevertheless discounted the overblown reports and rumors emanating from southern California. Indeed, he maintained at the very end of the San Diego affair just as he had at the beginning, "I know of no reason why the [Justice] Department should take any further action."

Although the federal government refused to intervene in San Diego, and Taft won neither California's votes nor reelection, the IWW continued to suffer at the hands of police and private citizens. No agency of government was prepared in 1912 to defend the civil liberties of citizens who flouted the traditions and rules of America's dominant classes.

Still, the IWW and its free-speech allies fought on. Pleading for funds and volunteers, they obtained money but precious few men. Even with a diminishing supply of volunteers and close to defeat, the Wobblies remained defiant.

Defiance was no substitute for victory. By October 1912, nine months after the inauguration of the free-speech fight, downtown San Diego remained vacant and lonely at night. "The sacred spot where so many I.W.W.'s were clubbed and arrested last winter," wrote Laura Payne Emerson, "lies safe and secure from the unhallowed tread of the hated anarchist, and in fact, from all other human beings." And she lamented, "They have the courts, the jails and funds. What are we going to do about it?"

If the battles in Spokane and Fresno demonstrated the effectiveness of nonviolence, San Diego starkly revealed the weakness of passive resistance as a tactic when the opposition refused to respect common decency and when no higher authority would intervene on behalf of the oppressed. Well before their defeat in San Diego, however, many Wobblies had had second thoughts about their organization's involvement in free-speech fights. At the time of the Spokane conflict, W. I. Fisher wrote to the *Industrial Worker*, "If we are to have a strong union we have to go to the job where the workers are and begin our agitation. . . . It is only where we control or are seeking control of the job that we can build up a lasting economic power." In 1911, during the Fresno struggle, Pacific Coast IWW representatives meeting in Portland voiced their opposition to unnecessary free-speech campaigns when more effective work remained to be accomplished in organizing and educating "wage slaves" on the job.

But the IWW could not avert further free-speech fights. In the far West and in other regions where migratory workers congregated, street speaking continued to be the most effective means for spreading the IWW gospel and for winning new recruits to the organization. After all, the migratories attracted to the IWW as a result of the 1909–12 free-speech fights would become the dedicated Wobblies who later spearheaded the IWW's successful penetration of the woods and the wheat fields during World War I. Other motives also kept Wobblies on their soapboxes. They were as much agitators as organizers, as much propagandists as labor leaders, and they needed their street corners and soapboxes in order to denounce capitalist society and "bushwa" morality. Wobblies also felt compelled to compete with the Salvation Army's street-corner preachers, who counseled the oppressed to be humble and content while awaiting their reward in heaven. In response to this advice, the IWW gospelers preached "a little less hell on earth" for exploited workers.

# 9

## Steel, Southern Lumber, and Internal Decay, 1909–12

As the IWW fought for free speech in the far West, it also struggled to bring labor organization to Eastern industrial workers and Southern woodsmen. As in the West, it appealed to the workers Carleton Parker described as social outcasts and outlaws, so in the East and the South it agitated among frustrated new immigrants, exploited black men, and poor Southern whites.

In 1909 no industry seemed less open and yet more attractive to the believer in militant industrial unionism than steel. That year the United States Steel Company had dealt the final blow to the existence of the Amalgamated Association of Iron and Steel Workers—an American Federation of Labor (AFL) affiliate composed largely of skilled American-born workers—which had been declining since its defeat in the 1901 steel strike. Thus, in 1909 neither skilled nor unskilled steel workers had an organization to defend their rights. Moreover, most steel companies, and United States Steel in particular, had established rudimentary welfare capitalism schemes in order to keep employees content. By skillfully mixing their labor force ethnically, promoting American-born workers, and dominating the steel towns' power structures (including police, courts, schools, and churches), employers created what David Brody has defined as "a situation of labor stability."

Yet the newer immigrant workers—Hungarians, Croats, Slovenians, Austrians, and Serbs, to name but a few of the diverse ethnic groups—were outside steel's labor consensus. They represented the instability inherent in the labor force. The companies exploited them, the skilled workers denigrated them, the mill towns ostracized them. Getting only the most backbreaking and lowest-paying jobs, the new immigrants lived in their noisome "Hunky towns" and "Dago villages." To these immigrant industrial workers, then, the IWW hoped to bring its program of direct action and its principle of industrial unionism.

Quite unexpectedly, an opportunity to reach the steel industry's unskilled workers soon presented itself to the IWW. On Saturday, July 10, 1909, workers at the Pressed Steel Car Company in McKees Rocks, Pennsylvania, received their biweekly paychecks. All day Sunday they reflected bitterly on their skimpy earnings, and on returning to work on Monday morning complained about their wages to foremen and timekeepers. In one department about forty workers refused to work until they received more explicit information about the company's method of calculating wage rates. That same evening employees met in a group to discuss their grievances before lodging a formal demand for redress with plant officials. On Wednesday morning, July 14, company officials declined to see them. At that juncture, 600 men in the riveting department walked out the factory door. By mid-morning only about 500 men, out of a total work force estimated at 3,500, remained on the job. These skilled workers soon faced a hostile and threatening force of strikers. The next morning the unskilled immigrants formed mass picket lines at all points of entry to the plant and kept the skilled men from reporting to work. By mid-afternoon on Thursday, July 15, 1909, the steel industry's carefully constructed "situation of labor stability" was under attack in McKees Rocks by an industrial conflict that involved the entire local labor force. Why?

McKees Rocks was much like the other steel towns in the Pittsburgh area. Situated on the left bank of the Ohio River six miles below Pittsburgh, in 1910 it had a population of 14,702, well over half of whom were foreign born. As in other steel towns, its workers were segregated ethnically. The immigrants lived in dreary ghettos lining the river "bottoms," while the native-born Americans lived on higher ground in town or across the river in Pittsburgh. Little contact existed outside the factory between these two major components of the labor force.

As in other steel towns a single company dominated the community. Long noted for its antilabor policies—by no means unique in the industry, but simply more stringently applied—the company, under the direction of president Frank Hoffstot, had by 1909 followed the trend set by United States Steel in using assembly line techniques of mass production combined with the principles of scientific management.

The Pressed Steel Car Company had never been known for good working conditions or high wages, and in both respects things seemed worse than usual in 1909. The Panic of 1907 and the ensuing business recession drastically reduced orders for new railroad cars, causing the company to lay off workers and to cut wages. Wages had not yet been restored to predepression levels in 1909.

Before he reduced wage rates in 1907, Hoffstot had also introduced a new assembly line production method that accelerated the pace of work through a piece-rate system. At the same time he devised a technique for pooling wages that penalized all members of a labor pool for time and production lost by any single slow worker. This new production system also penalized workers for delays caused by company failure to repair machinery or for breakdowns caused by vague instructions issued by plant superintendents. Although compelled to work at a feverish pace in order to satisfy the pool's production target, the men on the assembly line never knew what their actual piece rates would be and, in fact, usually found their weekly earnings well below expectations. Frank Kellogg, the professional social worker who directed the famous Pittsburgh Survey, discovered wage slips among McKees Rocks' workers that showed that some men received as little as $6.50 for ten days and two nights' work.

Working and living conditions added to the general discontent. Minimal plant safety precautions could not be relied upon. Many immigrants dwelled in the two hundred company-owned double houses. Renting for $12 monthly for four rooms, they lacked indoor plumbing and other amenities. Moreover, many working-class families had to take in lodgers in order to meet their monthly rent. Everywhere the immigrant turned in McKees Rocks, he encountered company agents who exploited him: boarding bosses who covertly raised his rent for company housing if he took in boarders, foremen who charged him for a job, special company police who tyrannized him.

Thus, despite the immigrants' lack of organization, the reserve labor army available locally, and the company's domination of the community, the men struck on July 15. They walked out of the factory in order to abolish the pooling system, to restore wages to pre-1907 levels, to demand a posted statement of wage rates and a written record of their earnings, and to obtain machinery through which to present future grievances. At the moment of the walkout, a union, let alone membership in the radical IWW, seemed the farthest thing from the immigrants' minds. Yet circumstances would soon draw Wobblies and immigrants into a marriage of convenience.

It was one thing for unorganized workers to strike, quite another to achieve their demands. McKees Rocks' strikers had more to contend with than most. Many lived in company houses from which they could be evicted—and eventually were. Community leaders rejected and despised them as aliens. The immigrants could not even rely on the complete support of their fellow workers, especially the skilled Americans. The Pressed Steel Car Company had its own Coal and Iron Police to disperse pickets and harass strikers; when private police proved deficient, Hoffstot could call on the local sheriff or, better still, the state police.

Pennsylvania's state police had been created at the behest of reformers anxious to abolish the use of private police forces during industrial conflicts. Yet in practice Pennsylvania's state troopers, or "Cossacks," as striking workers labeled them, worked to the advantage of employers. In the McKees Rocks dispute the state police protected the strikebreakers Hoffstot had obtained from New York's Pearl Berghoff Agency, a specialist in supplying scabs.

Despite the strength of the opposition, the strikers at first had considerable leverage. Ethnic solidarity impelled the community's unemployed men to join strikers on the picket lines rather than to take their places in the plant. Accustomed to a hard life in the Old World and to deprivation in the new, immigrants were better prepared than many American workers to endure the privations of a protracted conflict. Able to survive on less, they could fight longer. During the strike's initial stages, the American workers joined with the immigrants. Hoffstot's refusal to deal with any group of workers for a time kept immigrants and Americans united. Company arrogance also led influential sectors of the Pittsburgh community to sympathize with the strikers and to provide them with funds, as long as the industrial conflict in McKees Rocks could be kept within the limits defined by the skilled workers.

Under these circumstances, a skilled worker, C. A. Wise, an engineer in the axle department, emerged as the strike leader. Working with a Pittsburgh attorney named William McNair, Wise amalgamated the immigrants and the native-born Americans into a joint committee led by the so-called Big Six, which Wise dominated. Only four days after the walkout began (July 19), Wise and the skilled workers, much to the relief of the Pittsburgh press and the city's reformers, seemed in firm control of the conflict.

Hoffstot soon realized that his skilled employees would compromise the very issues basic to the immigrants' walkout. Indeed, as more and more Berghoff strikebreakers entered the community and violence became a distinct possibility, the skilled workers groped about for a settlement on almost any terms.

Not so the immigrant workers. Within their ranks were several men who had had some experience in European labor and radical movements. These men established the "unknown committee": a new executive body offering the kind of leadership the Big Six refused to provide. The "unknown committee" used tactics designed to limit the importation of strikebreakers. It formed mass picketing corps and special signal and watch groups to sound the alert when strikebreakers approached the community. These new, more radical leaders also issued threats to the state police; according to one reporter, they swore to "get" a trooper in retaliation for every striker injured or murdered.

When the conflict suddenly heated up, with violence flaring between immigrants and strikebreakers, Wise and the skilled workers rushed into Hoffstot's arms, announcing settlement terms on July 31. The unskilled immigrants saw no gain in the unexpected settlement, and so instead of returning to work they repudiated Wise and sought new leadership elsewhere. Enter the IWW.

Exactly how and when the IWW became involved in the McKees Rocks conflict remains unclear. During the strike's first weeks no mention of the IWW appeared in the commercial press, the *Survey,* or any other news sources. What is clear about the timing is that general organizer William Trautmann and the IWW appeared on the scene just when the differences between immigrants and Americans became irreconcilable.

It appears that the "unknown committee," influenced by its handful of European revolutionaries in exile, invited Trautmann and the IWW to McKees Rocks. But it is also possible that Trautmann, sensing the split within the strikers' ranks, simply saw an opportunity to promote the IWW's brand of radical industrial unionism. Whatever the case, by mid-August Trautmann and the IWW had assumed leadership of the immigrant strikers. On August 15 a crowd estimated at eight thousand gathered on Indian Mound, a hill overlooking the Ohio River where strikers met regularly, to hear Trautmann and other speakers. Trautmann addressed the audience in English and German; others spoke in nine different foreign tongues. All speakers sounded the same tocsin: solidarity and resistance. All emphasized the IWW slogan: "An injury to one is an injury to all." Yet the IWW had not assumed formal control among the strikers, effective power still being exercised by the radicals among the immigrants, although they accepted aid and advice from Wobblies.

Neither IWW assistance nor strike solidarity curtailed the importation of strikebreakers. The presence of rising numbers of Berghoff's men could have but one result: violence. On Sunday, August 22, immigrant strikers decided to act. They had been without jobs and income for more than a month; other men had taken their jobs and in some cases their homes. So early Sunday evening, as Berghoff's men returned to work, strikers sought to deter them from entering the plant. Words failing to impress the strikebreakers, fists and rocks followed. As fight after fight erupted, Coal and Iron Police, local sheriff's deputies, and state troopers became involved. When Sunday's battle ended, McKees Rocks counted six dead, six dying, and forty to fifty injured, mostly strikers. Within three days state troopers, acting under limited martial law, searched every immigrant's home, confiscating guns, knives, and weapons under terms of a state law that prohibited possession of weapons by aliens.

That strike violence occurred cannot be denied. To associate the IWW with violent outbreaks and to imply that IWW leadership instigated the slaughter of August 22, as has been done, is both unfair and naive. One observer at the

IWW-sponsored Indian Mound mass meetings reported that the keynote struck by all orators was for strikers to abstain from violence. "The reports of violence have been . . . greatly exaggerated," Paul Kellogg noted at the time.

Notwithstanding the IWW's pacific counsel and the strikers' orderliness, fear of violence enveloped the Pittsburgh area. Many feared that the IWW's Trautmann would be the leader who would provide the spark.

Wise and the skilled Americans saw in these anxieties the opportunity they had been seeking to terminate the strike. Everyone concerned—Wise, Hoffstot, and the reformers—feared the IWW-immigrant alliance. Only a prompt strike settlement, they now reasoned, would remove the cancerous Wobbly influence from the region. Hence Wise and Hoffstot made a second compromise agreement early in September. On September 8 a selected group of strikers, carefully screened by Wise and the local chamber of commerce, voted on the proposed settlement terms. Overwhelming approval resulted.

At the time of the settlement, most observers and participants hailed the terms, as did St. John, as a great victory for the strikers. Wise maintained that the men had won all their demands, and the *Survey* concluded that the "company practically agrees to the strikers' terms." Supposedly, Hoffstot agreed to restore the pre-1907 wage scale, modify the pooling system to the workers' satisfaction, establish minimum wages, post wage rates clearly, abolish all favoritism and graft in employment, and rehire all strikers without prejudice.

Careful scrutiny of the terms leads to a different conclusion. The company refused to raise wages immediately, and it did not agree to abandon the pooling system. Pressed Steel simply offered the strikers the status quo ante, which was what Wise and the skilled Americans had desired all along.

Upon perceiving what had really happened, Trautmann attempted to keep out the more than one thousand strikers not yet rehired. Again he planned to schedule mass meetings at Indian Mound in order to impress upon the immigrants the need for solidarity. Now, however, the gap between immigrants and native-born Americans had become so wide that, upon a complaint filed by Wise, local police arrested and jailed Trautmann. As usual, imprisonment of its leaders did not stop the IWW. No sooner was Trautmann settled in jail than Joe Ettor appeared in McKees Rocks to take the imprisoned general organizer's place. Industrial warfare seemed about to resume when over four thousand workers walked out again on September 15.

Now Pressed Steel employed its skilled workers to break the strike. Wise and his followers heckled and disrupted IWW strike meetings, demanded that the immigrants act like American citizens, and offered to lead the strikers back to work behind the American flag. In fact, on September 16 Wise's men, carrying a huge American flag at their head, led some two thousand workers toward the plant gate and the picket line parted, allowing the marchers to enter the factory unmolested. Thus ended the second walkout. The demoralized strikers returned to work, while Wise, in conjunction with company officials, dropped immigrant strike leaders from the payroll.

Hoffstot learned his lesson well. Instead of opposing all labor organization and treating his entire labor force autocratically, he now distinguished between the skilled and the unskilled, the native and the foreign. The strike over, Pressed Steel officials agreed to confer with the skilled workers' organization in order to save their company "from dealing with the radical and socialistic organization of the I.W.W." Before long Pressed Steel had the makings of a full-fledged company union.

The immigrant workers undoubtedly realized the extent of their loss before the IWW did. Once again IWW leaders believed their organization had fully demonstrated the primacy of economic over political action and the elemental advantages of direct action at the point of production. The Wobblies themselves looked forward to a bright future in the Pittsburgh area. Ettor and several IWW organizers were already at work organizing among workers in other district steel mills, and by late October Ettor waxed enthusiastic about the prospects for direct action. He reported success in organizing among Poles, Slovenians, Germans, Czechs, Hungarians, Croatians, and other nationalities. An IWW district convention held on October 10, Ettor noted, had established a Pittsburgh–New Castle District Industrial Council, which planned to issue an official publication known as *Solidarity*. (Whatever the McKees Rocks strike may have failed to accomplish, it did give birth to the IWW's official newspaper.) "From now on," concluded Ettor, "if I am not mistaken, things and men will move around here. History will be made, and, let us hope, so fast that we shall have no time to write about it."

Ettor was not entirely mistaken. Several weeks after he published his report from the "war zone," *Solidarity* hit the newsstands and the IWW became involved in steel industry labor conflicts at New Castle and at Butler, Pennsylvania. Wobblies lacked the time to write about their new activities, for local officials, disturbed by the outbreak of Wobbly-agitated labor unrest, had jailed the entire editorial and production staff of *Solidarity*. Management and public officials proved equally effective in squelching the strikes undertaken by new IWW recruits. If the McKees Rocks dispute had ended in partial success, those at New Castle and Butler ended in total failure.

Although *Solidarity* remained as a going concern for several years in New Castle, the same could not be said for the IWW as a labor organization within the steel industry. Try as they might, Wobblies never recaptured the spirit, or even the limited success, that was theirs at McKees Rocks.

What, then, had the IWW foray into the steel industry accomplished? It certainly demonstrated that the immigrant workers, so long neglected by craft unions, were good strikers and that they could be organized. Ethnic diversity and language barriers had proved no obstacle to IWW organizers, who did not patronize the foreigners the way the typical AFL organizer did. Given the anti-union structure of the steel industry and its mill towns, any labor union would have found it difficult to maintain stable organization among the immigrants. McKees Rocks proved that the IWW was not the union to do it, for it lacked the money, men, and administrative ability. Yet the IWW left an idea as its legacy. In the future steel workers would strive for the goal of industrial unionism that cut across the lines of nationality and skill.

\*  \*  \*

From 1910 to 1912 the IWW proved that other neglected workers could be organized and that racial as well as nationality differences might be surmounted by championing the cause of white and black workers in the South.

Few Southern workers were more abominably treated than those who toiled in the damp, isolated woods and mill towns of the Louisiana-Texas timber belt. Black or white, they led a miserable existence. Many resided in company towns where they were paid in scrip and required to buy necessities in a company store at inflated prices.

Naturally, these communities had almost no history of labor organization. In a painstaking study of Texas timber workers, Ruth Allen could find only one official mention of a strike before 1911. Sometime late in 1909 or possibly early in 1910, however, a "messiah" appeared in the region in the person of young Arthur Lee Emerson. A Southern-born Protestant, Emerson looked too gentle to be a labor organizer, let alone a Wobbly. Tall, thin, almost effeminately handsome, he carried the union gospel into the woods of Louisiana. Emerson apparently derived his faith in unionism from a brief experience lumberjacking in the Pacific Northwest, where he met dedicated Wobblies. Upon his return to the South, he immediately turned to labor organizing in order to raise Gulf Coast wages and working conditions up to the none-too-high Pacific Coast standards. After finding a job in a Fullerton, Louisiana, mill, he signed up 85 to 125 employees in his new union. Buoyed by this initial success, he traveled from place to place, signing on for a few days' employment—time enough to use the Wobbly tactic of organizing on the job.

Emerson soon discovered an ally in Jay Smith, another native-born Southern white Protestant, and the two roamed the woods of Louisiana and Texas signing up union members during the winter of 1910–11. They soon had enough members and sufficient locals to create a larger regional labor organization, and in June 1911 they founded the Brotherhood of Timber Workers (BTW). From headquarters in Alexandria, Louisiana, the BTW dispatched organizers and propaganda throughout the region. Membership soared. At one point in the BTW's brief history its membership ranged between 18,000 and 35,000.

At its birth, the BTW's link with the IWW was at best tenuous. Aside from the American Labor Union's 1904 attempt to organize the lumber industry and Emerson's experiences in the Northwest, only one other possible thread connected the BTW to the IWW. Covington Hall, Wobbly poet, songwriter, and essayist, a native Southerner of distinctly patrician ancestry, then resided in New Orleans, and from the first he volunteered his pen and typewriter in the timber workers' cause. Beyond this, the BTW differed drastically from the IWW.

Possibly bearing in mind the Southern environment, the BTW adopted a distinctly conservative constitution—so conservative in fact that many an AFL affiliate would have been shocked by its stolid tone. The constitution specifically ruled out violence as a tactic, it deemphasized the role of class conflict, and it proclaimed the BTW's desire to collaborate with employers. The union abided by the Southern code of race relations and segregated black members in separate lodges. It also provided in its constitution for rituals derived from the rural Protestant church (union meetings sometimes resembled revivals) and from America's popular fraternal orders. Only in the composition and nature of its membership did the character of the BTW diverge from that of the AFL.

Southern lumber operators wanted no part of this ostensibly conservative, even pragmatic, labor organization. When the Southern Lumber Operators' Association met in New Orleans in 1910, its Texas and Louisiana constituents decided to combat the emerging union movement. John H. Kirby, a man well suited for command in the struggle, assumed the lead in the fight against organized labor. Kirby's companies dominated the entire Southern lumber industry during those years. Incorporated in 1901, the Kirby Lumber Company controlled twenty-five plants with a total capitalization of $21 million; according to the 1906 *Southwest* magazine, "The Kirby Lumber Company is not only the largest enterprise of its kind in the State [Texas], but also in the South and possibly in the U.S."

Kirby directed a many-faceted offensive against the BTW in Texas and Louisiana. Whenever they had the power to do so, employers compelled workers to sign anti-union pledges. Lumber companies also resorted to an anti-union blacklist, although this violated Louisiana law. All lumber workers had to re-nounce allegance to the BTW, for refusal to do so would result in denial of employment and in blacklisting. Operators simultaneously played black and white workers off against each other. Employers replaced white workers with black strikebreakers; when blacks joined the union, however, employers sug-gested to their white workers that the BTW, by admitting African-American members, threatened the Southern pattern of race relations. Management also retained scores of hired gunmen and transformed many company towns into armed baronies.

As the BTW continued to recruit new members in 1910 and 1911, employers decided on a more forceful approach. In mid-May 1911 owners announced a decision to reduce all mills to four days' operation a week beginning June 1. If that failed to curtail union organizing and the union's demands for an eight-hour day and higher wages, the companies threatened to close all their mills for an indefinite period. The Southern Lumber Operators' Association thus considered putting more than twenty thousand men out of work. When show-downs and threats of a lockout brought no end to union agitation, in August 1911 the association shut eleven Louisiana mills employing three thousand men and empowered a special committee to order the closing of any of three hun-dred other properties in Texas, Louisiana, and Arkansas. Kirby publicly main-tained that his association fought socialism and anarchy, not organized labor. He even publicized his willingness to deal with the AFL, which, he claimed, recognized and respected private property. Kirby emphasized that his associ-ation would never bargain with the IWW.

Kirby's reference to the IWW at this particular time was in fact a red her-ring, for no formal link then existed between the BTW and the Wobblies, nor had IWW organizers yet been sent south. Not until April 20, 1911, almost two full years after Emerson and Smith began their organizing efforts, did men-tion of the BTW appear in the IWW press. Even then, all the IWW did for several months was to appeal to Southern lumber workers—who, by the way, did not read Wobbly publications—cautioning them to be moderate.

Kirby's favorable references to the AFL and his personal overtures to Sam Gompers were equally disingenuous. Employers liked to speak about negoti-ations with conservative, respectable American labor organizations when those organizations did not have the power to press labor-management bargaining. Lumber operators at that time had to deal with the BTW, not the AFL. By in-timating to the higher-paid, more skilled lumber workers that the BTW was linked to the IWW, which endorsed union integration, socialism, and violence, Kirby hoped to turn skilled men away from the union. Since the AFL had never had any influence or members in the industry, lumber workers would then return to the job without a union.

The association's strikebreakers, gunmen, black ists, and lockouts meanwhile took their toll on the BTW. As early as September 1911, association investigators reported that membership had fallen off sharply. The investigators also pointed out that the considerable number of black union members (estimated at 50 percent), created a general undercurrent of dissatisfaction among white BTW members. "It would therefore appear from a general summary," an Operators' Association investigator concluded, "that this Association has but to adhere strictly to the policy adopted and its members to give their full cooperation in order to ultimately clear the territory of socialistic agitators and to resume operations free and unhampered."

These association tactics, more than any other factors, drove the BTW's leaders to preach integration with blacks and affiliation with the IWW. Emerson and Smith realized that if African Americans remained outside the union, they would tend to scab. Hence, they advised the black worker, "The BTW . . . takes the Negro and protects him and his family along with the white wage worker and his family on an industrial basis." To the white worker they proclaimed, "As far as we, the workers of the South, are concerned, the only 'supremacy' and 'equality' they [the employers] have ever granted us is the supremacy of misery and the equality of rags. . . . No longer will we allow the Southern oligarchy to divide and weaken us on lines of race, craft, religion, and nationality." Having as great a need for financial support as it had for racial integration, the BTW moved closer to the IWW, the only outside labor organization willing to offer aid.

Southern workers also had a firm local basis for their resistance to the employer counteroffensive. Unlike the despised immigrant workers of the North or the unattached migratories of the West, Southern lumber workers belonged to a tightly knit local community. Small local farmers, lacking markets, often worked in the mills as family units. This community of sentiment and blood led several Louisiana lumber towns to elect socialist administrations, which protected union organizers and strikers from the worst excesses of company repression.

Union resistance nevertheless weakened. In February 1912 the Operators' Association ended its lockout and resumed operations with a largely nonunion work force bound by yellow-dog contracts. At this juncture the IWW actually entered the conflict. Seeking to instill new life into the BTW's ebbing spirit, Big Bill Haywood himself went south in the spring of 1912 to attend the BTW's second regional convention in Alexandria (May 6–9). Covington Hall joined him as an IWW representative. They pleaded with the disillusioned and dejected BTW delegates to maintain the struggle and promised IWW assistance if the BTW affiliated with the Wobblies. Haywood, in particular, pleaded with union members to transcend racial animosities, achieve real union integration, and meet employers with a black-white united front. Carried away by Haywood's enthusiasm, convention delegates voted to affiliate with the IWW and to move more firmly toward an integrated organization. In return, IWW national headquarters sent two veteran organizers, George Speed and E. F. Doree, south early in the summer of 1912.

Revitalized by its new alliance, the BTW once again struck to obtain higher wages and improved working conditions from Southern lumber operators. Again employers responded with a lockout and a lengthening blacklist. An army of strikebreakers went to work in the woods and mills accompanied by gunmen, whose function was to intimidate union organizers.

On Sunday afternoon, July 7, A. L. Emerson and several other BTW organizers held an unscheduled meeting near the premises of the nonunion Galloway Lumber Company in Grabow, Louisiana. Shortly before dusk a crowd began to gather, and Emerson climbed on the back of a wagon to address the farmer-laborers. Suddenly, three shots punctuated the heavy evening air. The crowd broke and ran for cover. Armed union men turned to defend their unarmed comrades and kin from the fire of guards shooting at them from concealed spots on company premises. Ten minutes and roughly three hundred rounds later, the shooting stopped. That evening saw three men dead, a fourth dying, and more than forty wounded. Three of the dead were union men, the fourth a company guard; the vast majority of the injured belonged to the BTW.

Immediately after the incident, Emerson and sixty-four union members, with the mill owner and three of his armed guards, were arrested. Grand jury proceedings began promptly, and on July 23 Jay Smith wired IWW headquarters, "Three true bills for murder against Emerson and sixty-four other union men and one true bill against each of them for assault with willful shooting. No true bill found against mill owners."

When IWW organizers Speed and Doree arrived in Alexandria, which they claimed to be 137 degrees "hotter than Hell," they found the "Iron Heel" very effective indeed. Expecting to witness an area-wide strike, they discovered a shattered labor organization. The Grabow incident had stifled labor militancy. The BTW now concentrated its slender funds and its diminished strength on defending imprisoned members. Speed and Doree soon learned why the strike had collapsed. Touring the timber belt to stir up union sentiment, they were tailed by company detectives and threatened by local citizens of anti-union sentiments.

While Doree and Speed agitated and eluded law officers and vigilantes, the indicted BTW members waited in prison before being brought to trial for murder. Not until October 8, three months after their indictment, did the state of Louisiana, with ample financial and legal assistance donated by the Lumber Operators' Association, bring to court the case of Emerson and eight other BTW members. A month later a local jury, apparently sympathetic to the union and unimpressed with the prosecution's evidence, acquitted Emerson and his codefendants.

The Iron Heel was not yet lifted from Dixie. As Emerson and his codefendants walked out of prison, IWW organizers Doree and C. L. Filigno, as well as BTW leader Clarence Edwards, marched in on charges of jury tampering. Now it was Emerson's turn to come to their defense. "I am going to enter into the fight again and fight harder than ever before," he pledged. As a matter of fact, Emerson wasn't much longer for the battle. Nor was the BTW-IWW alliance.

Just before the Grabow defendants went to trial, black and white BTW delegates to the 1912 IWW convention had installed their organization as the Southern District of the National Industrial Union of Forest and Lumber Workers. BTW delegates then returned south to resume their labor struggle under IWW auspices.

On November 11, 1912, thirteen hundred members of the union, now officially known as the NIUF&LW, struck the American Lumber Company, once a union concern but now a Santa Fe Railroad open-shop subsidiary at Merryville, Louisiana. The strikers demanded that fifteen men blacklisted because they had appeared as defense witnesses on Emerson's behalf be rehired. White and black Merryville workers presented a united front.

But racial solidarity proved of little value against determined company opposition. American Lumber employed the usual anti-union tactics: blacklists, strikebreakers, gunmen, and vigilante justice. More and more reports began to reach IWW headquarters concerning armed attacks on strikers as company gunmen and detectives resorted to a campaign of open intimidation. They kidnaped strike leaders, beating one and shooting another. Mob law enveloped Merryville as vigilantes sacked union headquarters and confiscated records and equipment. They also deported all union men, threatening them with death if any dared return to Merryville.

By the spring of 1913 the Southern lumber workers' cause seemed doomed.

Not even the IWW could offer hope or help. Little wonder then, that at the first convention of the NIUF&LW, which met in Alexandria on May 19, 1913, not a single delegate from the Northwest arrived and only twenty-four Southerners appeared. Worse yet, A. L. Emerson, pleading poor health, resigned as general organizer for the Southern district. His health was actually no worse than that of the organization he had founded: Both were finished as militant fighters. The Lake Charles murder trial and the Merryville strike coming so close on its heels had exhausted the Southern union financially and spiritually.

To put it bluntly, violence initiated by employers destroyed Southern timber unionism. In the last analysis, Southern timber workers turned to the IWW out of desperation. The Wobblies alone promised assistance to America's most despised and degraded workers. But in 1911 the IWW was a very frail reed on which to have to lean for survival.

✳  ✳  ✳

Since its reorganization at the 1908 convention under Vincent St. John's leadership, the IWW, despite a record of militant industrial activity, had made few substantial gains in membership. Nor had it achieved anything approaching internal stability. Wobblies had fought for free speech in Missoula, Spokane, and Fresno; they had struggled for improved working conditions at McKees Rocks and in Southern forests. But the IWW had failed to construct effective labor organizations in any of those places. Although the *Industrial Worker* reported on April 30, 1910, that sixty-six locals had been chartered since the 1908 convention, the IWW could not even hold a national convention in 1909, and one finally convened in June 1910 transacted no business of importance. At that 1910 Chicago convention, national organizer Trautmann offered few specific data on IWW membership. *Solidarity* sought to demonstrate organizational achievements by enumerating the IWW's sanctioned newspapers— by 1910, seven in number, including journals in Spanish, Polish, French, and even Japanese. St. John, in a letter to Paul Brissenden just after the 1911 convention, put the IWW's actual status into perspective. St. John noted that the general office had in an eighteen-month period issued sixty thousand dues books, but of that number only about one in ten, or roughly six thousand, represented members in good standing.

This dismal growth pattern led left-wing Socialist and erstwhile Wobbly Frank Bohn to title a July 11 article in the *International Socialist Review*, "Is the I.W.W. to Grow?" The essay opened by asking readers whether the IWW had a future, or only a past—and an inglorious one at that. A pessimist, Bohn held the triumph within the IWW of an antipolitical faction—the so-called philosophical anarchists, who made a fetish of attacking the Socialist party—responsible for the organization's lack of success. If the antipolitical element remained dominant, wrote Bohn, "the I.W.W. . . . is dead.'

Justus Ebert attempted to answer Bohn on behalf of the IWW. Writing in the *New York Call,* Ebert reminded his readers of how poorly the AFL had fared during its first decade, having a total annual income less than that of the IWW during its initial five years. Conceding that the IWW was not "likely to grow with the speed of a prairie fire," Ebert pointed to the organization's manifold militant activities from 1909 to 1911.

On the eve of the 1911 IWW convention, however, rumors seemed to substantiate Bohn's gloomy prophecy. One set of rumors contended that the convention majority would purge all advocates and practitioners of political action from the organization, thus converting the IWW once and for all into an anarcho-syndicalist cell composed of pristine believers. Another set of rumors implied that Western delegates, DeLeon's old "Bum Brigade," would dominate the convention, dismantle what little bureaucratic administration the IWW possessed, abolish the general executive board, as well as all national officials, and create in their place a form of "participatory union democracy."

One man even came to Chicago intent on burying the IWW as a labor organization. That man, William Z. Foster, had joined the IWW during the Spokane free-speech fight. A child of Philadelphia's slums, from which he had fled as a teenager, Foster had worked his way over and around the Western hemisphere as a sailor, ditchdigger, harvester, and general roustabout. A slight, earnest, intense individual, he demonstrated at an early age his penchant for radicalism and his flair for labor agitation and political polemics. Soon after his experience in Spokane and his enlistment in the IWW, Foster went to France. Traveling about Europe in 1910, he closely observed the tactics of the French labor movement. Six months in France deeply impressed the young American with what he called the tactic of boring from within, "the policy of militant workers penetrating conservative unions, rather than trying to construct new, ideal industrial unions on the outside." Foster resolved to return to the United States in order to propose using a militant minority to bore from within the established labor movement instead of building dual industrial unions outside the AFL.

Neither Foster, the decentralizers, nor the antipolitical fanatics disrupted the 1911 convention. Delegates never raised the political question, and the convention voted down an amendment asserting the futility of parliamentary action. Western proposals to abolish or minimize the power of the general executive board were roundly defeated, and the delegates managed, at least temporarily, to harmonize Western demands for increased autonomy and rotation in office with Eastern insistence on tighter organization and more bureaucratic, professional leadership. Thus far, no clear geographic divisions existed within the IWW. Opposition to centralized administration and to "autocratic" leadership usually came from Wobblies dissatisfied with what the administration was doing, not those who came from a particular geographic area. Westerners such as St. John, Haywood, Frank Little, and Richard Brazier, to name a few, struggled to create within the organization a more professional central leadership supported by higher dues, while Easterners such as Elizabeth Gurley Flynn, Ettor, and Arturo Giovannitti chafed at orders from general headquarters. Had the Westerners truly wished to dismantle the IWW's administrative machinery and put "participatory democracy" into practice, they certainly could have done so given their numerical preponderance within the organization.

Foster, not the so-called Western anarchists, had the most complete and well-thought-out proposals for dismantling the IWW as it existed in 1911. He proposed that the IWW relinquish its attempt to build a new labor movement, transform itself into a propaganda league, and then revolutionize the old unions by boring from within them. In his autobiography, Foster later claimed to have persuaded two Wobblies, Earl Ford and Frank Little, to his view of American labor's future. But the IWW's top officials—St. John, Trautmann, and Haywood—opposed Foster's plan. Rather than bring his resolution to the convention floor, where he realized he would suffer a resounding defeat, Foster resolved to agitate among the rank and file.

But Foster had only beat a strategic retreat. The chance to carry the organization with him came when a small faction of Western decentralizers nominated Foster for editor of the *Industrial Worker*. On November 2, 1911, he proclaimed his policy publicly in an editorial announcing his candidacy for editorship of the Western paper. Foster reminded the rank and file that, after seven years of struggle, the IWW still had only a minuscule membership, like other radical dual labor movements in England and Germany, and unlike the old unions in France, which had been captured by the syndicalists. He called on Wobblies to learn from the French workers' example, as Tom Mann, the radical British labor leader, was now learning in England, where he had recently declared against dual unionism and was "boring from within" the Trades Union Congress. Foster concluded his polemic by asserting, "I am satisfied that the only way for the I.W.W. to have the workers adopt and practice the principles of revolutionary unionism . . . is to . . . get into the organized labor movement and . . . revolutionize those unions."

The debate was soon on in earnest. Both the *Industrial Worker* and *Solidar-*

*ity* filled their columns in November and December 1911 with "boring from within" articles and correspondence, mostly anti-Foster in substance. J. S. Biscay offered the most thoughtful and complete rebuttal of Foster's position in the *Industrial Worker*. Like other Wobblies, Biscay pointed out that no exact analogy existed between the AFL and its European counterparts. What might be accomplished in Europe, in other words, could not so easily be achieved in America. "To start boring from within with all the craft unionists prejudiced already would mean the disbanding of the I.W.W., and hardly causing a ripple in the crafts. . . . To change our ideas at this time," Biscay reasoned, "would only spell defeat."

He might also have added that the European analogy broke down at other points. The established French, German, and English labor movements already contained a significant proportion of socialists and radicals in positions of influence ready to cooperate with the "borer," whereas the AFL, dominated by ardent foes of any form of labor radicalism, was prepared to rid the federation of such radicals at the first opportunity. The European syndicalists, whatever their country, did not advocate a form of trade unionism at odds with the prevailing structure of their nations' labor movements. In France, syndicalists did not take exception to the craft basis of the French labor movement; indeed, they supported it, and often favored craft unionism. That European developments did not in fact carry obvious lessons for American radicals was demonstrated by the experience of Bill Haywood, who visited Europe at the same time as Foster. Also impressed by European labor leaders, Haywood decided, while in France, that he would rededicate himself to working for the IWW upon his return to the States. The Wobblies reminded Haywood of the allegedly successful European syndicalists.

Foster's efforts were doomed to failure. Lacking support from any national IWW leader, he could scarcely carry his proposals effectively to the small, scattered organization membership. He could not even win the referendum vote for the editorship of the *Industrial Worker*. On December 16, 1911, Ben Williams closed *Solidarity*'s columns to discussion of Foster's proposition. "Why waste time trying to capture a corpse?" Williams noted.

Admitting defeat, Foster resigned from the IWW in February 1912, joined the Brotherhood of Railway Carmen, a craft union, and with Earl Ford founded the short-lived Syndicalist League of North America. Foster, of course, never captured the railroad brotherhoods for revolutionary unionism. Yet in 1919 Gompers allowed him to direct that year's steelworkers' organizing drive, an effort that craft union jealousies partially subverted. Soon thereafter Foster had enough of boring from within the AFL, which he left for the Communist party, becoming that party's major trade union figure.

But early in 1912, both Frank Bohn's question "Is the IWW to Grow?" and William Z. Foster's challenge became purely academic. Events in Lawrence, Massachusetts, revived the IWW and made it appear for a time a real competitor to the AFL as well as a distinct threat to the existing social order. Industrial conflict in Lawrence catapulted the Wobblies to national prominence.

# 10

## Satan's Dark Mills: Lawrence, 1912

Thursday, January 11, 1912, dawned cold and gray in the Massachusetts textile city of Lawrence. The city's woolen mills, huddled along the Merrimac River, appeared forbidding as the first rays of light accentuated the grimy snow along the river banks. Soon thousands of men, women, and children would leave their congested tenements and form a stream flowing slowly but steadily toward the mills. Many of these workers would arrive at the factories in a mood as sullen as the sky above them.

January 11 would be the first payday at Lawrence's textile mills since the state of Massachusetts's new fifty-four-hour law had gone into effect.* The last time state legislation had reduced hours (from fifty-eight to fifty-six) employers had maintained prevailing wage rates. Now, however, workers seemed confused and anxious. Most mills had posted notices warning of the required reduction in hours, yet many failed to mention wages. In short, neither the owners nor the managers of Lawrence's mills had prepared their employees for reductions in an already low wage scale.

In one mill a group of Polish women, upon opening their pay envelopes, cried, "Short pay!" left their looms, and walked out. That evening the *Lawrence Sun* reported, "Italian Mill Workers Vote to Go Out on Strike Friday—In Noisy Meeting 900 Men Voice Dissatisfaction Over Reduced Pay Because Of 54 Hour Law." The next morning, which was payday at most mills, employees arrived for work more sullen than they had been the previous day. About 9 A.M. an angry mob of Italians in the Wood Mill of the American Woolen Company, Lawrence's largest employer, deserted their machinery and ran through the mill demanding that other workers march out. As the Italians moved from one department to another they disassembled machinery, cut wires, blew fuses, and intimidated noncooperating workers into joining their walkout. The mob

* Although the new law limited the hours only of women and children, they composed a majority of the work force; reducing their hours of labor in effect also set a new maximum for skilled men omitted from the law's coverage.

surged down Canal Street along the Merrimac River. By evening the original few hundred strikers had increased their number to roughly ten thousand men, women, and children.

On Saturday those still at work accepted their pay envelopes without a murmur of protest. No violence flared. Some Boston papers reported, "Peace seems assured." Yet industrial warfare was close at hand, for on Saturday evening, January 13, the IWW's Joseph Ettor arrived in Lawrence.

For some years a small Italian IWW local had been functioning in Lawrence. At its meeting on January 10, the local decided, at the insistence of young Angelo Rocco, to invite Ettor to assist it in organizing mill workers and protesting low wages. No sooner was he in Lawrence than Ettor infused the immigrants with his own militancy. All night Saturday and all day Sunday, at meeting after meeting, he urged mill workers to strike for higher wages. By Monday he had them in an aggressive mood, and that morning, the start of a new work week, an immense crowd fired up by Ettor stormed City Hall. There a frightened mayor responded by calling out 250 local militiamen to disperse the mob and to patrol the mill district. Thus had peace ended in Lawrence, as its citizens began to choose sides in what would later become known as the great Lawrence textile strike.

A product of New England's industrial revolution, Lawrence was built on cotton and woolens. In 1845 the eminently successful business group known as the Boston Associates had selected one of the few remaining water-power sites along the Merrimac River, some 35 miles north of Boston, as an ideal location for a textile establishment. By 1912 Lawrence led the nation in the production of woolen worsteds, and in the American Woolen Company housed the largest, most profitable firm in the field. The city had a labor force of more than 35,000, and approximately 60,000 of 85,892 people living there depended directly on textile mill payrolls. But Lawrence was no paternalistic capitalist utopia. Perhaps, at first, when its employees were mostly native New Englanders, Lawrence could boast of excellent living conditions and a healthy, well-clothed working class. But from its origins, Lawrence, unlike the older textile cities in the region, attracted large numbers of immigrants. Its creation came roughly at the time of the potato blight, which forced poor peasant farmers by the millions off the land in Ireland and Germany.

For starving peasants, Lawrence represented an opportunity to work and to eat. The Irish and the Germans worked hard, ate skimpily, and lived frugally, and some of them thrived. Soon new immigrants arrived. From Lancashire and Yorkshire came skilled English textile workers; from the north came unskilled French-Canadians. They, too, worked hard, lived frugally, and sometimes thrived.

Europe's poor continued to look to America for opportunity. Lawrence's mills still demanded cheap labor. So, at the turn of the century, the poor began to arrive from Italy, Austria, Russia, and Turkey. Few of these new immigrants had had any experience in industry. Fewer still spoke English. By 1911, 74,000 of the city's 86,000 inhabitants were first- or second-generation Americans; southeast Europeans represented one-third of Lawrence's immigrant population, and for them room existed only at the bottom of the economic ladder.

Indeed, these new immigrants found life hard. Most worked in the textile industry, where an average annual income was $400 for heads of families, well below that needed for a minimal health and welfare budget. Yet women and children, who formed over half the labor force, received well below the average; in addition, the average wage for the unskilled, a large majority of the mill hands, seems to have been closer to $6 a week. During slack periods, which were quite frequent in the seasonal textile industry, wages fell even lower.

Hence, whatever economic and social security immigrants had in 1912 was based on sending wives, mothers, and children over fourteen into the mills. (Many parents falsified their children's ages and sent them into the mills at an even younger age.) Children of preschool age often were left in the care of neighboring women or went untended. At the age of fourteen, Lawrence's typical immigrant child left school, no matter what his or her grade or academic standing, and substituted a 6:45 A.M. to 5:30 P.M. mill day for his 9 A.M. to 3 P.M. school day.

Any careful observer could prove that Lawrence's living standards were low. Indeed, by 1912 four-story wooden tenements, erected with scarcely any open space separating one from another, had become Lawrence's most notable feature. Contractors jammed buildings so close together that people in adjacent houses used opposing walls for kitchen shelves. Lawrence, in fact, could claim some of the most densely populated blocks in the nation—blocks where frequent fires, filth, and vermin bore down heavily on the residents.

Mortality statistics reflected abysmal working and living conditions. Lawrence, with several other textile cities, led the nation in death rate per one thousand population. Like other textile towns, Lawrence had a shockingly high infant mortality rate. In 1909, the last year before 1912 for which figures are available, for every thousand births in Lawrence, 172 infants did not survive their first year. Tuberculosis, pneumonia, and other respiratory ailments stalked the adult mill workers, often cutting them down in the prime of life.

Such was immigrant life in Lawrence, Massachusetts, during the peak of Progressivism. Reform legislation had several times reduced the hours of labor for women and children; factory inspection acts had somewhat improved mill conditions. But working and living conditions remained otherwise virtually unchanged. Lawrence's immigrants would have been the last to know they were living in a "progressive" era.

Trade unions had never been a smashing success in Lawrence. Mill superintendents had effectively crushed all trade unions that emerged in their plants. At one time the Lawrence Central Labor Union had invited the United Textile Workers of America to organize the skilled workers. But the union president, John Golden, later remarked, "For years every beginning we have made in Lawrence has been instantly stamped upon by the mill superintendents and their subordinates." The shifting tides of immigration and the consequent changing complexion of the labor force created imposing obstacles to the process of union organization. Many immigrants resisted unionization, preferring semiformal nationality associations or church groups, while such craft unions as the United Textile Workers showed little desire to organize "foreigners."

From its birth in 1905 the IWW had tried to organize workers neglected by the craft unions, although the Wobblies could hardly claim greater success than John Golden. Unlike Golden and his union, however, they never ceased in their attempts to organize the immigrant masses of Lawrence. By 1910 the IWW had begun to build a dedicated following in Lawrence. In April of that year Local No. 20 of the National Industrial Union of Textile Workers (NIUTW) publicly boasted about its rising membership and its new headquarters, which included a five-hundred-seat auditorium, meeting rooms, a gym, and a game room. In January 1911, Louis Picavet, a local French-Canadian Wobbly, reported that Local 20 had joined with other Lawrence labor organizations to establish an Alliance of Textile Workers Unions. This alliance adopted the IWW's statement of principles, which emphasized the abolition of the wage system and social revolution. Lawrence Wobblies, according to Picavet, were doing some "boring from within." "The idea of meeting with the unions, even the conservative ones," he wrote, "can only result in good, because through our contact with them we can lead them first of all in a more progressive direction, and finally to the revolutionary conception."

Shortly thereafter, Local 20 initiated an active organizing campaign among textile workers. In August 1911, Local 20 began to lead Lawrence workers in a series of slowdowns and wildcat walkouts, which aimed to ease the work pace and to increase wages. Although few of these conflicts affected more than one mill, or more than a handful of weavers, Elizabeth Gurley Flynn pleaded with Lawrence's workers "to weave the shroud of capitalism." Despite the IWW's small total membership in Lawrence, by January 1912 most local workers knew of the organization's existence, aims, and local activities.

Still, on the eve of the 1912 strike no stable labor organization existed in Lawrence. The English-speaking skilled workers in the United Textile Workers' crafts claimed a membership of 2,500, but their somnolent locals scarcely disturbed employers. At best the IWW could lay claim to only 300 paid-up members. Thus, out of a work force of 30,000 to 35,000 in January 1912, only about 2,800 workers definitely belonged to trade unions.

By December 1911, however, the IWW had laid the basis for action in Lawrence, and the new fifty-four-hour law and the subsequent wage reduction offered Wobblies an opportunity for action that they did not hesitate to seize. When Ettor returned to Lawrence for the third time on January 13 to lead a spontaneous strike, he was no stranger to the town's textile workers, nor, for that matter, was the IWW an alien institution.

In the winter of 1912 Lawrence, Massachusetts, was America in microcosm. The textile workers represented both the new and the old immigrants, the skilled and unskilled. William Wood (president of the American Woolen Company) and the other mill directors typified one segment of the nation's industrial leaders; governor John Foss and the state legislature embodied the hopes of the Progressive era; John Golden and the United Textile Workers acted as surrogates for the "conservative" American labor movement, ever willing to accommodate the established order; and the IWW typified the radicalism of many Americans who felt that only revolutionary changes could correct the abuses of industrial capitalism.

Divided by nationality, craft, and religion, the textile workers seemed a weak adversary to pit against united employers. The older immigrants—Germans, Irish, French-Canadians, and most of the English—opposed the strike. Reflecting the sentiments of the more established skilled workers, John Golden did all in his limited power to break the IWW-led strike, exceeding some manufacturers in his condemnation of the immigrants' union tactics. Golden consistently sought to vitiate the IWW strike by offering himself and his union to the mill owners, the city officials, and the state authorities. For a price—company recognition of the skilled workers—Golden practically offered to break the strike.

In reality, Golden had precious little to offer anyone. For by the end of the first week of the dispute the IWW had brought unity out of diversity, order out of chaos. It was now to the IWW, and to it alone, that the mass of immigrant workers looked for advice and hope.

No man did more to unify and inspire the strikers than Joseph Ettor. Only twenty-six years old in 1912, he was already an experienced orator, organizer, and labor agitator. Born of Italian immigrant parents in Brooklyn in 1886, Ettor grew up in Chicago. From his father he heard tales of industrial warfare and revolutionary sentiments, and this early education directed him toward radicalism. A San Francisco iron worker by trade, Ettor soon became a Wobbly agitator by vocation, traveling up and down the West Coast visiting mining, lumber, and construction camps to organize for the IWW. During this period (1905–8) he became an adept soapboxer and one of the most popular Wobbly propagandists. The 1909 McKees Rocks strike brought him east, where he put to good use his command of the English, Italian, Polish, Yiddish, and Hungarian languages. After organizing among Pennsylvania's immigrant steel workers and coal miners, he turned up in Brooklyn to lead a strike by Italian IWW shoemakers. From Brooklyn he went to Lawrence.

The young but experienced Wobbly who arrived in Lawrence in the winter of 1912 was short and stocky, though nonetheless uncommonly attractive. He had flowing black hair, dark brown eyes, and high color; by no means handsome, his face yet seemed candid and youthful. Typically wearing a big, soft hat to one side of his head, a flowing Windsor tie, and a natty blue suit, Ettor had a touch of the artistic bohemian. Looking anything but a wage worker, he nevertheless magnetized laboring groups.

Arturo Giovannitti, poet, mystic, dreamer, and syndicalist, accompanied Ettor to Lawrence. Born of upper-middle-class parents in 1884 in Campobasso, Abruzzi, Italy, Giovannitti rejected his parents and his native land at the age of sixteen. Emigrating to America in 1900, he mined, kept books, and taught school in the New World. Not one for steady work, he knew what it was like to sleep in New York's doorways and starve in its streets. Born and raised an Italian Catholic, he flirted with Protestantism in America and for a time trained at a seminary. But he found his true ministry not with Jesus and Christianity but with Marx and socialism. In time he became a leader in the Italian Socialist Federation of New York. From Marxism he converted to romantic syndicalism and thence to "pure" revolutionary action (the propaganda of the deed), which he promoted in the pages of *Il Proletario,* an Italian syndicalist sheet. When the Lawrence strike erupted he hoped to become as popular among the strikers as his friend Ettor. Tall, robust, with a powerful voice, he played the mature intellectual to Ettor's boyish radical; where Ettor impressed audiences with his childlike enthusiasm, Giovannitti did it with a romantic, mystical intensity.

Even more important to the future of the IWW was the return of Big Bill Haywood to its front ranks during the Lawrence strike. Arriving in town on January 24, 1912, Haywood received the wildest demonstration ever accorded a vis-

itor to Lawrence, as thousands of strikers jammed the railroad station to welcome him. It was a moment fraught with great consequence for the Lawrence
strikers as well as for the IWW, which welcomed back a lost son.

A dominant figure at the IWW's 1905 founding convention, Haywood shortly thereafter was lost to the organization. In prison from 1906 through 1907
because of the Steunenberg case, he left prison a labor leader without a union,
a radical without an organization, and a revolutionary in an overwhelmingly
conservative society. Rejected by his old union (the Western Federation of
Miners) and unwilling to throw in with a divided IWW, from 1908 to 1910
Haywood crisscrossed the country propagandizing for socialism and keeping
only a minimal connection to the labor movement. In 1910 Haywood was a
Socialist party delegate to the International Socialist Congress in Copenhagen.
He traveled the radical speakers' circuit in Europe at the same time that William Z. Foster made his grand tour. But whereas Foster returned to America
dedicated to burying the IWW and "boring from within" the American Federation of Labor, Haywood came home convinced that his future lay with the
Wobblies.

Haywood's life, personality, and beliefs always had an enigmatic touch about
them. To conservatives, Haywood's was the voice of anarchy; to friends and
admirers, he was the epitome of sweet reason. To such trade union foes as Samuel Gompers, he was an inept propagandizer and a smasher of trade unions;
to his supporters he seemed to be an effective administrator and a talented labor organizer. To Mary Gallagher, a fellow radical, he was in every way a great
leader; to Ramsay MacDonald, the British socialist leader, he was a rough-hewn
agitator, splendid with crowds though ineffectual as an administrator. The fact
is that Haywood's life offers sufficient evidence to support any of these views.

His life, at least as much of it as can be reconstructed accurately, developed
in distinct phases, which appear to have flowed smoothly one into the other.
Beginning with few advantages in the way of family, education, or wealth,
Haywood had to earn his own keep at an early age. Born in Salt Lake City in
1869, left fatherless as a child, and never thereafter enjoying a secure home, he
sustained himself by picking up the various marginal jobs then open to a child
worker. By the age of fifteen he had become a hard-rock miner, and for the next
twelve years he worked in mining camps, seldom remaining in one place very
long. From these early experiences in an industry unusual for its labor solidarity as well as its labor violence he probably derived his beliefs about the
worker's place in American society and the irrepressibility of conflict between
capital and labor.

During the years 1896–1905, after marrying, raising a family, and settling down in Silver City, Idaho, Haywood served as a local union official and then as an officer in his international union. Service in the cause of trade unionism taught him the limitations as well as the advantages of the American labor movement. Aware of the movement's inadequacies, he became a crusader for industrial unionism and the socialization of American society. Before long the importance of his role as a labor leader diminished in comparison with his activities as a Socialist party politician. But seven years (1906–13) of Socialist party struggles left Haywood disillusioned with the ability of American Marxists to make a revolution in his native land. Recalled from the party's national executive committee in 1913, he began a new phase in his career: national leader of the apolitical, syndicalist, and revolutionary IWW. At last finding full satisfaction in his work, Haywood joined efficient union administration to the fire-eating, spellbinding rhetoric of revolution.

During these years—years in which the IWW experienced its most rapid growth—Haywood strove to give Wobblies their first taste of effective administration under a rationalized central office. But in between his tours of duty as a union official he devoted himself to agitation and to free-wheeling revolutionary oratory, impressing many observers with his antidisciplinarian, antiorganizational, anarchistic personality. His life was shadowed by violence, but few radicals ever expressed the doctrine of passive resistance so forcefully. An enemy of effete intellectualism, Haywood nonetheless had intellectual pretensions of his own. Although he might harangue strikers in working-class vernacular, he read widely (and deeply) and wrote with considerable skill. In his writings and speeches on economics, politics, sex, and religion, he stood midway between romanticism and realism, Victorianism and modernism. If he never wrote graceful and closely reasoned treatises, Haywood nevertheless unfailingly appealed to immigrant workers in the East and migrant workers in the West as well as to such intellectuals as John Reed and Max Eastman.

Unlike the more typical labor leader who opens his career as a radical, finds success, and becomes more conservative, Haywood began his union career conservatively, discovered success, and became radical. A man of many talents—administrator, organizer, agitator, speaker, writer—he developed none fully, which was perhaps his gravest deficiency.

But when Bill Haywood came to Lawrence in 1912, what most people saw was a giant of a man who was able to inspire solidarity among a cantankerous assortment of ethnic groups. Tall and broad-shouldered, with a pockmarked and scarred face set off by a patch over his right eye (which he had lost in a childhood accident), Haywood bore ample physical witness to the battles he had waged and the sufferings he had endured. With only his eye patch and soft Western hat to distinguish him from thousands of other workmen who wore the same blue shirt, plain tie, dull suit, and overcoat, Haywood would carry his immense frame to the speaker's platform, and, without stamping, pounding, bellowing, or bullying, use plain working-class language to carry his audience along with him.

In Lawrence, Haywood, Ettor, and Giovannitti had ample assistance from local Wobblies in leading the strike and organizing the workers. William Yates and Thomas Holliday, for example, provided what the two imported Italian agitators could not: knowledge of the textile industry, its workers, and its ways. A long-time official of the NIUTW, Yates was born in Lancashire, England, where at the age of ten he entered the cotton mills. For the next thirty-three years he labored in every branch of the textile industry. Arriving in the United States in 1900, he immediately joined the Socialist Labor party and the Socialist Trades and Labor Alliance and moved with them into the IWW. Thomas Holliday was also born in Lancashire. Like Yates, Holliday went to work in the mills at an early age, but in his case it was an American mill, his family having emigrated to America in 1887 when he was only five. He was one of the first IWW members in Lawrence and one of its few links to the skilled, English-speaking community of workers. Lawrence's new immigrants, similarly, provided their share of strike leaders.

The national IWW figures and the local strike leaders together produced organizational order out of anarchy. Enlisting men capable of speaking the native language of every striker and drawing representatives from every ethnic group involved, they created unified strike committees and relief committees. Structured on nationality lines and led by men already in the IWW or soon to join, these committees existed independently of the IWW. They operated on Haywood's advice: "There is no foreigner here except the capitalists. . . . Do not let them divide you by sex, color, creed, or nationality."

Led by Ettor, the strike committee promptly drew up its basic demands, which were few and limited in objective. The strikers asked for a 15 percent wage increase based on the fifty-four-hour week; double pay for overtime; elimination of the premium system (a system of bonus wage payments based on a speedup in production, which workers considered to be exploitive); and assurance that no discriminatory action would be taken against any worker who had walked out during the strike. In other words, there were no demands for union recognition or a closed shop, nor any mention of revolution.

Ettor taught the inexperienced immigrants the nature of industrial warfare. He devised special tactics to achieve the strikers' main immediate objective, which was to keep nonstrikers out of the mills. The strike committee organized mass picket squads, which, forming near the mill gates, would march around them without stopping, without slowing down, without resorting to open force or violence, and thus offering the police or militia no occasion to intervene. Any worker who desired to enter the mills had to endure the verbal insults shouted by thousands of fellow workers, many of whom were his neighbors. Social intimidation of this kind proved much more effective than physical violence. The strike committee also arranged regular parades during which thousands of workers would march through Lawrence's streets to music, singing the "Marseillaise" and the "Internationale."

Peaceful picketing, musical parading, and nonviolent coercion worked. The strike grew. By January 20, less than a week after it began, more than fourteen thousand workers had left the mills, which were now crippled. At first the mill owners declined to deal with the strikers. Lawrence's employers remained certain that, with the assistance of city and state authorities and given the workers' own ethnic and craft divisions, they could break the strike. So convinced of their chances for absolute victory were the mill owners that they had not bothered to make any provisions for the introduction of strikebreakers.

William Wood directed the antistrike coalition. Expressing complete surprise at the course of events, he called the strikers ignorant and irresponsible men who were unaware of the hard economic fact that employers could not pay employees for fifty-six hours' work when they labored only fifty-four hours. Wood and the other mill owners pleaded poverty. With Southern textile workers toiling longer hours for less pay, with textile imports increasing, and with tariff agitation in Washington causing business depression, how could Lawrence's wage rates be increased? "There is no cause for striking," Wood advised his workers.

Wood's imperviousness to the strikers' grievances was shared by Lawrence's dominant classes. Nothing better illustrated the existence in Lawrence of two separate nations—haves and have-nots—than the attitudes and policies of the city's elite. City judge Wilbur Rowell, attempting to answer what he deemed slanders on the city's reputation, reflected Lawrence's pervasive social myopia when he remarked, "It is a typical New England industrial city, with all the equipment and resources that are found in such a city for generous and noble life, and for the sympathetic relief of weakness and suffering." The generous and noble life apparently included the one-penny school lunches of molasses and bread that Lawrence granted the children of its working classes. As Rowell and his class surveyed the strike scene, they necessarily concluded that industrial conflict had been imported into a peaceful New England town by outside agitators—the age-old rationalization of exploiters shocked by the rebellion of the natives.

Other Lawrence leaders were less solicitous. Mayor Scanlon had called out the local police and militia immediately upon the strike and soon thereafter requested state militia. He also purportedly hired Sherman Agency private detectives to keep the strikers and Wobblies under surveillance. Local priests joined the antistrike coalition. Father O'Reilly, the leading Irish-American cleric, condemned the IWW in his parish calendar for misleading "ignorant" immigrants, and a French-Canadian priest advised a jeering crowd of seven thousand strikers to return to work. Catholic priests also visited their East European immigrant flock to warn them that continued disobedience to employers would lead to damnation. Some of Lawrence's better citizens even engaged in criminal conspiracies to break the strike. State authorities, though less concerned than Lawrence's officials with the textile manufacturers' interests, proved equally anxious to remove the IWW's influence from the city.

Governor Foss and the state legislature sought to bring strikers and employers together in mutual negotiations that would end the conflict on the basis of a compromise that altogether excluded the IWW. Foss, for example, publicly professed his desire to cooperate with John Golden and the craft unionists. But that proved impossible, for Golden had no influence with the strikers, and the manufacturers disliked the craft unionists as much as the Wobblies. Unable to mediate the dispute himself, the governor asked strikers and employers to submit their respective cases to the State Board of Conciliation and Arbitration. Lawrence's employers declined to do so. Finally, on January 29, Foss beseeched the disputants to accept a thirty-day truce during which the employers would pay the fifty-six-hour wage and the workers would return to the mills, while he, Foss, adjudicated the outstanding grievances. The owners leaped at this opportunity to resume full production. Golden and the United Textile Workers proved equally anxious to end the strike before the IWW's inroads among the workers deepened. But the strike committee firmly and flatly rejected the governor's offer. How could it resume a strike after a month-long truce if Foss failed to arrange a settlement satisfying the workers' demands? Ettor and several strikers had already presented their demands directly to Wood, who had rejected them out of hand.

Although the state did little to assist the strikers, it did a great deal to aid employers. It sent militia to Lawrence, and Massachusetts soldiers proved no different from those Wobblies had encountered in other states during other strikes. Ostensibly sent to protect lives and property, the militia usually interfered with the strikers' civil rights. One Boston Brahmin on militia duty in Lawrence informed a reporter, "Most of them [militia] had to leave Harvard for it, but they rather enjoyed going down there and having their fling at those people!"

Despite the nature of the opposition, the strikers held firm. For a time, at least, they had caught the Wobbly spirit, the same spirit that had carried the IWW through the battles at Spokane and Fresno and was even then carrying it through the brutal San Diego struggle. Walter Weyl noted "a new halting self-confidence breaking through the mists of apathy [among the strikers]. The souls behind these white faces were beginning to stir." "We are a new people," said one striker to another observer. "We have hope. We never will stand again what we stood before." Such faith enabled the strikers to surmount all the tactics used against them, including the manufacture of stories of violence.

The Lawrence strike began with violence. On Friday, January 12, Italian workers had undeniably run amok through the Wood Mill. Later that same day strikers had shattered factory windows. By Monday, January 15, strikers had already clashed openly with local police and militia. A group of strikers had marched toward the Pacific Mill to call on the operatives inside to join the walkout, and the militia, assisted by Lawrence firemen, had met the marchers with blasts of icy water from a high-pressure hose. During the ensuing turmoil, the mob scattered, flinging ice at the enemy as it retreated. That, in brief, was the first "bloody" battle of Lawrence.

Violence was certainly not among the objectives of Ettor, the Wobblies, and the strike committee. Indeed, as the Wobblies and the members of the strike committee asserted firmer influence among the strikers, violence diminished. But reporters and their publishers, eager to sell copy, did their best to manufacture stories and headlines about clashes between strikers and soldiers. Some of Lawrence's "better" citizens added to the rumors of violence. On Saturday, January 20, the police, acting on an anonymous tip, found dynamite at several locations, including a cache next to the printing office where Ettor received his mail. The newspapers immediately proclaimed the strikers guilty of a conspiracy to blow up Lawrence. Much to the dismay of the IWW's critics, it turned out that John Breen, a successful local businessman and school board member, had planted the dynamite in order to turn sentiment against the strikers. In May 1912 a local court tried, convicted, and fined Breen $500. Not long after this conviction, a contractor for the American Woolen Company admitted that the dynamite scheme had been arranged at company president Wood's suggestion. But the second confessed dynamiter committed suicide before Wood could be brought to trial, and the eminent Bostonian eluded justice.

Employers, local officials, and newspapers continued to seek out or to create strike violence. Stories spread to the effect that Italian strikers threatened nonstrikers with "Black Hand"* retribution. Yet law officials never uncovered any solid evidence to prove physical intimidation by Wobblies or strikers.

Nevertheless, a *New York Times* headline proclaimed on January 30, 1912, "Real Labor War Now in Lawrence." Behind the headline was the first outbreak of strike violence in two weeks. On the morning of January 29, irate strikers had spontaneously thrown ice and rocks at streetcars carrying nonstrikers to work. Local authorities now sought to make the most of a minor disturbance. That evening, as the IWW led one of its regular parades down Lawrence's streets, the police were in an ugly mood. Parading, singing strikers soon found themselves confronted by determined and barricaded policemen. Both sides began to push and shove, and in the resulting turmoil one officer was stabbed and a young Italian striker, Annie LoPezzi, was shot and killed. Unhesitatingly, yet without evidence, the police accused the strikers of both deeds. A few days after the incident the police had captured an alleged murderer, a man named Joseph Caruso, and his alleged accomplices and co-conspirators, Ettor and Giovannitti, who were accused of inciting, procuring, counseling, and commanding an unknown person to commit murder. Despite the flimsiness of their evidence the police accomplished their objective: the imprisonment of Ettor and Giovannitti, who, from their arrest in late January until their trial the following autumn, remained in prison and hence unable to lead the strike.

With the strikers' leaders in jail, Lawrence's employers expected the walkout to collapse. But city officials and mill owners could not have been more wrong. Haywood, Trautmann, and Flynn more than adequately replaced the imprisoned leaders, and with the conflict more than three weeks old, the strikers had had time to produce leaders from their own ranks.

All the headlines and rumors of violence meanwhile operated to the advantage of the strikers and the IWW. Strikers, not soldiers, had died. Innocent men had been imprisoned for a crime they apparently had not committed, and in jail Ettor and Giovannitti could play the roles their dramatic personalities craved to fill: martyrs sacrificed to the cause of human justice and equality. From all sides and all classes, sympathy and words of encouragement rained down on the "persecuted" strikers, who suddenly discovered allies they never knew they had.

* A Mafia organization supposedly brought to America by Sicilian immigrants.

By stressing nonviolent strike tactics, the Wobblies did their best to preserve the loyalty of their newfound allies. Only a short time before Lawrence, Haywood had lectured New York Socialists on the need for sabotage and the imbecility of obeying capitalist laws and bourgeois courts. In Lawrence, faced with actual industrial conflict, he offered quite different counsel. "Can you weave cloth with the bayonets of your militia, or spin with the clubs of your policemen?" he asked employers. The workers, he said, would simply keep their hands in their pockets, weave no more, and let the soldiers go naked.

In Lawrence, IWW propagandists did not have to emphasize the inevitability of class conflict or the hostility of the state. The facts spoke for themselves, and the strikers could draw their own lessons. The actions of employers, city officials, and the militia demonstrated better than any IWW speaker or pamphlet the realities of class warfare.

The IWW's main problem in Lawrence was to obtain strike funds. With about 23,000 men, women, and children out of work for nine weeks, and another 30,000 or more dependent on their earnings, strike relief posed no small problem. The IWW itself lacked a substantial treasury, and neither the Lawrence Central Labor Union, which was hostile to the IWW, nor the usual local charitable agencies could be expected to contribute generously. The fraternal, religious, and mutual aid societies established by the city's various ethnic organizations, regardless of their views on the strike, could not refuse aid to fellow nationals. But throughout the protracted conflict the IWW shouldered the main burden of relief.

It did so masterfully. The strike committee organized an elaborate system directed by a relief committee composed of representatives of all the nationalities caught up in the struggle. Each ethnic group also had its own special relief committee. These committees investigated the needs of applicants, provided soup kitchens for single men, and furnished food or store orders for families. The committees provided for fuel, shoes, medical assistance, and, in some cases, even rent.

But the strike committee's well-conceived and well-organized relief operation relied almost entirely on financial contributions from outside Lawrence. Here the IWW's organizers and its general headquarters proved most useful. Using every contact they had with other labor organizations, socialist groups, and radicals, the Wobblies solicited funds. Solicitation was made all the easier by the arrogance of the mill owners and the obstinacy of city officials. Every time Wood or another employer rejected negotiations, contributions to the strikers' cause increased.

The IWW also hit upon a perfect scheme to increase newspaper publicity and to lessen the local relief burden. At the end of January, Italian Socialists in New York suggested that the strikers' children be cared for by families outside the strike zone, as had been done on occasion in France, Italy, and Belgium. The *New York Call* publicized the idea, and within three days four hundred New Yorkers offered to take one or more of Lawrence's strike children. On February 11 New York reformers arrived in Lawrence to pick up the first group of 119 children, aged five to fifteen, for distribution to foster parents. When the refugees' train arrived later that day at New York's Grand Central Station, a huge crowd, composed mostly of immigrant working people, greeted the children. "The children marched down the platform," wrote an observer, "four in a row, holding hands, all dressed much alike in their new cloaks and caps. First, there was silence, then a curious emotional wave passed through the crowd . . . followed by a steady roar of cheers."

No one could have dreamed that this new tactic would work so well. Not only did the removal of the children ease the relief problem in Lawrence, but it also gained the most remarkable national publicity. Nothing, after all, was more calculated to increase sympathy for the strikers' cause than the sight of undernourished children removed from their parents' homes because of industrial warfare. To take advantage of this publicity and sympathy, the IWW organized more children's pilgrimages.

The Children's Crusade worked much *too* well in the view of Lawrence's mill owners and public officials. When children quit school to work in the mills, or when immigrant parents left very young children at home untended while they worked in the mills, no city official or local employer cried neglect. But now that the IWW sent these same children out of Lawrence to good homes with the guarantee of ample food, medical care, and supervision, the owners and the officials screamed neglect. They decided to halt the children's exodus at almost any cost. The militia commander posted an order on February 17 to the effect that no child could leave town without his parents' written consent. When the strike committee obtained the necessary written statements, the city marshal announced on February 22 that no more children would be allowed to leave Lawrence—period.

This ruling led to what proved to be the strike's turning point, for on February 24 a group of Philadelphia socialists arrived in Lawrence to pick up some two hundred children for transport back to Philadelphia. Well aware of the marshal's February 22 edict, the Philadelphians intended to challenge and defeat it. Eager to stand on solid legal ground, they obtained the written permission of the parents involved and even took some of the children's mothers to the train station. As the Socialists, the children, and their mothers proceeded toward the special car obtained from the Boston and Maine Railroad, the local police acted. Two members of the Philadelphia Women's Committee described what followed: "The police . . . closed in on us with clubs, beating right and left, with no thought of children, who were in the most desperate danger of being trampled to death. The mothers and children were thus hurled in a mass and bodily dragged to a military truck, and even then clubbed, irrespective of the cries of the panic-stricken women and children."

Newspapers and magazines made the entire nation witness to the arrogance, stupidity, and brutality of Lawrence's employers and public officials. Governor Foss ordered an immediate investigation. Socialist congressman Victor Berger demanded a congressional investigation, which resulted in hearings in Washington at which the strikers obtained still wider publicity. The relief committees no longer had to worry about outside contributions.

Eight weeks of industrial conflict had brought no break in the strikers' ranks. In early March they appeared stronger than ever. Nationwide support and sympathy almost inundated the strikers. Unable to operate at capacity, Lawrence's mills could not fill spring orders. Meanwhile, a Democratic Congress had begun to investigate a strike that involved staunch Republican mill owners. Given these circumstances, the employers beat a strategic retreat. Finally, on Saturday, March 12, the strike committee obtained a satisfactory settlement proposal from the American Woolen Company. The agreement provided a flat 5 percent wage hike for all pieceworkers; 5 to 25 percent increases for all hourly rated employees, with the highest percentage going to the lowest-paid workers; time and a quarter for overtime; no discrimination against any striker; and reforms in the premium or bonus system. Two days later at an excited mass meeting the strikers voted to end their walkout and accept the proposed settlement.

The workers had thus achieved their four original demands. As Haywood gloatingly remarked, "Passive, with folded arms, the strikers won." He later said to the even more gleeful immigrants, "I want to say . . . that the strikers of Lawrence have won the most signal victory of any organized body of workers in the world. You have demonstrated, as has been shown nowhere else, the common interest of the working class in bringing all nationalities together."

For Lawrence and for the New England textile industry, however, the settlement failed to bring peace or a sense of security. An uneasy fear lingered. The IWW remained in Lawrence, and to mill owners, public officials, and federal investigators that labor organization seemed to be the spearhead of a threatened social revolution. Textile industry employers throughout New England raised wages—partly in fear of the IWW, partly to arrest further industrial conflict, and partly to remove the possibility of social revolution.

The legal proceedings arising out of the Lawrence strike, especially the Ettor-Giovannitti case, also aroused anxiety in New England. All that spring and summer the IWW organized its Ettor-Giovannitti defense campaign. All available Eastern organizers, and some from the West, were put to work on it. Some of the effort that should have been devoted to solidifying the organizational gains achieved in Lawrence went instead into legal defense activities, which brought no new members to the organization. The closer the trial came, the more energy the IWW expended on it. On September 15, 1912, 35,000 workers, including 13,500 who traveled from Lawrence to Boston on two Red Specials, assembled on the Boston Common to protest the scheduled trial and to threaten an industry-wide general strike. Later in the month, on September 28, Lawrence textile workers spontaneously walked out of the mills. The rank and file continued to advocate a general strike, despite the opposition of Local 20's officials and of the imprisoned Ettor and Giovannitti.

On September 30 the two accused Wobblies were brought before the bar of justice at—of all places—the site of America's earliest witch-hunt, Salem. For fifty-eight days the trial dragged on, ending on November 26, when Ettor and Giovannitti made their final impressive speeches. Ettor informed the jury, "I neither offer apology nor excuse; I ask no favors; I ask for nothing but justice in this matter." Giovannitti proved even more eloquent, closing with these words: "And if it be that these hearts of ours must be stilled on the same death chair and by the same current of fire that has destroyed the life of the wife murderer and the patricide and parricide, then I say that tomorrow we shall pass into a greater judgment, that tomorrow we shall go from your presence where history shall give its last word to us." The jury thought so highly of the defendants' closing arguments and so lightly of the state's evidence that it acquitted Ettor and Giovannitti.

At first the IWW seemed to have achieved an even more remarkable triumph in its hold upon Lawrence's immigrants and in the establishment of a stable, effective industrial union. As late as mid-September 1912 the IWW claimed about sixteen thousand paid-up members in Lawrence's mills—an impressive achievement in a formerly anti-union city. In August an IWW leader noted how wrong were the commentators who had said "that the workers [in Lawrence] would be satisfied with butter instead of molasses on their bread and the revolutionary movement would be at a standstill. . . . Nothing could be farther from the truth," he went on. "The unions are growing by leaps and bounds . . . and the work of adding recruits goes merrily on." Yet in the last analysis the pessimists proved correct in their impressions of the immigrant workers' basic desires and in their forecast of an IWW decline. Why?

Most analysts of the IWW and of the Lawrence strike have found a simple explanation for the organization's failure to preserve the gains it had achieved during the heat of the battle. The traditional version asserts that the IWW "was more interested in winning converts for the revolution than in building a day-to-day collective bargaining agency." That the IWW preached the irrepressible class war is certainly true; that it preferred revolution to bread-and-butter gains is less true. Haywood and other IWW leaders advised strikers to accept the March 13 strike settlement, and it was Ettor and Giovannitti who, in September 1912, counseled Lawrence's rank and file against protest strikes.

Other reasons must be sought for the IWW's eventual failure in Lawrence, and they are not all that hard to find. Late in 1913 Selig Perlman, then working for the Commission on Industrial Relations, investigated labor conditions in Lawrence, specifically as they related to the IWW. He had no problem locating the causes of the organization's difficulties. Perlman discovered that employers regularly infiltrated spies into the union and that local newspapers just as regularly printed false and unfavorable articles about the IWW. Manufacturers also manipulated the labor market to the union's disadvantage: In periods of unemployment the mills continued to advertise for labor outside Lawrence in order to flood the local labor market. Employers, Perlman also found, consciously played one nationality off against another, and with considerable success. The favored nationalities, for example, received higher wages, rapid promotions, and a share in municipal patronage and power.

A report presented to the IWW by Thomas Holliday of Local 20 in March 1913 indicates that Perlman's assessment was remarkably accurate. Holliday reported that Lawrence's employers had initiated a temporary depression—the closing of local mills to which Perlman had referred—that threw thousands of immigrants out of work. A nationwide recession had developed, and Lawrence Wobblies suffered considerably. A local union official reported sadly, "Reaction . . . has been busily at work within the ranks of Local Union No. 20 sowing the seeds of dissension and despair."

One final factor militated against IWW success in Lawrence. Out of a sense of despair caused partly by their exploitation by employers and partly by their total rejection by Lawrence's elite, the new immigrants had turned to the IWW. When the IWW could not resist exploitation or alter the attitudes of the local ruling class, for reasons Perlman enumerated, the immigrants drifted out of the organization.

But in the early spring of 1912 no one, either inside or outside the IWW, could foresee how few members the organization would have in Lawrence only a year later, or how completely paralyzed the IWW would be at the time in the industrial Northeast. After the well-publicized events in Lawrence, outsiders still feared and exaggerated the IWW's power. And the Wobblies, gloating over their victory, also exaggerated the effects of the Lawrence conflict.

To the convinced Wobbly, 1912 seemed like the dawn of a new, freer era. The IWW, indeed, conducted more strikes and free-speech fights from 1912 to 1913 than at any other time in its pre–World War I history. In the midst of the San Diego struggle and only two weeks after the triumph in Lawrence, the *Industrial Worker* boasted, "The revolutionary pot seems to be boiling in all quarters. The day of transformation is now at hand."

Wobblies had suddenly discovered that their tactics worked. In the past they had preached but not practiced industrial organization and direct action at the point of production; now they had started, as in Lawrence, "to practice what we preached."

Wherever Wobblies chose to look in the summer of 1912 they could see organizational activity. E. F. Doree boasted of four thousand Wobblies out on the Grand Trunk Pacific in Canada, fifteen thousand in eleven New Bedford textile mills, fifteen thousand timber workers in Louisiana and Texas, and two thousand auto workers in Cleveland. An IWW organizer in Vancouver, Canada, reported with equal enthusiasm that the organization had established five new locals in Vancouver and that the impact of IWW agitation was being felt all over British Columbia.

This euphoric optimism carried right on through to the seventh IWW national convention, which met at Brand's Hall in Chicago September 16–26, 1912. Forty-five delegates from all over the United States and Canada attended. Although some signs of decentralist sentiment appeared, no ideological or sectional lines divided the delegates. Indeed, delegates from Portland, Oregon, came to the Chicago convention with proposals for tightening and centralizing the IWW's methods and structure. So much for the alleged commitment of Western Wobblies to primitive frontier individualism and to rank-and-file participatory democracy. So advised, the convention voted to encourage the appointment of more professional organizers who would recruit on the job and maintain accurate and complete membership records.

Most Wobblies returned home from the convention enraptured about their organization's future. James P. Cannon, one of the younger Wobblies then rising to prominence in American radical circles, thought the organization's rapid growth had ended internal strife and dissension forever. "Nor was there any reaching out for respectability," Cannon wrote. "Every man was a 'Red,' most of them with jail records, too. . . . Here was an assemblage which, to a man, rejected the moral and ethical teachings of the existing order, and had formulated a creed of their own which begins with Solidarity and ends with Freedom."

But in 1912 freedom and solidarity were farther away than most Wobblies suspected. Still transfixed by their success at Lawrence, they forgot the relative paucity of the IWW's total membership and the bankruptcy of its treasury. Swept away by the growth and successes of 1912, they would be ill prepared to meet the decline and defeats to come their way in 1913.

# 11

## Satan's Dark Mills: Paterson and After

History never repeats itself precisely. To paraphrase Hegel's famous aphorism, similar historical events occur first as success, next as failure. This, much to its regret, the IWW learned in 1913.

In 1913 IWW organizers directed a walkout begun by rebellious textile workers in Paterson, New Jersey, just as they had done the previous year in Lawrence. In Paterson, however, the industrial conflict ended in defeat, and the IWW's failure there presaged its bleak future among the immigrant workers of the industrial Northeast.

Like Lawrence, Paterson in 1913 was an old, established industrial city. About 20 miles from New York City and less than 100 from Philadelphia, it sat astride the most compact domestic market in nineteenth-century America. By the second half of the nineteenth century, Paterson, taking advantage of all its geographic attractions, had become one of the Northeast's more significant small industrial centers.

By 1913 Paterson led the nation in silk production. More than three hundred mills and dyehouses employing about 25,000 men, women, and children (out of a total of about 73,000 working men, women, and children in the city) dyed and wove the fine as well as the cheap silks demanded by New York's garment industry. Once a producer of only the finest high-grade and high-cost silks, Paterson, compelled by changes in the structure of the market, had turned to the manufacture of cheaper silks, which could be produced on larger, more efficient looms operated by women and children.

Like other industrial cities of its size, Paterson had a polyglot population. At first its people consisted largely of native-born Americans of British and Dutch stock. Then, in the 1840s and 1850s, the first waves of Irish and German immigrants reached the city. Even after the Civil War the Irish, the Germans, and some Englishmen continued to settle in Paterson. Toward the end of the century eastern European Jews and southern Italians started to arrive in significant numbers, and they continued to do so right up to the strike year of 1913.

Working conditions in Paterson did not differ materially from those in Lawrence. Work was hard—ten hours daily—and the mills were dirty, stuffy, and noisy. The people who toiled inside were like the laborers of Lawrence: Men and women worked alongside adolescent boys and girls (over fourteen).

Wages conformed to the pattern prevalent elsewhere in the textile industry. Paterson's average wage for skilled workers in 1913 was $11.69 a week. The unskilled, of course, received much less—closer to $6 or $7 a week. The number of unskilled, especially women and children, at work in the industry was rising rapidly in proportion to the total number of employees.

But even family labor failed to provide Paterson's immigrants with comfort or security. Although the city's slums did not match the worst in Lawrence, the housing of many workers was still, in the words of Paterson's leading rabbi, "distinctly bad." Housing aside, the unskilled immigrants lived on the margin of economic security: Seasonal and technological shifts frequently left them jobless, competition from low-wage mills in Pennsylvania threatened their wage scale, and the abundant supply of cheap immigrant labor exercised relentless downward pressure on their wage rates.

There were also important differences between Lawrence and Paterson. In Paterson, unlike Lawrence, no single company dominated the city's economy, and numerous small mills ruthlessly competed with the larger manufacturers. Paterson also had fewer significant nationality groups among its new immigrants. In both textile towns, however, wages were low and immigrant families sent their children into the mills in order to supplement income. In short, Paterson, like Lawrence, contained within itself the social dynamite that, given the spark, could explode into industrial warfare. Paterson had long been a favorite target for IWW agitators. From the IWW's founding in 1905, not a year passed without some organizational activity in the city. The 1908 convention that established the National Industrial Union of Textile Workers (NIUTW) met there. But over the years IWW efforts to penetrate the silk industry met with little success, for Paterson's employers were as hostile to trade unions as were Lawrence's, and they had been equally successful in beating back union threats. Although silk workers belonged to several craft unions affiliated with the United Textile Workers (UTW), these unions were neither active nor effective. On the eve of the 1913 strike Paterson was fairly unorganized.

At one time Paterson's silk manufacturers had faced little competition. This was no longer so in 1913. Technological innovation and changing demands brought an intensive competition to the silk industry, much more bitter than that faced by Lawrence's American Woolen Company. In the mid-1890s engineers had perfected a high-speed loom that could be operated by

women. Simultaneously, demand increased for the cheap silk turned out by
the new looms, thereby providing manufacturers of cheap-grade silks with
larger profits on their investments than could be had by Paterson's producers of fine silks. The cheap silk industry also moved to the coal-mining communities of eastern Pennsylvania, where a large female labor force sought
work at low wages. Paterson's weavers had traditionally worked only one or
two jacquard looms, which turned out fine silk. The Pennsylvania women,
however, tended four looms and produced considerably more silk per unit
of labor than their Paterson competitors. The ensuing technological innovations destroyed traditional working patterns in Paterson. An industry once
composed largely of well-paid skilled weavers fast became one with more and
more low-paid women workers. Weavers who once tended two looms now
worked three or four.

Considerations other than wages made weavers discontented with the four-
loom system. Many weavers considered the obligation to tend four looms in
poorly illuminated mills to be too much of a strain on their eyes and nerves.
Others feared that the general introduction of the four-loom system would
engender rising unemployment, create a reserve labor army anxious for work
at any price, and thus ultimately undermine prevailing wage rates. When one
man or woman could do the work formerly done by two or three hands, how
could Paterson provide jobs enough for all its workers?

When silk workers asked for shorter hours or higher wages, employers pleaded poverty. Paterson's manufacturers claimed, and with some justice, that their
wages were higher than those paid in any other American silk-making community. Moreover, New Jersey state law limited the workers to a fifty-five-hour
week, while out-of-state competitors worked their employees from fifty-seven
to sixty hours. How, asked Paterson's employers, could they meet their workers' demands when concessions would place them at the mercy of competitors in other states with lower wage rates and weaker labor laws?

Paterson's workers refused to accept their employers' case for the status quo.
Early in 1912, when several local mills introduced the four-loom system, the
weavers rebelled. They demanded either increased piece rates or the elimination of the multiple-loom system. At first only the skilled workers allied to the
AFL craft unions protested. Instead of supporting the protest, the UTW placed
itself at the mercy of the employers' sense of justice. Nothing coming of UTW
efforts to improve working conditions, Paterson's workers looked elsewhere
for union leadership.

At that particular time the IWW was fully occupied in Lawrence. Not so
Daniel DeLeon's then-insignificant organization, the so-called Detroit IWW.

DeLeon's right-hand man, Rudolph Katz, rushed to Paterson to lead the rebellious local workers. Under Katz's leadership more than five thousand workers came out on strike. Coming during the peak production season, the walkout caused several mills to settle on union terms—largely an increase in wages and limited recognition of the union.

These gains proved short-lived. The larger mills never negotiated with the strikers; instead, they used their influence to have Katz jailed for six months, and then proceeded to smash the leaderless strike. The smaller manufacturers, who had settled with the union, broke their contracts as soon as the busy season ended. DeLeon's IWW never had a chance in Paterson. Not only was it fought by employers, but both the AFL craft unions and the Chicago IWW opposed it as well.

As 1912 ended, Paterson's basic industrial relations problem remained unresolved. Employers continued to introduce four looms, hire women at lower wages, and slash piece rates.

Finally, in January 1913, the decision by Doherty and Company, the largest mill in Paterson, to introduce the four-loom system in a plant traditionally run on the two-loom pattern brought the city's festering discontent to a head. At once Doherty's skilled weavers protested. Yet when Doherty responded by asserting that external competition dictated the introduction of the four-loom system, the protesting craft unionists did nothing more.

With Lawrence out of the way, the IWW was now ready to move in. Early in January an IWW leader reported to *Solidarity* that Paterson Local 152 had been doing good work agitating for an eight-hour day and for the abolition of the four-loom system. The IWW, he added, should be able to make Paterson's bosses sit up and take notice. Local 152 appealed to workers by arguing that the eight-hour day would compel employers to hire more workers, and that once the reserve labor army shrunk in size, workers could compel employers to grant "more wages, better treatment, better light." Refuse to run more than two looms on broadsilk, more than one loom on silk, the IWW agitators advised, but "organize your forces. Act together. When we get ready we will set the date and refuse to work longer than 8 hours."

As the IWW sent its message throughout the city, it stimulated further discontent among Doherty employees, who, late in January, walked out spontaneously. This time, however, they did not lack leadership or organization. Local 152 immediately offered help and set about widening the original walkout initiated by only a handful of workers. By February 1 the IWW succeeded in making the Doherty walkout plant-wide. Strike leaders now reasoned that unless Paterson's other mill hands came out and shut down all the city's mills, the Doherty strike would collapse. Calling on the workers in every mill and dyehouse to strike on Tuesday morning, February 25, Wobbly organizers advised, "It is far better to starve fighting than to starve working." On the morning of the 25th workers began to walk out of Paterson's silk mills, and in the days that followed more and more workers came out. They left at the rate of almost 1,200 a day, until 25,000 workers were out and Paterson's silk industry had been shut down tight. At this point the strikers made only two specific demands: an eight-hour day and a $12 minimum weekly wage for dyehouse workers (the filthiest and least desirable employment in the industry).

In Paterson, as in Lawrence, the strikers were divided by nationality and craft. Again, the previously unorganized and less skilled new immigrants walked out first, followed, though somewhat reluctantly, by the skilled English-speaking workers. Throughout what was to prove a protracted conflict, the two groups of strikers maintained a shaky alliance of convenience, ready to crumble at the first shock. In the past the English-speaking workers had never shown any inclination to cooperate with the immigrants who labored alongside them in the mills. Secure in their established craft unions with their higher wages, the skilled workers were patronizing to their foreign colleagues. One veteran AFL craft unionist told the Commission on Industrial Relations that the trouble in Paterson "was too many immigrants coming into the silk trade that did not thoroughly understand the working of our organizations, or had not become Americanized." He contended that the AFL could not organize Paterson's "unamerican" immigrants.

Elizabeth Gurley Flynn, one of the most active IWW agitators during the Paterson struggle, clearly recalled the city's tenacious ethnic divisions. She found the immigrant broadsilk weavers and dyers, though largely unorganized and unfamiliar with unionism, easy to stimulate to aggressive activity. But the English-speaking ribbon weavers, with thirty years of craft union traditions behind them, responded to the IWW-led walkout only after three weeks of actual conflict. Even then they continued to exert a conservative influence on the mass of immigrant strikers. John Reed, then a young reporter fresh out of Harvard and making his first contact with the realities of the class struggle in America, carried away from Paterson the same impressions as Flynn. Upon asking a young Jew which nationalities were united in the strike, Reed obtained the following reply: "'T'ree great nations stick togedder like dis.' He made a fist. 'T'ree great nations—Italians, Hebrews, and Germans.'" How about Americans? Reed inquired. "The Jew shrugged his shoulders, grinned scornfully, and answered: 'English peoples not go on picket line. Mericans no lika fight!'"

"The degraded and ignorant races" went out on Paterson's picket lines and got clubbed partly because they rebelled against miserable working conditions and partly because the IWW organized their rebellion. The AFL never came forward, at least not to organize the immigrants. "Instead," wrote social investigator John Fitch, "came Haywood . . . Flynn, [Patrick] Quinlan, [Carlo] Tresca*—empty handed, with neither money nor credit nor with the prestige of a 2,000,000 membership, but willing to work and to go to jail. They have put into the 25,000 strikers a spirit that has made them stand together with a united determination for a period that must have tried the souls of the strongest."

When the IWW organizers and agitators arrived in Paterson, Silk Workers Local 152 had only about nine hundred members. Two weeks after the strike began, the union had more than ten thousand new members. The IWW immediately set about organizing the silk strikers into an effective force. First, it created a strike committee comprising two delegates from each shop (six hundred members at full strength) to administer the conflict. As in Lawrence, the majority of committee members at first were nonunion, non-IWW. When inquiring journalists asked the strikers who their leaders were, the workers shot back, "We are all leaders." The IWW organizers—Haywood, Flynn, Quinlan—served in a purely advisory capacity.

With the strikers organized, Wobbly agitators could go about their work more effectively. Precisely what they did has been described by Flynn, according to whom the agitators' primary goal was to educate the strikers. Sounding almost like John Dewey, she noted that "education is not a conversion, it is a process." IWW speakers, she observed, sought to transcend the prejudices of a lifetime: prejudices on national issues, prejudices between crafts, prejudices between men and women, prejudices between ethnic and religious groups. The Wobblies attempted to convert the immigrants from their diverse Old World religions to a new single-minded faith in the class struggle, to make the strikers forget that their walkout was over a few cents more or a few hours less, "but to make them feel it is a 'religious duty' for them to win that strike." One overriding goal underlay the IWW's work in Paterson, Flynn declared: "To create in them [the strikers] a feeling of solidarity" as part of the long process of instilling "class spirit, class respect, class consciousness."

Neither the IWW organizers nor the strike committee ever lost sight of the walkout's immediate objectives. From the first, the strike committee offered to confer with employers in order to settle the dispute. Similarly, the separate

* An Italian syndicalist, romantic radical, and lover of Elizabeth Gurley Flynn, Tresca was an antifascist purportedly assassinated by Mussolini's agents in America in 1943.

shop committees approached their respective employers to probe the possibilities of reaching an equitable accord. Within the larger strike committee, a smaller executive body of twenty—all IWW members, but also all local Paterson men—handled the preliminary negotiations. The various shop committees' most basic demand was the eight-hour day. One strike leader afterward remarked, "I know positively had the manufacturers at the time of the strike granted an eight-hour day the strikers would have thrown all other grievances aside." But once the strike had erupted they asked for more. They demanded time and a half for overtime, minimum-wage levels for the less skilled (particularly the dyehouse workers), increases in the general piece rates, abolition of the three- and four-loom system in broadsilk, and several minor items. As in all IWW-led strikes, the workers did not insist on union recognition or on the closed shop.

The IWW's administration of the Paterson struggle differed in no basic respect from what it had been in Lawrence. Picket squads assigned to each of the mills marched continuously up and down the sidewalks in front of the factory gates with every intention of psychologically intimidating men and women who might have considered breaking the united front by reentering the mills. (Physical violence, however, always remained a possibility.) Every day for seven months, in the face of policemen's clubs, detectives' pistols, and rough weather, the pickets performed their function.

IWW agitators ensured that the strikers' ranks remained united. Flynn explained how this was done. Sunday was the crucial day: "If on Sunday," she said, "you let these people stay at home, sit around the stove without any fire in it, sit down at the table where there isn't very much food, see the feet of the children with shoes getting thin, and the bodies of the children where the clothes are getting ragged, they begin to think in terms of myself and lose the spirit of the mass and the realization that all are suffering as they are suffering. You have got to keep them busy every day in the week, and particularly on Sunday, in order to keep that spirit from going down to zero." Which was why the IWW held constant meetings that were more in the character of high school pep rallies than serious war councils. This was why every Sunday the IWW would lead a march to Haledon, a small socialist-administered township just outside Paterson's city limits, where strikers could picnic, listen to radical oratory, and sing without fear and without police interference.

The IWW once more pledged to wage a nonviolent struggle. In Paterson, as in Lawrence, it insisted that strikers could gain victory simply by keeping their hands in their pockets. Again, it advised its followers that bayonets and clubs could not weave silk. "We believe the most violent thing the worker can do," local IWW leader Adolph Lessig said, "is when they quit work."

Numerous witnesses testified to the effectiveness of the IWW's peaceful methods. Paterson's Rabbi Leo Mannheimer paid tribute to the leadership of Haywood, Flynn, Tresca, and the others, who held in check an army of 25,000 for thirteen weeks. "Had they been preaching anarchism and violence," the rabbi wrote, "there would have been anarchism and violence." Instead, excepting a few broken windows, there had been no destruction of property, and certainly no destruction of lives. Passive resistance had been the strikers' weapon, Rabbi Mannheimer concluded.

From the attitudes, policies, and actions of Paterson's employers and its leading citizens, one would never have known that nonviolent industrial conflict was being waged. Paterson's manufacturers and local elite made Lawrence's appear almost benevolently enlightened. They hired armed private detectives to patrol the mills and intimidate the strikers. Manufacturers had one overriding aim, according to Rabbi Mannheimer, and that was "to starve the strikers into submission, so that they will return to the mills disheartened."

Following what had by then become a time-honored American practice, Paterson's employers proclaimed their belief in decent, honest, God-fearing American trade unions and their desire to protect decent men and women from intimidation by hoodlum, radical, un-American unionists. But any reasonably astute observer saw through employer propaganda. If pinned down, John Fitch observed, "the employers admit that they are opposed to unionism as such, and not to the I.W.W. alone." If unionism could not be resisted, however, employers preferred the AFL to the Wobblies.

Paterson's dominant groups agreed with the employers' anti-union sentiments. Mayor Andrew McBride claimed the conflict had been caused by out-of-town agitators who preached "unamerican" doctrines to gullible and confused immigrants. The editor of the *Paterson Press* suggested that the city handle the IWW with the same dispatch San Diego had demonstrated in the previous year's free-speech fight. "The sooner the I.W.W. outfit leave town," he informed his readers, "the better it will be for all concerned, *no matter how it is accomplished*" (italics added).

The city authorities thus decided to drive the "outside" agitators out of Paterson—subtly if possible, forcibly if necessary. A specially established group of local clergymen (excluding Rabbi Mannheimer), founded with the blessings of the board of aldermen, sought to bring employers and employees together on an individual, nonunion basis. But because the IWW refused to recognize the clergymen's version of the Golden Rule, most Paterson preachers came to agree with laymen that the Wobblies should never have been permitted into town, "but having come they should be driven out."

Perhaps one way of driving the Wobblies out was to invite the AFL in. Although manufacturers made no direct overtures to an AFL union, Paterson's press, pulpit, and municipal officials invited Gompers's organization in to help stymie the Wobblies. The Paterson central labor organization, an AFL affiliate, tried to arrange a peace conference between employers and strikers. Just as local AFL men had almost completed their arrangements, however, Flynn warned the strikers against following AFL "fakirs and grafters." She proposed instead that the strikers cooperate with the central labor council if that body would endorse a twenty-four-hour sympathy strike—a demand no AFL affiliate could possibly accept. The first AFL peacemaking venture proving a failure, the town fathers invited John Golden and the UTW to organize the strikers. At a time when every meeting hall in Paterson had been denied the IWW, John Golden, Sarah Conboy, and their AFL associates obtained the local armory to plead their case. On the evening of April 16, and with the conflict now two months old, thousands of Paterson strikers flocked to the armory to hear what the UTW-AFL had to offer. When Conboy and Golden stepped to the platform, boos, hisses, and catcalls echoed across the cavernous building for fully forty-five minutes. The local police finally drove the strikers out of the armory, leaving the UTW-AFL, in the words of one observer, "in possession of a vast emptiness."

Another way of driving the IWW out seemed simpler and more expedient. The day after the general strike began, Paterson's police arrested Flynn, Tresca, and Quinlan and closed every hall in town to the strikers. The following evening police arrested a socialist named Frederick Sumner Boyd for having read at a strike meeting the free speech clause of the New Jersey state constitution. Later, at the station house, police chief Bimson asked the socialist what strange law he had been reading. Boyd replied, "Why, chief, that was the constitution of New Jersey. Never hear of it before? I thought not." Day after day the police interfered with strike meetings, confiscated socialist newspapers and strike literature, and arrested strikers by the score. Any Wobbly who dared speak in Paterson courted arrest and imprisonment. Paterson's police, trying to learn from Lawrence's mistakes, arrested not two men but every leader it could lay its "legal" hands on and 1,850 of the strikers.

The arrests went on, as did the beatings and clubbings. On April 19, company detectives shot and killed Modestino Valentino, an innocent bystander to a scuffle between pickets and scabs. Justice never visited the silk manufacturers' gunmen. A week later local prosecutors indicted Tresca, Flynn, Quinlan, and Lessig on insubstantial charges, and on May 10 a Paterson jury convicted the socialist editor Alexander Scott of sedition—that is, of criticizing the city police—and sentenced him to one to fifteen years in prison. Shortly thereafter, Frederick Sumner Boyd found himself in prison on sedition charges. On July 13 a strikebreaker shot and killed Vincenzo Madonna, an IWW striker, and murder again went unpunished. There seemed to be no end to the injustices committed by Paterson's lawfully constituted authorities. Unhappy about the IWW meetings in Haledon, on July 19 Paterson's police instigated a riot there in order to arrest Haledon's socialist mayor on the pretext of "unlawful assemblage and malfeasance in office."

John Reed had first arrived in Paterson one morning at sunrise to find the city's streets gray, cold, and deserted. The police soon appeared, and a little later the pickets came out. Then came the rain, compelling Reed to seek shelter on a nearby porch, whereupon the police attempted to drive him off the porch and back again out into the downpour. When Reed refused to desert his shelter, a policeman promptly placed him under arrest. The young reporter found himself in a jail cell, about 4 feet wide by 7 feet long, with an iron bunk hung from one side, "and an open toilet of disgusting dirtiness in the corner." Here, in jail, Reed learned how the strikers endured Paterson-style justice. While he paced nervously in his tiny cell, forty pickets joined him in the lockup, two to a cell. Joking and laughing, the forty new arrivals lifted and slammed heavy iron beds against metal walls, causing a commotion that to Reed sounded "like a cannon battery in action." For Wobblies it was simply another jail battleship. The prisoners also cheered the IWW, Haywood, Flynn, and Tresca, the Italians among them singing constantly right up until their release.

But the strikers could not exist solely on true belief. As the conflict wore on, through spring and early summer, the strikers grew hungrier. As always, the IWW's own resources were limited. Socialists, craft unionists, social reformers, and sympathizers had to provide the bulk of material assistance for the conflict. Fortunately, in Paterson, as in Lawrence, every repressive measure taken by the IWW's enemies brought increased aid to the strikers. Still they needed a cause célèbre like Lawrence had had in the Children's Crusade, which Paterson, after three months of industrial warfare, still lacked.

John Reed and New York's Greenwich Village intellectuals intended to provide this essential ingredient for Paterson's silk workers. During a gathering at the home of Mabel Dodge Luhan, the salon hostess and radical dilettante, Big Bill Haywood complained bitterly about the lack of publicity the Paterson strikers were getting in New York. Not to be outdone in radical rhetoric by her special guest, Luhan suggested, "Why don't you bring the strike to New York and *show* it to the workers?" "Well, by God There's an idea!" Haywood responded. "But how? What hall?" Then, as Luhan recalled in her memoirs, a young man in the salon burst out, "I'll do it! My name is Reed . . . we'll make a Pageant of the strike! The first in the world."

Thus did John Reed hope simultaneously to save the strikers from certain defeat and to make the IWW the link between New York's radical "new" intellectuals and the "new" working-class revolutionaries, who together, in Nietzschean fashion, would leap out of their times, transcend the prevailing structure of society, and transform the values of bourgeois America.

Reed worked day and night to bring off his dream. He recruited other intellectuals, artists, designers, stage directors, voice experts, and anyone else he could make use of. Together they drilled Paterson's conglomerate strikers into a unified theatrical company that could sing with one voice and act with some feeling. Finally, June 7, the day of the pageant, arrived. Thousands of strikers marched out from Paterson, crossed the Hudson River, and paraded through Manhattan to the old Madison Square Garden, where an immense sign blazed the letters *IWW* across New York's skyline. Inside thousands of spectators looked down upon a flaming red stage set. Waiting for the pageant to open, the expectant audience chanted strike slogans and thundered out IWW songs. Silence finally settled on the Garden as the silk workers came on stage to re-enact Reed's version of industrial warfare. Whistles blew, pickets marched, cheered, and sang; police harassed the innocent; the strikers held fast. Even murder reappeared on the stage, as the strikers dramatized the gratuitous slaying of Modestino Valentino and the mass funeral that followed. At the pageant's close, Haywood, Flynn, Tresca, and Quinlan ended the strike drama with a reenactment of their standard Paterson oratory. As the striker-actors left the stage, a band struck up the "Marseillaise" and the "Internationale"—which the audience bellowed out in a swelling chorus. So ended Reed's strike pageant, the first and last such event the world has seen.

From the next morning on, the strike went downhill; the pageant proved to be its climax, the rest was anticlimax. Reed had promised money for the strikers—thousands of dollars to feed, clothe, and shelter them—and now he couldn't deliver on his promise. Flynn vividly recalled the aftermath: "This thing that had been heralded as the salvation of the strike, this thing that was going to bring thousands of dollars to the strike—$150 came to Paterson, and all kinds of explanations."

After the financial fiasco of the pageant, cracks appeared in the strikers' previously solid wall. As June passed into July and July into August, the cracks widened into gaping holes. First, the skilled English-speaking workers, always more moderate than the mass of immigrant strikers, tried to exert their power on the strike committee to arrange a compromise shop-by-shop settlement. Next the Socialists and the Wobblies, previously united in support of the strike, began to tear at each other's throats. All the while the strikers contended with hunger—"hunger gnawing at their vitals; hunger tearing them down."

When employers proposed a shop-by-shop settlement in early July, the skilled ribbon weavers leaped at the opportunity to return to work. The IWW leaders, however, insisted that the great majority of strikers must receive some concessions before the walkout ended. But now the more conservative workers turned IWW principles against the Wobblies. "We are the silk workers," the ribbon weavers said. "You are simply outside agitators. You can't talk to this strike committee even."

During the conflict's first months Socialists and Wobblies had displayed almost perfect harmony. Wobblies did most of the agitating and organizing; Socialists provided most of the publicity, sympathy, and money. Paterson's strikers had no better friend than the Socialist *New York Call.* To some American radicals Paterson demonstrated beautifully the need for both kinds of working-class action: direct and political.

Cooperation faltered as hunger and pessimism spread. The old submerged grievances and conflicts separating IWW syndicalists from Socialist politicians soon rose to the surface. By July, Socialists joined the more moderate English-speaking strikers (some of whom were themselves Socialists) in supporting compromise shop-by-shop agreements. The local Socialist paper began to advise strikers, "Industrial action has failed; now try political action." As the strike weakened, the earlier Socialist support of IWW leadership turned to criticism. The *New York Call,* originally a leading advocate of the strikers' cause, became its most outspoken critic. When confused strikers asked John Reed why Socialists no longer supported them, he had no answer. "All I could say," Reed later wrote, "was that a good share of the Socialist Party and the American Federation of Labor have forgotten all about the Class Struggle."

By mid-July, with Quinlan and Boyd in prison, Flynn finally released after a jury deadlock, Haywood and Tresca awaiting trial in the fall, and hundreds of other strikers either in jail or out on bond, the silk workers held on only by the skin of their teeth. Although the manufacturers had also begun to weaken by July, finding themselves unable to fill profitable orders for the coming fall fashion season, they remained united. United, the employers could take advantage of the breaks developing in the strikers' ranks.

The strike collapsed in a fashion that was all too predictable. The English-speaking skilled workers cut their less-skilled comrades adrift. On July 18 the ribbon weavers notified the strike committee, "We have drawn out of your committee. We are going to settle our strike to suit ourselves. We are going to settle it shop by shop." With the ribbon weavers' secession, the strike committee decided, without taking a referendum vote, to allow the remaining strikers to return to work on the basis of individual shop agreements, whatever the terms. By July 28 everybody was back at work, and nobody had obtained much of an improvement in wages or working conditions.

Flynn later asserted, "If the strikers had been able to hold out a little longer by any means, by money if possible . . . we could have won the Paterson strike." But, as she argued, the Socialists who had the funds offered only criticism and complained about Wobbly ingratitude.

Flynn, in a postmortem on Paterson, explained why the IWW could achieve short-run coalitions with immigrant industrial workers yet could not maintain their commitment over the long haul. To Flynn a labor victory in order to be meaningful had to be two-sided: Workers must gain economic advantage but they must also achieve the revolutionary spirit. If a strike could achieve only one objective, she argued, better to gain in spirit than in economic advantage. But even Flynn perceived that if the IWW offered strikers only revolutionary spirit and no bread, its appeal would be too circumscribed. Consequently, the IWW conducted its strikes, like the one in Paterson, pragmatically. It followed no hard and fast rules. If the strikers wanted higher wages, shorter hours, and better conditions, IWW organizers let them fight for them. If they wanted agreements (not time contracts) with their employers, IWW leaders let them negotiate for them. The IWW organized, agitated, and advised, but the strikers, most of whom in Paterson and elsewhere in the East did not understand or accept hard-core IWW doctrine, finally made the decisions. If the strikers failed to learn from action, or if they decided wrongly, there was nothing IWW leaders could do.

Had the IWW organizers in Paterson been prepared to offer the correct advice and exert the proper control, the result for both the strikers and the IWW might have been different. Unfortunately, Wobblies did not necessarily give strikers wise counsel. Paterson's workers had sought to earn a few cents more and work a few minutes less each day. But to Flynn and Haywood, among others, if the strikers returned to the job with material gains but "with the same psychology, the same attitude toward society," they would have won only a temporary triumph, not a lasting victory. This IWW commitment to larger revolutionary principles and goals, this desire to inculcate Marxist ideology among immigrant workers, made it difficult, if not impossible, for Wobblies to maintain permanent organization among workers whose needs were short run and whose ideological commitment was minimal.

Only an IWW true believer could perceive a victory in Paterson. During the peak of the strike more than ten thousand silk workers had enrolled in the IWW; less than six months later the most optimistic estimate was fifteen hundred members in good standing, and in the following months that fifteen hundred steadily shrank. The NIUTW took sick after Lawrence; after Paterson it died. When the IWW failed to deliver improved working and living conditions to Paterson's immigrants, they, like Lawrence's immigrants, found security in their families, ethnic associations, and religious groups. For them, the IWW was never a home, never a true belief, never the kind of cause that merited absolute sacrifice. For a time the IWW had simply offered Paterson's workers hope for an immediate improvement in their wretched lives.

Paterson was not the sole IWW failure in 1913. Its pattern was repeated elsewhere with similarly dismal results. During the summer of 1912 the IWW had begun to agitate among the unskilled workers in the thriving rubber factories of Akron, Ohio. At first it made little progress in organizing among the industry's twenty thousand workers, many of whom were native-born Americans from the hills of West Virginia, Kentucky, and Tennessee. Early in February 1913, however, just as the Paterson strike was beginning, the IWW announced a meeting for Akron rubber workers interested in more of the good things in life. Shortly after this notice, 300 men walked out of the Firestone plant, demanding higher wages. At that point the IWW could claim no more than 150 members in Akron; indeed, the 300 Firestone strikers knew almost nothing about the IWW as a radical labor organization. In Akron, as in Lawrence and Paterson, the Wobblies quickly promised to provide strikers with leadership and aid. By February 15 the more than 3,500 men and women who had by then walked out of work gladly accepted IWW leadership. As usual, the strikers demanded not revolution but bread, a sentiment that an IWW leaflet turned into the slogan, "Less booze for the bosses! More bread for the workers!" By February 18 IWW agitation had increased the strikers' ranks to fourteen thousand, mass picketing had shut down the city's major rubber plants, and the Wobblies proclaimed complete control of the walkout.

Only a week later, Akron's employers and public authorities responded to the IWW threat with outright repression. Police broke the picket lines and escorted strikebreakers to work. They arrested IWW leaders and clubbed protesting strikers into submission.

After the repression began in earnest, the strikers' ranks began to splinter, and local AFL affiliates joined the crusade against the IWW. Finally, on March

31 the strike committee, making no mention of higher wages, shorter hours, or better conditions, reported that the walkout had been terminated.

At least one IWW organizer learned something from Akron. Writing in *Solidarity*, Frank Donovan commented, "A spontaneous strike is a spontaneous tragedy unless there is a strong local organization on the spot or unless a strong force of outside experienced men are thrown into town immediately."

Yet the lesson did not sink into the IWW's consciousness immediately, for that June Wobblies conducted a poorly coordinated strike of six thousand workers at the Studebaker auto plant in Detroit. Again the IWW simply assumed leadership of a spontaneous rebellion. After framing the usual material demands and advising the strikers regarding tactics, the Wobblies directed a strike as unsuccessful as the others it led in 1913, and even shorter in duration.

Successive defeats at Akron, Detroit, and Paterson made the IWW's future appear so dim that the editor of *Solidarity* suggested that perhaps the organization had better forget about leading large-scale, protracted industrial conflicts. Instead, he recommended the use of short, sharp fights "which require little financial aid . . . as more effective in dealing with the powerful forces of organized capital."

Only one bright spot illuminated an otherwise bleak IWW landscape. In April 1913 the Marine Firemen, Oilers, and Water Tenders' Union, claiming 25,000 members and effective control of ships on the Atlantic and Gulf coasts, voted to affiliate with the IWW. It would remain the one stable and effective IWW organization outside the Western states.

Apart from this, in the summer of 1913 the IWW seemed on the verge of disintegration. That year's membership referendum on the election of national officers and the adoption of constitutional amendments counted only 2,800 votes. Open dissension broke out among Wobblies on the West Coast, where civil war threatened the future of the *Industrial Worker*. Things became so bad that at a July meeting the general executive board, by a unanimous vote, suspended Walker C. Smith as editor of the Pacific Coast paper. Most likely, board members had decided that Smith's editorial series endorsing sabotage and his attacks on the IWW's national administration, combined with his demands for organizational decentralization, injured the IWW's image and its stability. That September the *Industrial Worker* ceased publication, which was not to be resumed until April 1916.

On the eve of the September 1913 national convention, even Ben Williams questioned the IWW's future as a labor organization. "At present we are to the labor movement," wrote Williams, "what the highdiver is to the circus. A sensation, marvelous and ever thrilling. We attract the crowds. We give them thrills, we do hair-raising stunts and send the crowd home to wait impatiently for the next sensationalist to come along. As far as making Industrial Unionism fit the everyday life of the workers we have failed miserably."

The 1913 convention did nothing to quiet Williams's fears. After it was over, he saw an organization rent by conflict between those who advocated industrial organization and competent leadership and those who argued for complete local autonomy (decentralizers) and rank-and-file plebiscite democracy. To the labor economist Robert Hoxie, who also attended the 1913 convention, the sessions revealed the IWW as pathetically weak. After eight years in existence it could not claim more than fourteen thousand members, nor could it pretend to have founded a stable organization in any large industry, he observed. The IWW, Hoxie contended, "instead of being the grim, brooding power which it is pictured in popular imagination, is a body utterly incapable of strong, efficient, united action and the attainment of results of a permanent character; a body capable of local and spasmodic effort only . . . it has no present power . . . of constructive action." As a directly effective social force, Hoxie found the IWW useless.

At the end of 1914 the IWW appeared about to wither on its own radical vine. A frail plant, it had originally taken root and bloomed in the arid soil of the American West. Transplanted to the East, its roots never took firm hold; its blossoms withered in Lawrence and died in Paterson and Akron. After its failure in the industrial East, all that seemed left for the IWW was to return to the Western environment that had spawned it. This is what the Wobblies began to do in 1913 and 1914. Within three years the IWW's radicalism would once again be an effective social force.

# 12

## Back to the West, 1913–16

The years 1913 and 1914 were not good ones for the American worker. Nor were they any better for organized labor, and least of all for the IWW. The legislative reforms of president Woodrow Wilson's New Freedom, which passed Congress in the summer of 1913, coincided with the onset of what had by then become a typical American cyclical depression (as in 1873 and 1893). As business inventories rose, capital investment slackened, and production declined, union membership fell. For the IWW, depression only aggravated the internal disorders wrought by industrial defeats in Paterson and Akron, the collapse of the *Industrial Worker,* and the sectarian schisms always ready to fragment the organization's shaky structure. Not until European war orders reached America late in 1915 would the economic environment improve for business, organized labor, and simultaneously for the IWW.

Even in the bleak years 1913 and 1914, however, the IWW sowed the seeds of discontent that it would harvest in the bumper years to follow. A labor riot in Wheatland, California (1913), a union explosion in Butte (1914), and the execution of an IWW martyr in Salt Lake City (1915) cultivated the soil of the American West for a harvest of hate.

Few workers in America were better adapted to the doctrines and tactics of the IWW than the migrants who followed the harvest on the West Coast, from the fruit and hop fields of Washington and Oregon to the ranches of California's San Joaquin, Central, and Imperial valleys. No workers were more mistreated by their employers, and none so lacked the elementary amenities of a decent life: a home, a family, an adequate diet.

They also displayed all the wretchedness of life within such a culture. To men, women, and children who received little from the society that spawned them, used them, and discarded them, *country, flag,* and *loyalty* were all meaningless terms. Investigating migrants for California, Carleton Parker found them sullenly hostile, and "ever . . . ready to take up political or legal war against the employing class." In short, they were fine recruits for the IWW's total war on capitalism, the American system, and "bushwa" law and morality.

Yet labor organizers, including those from the IWW, found the migrants difficult to organize. Moving from place to place and from job to job, the casuals were hard to contact and harder still to keep in a stable labor organization. Often unemployed and always poorly paid, they could seldom pay dues regularly enough to maintain union membership in good standing. Thus before 1913 all efforts to organize West Coast migrants, whether by the American Federation of Labor (AFL) or the IWW, failed.

Not that the IWW did not seek to recruit the casuals. From headquarters in Spokane, Seattle, Fresno, and other West Coast cities, Wobblies vigorously propagandized among the migrants. Despite the West Coast free-speech fights and incessant propaganda, however, no significant increase in IWW membership among migrants could be discerned before 1913.

But Western Wobblies persisted and eventually found an organizing technique that seemed to work. From such IWW locals as those in Redding, Sacramento, Fresno, Bakersfield, Los Angeles, and San Diego, they sent a continual stream of literature and what came to be known as "camp delegates" into the countryside. The camp delegate took the IWW local directly out onto the job. He would find work among the migrants, talk up the IWW to them, sign up those interested in the organization, and then send the names, initiation fees, and dues to permanent local headquarters in the nearest town. Each of the central, or permanent, California locals dispatched job delegates out into the field, where they continually agitated and organized on the job, carrying IWW dues books and stamps, red cards, songbooks, and leaflets. The camp or job delegates literally carried a union local under their hats. This provided the backdrop for an incident at Wheatland, California, in August 1913 that gave the IWW the publicity it so desperately sought and the increased influence among the migrants it so ardently desired.

The Durst Ranch at Wheatland, described by IWW attorney Austin Lewis as "an open air factory," was in 1913 the largest single employer of agricultural labor in California. In the summer of 1913, as he had done every year just before harvest time, E. C. Durst advertised extensively for hop pickers, promising them ample work and high wages. The workers came: footloose, native-born migrants; immigrant families uprooted from communities in Europe and Asia; and even some middle-class boys and girls out from California's cities for a summer of "fun" and a chance to earn some money in the healthful countryside. By the end of July, some 2,800 men, women, and children had reached Durst's ranch.

What they found was not what Durst had promised. Work was not ample, wages were anything but high. Working and living conditions were even worse. As usual, in order to keep wages down Durst had advertised for more pickers than he needed. Never posting a flat piece rate for picking, he altered it daily. When the pickers were abundant, the rate declined; when they were scarce, it rose. More than two thousand of them camped on a barren hillside—some in tents (which Durst rented at $2.75 per week), some in topless canvas squares, some on straw pallets. Men, women, and children shared eight small, unkempt toilets, which in the course of an average day overflowed with human waste and insects. Filth, germs, and disease abounded. Out in the hop fields, conditions were no better, probably worse. Work began on July 30, and for the next week the temperature hovered near 105 degrees. Drinking wells were a mile from the harvest site, and Durst refused to provide his pickers with water.

Against this background, on Friday, August 1, a handful of pickers began to agitate among the great mass to demand an improvement in working and living conditions. Mostly Wobblies, these agitators found a ready audience for their message, which stressed direct action to redress the pickers' primary grievances. In Richard "Blackie" Ford, a veteran Wobbly, the migrants discovered an able leader. Ford and the other Wobblies persuaded the pickers to agree on a list of demands to be presented to Durst. The migrants called for uniform minimum wages, free water in the fields, and decent camp conditions. Durst chose not to listen to his employees, who, in turn, became more discontented and more militant. Wobblies circulated throughout the camp stirring that discontent, holding irregular small meetings on Saturday, August 2, to demonstrate the migrants' solidarity, and planning to culminate their agitation at a mass meeting scheduled for late Sunday afternoon.

At 5 P.M. Sunday, August 3, as a hot sun beat down on Durst's ranch, the IWW-sponsored mass meeting opened peacefully. Blackie Ford suggested that the pickers consider a general strike, which, granted worker solidarity, would compel Durst to meet the migrants' demands. In the midst of his oration he dashed into the crowd, lifted a sick baby from the arms of its mother, and, holding it before the assembled pickers, cried out, "It's for the life of the kids we're doing this."

While Ford thus dramatized the pickers' plight, Durst panicked. Unsure about what two thousand agitated migrants might do and less sure of what was actually being done at the mass meeting, Durst did precisely what other employers threatened by the IWW had done in the past and would do in the future: He turned to the law, calling in the Yuba County district attorney, the sheriff, his deputies, and a special posse. As the agents of the law sped to the scene of the meeting (some of them traveling in Durst's private car), the migrants were in the middle of a rollicking IWW song, "Mr. Block," written by Wobbly bard Joe Hill. Coming closer to the meeting ground, the authorities could pick up the words of the song, which derided the nonunion worker who accepted the American success myth. "Poor Block," the last verse ran,

> he died one evening, I'm very glad to state:
> He climbed the golden ladder up to the pearly gate.
> He said, "Oh, Mr. Peter, one word I'd like to tell,
> I'd like to meet the Astorbilts and John D. Rockefell."
> Old Pete said, "Is that so?
> You'll meet them down below."

As the law officers arrived at the meeting ground, what followed was perhaps inevitable. Durst expected the outnumbered authorities to disperse the crowd. Carrying out his wishes, a group of deputies approached the speaker's platform to arrest Ford, while another deputy, in an effort to intimidate the crowd, fired his shotgun in the air. The simultaneous attempt to seize Ford and the unwarranted warning shot transformed an orderly audience into an unruly mob. Before the violence subsided four men—District Attorney Manwell, a deputy sheriff, a Puerto Rican worker, and an English boy—lay dead; many more were wounded or beaten.

Although public officials and California's newspapers declared the IWW responsible for the bloodshed at Wheatland, Austin Lewis rightly pointed out that the labor discontent at the Durst Ranch had grown spontaneously. The violence could not be ascribed to the IWW. It was instead, as Lewis claimed, the natural emotional result "of the nervous impact of the exceedingly irritating and intolerable conditions under which those people worked."

Yuba County's public officials and the press nevertheless charged the IWW with responsibility for the bloodshed. As a result, deputies and Burns detectives traveled up and down California with John Doe warrants charging anonymous individuals with assorted crimes, including inciting to riot and first-degree murder. Wherever the deputies or Burns men discovered a suspicious migrant or an IWW suspect, they served process and locked him in jail. In one small town after another migrants were locked up beyond the reach or discovery of defense counsel.

Because someone had to be punished for the August 3 bloodshed at Durst's ranch, and because no official agency would dare reprimand the public officials most responsible, California decided to punish the IWW. Yuba County officials indicted Ford and Herman D. Suhr, a mentally retarded Wobbly also active at Wheatland, for the murder of District Attorney Manwell and the deputy sheriff. Except that Ford and Suhr were physically present at the time and place of the alleged murders, their role did not differ materially from that played by Ettor and Giovannitti in Lawrence a year earlier. Both had consistently advised the hop pickers to refrain from violence, and neither man had been observed by witnesses to have attacked or killed any person. From the day of their arrest until their trial on January 24, 1914, California's newspapers featured stories connecting the IWW with crop destruction, sabotage, violence, and even murder. To be sure, IWW agitators' hyperbolic rhetoric of class warfare did little to counteract the organization's negative public image; indeed, it worsened it. All this made the jury's verdict of guilty as charged in the Ford-Suhr case inevitable. The two Wobblies were sentenced to life imprisonment in Folsom State Penitentiary.

The conviction and imprisonment of Ford and Suhr did not end the tumult caused by the Wheatland incident. The Wobblies promptly organized a movement to secure from governor Hiram Johnson a pardon for the two prisoners. The pardon campaign backfired. Although Johnson agreed that justice had been less than perfect during the trial, he could not readily pardon individuals who belonged to an organization that counseled direct action, encouraged sabotage, and waged unremitting class war.

Johnson and the California Progressives who had placed him in office realized that more than legal repression would be needed to rid their state of the IWW menace. The Progressives sought to restrict IWW influence among migrants by reforming work conditions on California's ranches. Governor Johnson initiated a special investigation of migrant labor conditions by the State Immigration and Housing Commission, which the labor economist Carleton Parker directed and brought to completion in 1914. Parker's investigations at Wheatland and elsewhere in the state led him to sympathize with the plight of the migrants, although he remained hostile to the IWW. The commission thus proposed that the state regulate conditions more effectively, using the power it already had to set sanitary and living standards for California's migrant labor camps. It also suggested that employers could best combat the IWW by improving working conditions, and it warned migrants that strikes, sabotage, and violent demonstrations would bring no improvement to their lives.

But commission-instigated reforms and suggestions did not liberate California from the IWW. Migrants drew their own lessons from Wheatland. When they had been peaceful and tolerated exploitation, the state and its Progressives had neglected them. When they turned to the IWW and confronted employers as an organized force, public neglect changed to public concern.

If anything, Wheatland increased the IWW's attraction to California's migrants. When Paul Brissenden investigated California labor conditions for the Commission on Industrial Relations in August 1914, he discovered forty IWW locals and a total membership of about five thousand, of whom half were "missionary revolutionists" who passed the message on and organized on the job. One California Wobbly proudly informed Brissenden, "Three or four years ago I had a hard time to get those scissorsbills working stiffs to even listen to the I.W.W. dope. Now it's easy. They come around and ask for it."

That was precisely what California's public officials and private employers feared. The Commission on Immigration and Housing, led in 1914–15 by the Progressive reformer Simon Lubin, sought by further improving conditions in California's "factories in the fields" to limit the IWW's influence among migrants. Failing in that, the commission thought in terms of using federal penal power to suppress the IWW. By the summer of 1915 California officials had already succeeded, in cooperation with officials of the states of Washington, Oregon, and Utah, in obtaining a special agent from the Department of Justice to assist them in an investigation of the IWW's activities in the West. Lubin later reported to United States attorney general Thomas Gregory that the West Coast investigation had established, among other findings, that the Wobblies preached and practiced sabotage, property destruction, arson, and violation of federal laws, and even threatened public officials with assassination.

But Gregory and the Justice Department read Lubin's 1915 report skeptically, taking it as simply another neurotic local reaction to a limited radical threat. Only two years later, however, with the United States involved in a bloody war, the Justice Department would treat Western accounts of an IWW-posed threat to national security more seriously. In 1917, Westerners like Lubin would obtain the federal suppression of the Wobblies that they had unsuccessfully demanded in 1915.

\* \* \*

Only a year after the Wheatland incident the IWW returned to Butte, Montana. In 1914 Butte was one of the most solid labor union cities in America. The unionism that dominated there bore slight resemblance to the radical miners' unionism of the late nineteenth century or to the IWW's original impact on the city's labor movement from 1905 to 1907. By 1914 the more moderate form of trade unionism associated with AFL affiliates had come to prevail among Butte's workers, the miners included. This would make the IWW's return to the city more surprising—and also more disruptive.

Local 1 of the Western Federation of Miners (WFM) had long controlled Butte's labor world. With eight thousand members it was the largest local in the WFM as well as in the city. Impressive in its economic power before 1905, it had begun to atrophy afterward as the Anaconda Copper Company established its own economic hegemony. Once Anaconda emerged triumphant over its business rivals, the union's ability to influence working conditions diminished. Wages stabilized, hours of work grew longer—in some cases the seven-day week prevailed in the mines and smelters—and safety conditions deteriorated.

Conservative though the unions and their members seemed in 1914, Butte nevertheless had a long and deep radical tradition. The city's voters, in fact, had elected a Socialist administration in 1913, and the Socialists controlled the strongest party organization in Butte. Although the WFM's secession from the IWW in 1907 had undermined the Wobblies' influence in Butte, the miners retained an abiding faith in the principle of industrial unionism, which gave the IWW a prestige it lacked in some other industrial communities. It was only a matter of time before Butte's radical past would reassert itself.

The radicals had not vanished. One of them, Thomas Campbell, who would play a key role in Butte's tangled labor history from 1914 to 1920, attended the 1911 WFM convention as a delegate from Butte Local 1. He departed from the convention convinced that the AFL and the incumbent WFM administration were treacherous, and he hoped that Butte's miners would soon find "that the organization known as the IWW have got the key to the situation . . . in spite of the treachery and trickery of the labor fakers of today." The "treachery and trickery" to which Campbell alluded made him and his fellow radicals cautious. This became especially apparent after 1912 when company-influenced (if not dominated) conservatives seized effective control of Local 1, which was by then completely permeated with agents working for Anaconda and Con F. Kelley, manager of Anaconda's Butte mines. Even those who were not actually labor spies received special benefits from the company if they voted and behaved properly. As "company" men they received special leasing arrangements and better working areas in the mines.

With conservatives in the union saddle, the mine operators rode roughshod over their more militant employees. Local 1, for example, failed to protest the company's discharge of two hundred to three hundred Socialist Finnish miners. Any miner or union member who complained about company influence was apt to be labeled a Socialist, Wobbly, or anarchist and thrown out the window of the union's hall.

Company domination of Local 1, however, caused increasing numbers of union members to become dissatisfied with the lack of union democracy and with the heavy assessments placed on Butte's miners to support strikers elsewhere. Most important, the miners grew disenchanted with their organization's inability to improve working conditions in Butte.

How the mass of miners felt about these developments became apparent on June 13, 1914, which was Miners' Union Day and a legal holiday in Butte. Traditionally, *all* the city's miners paraded through the downtown area, after which they celebrated with an orgy of oratory, machine-drilling contests, boxing exhibitions, and drinking bouts. But on June 13, 1914, only four hundred of the eight thousand local miners came to the parade; even the police, who usually accompanied the paraders, refused to march. The nonparticipating miners lined the streets along the parade route prepared to attack the company men who controlled Local 1. Before the paraders could proceed very far, a mob of angry onlookers surged in upon them and forced the marchers to flee for shelter. Suddenly, a member of the mob yelled, "Let's destroy the Hall!" (Local 1's headquarters). Storming the building, the enraged miners destroyed everything in sight, throwing a piano out the window, followed by books, furniture, and two safes.

The destruction accomplished, the rebellious miners turned to the task of construction. Insurgent leaders decided to establish a new union entirely independent of Local 1, and they planned an early referendum on the question open to all miners. The referendum went off peacefully as scheduled, with 6,348 miners declaring against the old union and only 243 voting in favor of it. The new organization, called the Butte Mine Workers' Union, was unaffiliated with the WFM, AFL, or IWW.

The creation of the independent union only worsened Butte's labor turmoil. Anaconda officials and the officers of Local 1 were naturally displeased. So, too, were Charles Moyer, president of the WFM, and Samuel Gompers. Company officials, Local 1's leaders, Moyer, and Gompers all blamed the IWW for Butte's labor problems. Instead of seeking to appease the miners in the new union or trying to reform and rebuild Local 1, Moyer joined the discredited local union officials in combating the insurgents.

Apparently unaware of the depth of local hostility to himself and to his organization, Moyer arrived in Butte on June 23 hopeful of converting the miners to his view and regaining their loyalty to Local 1. Instead, he met hate—deep, unreasoning, and violent. Few miners showed up for his talk that evening at the old union hall. Most miners instead gathered on the sidewalk outside to shout imprecations and threats at the WFM president. Nevertheless, Moyer tried to speak—that is, until a shot rang out somewhere in the hall. Shooting suddenly erupted on all sides; as one man fell dead outside on the street, the anti-Moyer mob grew infuriated and attacked the union hall, placing it under total siege. Moyer and his supporters fled for their lives out a back exit, while an armed crowd, estimated at 150, blazed away at the hall from the front sidewalk. After Moyer and his group completed their escape via the rear fire escape, the mob entered the hall, placed dynamite charges in it, and blew it sky-high.

Again, no local officials opposed the miners' destructive wrath. That whole evening the anti-Moyer miners had Butte to themselves, while non-working-class residents, expecting the worst, barricaded themselves at home. Throughout that explosive day and evening Butte's socialist mayor, Lewis J. Duncan, advised Montana's governor that all would be well if only the authorities left the miners alone.

Once again, Moyer, Gompers, and Anaconda officials blamed the IWW for Butte's troubles. It was true, particularly after the June 23 dynamiting of the union hall, that IWW agitators had taken to the streets with increased vigor. It was also true that several of the local insurgent leaders, notably Tom Campbell and Joe Shannon, were by then probably IWW members, and militant ones at that. But to contend that two hundred Wobblies in a propaganda league, the only official organization maintained by the IWW in Butte in 1914, were responsible for all the city's turmoil and tension is to stretch a point. After all, the new independent miners' union claimed 5,400 members, and even IWW sympathizers agreed that no more than a hundred of these were Wobblies. In fact, some of the demonstrators Moyer took for Wobblies were probably private detectives who had infiltrated either Local 1, the independent Mine Workers' Union, or the IWW propaganda league.

After the violence of June subsided, the Butte Mine Workers' Union exercised firm control over mine labor. It denied work to nonmembers, it summarily deported or tried its opponents, and it applied for and won membership in Silver Bow County's central labor organization.

Neither Moyer, Gompers, nor Anaconda officials enjoyed these new developments. Gompers considered labor conditions in Butte deplorable, and on August 30 he suggested to Moyer that Montana's governor might well exercise his power to repress the insurgent miners. The AFL president attacked Butte's insurgents simultaneously on several fronts. He ordered Butte's central labor organization to deny the rebels a seat, he advised various international union presidents to weed troublemakers out of their locals in Butte, and he even agreed to sanction the governor's use of military police power. Not

until the morning of August 31, however, when insurgent unionists dynamit-
ed the "rustling" shack at a local mine, did the rebels' opponents have an opportunity to retaliate. Even before the smoke cleared from the area of the shack,
the county sheriff had issued warrants for the arrest of miners' union officials,
and he had also wired the governor requesting troops. The next day, September 1, militia arrived in Butte to place the city and the county under martial
law as directed by the governor.

Before a state supreme court decision finally lifted martial law several months
later, the troops had crushed the Mine Workers' Union as an effective labor
organization. No sooner had they arrived in Butte than their commander prohibited all street meetings (except those of the Salvation Army), censored local papers, closed the Socialist press, and arrested insurgent union leaders. The
arrested men were held incommunicado, without bail, and were tried by military courts without a hint of due process. When the militia finally withdrew
from Butte at the end of 1914, what had once been the strongest miners' union
in the West was no more.

Moyer and Gompers proved to be their own worst enemies and the IWW's
best allies. Not only had they failed to end the IWW's influence in Butte, but
they inadvertently destroyed the remainder of Local 1's strength and undermined the power of other local AFL affiliates. Their hysterical charges of IWW
influence and conspiracy presented Kelley and the governor with a firm foundation on which to erect their repressive anti-union policies. Moreover, Moyer's and Gompers's endorsement of corrupt local union officials and even
military repression turned Butte's miners completely away from the WFM and
the AFL. When unionism returned to Butte full strength during World War I,
it would come in the form of a large independent miners' union and a smaller IWW local, which, because of their antagonism toward the WFM and AFL,
cooperated closely. After 1914 the outstanding miners' union leaders in Butte
would be either IWW members or fellow travelers. The developments in Butte
would leave even larger implications for the IWW's future among Western
miners. Moyer's mistakes there, soon compounded elsewhere, opened the
entire Western nonferrous mining industry to IWW influence and penetration, which would reach its peak in the war years.

✳ ✳ ✳

On Saturday evening, January 10, 1914, two armed, masked men entered the
small Salt Lake City grocery of John G. Morrison. Morrison was alone in the
store with his two teenage sons, Arling and Merlin, who were helping their father close shop for the evening. One of the masked men shouted at the eldest

Morrison, "We've got you now," and then one of them shot directly at the grocer. A frightened Merlin rushed into hiding as his father fell, and his older brother Arling seized a gun and returned the fire. At this point, the two gunmen turned their revolvers on Arling and pumped three bullets into his body, killing him almost instantly. Leaving one dead youth, one dying man, and one terrified boy, the assailants fled from the grocery without taking money or merchandise. Later that same evening, John Morrison died, leaving behind no clue to his murderers.

Three days later, on January 13, Salt Lake police claimed to have a prime suspect in custody. The same night that the two Morrisons had been killed an itinerant worker had appeared in a local doctor's office, asking to be treated for a gunshot wound in the chest, which he claimed to have received in a quarrel over a woman. Just three days later, the doctor, named McHugh, reported this case to the police, who, with the doctor's cooperation, seized the suspect at his boarding house, where he was still in bed recovering from the January 10 gunshot wound. (During the arrest the police shot the wounded man in the hand.) On January 22 the suspect, now identified as Joseph Hillstrom, alias Joe Hill, pleaded "not guilty" to murder charges. Six days later, at a preliminary court hearing, witnesses in the neighborhood of the murder identified Hill as one of the masked murderers whom they had seen flee from the grocery. The court bound him over for trial on June 10.

Up to that point, there was nothing unusual about the case. A brutal pair of murders had occurred and the police were naturally eager to locate a suspect in order to satisfy the public's clamor for vengeance. Just such a prime suspect had appeared in the person of Joe Hill, an unemployed itinerant worker, who had also been shot the evening of January 10 (as had one of the murderers) and who refused to provide himself with an alibi, insisting that he could not do so when a woman's honor was at stake. Ordinarily, an unimportant man like Hill might have been promptly tried, convicted, and executed without a whisper of protest. After all, who was Joe Hill?

In January 1914 few Salt Lake residents could have answered that question. At first, even Salt Lake's police had little information about their suspect. Perhaps a few Wobblies knew something about Hill, but even in their case knowledge about him was limited. Many Wobblies claimed to know Hill but, as a matter of fact, they knew his songs, not the man. As the first IWW account of Hill's arrest commented, "Wherever rebels meet, the name of Fellow Worker Joe Hill is known. Though we may not know him personally, who among us can say he is not on speaking terms with 'Scissor Bill,' 'Mr. Block' the famous 'Casey Jones' and many others in the little red song book?"

Answers to that question were soon forthcoming. Born in Sweden, October 7, 1879, Joel Hägglund, the man who became famous as Joe Hill, emigrated to the United States in 1902. For ten years he worked itinerantly, stacking wheat, laying pipe, digging copper, and working at sea. As he worked and traveled across the United States, he composed songs, poems, and idle verse. His name was changed to Joseph Hillstrom, and then to plain Joe Hill. These name changes reflected his changing interests. Sometime in 1910 Hill became interested in labor affairs and radicalism, taking out a membership card in the San Pedro local of the IWW and becoming, later that year, an active agitator in the Portland area. In 1912 he participated in the San Diego free-speech fight. His wandering eventually took him to Utah, where, at some time in 1913, he labored in the Bingham Canyon copper mines and also for a local construction company. Joe Hill agitated and organized, possibly participating in two IWW-linked strikes that occurred in the Salt Lake City vicinity. At the time of his arrest and indictment he was unemployed and not representing the IWW in any capacity.

Whatever they may have been, the exact circumstances that brought Joe Hill to Utah and kept him there transformed him from an obscure Wobbly bard into a legendary martyr. In April 1914, more than three months after Hill's arrest, the IWW first became interested in his case, forming defense committees, soliciting funds, and all the while asserting that Hill was being prosecuted not for having murdered the Morrisons but simply because he was a Wobbly.

Even before his case came to trial, Joe Hill had been convicted in the court of public hysteria. The pretrial proceedings and the ensuing trial violated many of the basic principles of due process. From the time of his arrest until the trial began, Hill lacked legal assistance. Police and press created a hostile environment that reduced the already minimal prospects for a fair trial. Later the trial judge repeatedly favored the prosecution and hampered the defense. No witness ever absolutely identified Hill as the murderer, no motive was ever introduced to account for the crime, no bullet could be found to link Hill to the killer allegedly wounded in the grocery, and no gun could be located to connect Hill with the murder of either the grocer or his son. Yet on June 26, 1914, a jury found Joe Hill guilty, and on July 8 a judge sentenced him to death.

Verdict and sentence merely served as an introduction to the Joe Hill case. For the next year and a half a defense campaign of international proportions rallied support for Hill. From Salt Lake City to San Francisco, from New York to Washington, D.C., from Stockholm to Berlin, his sympathizers protested the verdict and demanded a pardon. Thousands of letters and telegrams of protest reached Utah governor William Spry. Although the defense campaign finally failed to save Hill's life, it did produce a myth and a martyr. Stories spread concerning Hill's incredibly exemplary character.

Hill himself added to the martyr myth by writing a series of letters while in prison awaiting his execution. They reveal a man and a mind warmly human and willing to face death with wry humor and pathos. They also reveal the mind of a man who knew how to play the role of martyr. To Elizabeth Gurley Flynn, he emphasized his own insignificance: "We cannot afford to drain the resources of the whole organization and weaken its fighting strength just on account of one individual—common sense will tell you that. . . . There will be plenty of new rebels come to 'fill the gaps,' as the war news puts it, and one more or less does not count any more than it does in the European War." Hill played his role to the very end. On November 18, the eve of his execution, he wired Haywood, "Good-bye, Bill. I will die like a true blue rebel. Don't waste any time in mourning. *Organize.*" Then he wrote his last will:

My will is easy to decide,
For there is nothing to divide.
My kin don't need to fuss and moan—
"Moss does not cling to a rolling stone."
My body? Ah, if I could choose,
I would to ashes it reduce,
And let the merry breezes blow
My dust to where some flowers grow.
Perhaps some fading flower then
Would come to life and bloom again.
This is my last and final will,
Good luck to all of you.

On November 19, 1915, a Utah firing squad executed Joe Hill. Hill received a martyr's funeral. Taken to Chicago, his body was buried at Waldheim Cemetery alongside the graves of the Haymarket anarchists. Haywood, an American labor radical, and Big Jim Larkin, an Irish labor radical, spoke the last words over his grave. Larkin declaimed, "Let his blood cement the many divided sections of our movement, and our slogan for the future be: Joe Hill's body lies mouldering in the grave, but the cause goes marching on."

Joe Hill arrived in Utah an insignificant migrant worker; when his corpse departed the state two years later, he was internationally proclaimed as a martyr to labor's cause. He was, according to the later song of Alfred Hayes and Earl Robinson, the Joe Hill "who had never died." For the next fifty years Wobblies, novelists, playwrights, and poets kept the memory of the rebel Swedish immigrant alive. In that period many Wobblies tried to emulate Hill's appeal for self-sacrifice, and several met comparable fates.

We shall probably never have definitive proof as to whether Hill was guilty or innocent of the crime for which he was executed. Suffice it to say that his guilt cannot be proved beyond a reasonable doubt, nor can his innocence be positively established. What he had once done or believed in became unimportant after his arrest, trial, and execution. What became important was how Wobblies, radicals, and others felt about him; for all Wobblies, most radicals, and many other Americans, Hill became symbolic of the individual sacrifice that made a revolutionary new society possible. In death, Joe Hill became a symbol, and, as a symbol, he assumed more importance than he had ever had as a living man.

✳   ✳   ✳

Much more important to the future of the IWW than the exciting and explosive incidents in Wheatland, Butte, and Salt Lake City was the tedious agitating and organizing the Wobblies had begun among the migratory harvesters in the plains states. Every summer thousands of men and boys fanned out from Chicago, Kansas City, Sioux City, and the twin cities of Minneapolis and St. Paul to follow the wheat harvest from Texas north across the plains to southern Canada. Like migratory farm workers everywhere, they worked long hours for minimal pay and execrable room and board.

Like the migratories of the West Coast, those of the plains states lacked wives, families, homes, roots; nothing tied them to society; their alienation, if frequently unconscious, was nevertheless complete. They seemed perfect recruits for the IWW's gospel, as one Wobbly, who saw in them the last, best chance for establishing the One Big Union, asserted: "Nowhere else can a section of the working class be found so admirably fitted to serve as scouts and advance guards of the labor army. Rather, they may become the guerrillas of the revolution—the *franc tireurs* of the class struggle."

Yet the migratories of the plains were as hard to organize on a stable basis as their counterparts on the West Coast, and for the same reasons. After experimenting with new methods of recruitment during the 1914 summer harvest, Wobblies planned to make this issue the major order of business at their approaching national convention. At a convention otherwise marked by pessimism and failure, IWW delegates adopted a motion presented by Frank Little to call a conference early in 1915 bringing together members from different locals bordering the harvest district in order to determine ways and means to combine the organization's previously spasmodic efforts to organize the harvesters. The IWW press continued the discussion, as numerous Midwestern Wobblies offered suggestions on how best to organize the harvest hands. All the pleas and advice stressed job organization. Revolutionary pronouncements, one editorial concluded, were useless without organization at the point of production. "Around the 'job,' distasteful, monotonous, and gruesome as it actually is in many instances, center all our revolutionary aspirations," the editorial went on. Haywood, elected general secretary at the 1914 convention upon St. John's retirement from office, made organization of the migratories his first order of business. He announced the formation of a Bureau of Migratory Workers to assist the harvesters in improving their working conditions, and he scheduled two organizational meetings for IWW leaders and migratories to be held in Kansas City in April and May 1915.

On April 15, 1915, harvest workers and Wobblies from points as far apart as Des Moines, Fresno, San Francisco, Portland (Oregon), Salt Lake City, and Minneapolis descended on Kansas City to found an IWW harvest workers' organization. These delegates promptly created the Agricultural Workers' Organization (AWO Local 400), composed of all local unions whose members worked in the agricultural districts of the United States and Canada. That done, the delegates provided for a general secretary-treasurer as the AWO's presiding official, and for field delegates, counterparts to the West Coast's job delegates. Significantly, the Kansas City meeting resolved to ban street speaking and soapboxing as methods of organization; delegates seemed more interested in members and dues than in propaganda and revolutionary rhetoric. Before adjourning the delegates chose Walter T. Nef as general secretary-treasurer and elected a five-man executive board to assist him. Haywood promised Nef, his executive advisers, and the delegates adequate financial support to launch their venture, and they left Kansas City with high hopes.

Those hopes were soon to be justified, for the destiny of the AWO lay in able hands. Nef was an experienced, dedicated, no-nonsense Wobbly. He had already organized on both coasts, as well as in the wheat belt. He had worked in construction, lumber, longshoring, and mining, as well as in agriculture. He was a builder, not a booster; an organizer, not a propagandist. He promptly established a $2 initiation fee, high by IWW standards but necessary to the creation of a stable organization. If the union was sufficiently important, Nef argued, the worker would pay to belong to it and to make it function effectively.

Nef's immediate objectives were limited. The AWO entered the harvest fields to demand a better deal today, not revolution tomorrow. A ten-hour day, a minimum wage, premium pay for overtime, good board, and clean beds with ample bedding—this is what the AWO sought in the summer of 1915. By August, during the Kansas harvest, the AWO had achieved many of its demands, and with some optimism it began to draw up stronger demands for the approaching Northern harvest. Rising membership rosters and increasing revenue made it possible for Nef to announce on August 7 the opening of a permanent AWO central office in Minneapolis. From that office Nef sent one hundred job delegates out into the field, who brought in at least one hundred new members a week. By September the AWO counted fifteen hundred members in North Dakota alone and another three hundred to five hundred in South Dakota. As the harvest season moved toward its close, the AWO reported weekly membership increases. At the end of the harvest, when it held a second convention in Minneapolis (November 15–16), the AWO claimed a minimum of three thousand members.

Optimism spread from the AWO to the remainder of the IWW. Ben Williams later recalled 1915 as the first time in his ten years with the organization that the IWW had ample funds: sufficient money to rent a large general office on Madison Street in Chicago, where it also established a printing plant and editorial offices for foreign-language sheets while planning future consolidations of IWW operations within the expanded and suddenly affluent general headquarters.

Nef and the AWO meanwhile proposed grander projects for the immediate future, suggesting, among other things, the establishment of permanent AWO branch headquarters in Omaha, Sioux City, and Kansas City, from which job delegates could more efficiently organize the 1916 harvest. Nef now planned to organize corn harvesters and loggers as well. On December 12–13, 1915, fifty-five IWW delegates, meeting in Sacramento, founded a California branch of the AWO, patterned exactly after its Minneapolis parent. Before long, Minnesota lumberjacks as well as the entire Spokane lumber workers' local had taken out membership in Nef's organization. With an adequate surplus in its treasury and with more than two thousand paid-up members, the AWO's future looked bright.

Nef's lieutenants moved into the wheat fields in 1916 with the same tactics they had taken in 1915: organization on the job and immediate improvements in working conditions. Business was never better for them. In July the AWO took in four thousand new members, with the expectation of another six thousand in August. By late August it claimed over twelve thousand members and job control over many harvesting machines and farm districts, where wages and hours met AWO standards. As the money and the members rolled in, IWW general headquarters grew ecstatic over its harvest campaign. On September

30, 1916, *Solidarity* devoted an entire issue to the activities of the harvest hands. The AWO closed the 1916 harvest season twenty thousand strong, apparently having proven that with the proper tactics and the necessary leadership, migratory workers could be organized.

Nef and Haywood dreamed of using the AWO's successes as a basis from which to penetrate other industries, although they disagreed sharply about what should be the AWO's precise role. His differences of opinion with Haywood led Nef to resign as AWO general secretary-treasurer in November 1916 and to move to Philadelphia, where he established an IWW office patterned after the AWO. Nef proposed to recruit Philadelphia workers regardless of their particular industry for his organization, until the IWW had established stable industrial unions in all areas. He did not choose Philadelphia by accident. In April 1916 the IWW had over three thousand members in good standing in a local branch of the Marine Transport Workers' Union, which had full job control on the city's waterfront—the kind of closed shop and wage agreements the AFL unions prided themselves on achieving.

Everywhere a Wobbly looked in 1916 he saw revived organizational life—in the wheat fields of the Midwest, the orange groves of southern California, the Douglas fir forests of the Pacific Northwest, the north woods of Minnesota, Philadelphia's waterfront, Chicago general headquarters, and most spectacularly of all in the vast Mesabi Iron Range of northern Minnesota, where, in the summer of 1916, the IWW waged its most spectacular strike since Lawrence and Paterson.

# 13

## Miners, Lumberjacks, and a Reorganized IWW, 1916

The year 1916 found the IWW's fortunes at floodtide. Fresh from their triumphs in the wheat fields and with funds to support their activities, Wobbly organizers inundated the mining and lumber regions of northern Minnesota, the forests of the Inland Empire and the Cascades, and the wheat, fruit, and hop fields of Washington and Oregon.

Some 75 miles north of Duluth, Minnesota, in one of that state's most isolated regions, lies a group of low hills, surrounded by great wastes of land, covered only with the charred, blackened stumps of a once magnificent pine forest. The hills extend for 50 miles, east and west, hiding an immense mineral treasure beneath their blackened bosoms. From steep shafts driven a thousand feet below the earth's surface, miners with dynamite, drill, pick, and shovel labored to bring forth 2 million tons of hard iron ores annually; above ground, giant steam shovels tore at the earth's crust, stripping away over 20 million tons of soft iron ore each year. These underground and open-pit mines of Minnesota's Mesabi Range fed the insatiable steel mills in Gary, Youngstown, and Pittsburgh.

As mineral wealth poured out of the Mesabi Range, large corporations entered. The nation's leading steel companies took possession of the range's primary ore bodies; by 1902 the Oliver Mining Company, a subsidiary of United States Steel, was the largest single operator on the range.

Unlike other isolated mining districts, the range was never blighted by company towns. Instead, small independent frontier communities grew and flourished, keeping pace with the mining industry's own expansion. By 1916 over sixty thousand people lived in the five range towns, which together formed an integrated community. (Virginia and Hibbing, the two largest towns, claimed populations of fifteen thousand each.) Although not controlled by the mining corporations, the cities depended heavily on company prosperity. Local merchants and professionals catered to working-class families; municipal governments, using taxes wrested from protesting mining companies, provided their residents with paved, brightly lit streets, gracious public buildings, and fine schools.

Behind the carefully constructed façade of white ways and public edifices, however, the commonplace sores of life in urban America festered. Although local wages and earnings appeared high, the cost of living in these isolated mining communities was equally high.

Ethnic divisions added to the miners' problems. Always short of labor, employers had introduced successive immigrant groups into the range's labor force. First came the Irish, Cornish, and Scandinavians, many of whom brought previous mining experience to their work in the deep shafts. After 1905, as open-pit mining expanded and the demand for unskilled labor increased, Finns, followed by eastern and southern European immigrants, entered the labor force. By 1912 over thirty different tongues could be heard in the range's cities, and the diverse ethnic groups had fallen into distinct camps. The earliest arrivals had become mine captains, shift bosses, skilled, highly paid workers, and, on occasion, successful local businessmen. The latecomers did the dirty work and were exploited by those who had preceded them to the range.

The IWW had sporadically sought to organize the Mesabi Range's immigrant miners. In 1913, for example, Frank Little, James Cannon, and E. F. Doree carried the Wobbly gospel north. Starting in Duluth among dock wallopers and ore handlers, they planned to move north and west to the range communities. But in August local Duluth businessmen kidnaped Little, and although other Wobblies later rescued him, such repressive tactics kept the IWW from gaining recruits in the district.

During the next three years, as Agricultural Workers' Organization (AWO) triumphs pumped new life and fresh money into the IWW, Wobblies carefully watched labor developments on the range. On February 7, 1916, an AWO report concluded, "The Finnish organizer is up on the Range, and expects good results as soon as the weather gets a little better." Several days later, Walter Nef noted that the Metal Mine Workers' Industrial Union of the IWW had just been established as Local 490 and that it included within its jurisdiction the iron miners of northern Minnesota. At about the same time, radical Finns contacted Nef to request south Slav and Italian organizers. Unless Italian and Slav organizers came, they warned, self-defeating, spontaneous strikes would erupt. Almost one month later to the day, a spontaneous miners' revolt erupted.

Throughout May, as underground miners watched production rise and the cost of living soar, they expected a wage increase. But on June 2 the workers at the St. James, an underground mine near Aurora, were sorely disappointed as their monthly paychecks showed no increase. The next morning, as these miners congregated in the dry room to change into working clothes, they discussed their low wages. Led by Joe Greeni, an Italian miner, the others agreed not to work until the contract system* was abolished and they received a $3 daily minimum. That evening the members of the day shift returned to the mine shaft and brought the night shift miners out with them, closing the St. James tight. Both shifts, some eighty men, then paraded toward a meeting hall in Aurora. On their way, more and more miners joined the parade, until four hundred men in all entered the hall. A spirit of solidarity surged through the miners, who, without any labor organization or outside leadership, voted to strike. The initial walkout spread rapidly. By the end of June, two-thirds of the range's working force, or ten thousand out of fifteen thousand miners, had walked out, including 85 percent of the underground workers. The conflict indirectly affected another fifteen thousand district workers as it spread to the adjacent and subsidiary Vermillion Range.

Underground miners had walked out first because their grievances were deeply felt and because they outnumbered the surface workers. Complaining that the contract system of wage payments exploited them, the miners accused the mine captains of giving the most productive locations to workers who paid them off in money, cigars, and women. Some miners even asserted that in return for good working positions in the mines, the captains had demanded sexual liberties from the workers' wives and daughters.

Exploitation under the contract system wore many faces. Workers never knew how much they had earned until they received their monthly paychecks. Piece rates fluctuated constantly, while the charges levied on the miners for supplies rose regularly. A worker expecting to average $3 or $4 a day might end the month with as little as $1.60. Two Department of Labor mediators who investigated the conflict were appalled by the absence of uniform wage rates, especially among the employees of the Oliver Mining Company. The mediators also noted that, although mining companies had advanced wages before the 1916 strike, the cost of living had risen twice as rapidly as wage rates, which led an immigrant miner with a wife and seven children to complain, "Children go to church and priest like to see wife dressed nice like American ladies, and children like American children. I like too but can't. . . . The mining captains give all the good places to single men who can go to the saloon with them and buy cigars . . . but we married men can't do that and so we don't get $4 places."

To abolish the contract system, to secure a minimum wage, and to liberate themselves from company exploitation, the miners struck. Aware that they

---

* Foremen acted as hiring agents and set the wages based on the quantity of ore dug, not the number of hours worked. Desirable mining locations were thus placed at a premium.

lacked organization and leadership, the strikers turned first to the American Federation of Labor (AFL) and the Western Federation of Miners (WFM), but both failed to respond to the miners' overtures. Only at this point did the strikers request assistance from AWO headquarters in Minneapolis. Now Walter Nef officially placed the IWW in the dispute by dispatching organizers to the range.

What was the actual role of the IWW? On one point the evidence is incontrovertible: The original walkout at the St. James mine occurred without IWW intervention. But from that point on the IWW kept the strike going, and indeed helped it spread. The IWW achieved its aims not by coercion but by giving the striking miners leadership, funds, and publicity. As had already been the case in Lawrence and in Paterson, Wobblies transformed a spontaneous revolt into a full-scale industrial conflict. In all three instances, IWW headquarters had been advised of employee discontent on the eve of the strikes, and in all three instances the IWW instantly had organizers on the spot. The IWW had six to eight organizers on the Mesabi Range by June 6, and thereafter Nef and Haywood recruited further assistance for the strikers, especially among Wobblies who could speak Italian, Polish, and other eastern European languages.

Few as the IWW harvesters may have been, they nevertheless reaped a bumper crop of union members. Before the strike was a week old, the miners had established the first range local of Metal Mine Workers' Union No. 490; by July 1, Nef counted four thousand IWW members on the range. As IWW prospects brightened, Haywood and Nef pleaded for more organizers to work the Mesabi Range. By mid-July the IWW had sent thirty-four organizers, the most it had ever employed in any single conflict. By then the IWW had also helped the local miners to print a *Strike Bulletin* to present their viewpoint, which never appeared in the region's newspapers, and also to establish a central strike committee composed entirely of local miners, which had ultimate responsibility for all negotiations with employers.

The IWW's role in the Mesabi Range strike was not the only similarity with the conflicts at Lawrence and Paterson. Minnesota employers used familiar tactics to break the strike. The mining companies controlled the local sheriff's office, the range police chiefs, and the St. Louis County authorities (situated in Duluth), and they maintained significant influence with governor J. A. Burnquist. Not satisfied with the ability of public authorities to control the strikers, the companies also hired more than 550 private armed police of their own, whom Sheriff Meining appointed as deputies, thus investing private gunmen with public authority.

The mining companies and their local supporters regularly accused the miners of plotting property destruction, the subversion of middle-class morality, and violent political revolution. To prevent this alleged insurrection, local police practiced savage repression. When strikers marched on a public highway accompanied by a band, Sheriff Meining dispersed them for disturbing the peace and jailed six IWW organizers on unspecified charges. The sheriff, so disturbed by parade noises, showed no such concern when company gunmen disrupted peaceful union meetings and placid picketers. From the isolated range down into Duluth, officials denied the strikers access to any public communication, while the private company guards established a veritable reign of terror.

Repression reached its climax on July 3 when a posse, consisting largely of company guards deputized by Sheriff Meining, forcibly entered the Biwabik home of striker Philip Masanovitch to search for an illegal still. The "deputies" treated their suspects, including Masanovitch's wife, roughly. An altercation ensued during which two men, one of whom was a deputy, were killed. Easily subduing their enraged antagonists, the armed guards immediately arrested five occupants of Masanovitch's home on first-degree murder charges. Later that same day seven IWW organizers, including James Gilday, Joseph Schmidt, Carlo Tresca, and Sam Scarlett, charged with being accessories to the murder, were arrested in the town of Virginia, miles from the scene of the incident. It was the Ettor-Giovannitti affair all over again.

In Minnesota, as in Massachusetts and New Jersey, repression, murder indictments, and arrests failed to disrupt the strike. The IWW sent new organizers to replace those in prison, taught local miners to manage their own union and their strike committees, and used the repressive incidents to win publicity, sympathy, and funds for the strikers' cause. The strikers, though opposed by the companies, the county authorities, the Duluth press, and even the governor, now found they had important allies of their own.

The most important of the strikers' allies were the mayors and businessmen of the range communities. As the conflict dragged on and the violence increased, elected town officials decided to intercede. On July 7 they called a public meeting at Virginia to discuss the tense local situation. At the meeting, which was attended by the strikers' committees, local officials, and range businessmen, one miner after another testified about his exploitation by mine captains and about the low wages that made a decent life impossible for most immigrant families. Every request the strikers placed before the meeting sought to redress a specific grievance: an eight-hour day (portal to portal), abolition of the contract system, a $3 minimum for underground work and $2.75 for surface labor, and so on.

Aware of the moderate nature of the strikers' demands, local businessmen and public officials sympathized with the miners' cause. One Hibbing businessman, himself a former immigrant workingman who had made good, told the miners that every man at the Virginia meeting supported them. Every laborer, this man proclaimed, "should have sufficient money to clothe his family well, so he can feed them, so he can educate the children, and so he can have a comfortable home, and sufficient to save for his old age."

The range mayors tried to negotiate with the companies on behalf of the strikers to obtain a decent living for every local miner. The companies, however, rejected all peace overtures. They preferred victory to negotiation. Thus, employers refused to meet municipal officials, and, in order to justify their own repressive tactics, they continued to accuse the strikers of being IWW anarchists and dangerous revolutionaries. But company intransigence only gained the strikers additional support. The Minnesota State Federation of Labor, though hostile to the IWW, now endorsed the strike. Frank P. Walsh, former chairman of the Commission on Industrial Relations, and his close friends George West and Dante Barton, used their special creation, the Committee on Industrial Relations, to flood the metropolitan press and middlebrow journals with prostrike literature. The IWW, of course, continued to send funds and organizers.

Unable to bring employers to the bargaining table, the strikers and their allies finally turned to the federal government. On July 19 four local mayors and Fluvio Pellinelli, representing the strike committee, sent identical telegrams to secretary of labor William Wilson requesting federal mediation. Simultaneously, Dante Barton, George West, and Louis F. Post urged Wilson to accede to the request, and, more particularly, to appoint Hywel Davies, a former Tennessee coal miner, as a federal mediator. Only two days later, on July 21, Secretary Wilson ordered Davies and W. R. Fairley, an Alabaman with mining experience, to the range to attempt federal mediation.

Davies and Fairley reached the range on July 27 and immediately conferred with the local mayors and with the strikers' central committee. Afterward they contacted company officials. Davies and Fairley proved, at least to their own satisfaction, that the strikers' grievances were legitimate, that the strike had erupted spontaneously, that the IWW had agreed to peaceful, pragmatic negotiations (even without IWW participation), and that the companies in conjunction with county officials had violated wholesale the strikers' constitutional rights and had established brutal repression across the range.

Although the mediators, unlike some others who would later investigate IWW-associated conflicts, sympathized with the strikers and favored their cause, they, too, failed to bring the companies to the bargaining table, let alone to terms. So ineffectual was federal mediation that, on September 9, the strike committee proclaimed, "We consider it a crime . . . that up to the present time no attempt has been made thru the mediators . . . to bring about a conference between the men and the companies." At which point Davies and Fairley could only bicker about the strikers' unwillingness to make sworn statements or to face publicly the accused foremen and captains.

With winter approaching and with federal mediation a failure, the strikers' resistance weakened. The IWW had begun to worry more about the future of its imprisoned leaders charged with murder than about the result of the conflict. Not unexpectedly, on September 17 the range branches of the Metal Mine Workers' Industrial Union voted, without even notifying Davies and Fairley, to call off their strike.

Yet the strikers' failure was more apparent than real. By mid-October even the Labor Department agents perceived that the strike had frightened employers into granting concessions. By January 8, 1917, Davies and Fairley boasted that, with the exception of the Oliver Company and several smaller ones, most of the employers had advanced wages for a second time on December 15 and had also consented to comply with the mediators' recommendations concerning rationalization of the contract system and the elimination of exploitation in employment.

With the end of the strike and the companies' ensuing improvements in wages and working conditions, the IWW's locals on the range atrophied. Wobblies nevertheless took pride in the improved conditions they had helped win for the miners and in the spirit of solidarity they believed they had inculcated among the range's workers. A solid core of Finnish and Slovenian Wobblies remained active, the Finnish-language paper *Socialisti* transformed itself into an IWW sheet, local Wobblies produced a Slovenian IWW paper, and Haywood even provided two permanent paid organizers to work on the range. The IWW expectantly awaited the spring and summer of 1917, when the miners, with better weather, would once again be ready to fight their employers under IWW auspices. Content that it had planted the seeds of industrial unionism and syndicalism on the Mesabi Range, the IWW devoted itself to securing the freedom of its imprisoned leaders and the poor immigrants incarcerated with them in a Duluth jail.

The IWW spared no effort and no expense in defending the indicted prisoners. At first, Haywood, Flynn, and Ettor beseeched Frank Walsh to act as defense attorney. When Walsh begged off, they obtained O. N. Hilton, a Salt Lake City attorney who had made a reputation defending radicals by his handling of the Joe Hill case and other labor trials involving the WFM. Flynn and Ettor, however, continued to plead with Walsh and other influential reformers to aid the Duluth defense.

Luckily, the IWW needed no additional legal talent. On December 15, five days before the Minnesota murder trial was scheduled to open, IWW Chicago headquarters learned that Tresca, Scarlett, Schmidt, Mrs. Masanovitch, and another immigrant worker had been freed, that the cases against James Gilday and Joe Greeni had been dismissed, and that Phil Masanovitch and two other immigrants had received indeterminate sentences, with eligibility for parole at the end of a year.

In December 1916 all IWW leaders were satisfied by the outcome of the Mesabi Range legal defense effort. Indeed, they were glad to have the Minnesota cases out of the way so they could devote the organization's resources to defense of another large group of Wobblies about to be tried for murder in Everett, Washington. Many of those who had just been involved in the Duluth proceedings, including Haywood, Flynn, and Harrison George, would also work together to secure the acquittal of the Everett defendants, under indictment in a case that derived from the IWW's renewed organization work among the lumberjacks of the Pacific Northwest.

The Pacific Northwest's lumber industry had undergone few changes since 1907, when the IWW first attempted to penetrate it in that year's unsuccessful walkout by Portland mill workers. In the years following the 1907 Portland strike the IWW struggled, without success, to organize the Northwest's lumber workers. Street-corner meetings, soapbox orations, and free-speech fights—all city-centered activities—accomplished precious little in the way of reaching lumber workers who toiled in the region's isolated logging camps. Unable to improve the lumberjack's working conditions through free-speech fights, the Wobblies went out on the job as camp delegates to carry their gospel directly into the logging camps, where they could wage the economic struggle at the point of production. As usual, if the IWW made revolutionists, it gained few recruits and less power in industry; if it gained members and industrial power, it lost its revolutionary fervor. Initially, in the lumber industry it possessed neither industrial power nor revolutionary recruits.

Employers nevertheless took seriously the IWW threat to their interests, and kept themselves well informed about Wobbly plans and progress. "A concerted effort should be made to thwart the efforts of this organization," one employer warned, "for if they are allowed to continue, and increase in numbers, sooner or later it means serious trouble."

That employers meant to eliminate the IWW from the Northwest was demonstrated by three events. First, the employers established the West Coast Lumbermen's Association in the summer of 1911, merging three regional trade associations. Originally organized to combat business insecurity and competitive malpractices, the new association united most effectively on anti-union measures. Second, most of the West Coast lumber companies now began to employ private detectives on a regular basis, and also often stationed sheriff's deputies on company premises. Third, in 1912 employers persuaded local federal officials to investigate the IWW for alleged illegal activities, though businessmen were dubious that any federal official "can be found with nerve to press proceedings." (Six years later such doubts would seem quite mistaken.)

Hard as employers combated the IWW from 1910 to 1912, they could not entirely stymie the Wobblies, particularly after the IWW's victory in Lawrence resurrected the organization. The spring of 1912 saw the Wobblies lead mill workers in the Puget Sound region in a strike for higher wages and the eight-hour day. Defeated in the mill towns by the combined opposition of AFL-affiliated central labor councils and vigilante justice (organized by private citizens and endorsed by public officials), the IWW hoped for better luck out in the woods.

Logging camps, however, were as well prepared as mill towns to fight the Wobblies. When word of urban labor disturbances reached the interior, camp foremen began to screen new workers more carefully. Private detectives again found plentiful employment in the industry, and the Lumbermen's Association, in conjunction with the Employers' Association of Washington State, influenced public officials to hound Wobblies, both in and out of town. By mid-May 1912 employers had completely repulsed the IWW's invasion.

From 1913 to 1915 the IWW declined in the Northwest as it did elsewhere in the nation. The IWW could do little to combat economic recession, vigilant employers, private detectives, and vindictive vigilantes. But war orders ended economic stagnation in 1915 and 1916, the labor market tightened, and the IWW, fresh from its wheat-belt victories, its treasury replenished with the AWO's funds, resumed its aggressive organizing tactics in the Northwest. In 1916 the class struggle in the Northwest entered a more virulent and ominous phase.

The Spokane Lumber Workers' Local formally affiliated with the AWO in February 1916 and—suddenly obtaining money for its usually empty treasury—initiated an intensive organizing campaign among the Inland Empire's workers. That summer the organizing impulse also reached the West Coast, when several hundred IWW lumber workers met in Seattle on July 3 to plan for "a vigorous and aggressive campaign of organization in the lumber industry" that would emphasize job organization and concrete material demands.

As the IWW pressed its organizing drive, employers counterattacked. As early as January 11, 1916, the Washington Employers' Association brought district lumbermen together in Seattle to discuss the threat raised by unionism. By June employers had welded a united front up and down the West Coast to fight not just the IWW but all organized labor. At a July 18 meeting in Portland, lumbermen unanimously decided to commit themselves to the open shop and to found the Lumbermen's Open Shop Association.

By November 1916 the employers' offensive had prevailed even in San Francisco, a union stronghold, and the Puget Mill's San Francisco office informed its men in the field in Washington State, "The principal thing to look out for now is to see that we keep a goodly *number* of *non-union* men always on the job, so that the unions will not have a chance to again get control."

Yet by 1916 lumbermen came to understand that it took more than blacklists and repression to defeat unions. "This bringing men in at night and putting them into a cabin in a dark hole, with no bed, no bed clothes, no light, no heat, no anything of that kind, is altogether played out," the Puget Mill's manager wrote, and then added, "Men expect different things altogether nowadays." His company decided to give its employees those "different things," primarily better bunks, bedding, and board, partly because they reduced labor discontent and partly because they decreased accidents, production delays, and operating expenses. The Merrill Ring Company was even more solicitous of its employees, causing a Wobbly organizer to observe, "The bunk house is perhaps the best on the coast. . . . The cooks are instructed to feed the men an abundance of clean, wholesome food, and there is a long list of good rules. . . . With a few improvements, such as furnishing bed clothes, these camps would even be tolerated by an I.W.W."

Organized labor in the Northwest could find solace only in its strength in Everett, Washington, a booming mill town at the mouth of the Snohomish River on the northern part of Puget Sound. There, even during the dark recession days of 1913–15, unions had retained some power, the shingle weavers* local, for instance, obtaining union shop contracts from Everett's manufacturers. "We understand that Everett is the only union town in the State," a lumberman commented in 1916. "It is about time," a lumber industry execu-

* Mill workers who produced building shingles.

tive suggested, "that conditions are changed." This employer determination to alter conditions in Everett would soon bring the city's businessmen and the IWW into a bloody confrontation.

The 1916 employers' open-shop drive had not bypassed Everett; it simply took a different form there: brutal, violent, and ultimately fatal. On May Day, 1916, the city's unionized shingle weavers (affiliated with the AFL, not the IWW) walked out to protest their employers' refusal to increase wages, which had been cut eighteen months earlier during the recession. Easily identifiable by the fingers they had lost to mill saws, Everett's shingle weavers demanded a share of the lumber industry's new prosperity. Although during earlier labor struggles in Everett the city's employers had been internally divided and unaligned with management interests outside the city, now, in 1916, Everett's mill owners presented a united front and drew upon support from both the state employers' association and the lumbermen's association. This new alignment of forces encouraged Everett's employers to smash the union and to establish the open shop in the city. Resolute mill owners thus hired armed professional strikebreakers to assist them in reopening the mills, and as smokestacks once again darkened the city's sky, resistance among the strikers ebbed. By midsummer many shingle weavers had returned to work without their union.

With the AFL shingle weavers beaten, the IWW intervened to see what it could salvage from the wreckage. Already well known and widely feared by Everett's employers and citizens, Wobblies for several years had maintained a small local headquarters that provided the city with soapboxers and radical literature. Haywood himself had addressed a large Everett audience in 1913, and Seattle, an IWW hotbed, was just down the Sound from Everett. In the summer of 1916, Seattle came to Everett in the person of James H. Rowan and other IWW agitators. When city officials arrested the agitators, the IWW threatened Everett with "a drastic dose of direct action."

Already triumphant in their conflict with the AFL shingle weavers, Everett employers were not about to open their industry to the IWW. They thus decided to test San Diego's anti-IWW tactics in the Northwest. The local Commercial Club, dominated by the mill owners, organized a vigilante group, which, when denied city cooperation, called upon Donald McRae, the county sheriff, who promised to deputize five hundred volunteers to protect Everett against invasion by outside agitators. Under McRae's leadership, the city's soldier citizens—junior executives, white-collar workers, petty bureaucrats— harassed the Wobblies, breaking up street meetings, pulling Wobs off trains and trolleys, beating them and deporting them.

As more and more Wobblies came north to Everett, the Commercial Club and Sheriff McRae resorted to San Diego–style measures. On October 30 forty Wobblies arrived on a boat from Seattle prepared to talk their way into Everett's jail. They never even had a chance to begin: McRae and his armed deputies met the Wobs at the boat dock, clubbed them, and escorted them directly to the city jail. That night deputies removed the prisoners from jail and took them to Beverly Park, a local forest preserve, where they stripped their captives and made the Wobblies run a gauntlet of several hundred vigilantes, who delighted in beating the naked prisoners with guns, clubs, and whips. To Wobblies the events of October 30 soon became known as the Everett Massacre. But the "massacre" would pale into insignificance compared to events of the following week.

As reports of the Beverly Park incident trickled back to IWW headquarters in Seattle, Wobbly leaders there decided to stage a mass invasion of Everett in order to confront the vigilantes with the power of numbers. Before long, several hundred loggers, itinerants, unemployed workers, radicals, and even a few young students had volunteered to fight in Everett for free speech and for the right to organize unions. Sunday, November 5, was set aside as the day to challenge Everett. As Sunday approached Wobblies made their way to Everett, the main body, about 250 strong, chartering a small steamer, the *Verona*, to carry them up Puget Sound. On the morning of November 5, a boisterous, happy bunch of workers, who might well have been out on a Sunday pleasure cruise, sang merrily as their boat glided up the Sound.

Everett's employers and vigilantes meanwhile had decided to accept the IWW's challenge and to meet force with force. Informed by private detectives of all the IWW's plans, the Commercial Club knew in advance about the voyage of the *Verona*. Down to Everett's docks marched the vigilantes, deputized by McRae, and armed with rifles, shotguns, and pistols. Fortified with whiskey and motivated by self-righteous notions of civic pride and respect for the law, McRae's deputies concealed themselves in a warehouse and in several small tugboats, forming a semicircle around the dock where the *Verona* was expected to land. Soon the concealed deputies, as well as a large crowd that had gathered high on a hilltop above the harbor, heard the strains of song drift across the harbor. "Hold the fort for we are coming, Union men, be strong," the Wobblies sang. As the *Verona* slipped into its dock and sailors made fast the ship's lines, McRae and two other deputies exchanged heated words with the "invaders." Suddenly a shot rang out, and then the sound of gunfire burst out in all directions. Caught in a deadly crossfire, the men aboard the *Verona* panicked, almost capsizing the boat, some of the Wobblies indeed falling overboard and probably drowning. Finally, at least one Wobbly aboard the ship had the good sense to order the boat's lines cast loose and its engines reversed. Still under constant fire, the *Verona* steamed out into the bay, and as it glided away from Everett, four men lay dead on its decks, one was dying, and thirty-one others were wounded. An unknown number of passengers had also fallen into the water, their bodies washed away, unknown, unidentified, and unmourned. On the dock, one deputy lay dead, another lay dying, and twenty were wounded. Thus ended Everett's "Bloody Sunday."

To this day no one knows with any certainty who fired the first shot. Nor does anyone know whether the wounded deputies were shot by Wobblies or by their own allies. Who fired the first shot is really unimportant. What is significant is that public authorities and private citizens had attempted to deny Wobblies their constitutional right to land at a public dock and to speak in Everett. Of further significance was the refusal of federal authorities, despite appeals from Haywood, the AFL, and influential West Coast reformers, to intervene on behalf of the rights of American citizens, who happened to be powerless workingmen.

This genuine "Everett Massacre," however, proved a blessing in disguise for the IWW. Already the beneficiary of national publicity resulting from the Mesabi Range strike and the murder trials there, the IWW now received the same treatment on the West Coast. Washington State's workers learned that the IWW was willing to fight and die for the principle of labor organization and that it was willing to go where AFL affiliates feared to tread. Repression in Everett, instead of capping the employers' open-shop drive, only served to make businessmen more anxious about labor problems.

The United States entered World War I in the spring of 1917, just as the Wobblies accelerated their own domestic class war. One conflict would feed on the other, and there would be no real victors among the contestants, abroad or at home, though the Wobblies would suffer the gravest defeat. In late 1916 and early 1917, however, the IWW viewed its future with unabated optimism. Exhilarated by the struggle on the Mesabi Range, united in adversity by the Everett Massacre, and revived financially by the AWO's growth, the IWW proposed at its 1916 convention to create the structure of an effective labor organization. Indeed, that convention would be the most important held by the IWW since 1908, when the "direct-actionists" had seized control of the organization.

As the IWW general executive board began to plan for the coming national convention in the spring of 1916, a new sense of purpose prevailed among its members. At its April sessions the general executive board concluded that the IWW had completed its preliminary phases of agitation and education. Now it could embark on its final phase: organization and control of American industry. General executive board members decided that the chaotic, mass mixed unions should become relics of the past, that the AWO should become an industrial organization for agricultural workers, and that nonagricultural workers recruited by the AWO should be organized as soon as feasible into industrial unions in their respective industries. Moreover, in order to limit the AWO's recruitment of nonfarm workers, the general executive board proposed to establish separate recruiting unions that would organize workers in all industries lacking separate locals.

The first thing that impressed Ben Williams, editor of *Solidarity,* when the 1916 convention opened on November 20 at Bush Temple in Chicago, was the absence of the soapboxer. "The I.W.W.," Williams commented, quoting a delegate, "is passing out of the purely propaganda stage and is entering the stage of constructive organization."

Haywood and the general executive board dominated the proceedings. Gratified by the accomplishments of the AWO but determined to reassert the authority of general headquarters, Haywood proposed to use the success of the AWO to nurture well-endowed industrial unions. In a burst of exuberance, Haywood prophesied that "the rest of the world will soon be asking the Industrial Workers of the World, What are we going to have for breakfast in the morning?" To achieve the industrial control and discipline necessary to dictate the world's breakfast menu, Haywood recommended, first, that all IWW administrative, printing, and publishing operations be consolidated in Chicago; second, that a general recruiting union, responsible to and controlled by general headquarters, be created to serve as a clearinghouse that would later refer new recruits to their proper industrial unions. The general executive board accepted his recommendations and added some of its own, including a proposal to abolish the office of general organizer—then held by Joe Ettor, who had just resigned after several years in that position—and leave its functions in the hands of the general secretary-treasurer (Haywood). It also suggested that national industrial unions, autonomous institutions in theory but impotent in practice, be replaced by simple industrial unions, which like all other subordinate bodies would then become subject to direct control by general headquarters. All the proposed internal reforms aimed at a single objective: to centralize the IWW's operations and to make field work subject to discipline by the elected administrators and their staff functioning out of national headquarters. The IWW's unexpected affluence also enabled the proponents of organizational centralization to offer, for the first time in the IWW's history, decent salaries to national organizers and officers.

When the convention adjourned *sine die* on December 1, Haywood found himself commander-in-chief of an expanding empire. No other figure remained within the organization to challenge his power. St. John followed the lure of gold, prospecting in New Mexico. Joe Ettor, now resigned, was destined to find a new career as a small-time entrepreneur. Elizabeth Gurley Flynn, then occupied full time with the defense of the Mesabi and Everett defendants, was on the verge of an irreparable rupture with Haywood and with the IWW. Ben Williams had just resigned as editor of *Solidarity* and was soon to be replaced by Ralph Chaplin, Haywood's hand-picked candidate. Walter Nef, the guiding genius of the AWO, had previously been forced out of that organization, even before the 1916 convention limited its power, and he was now laboring obscurely as an organizer on the Philadelphia waterfront.

What had happened was simple, if not at first clear: The flamboyant agitators and propagandists of the past had been replaced by less well-known but more effective labor organizers—all under Haywood's control. Even Ben Williams, no friend of Haywood, conceded in January 1917 that the changes wrought by the 1916 convention were "designed to promote a better system and more efficiency in the work of the organization. If the tendency towards centralization does not become extreme, the I.W.W. . . . took a long step forward toward the formation of the new society within the structure of the old."

On the eve of America's entry into World War I the IWW stood poised to open a new and more successful chapter in its history. It appeared ready to generate a sense of solidarity and a spirit of organization among workers long neglected by the trade unions. The IWW hoped to accomplish what no other American labor organization had ever done, or even attempted: effectively organize America's disinherited and dispossessed.

# 14

## The Class War at Home and Abroad, 1914–17

Sitting behind his large rolltop desk at IWW headquarters on Chicago's West Madison Street early in 1917, William D. Haywood was a happy man. To Ralph Chaplin, then editor of *Solidarity*, Haywood seemed more self-assured than ever, more firm in voice, and more youthful in appearance as he worked amid busy clerks and harried secretaries. Big Bill, Chaplin later recalled, suddenly seemed to be "a revolutionary tycoon whose dream had come true." Haywood's exuberant, boyish enthusiasm infected everyone at IWW headquarters, an office teeming with activities as its occupants prepared to "build their new society within the shell of the old."

A war-generated economic boom had produced the resurgence of both Haywood and the IWW. With production rising and labor increasingly scarce, employers hesitated to sacrifice profits to anti-union principles. The IWW now not only organized successfully but won material improvements for its members. Although statistics concerning the organization's membership growth between 1916 and late 1917 are at best imprecise, it seems likely that during this brief period the IWW more than doubled its membership, from roughly 40,000 in 1916 to 100,000 or more at one point in 1917.

America's entry into the war in April 1917 further tightened the labor market, opening attractive opportunities for assertive IWW organizers. As Woodrow Wilson brought the nation into war, the IWW marshaled its labor armies for another round in the irrepressible class war between labor and capital. Yet at the same time other Americans viewed the emergency as an opportunity to destroy the IWW.

The IWW had always preached revolution, antimilitarism, and antipatriotism. Neither the war in Europe nor American intervention in that war caused the Wobblies to alter their ideology. Aware that workers and their families received a steady diet of patriotic shibboleths in school, factory, and community, IWW journals did their best to counteract the rhetoric of Americanism. "Love of Country?" asked the *Industrial Worker*. "They [the workers] have no country.

Love of flag? None floats for them. Love of birthplace? No one loves the slums." Let those who own the country fight, Wobbly soapboxers declaimed.

Instead of going abroad to slay capitalist-created dragons, Wobblies were advised to remain at home in order to fight their bosses in the only worthwhile war: the class war. When American forces threatened to invade Mexico in 1914, Haywood told a New York City protest meeting, "It is better to be a traitor to your country than to your class."

While the IWW criticized patriotism and opposed war as an instrument of national policy, it offered no program to end war or to keep its members out of military service. About all it could do, and ever did do, was grind out antiwar propaganda and bar membership in the organization to any worker who enlisted voluntarily in any branch of the military service.

The IWW's lack of a specific strategy to oppose war did not mean that the organization substituted antiwar propaganda for realistic policies. It reflected instead the IWW's own estimate of the weaknesses of American antiwar factions. Wobblies spread their antiwar propaganda so profusely because they perceived how patriotic, even jingoistic, most workers were. The IWW also criticized the antiwar crusades of American pacifists and Socialists as ineffectual movements lacking economic and social substance. Pacifists, in their view, engaged in wishful thinking, substituting pious platitudes for realistic policies, Christian beatitudes for real power.

The outbreak of world war in the summer of 1914 revealed both the IWW's realism and its utter inability to devise an effective response. "We had no reason to expect a different turn of events," *Solidarity* commented when it heard the war news. European workers had acted much as the IWW feared they would: Nationalism transcended class, patriotism blighted politics. Though condemning the European war, the IWW did nothing to change American foreign policies. While the nation remained at peace, the IWW pursued its customary business of organizing workers, leaving peace crusades in other hands.

Explaining to an enraged reader of *Solidarity* why the IWW refused to take antiwar pledges or to join peace crusades, Ben Williams argued that pledges, resolutions, and crusades, unsupported by economic control and power, would not stop war if war was what the masters wanted. Not only did the IWW sense that America would eventually enter the war, but Williams prophesied what in 1914 seemed even more fantastic. While European and American radicals, as well as liberals, regarded tsarist Russia as a major threat to the progressive forces of the Western world, Williams hailed Russia as a revolutionary force. "At the risk of shocking some of our readers," he wrote, "we are offering to bet on Russia as *the hope of Europe*."

For the next three years, as Wilsonian diplomacy drew America into the maelstrom and Williams awaited a Russian revolution, the IWW pursued its organizing campaigns and Wobblies discussed what the IWW should do when war came. These discussions reached a peak on the eve of American intervention. Anxious for action, a Spokane IWW official suggested that the organization emulate the example of its Australian fellow workers who went to prison rather than wage a capitalistic war. Specifically, he recommended a vigorous antiwar campaign and a twenty-four-hour protest general strike. Speaking for majority sentiment, Ben Williams opposed "meaningless" antiwar gestures. "In case of war," he advised, "we want the One Big Union . . . to come out of the conflict stronger and with more industrial control than previously. Why should we," he asked, "sacrifice working class interests for the sake of a few noisy and impotent parades or antiwar demonstrations? Let us rather get on the job of organizing the working class to take over the industries, war or no war, and stop all future capitalist aggression that leads to war and other forms of barbarism."

In February 1917 James M. Slovick, secretary of the Marine Transport Workers' Industrial Union, glimpsed the IWW's future. Writing to Haywood for advice, Slovick recommended that the IWW declare a general strike if a declaration of war against Germany passed Congress. He granted all the usual objections to his recommendation. Fearing destruction of the IWW in any event, Slovick saw no sound reason for the organization to equivocate its antiwar position. Haywood spurned Slovick's suggestion, advising the Marine Workers' official that the general executive board could not constitutionally act upon the request of a single member.

Between February 1917 and America's declaration of war on April 4, the IWW followed a course midway between that recommended by Slovick and that suggested by Williams. In line with Williams's advice, the IWW concentrated on organizing harvest hands, copper miners, and lumber workers. Yet on March 24 *Solidarity* did what Slovick had demanded: It distinguished the IWW from the labor organizations that sanctioned war. In a box on page 1, the paper published "The Deadly Parallel," placing side by side in boldface type the IWW's 1916 declaration against war and the AFL's pledge to offer devoted and patriotic service to the American nation in case of war. Then, beneath an estimate of the war's casualties, *Solidarity* commented, "Ten million human lives stand as a monument to the national patriotic stupidity of the working class of Europe! Who will be to blame if the workers of America are betrayed and led into the bloodiest slaughter of history? Who?" The question answered itself.

On April 4, however, academic discussions and rhetorical questions ended for the IWW. America was now at war. What, indeed, would the IWW do? Wobblies themselves wondered. Members all over the country turned to their regional headquarters or to Chicago for guidance. IWW leaders, of course, sought to enlighten their followers. At first, they counseled and followed a consistent course. Playing down antiwar propaganda, they concentrated upon what *Solidarity* called "the great work of ORGANIZATION." Even Frank Little, later to become notorious as the IWW's most bitter foe of war, limited his comments to advice that workers "stay at home and fight their own battles with their own enemy—the boss."

Although the IWW took no specific antiwar actions, it refused, unlike the AFL and most other labor organizations, to sanction Wilson's crusade. At the time this took courage. (The Socialist party also adopted an antiwar resolution in 1917, causing an influential group of intellectuals to secede from the party and become Wilsonians.)

Soon, however, the IWW faced an issue more difficult to resolve than that of war or peace. Forced to adopt a position on the draft question, IWW leaders equivocated. On May 3, Haywood, writing to Frank Walsh, noted that the IWW, though opposed to the war, had established no precise antiwar program. "What our steps will be in the event of members . . . being conscripted," wrote Haywood, "has not yet been determined. While being opposed to the Imperial Government of Germany, we are likewise opposed to the Industrial Oligarchy of this country, and instead of fighting to continue it, we will always be found fighting in our small way for the restitution of the rights of the working people." That, however, did not amount to a policy on conscription.

Before the enactment of the draft law, the *Industrial Worker* had offered a poetic solution:

> I love my flag, I do, I do,
> Which floats upon the breeze,
> I also love my arms and legs,
> And neck, and nose and knees.
> One little shell might spoil them all
> Or give them such a twist,
> They would be of no use to me;
>     I guess I won't enlist.

*[handwritten note: they don't want to risk their bodys for war, bodys that they use for Labor work.]*

Yet anti-enlistment poetry provided an inadequate guide for Wobblies who wanted to know what to do when their draft boards beckoned. Did the IWW have an official policy?

Several influential Wobblies thought the organization should oppose conscription. Most militant and outspoken of these was Frank Little, who traveled across the West organizing workers and criticizing the draft. Richard Brazier, West Coast organizer and a new general executive board member, also suggested to Haywood on May 26 that the board take a definite stand on the issue; Brazier advised Wobblies to declare their conscientious objection to war and their willingness to resist conscription. These antiwar militants apparently forced a special general executive board meeting in mid-July that considered anticonscription tactics. What happened at that meeting is unclear. Yet evidence indicates that the militants were defeated at the session and that Haywood won majority approval for the IWW's equivocal war policies. But Ralph Chaplin, one of the defeated militants at the general executive board session, continued to publish antiwar pleas in *Solidarity*, including a July 28 special anticonscription feature that concluded, "All members of the I.W.W. who have been drafted should mark their claims for exemption, 'I.W.W.; opposed to war.'"

Yet roughly 95 percent of the eligible Wobblies registered with their draft boards, and most of those served when called. Some apparently entered the service in the hope that they could foment antimilitarism from within. On the other hand, most of those who resisted conscription did so for ethnic reasons—primarily the Finns on the Mesabi Range and the Scandinavians in Rockford, Illinois.

The IWW's cautious reaction to war and to conscription failed to protect the organization from the waves of wartime hysteria that swept across America. As the IWW increased its economic power during the first months of American involvement in the war, employers, faced with an increasingly assertive labor force, struck back against the Wobblies. Using the war emergency as a pretext and accusing the Wobblies of sedition, businessmen enlisted public opinion and government power to repress the IWW.

Wobblies had premonitions of the threat war posed to their organization. Since the IWW's birth in 1905 public authorities had sought to proscribe or repress it, and since the 1912 San Diego free-speech fight the federal government had been drawn intermittently into the struggle to outlaw the Wobblies. World War I, as far as businessmen and public officials were concerned, quite obviously transformed the IWW's subversive potentialities into living realities. Many Wobblies realized this.

They also realized that never had things looked so propitious for successful organizing among harvesters, copper miners, and loggers. Profit-conscious employers would think twice about stimulating employee dissatisfaction by interfering with labor organizers or by discharging IWW members summarily. Federal officials, eager to achieve full war production, would urge private employers to improve working conditions and to avoid anti-union crusades. Indeed, as both union membership and wages rose, the IWW could take credit for these improvements, further heightening its appeal to prospective members.

IWW publications and private correspondence among Wobblies reflected their perceptions of the war as both a threat and an opportunity. A Washington State member, for instance, wrote just a few days after the American declaration of war, "I hope this damn war business is not going to set us back, as the prospect for the I.W.W. looks very bright."

If the IWW was to be repressed during the war, it would not be for offering rhetorical opposition to America's involvement. Nor would it be for encouraging sabotage, sedition, and subversion. Repression, if it came, would be a result of IWW struggles to organize workers. Rather than squandering precious resources in fighting against United States involvement in the war, the IWW intended to use all its strength to fight what Haywood labeled America's "industrial oligarchy."

Planning to hit its enemy where it hurt most—in the pocketbook—the IWW concentrated on industries where it had already demonstrated some strength. Quite fortuitously, those industries happened to be vital to the nation's war effort. American and Allied soldiers could not fight without food; without lumber, the military could not house recruits, transport them across the ocean, or challenge German pilots for control of the skies; without copper, production of military hardware was hampered and wire essential to battlefield communication lines was impossible to obtain. It is most significant, then, that in the spring and summer of 1917 IWW strikes affected the wheat fields, the forests, and the copper mines.

The IWW's resurgence as a labor organization had begun in the summer of 1915, it will be recalled, with the Agricultural Workers' Organization (AWO) triumphs in the wheat belt. As war increased the demand for wheat and conscription diminished the available labor supply, the Agricultural Workers' Industrial Union (AWIU) looked forward to 1917 as its best year. At its annual convention in May 1917, the AWIU heard reports that the Farmers' Nonpartisan League of North Dakota* was anxious to meet with IWW representatives. A. C. Townley, president of the Nonpartisan League, had proposed that five league delegates confer with an identical number from the IWW to decide on wages, hours, and working conditions for the approaching harvest season.

Two months later, in July 1917, just before the Dakota harvest season began,

* A radical agrarian group committed to public ownership of grain elevators and railroads, among other reforms, and a potent political force in the Dakotas.

the IWW announced a tentative agreement with the Nonpartisan League. For the first time, IWW headquarters promised, a uniform wage scale (unspecified) had been established for the harvest hands, which the league voted to recommend for adoption by North Dakota's farmers. In order not to upset traditional IWW sanctions against signed agreements or customary agrarian, antilabor individualism, the agreement between the AWIU and the league remained verbal and tentative.

Tentative though the agreement was, and though honored as much in the breach as in the practice, it nevertheless benefited the IWW. The following year (1918), when Thorstein Veblen investigated the farm labor situation at the behest of the federal government's Food Administration, Veblen discovered no sharp hostility between grain farmers and Wobblies, nor did he uncover any IWW disloyalty or opposition to the government's war efforts. Whatever violence and labor conflict affected the grain belt, Veblen continued, was introduced by urban-based commercial clubs, bankers, editors, and politicians.

Although the IWW encountered no bitter-end employer opposition in the wheat fields, it faced an entirely different situation in its attempts to organize the harvesters and loggers of the Pacific Northwest.

The IWW's appeal to labor in the Northwest resulted from the refusal of employers in that region to alter unacceptable working conditions or to bargain with moderate AFL affiliates. As president Woodrow Wilson's Mediation Commission reported in 1918, the IWW filled the vacuum created by the employers' obdurate antilabor policies. Seizing on the loggers' desire to be treated with dignity, which in the lumber industry meant largely the eight-hour day, decent bedding, and wholesome board, the IWW made its red card common throughout the Pacific Northwest. Even before America entered the war the IWW had initiated an organizing drive in the Northwest patterned after the AWO's successful tactics. First organized as a branch of the AWO, by March 1917 the lumber workers were strong enough to go their own way. At a special convention held in Spokane on March 4–6, 1917, the lumber workers established a six-thousand-member IWW industrial union: Lumber Workers' Industrial Union No. 500. To its Spokane central headquarters this union soon added branch offices in Seattle and Duluth.

That spring, as the ice in the rivers and lakes of the short-log region of northern Idaho and eastern Washington thawed, the IWW wisely chose to take its members off the job, leaving Idaho's rivers clogged with logs and its mills starved for fresh supplies of raw material. Rather than combat this unexpected strike and thus lose a favorable market opportunity, employers conceded the union's demands, giving Wobblies higher wages and an eight-hour day.

The IWW success in the Inland Empire proved infectious. From headquarters in Spokane, the IWW moved against the fruit, vegetable, and wheat farmers of eastern Washington, and from its Seattle headquarters, the lumber workers' union planned to organize the Douglas fir industry west of the Cascades.

Employers and public officials in the Northwest became so fearful of the IWW that by mid-June 1917 panic pervaded the region. As a result of IWW pressure in his state's farm and logging districts, Washington governor Ernest Lister had already appointed a special committee, including the president of the state Federation of Labor, to investigate local labor conditions. On June 19 the United States attorney for the eastern district of Washington asserted that the IWW had made preposterous demands on the region's farmers, which could not possibly be granted.

The labor situation in the Northwest continued to deteriorate. Reports filled the IWW press describing region-wide walkouts by lumber workers aimed at securing the eight-hour day and wages in line with the prevailing inflationary trend. Federal attorneys in Washington and Idaho noted a rising tide of IWW threats to the peace and security of the Northwest. The AFL joined in the clamor for action, reviving its long-defunct Brotherhood of Timber Workers and laying plans for a sweeping strike in the Douglas fir industry. Since IWW crews had been striking intermittently since mid-June, Wobbly leaders decided that, rather than allow AFL officials to assume credit for any future walkouts, the IWW should declare its own industry-wide walkout, effective July 17. It was in response to the IWW's strike call that thousands of men left their jobs and partially paralyzed the lumber industry.

Although the IWW's critics stressed the violent, anarchic aspects of the ensuing strike, Wobblies themselves insisted on absolutely passive resistance. Strike leader James Rowan warned Wobblies to be leery of men who advocated violence and who infiltrated the organization in order to serve as agents provocateurs.

As the IWW's strike for the eight-hour day gathered momentum, employers had important decisions to make. They could choose voluntarily to go on an eight-hour day and thus avert employee discontent, or they could remain on minimum ten-hour shifts. They could fight or woo labor jointly, or each employer could go his own way, as had been traditional in the lumber industry. Yet even before the IWW general strike began on July 17, lumbermen had made cooperative plans to cope with their labor problems. At a July 17 Seattle meeting, the industry's top executives decided, despite some dissent, to refuse to grant the eight-hour day.

8 hour denial

To maintain the customary ten-hour day, employers established the Lumbermen's Protective Association on July 9, 1917. The association's leaders threatened firms that refused to join with business boycotts and pledged to penalize any member company that granted the eight-hour day. Companies joined the association—sixty of them the day it was formed, including Weyerhaeuser, the industry's giant—because they suddenly realized that the IWW had established an effective organization among the loggers. As Alex Polson, one of the most individualistic and difficult of lumbermen, explained it, "If it were not for the I.W.W. menace to our country I never would have attended the meeting [July 9] . . . nor permitted them to use my name on the committee. It is to beat this organization [the IWW] that I think our company should stay with them [the Protective Association] right down the line to the last ditch."

Neither the Protective Association nor employer-hired detectives and deputies repulsed the IWW eight-hour movement. Reports reached the Department of Labor on July 19–20 describing widespread strike activity in the Northwest. E. G. Ames of the Puget Mill Company declared that the lumber and logging business of the Grays Harbor district was practically paralyzed.

AFL tactics made the lumbermen even unhappier While employers attempted to protect the "loyal" majority of their workers against subversive labor agitators, AFL affiliates tried to use the crisis to enroll lumber workers in the Brotherhood of Timber Workers. But employers showed as little love for the "patriotic" AFL as for the "subversive" IWW.

Unwilling to grant their employees an eight-hour day, even more unwilling to deal with unions, including AFL unions, lumbermen had no choice but to fight the strike to the bitter end. Using Pinkertons, local sheriffs, state officials, federal attorneys, and ultimately the federal government, employers could partially offset the effectiveness of the IWW-led strike. In a tactical response the IWW, in late August, sent its members back to work with orders to strike on the job. Thereafter when workers malingered, soldiered, or walked off the job without warning, employers found themselves impotent. Once they would simply have replaced unsatisfactory men with a new work crew; in wartime this could not be done.

Even with the IWW general strike an apparent failure, the Washington State Council of Defense nevertheless reported gloomily in late September that logging camps were operating at only 50 percent of capacity and mills at 60 to 65 percent, scarcely sufficient in either case to satisfy wartime demands. The council found more workers joining the IWW and the AFL, and it warned that if operators maintained their unyielding opposition to a shorter workday, costly strikes and labor inefficiency would worsen.

In the lumber industry, at least, the IWW appeared to be waging its class war effectively. But Wobblies, like the Allies and the Central Powers, fought their war on more than a single front. While clashing with lumber operators in the Pacific Northwest, the IWW simultaneously carried the struggle to copper barons in Montana and Arizona.

If lumber workers had legitimate grievances, so did copper miners. Nowhere was this clearer than in Butte, Montana, once a miners' union stronghold but in April 1917 an open-shop city for miners. No copper miner could get work without his rustling card, and none received his card if he participated in union affairs. Since the labor explosion that rocked Butte in 1914, few miners looked to Charles Moyer's organization, the International Union of Mine, Mill and Smelter Workers (IUMMSW),* or to its parent AFL for assistance. For three years the rustling card, Pinkertons, company gunmen, and union rivalries closed Butte's mines to organized labor. Then the war came, and in Butte, as elsewhere, prices rose, profits increased, and the labor market tightened. Now even the smallest spark could set off the city's highly combustible labor force.

That spark flashed literally on June 8, 1917, when a fire broke out at the shaft bottom on the 2,400-foot level in the North Butte Mining Company's Speculator mine. Flames roared through the shaft and tongues of fire seared its crevices and crannies, turning the whole mine into an inferno. Men fled in all directions. A few fortunate ones succeeded in breaking through heavy concrete bulkheads designed to limit trespass; most miners were trapped by these unbreakable barriers. Wherever they fled in the shaft, the miners were pursued by the flames and the poisonous gases released by the intense heat. In the end, 164 men roasted to death in the hell known as the Speculator mine.

Seething with indignation, Butte's miners reacted to the tragedy. Led by IWW men, notably Tom Campbell and Joe Shannon, the only leaders the miners now trusted, the workers organized a new independent union, the Metal Mine Workers' Union (MMWU), in order to transcend traditional IUMMSW-AFL-IWW rivalries. Its nominal independence notwithstanding, the MMWU was dominated by the Campbells and the Shannons (IWW militants), and many among its rank and file promptly obtained red cards. IWW headquarters meanwhile wasted no time in dispatching organizers to Butte. The simmering labor pot boiled over on June 11, when ten to twelve thousand miners led by Wobblies  walked off the job to demand better working conditions, a $6 minimum daily wage, union recognition, and abolition of the rustling card.

Miners answered their employers' recalcitrance not with violence, sabotage, or anarchy, but with moderation. On June 20 an official of the MMWU asked Labor Secretary Wilson to initiate a federal investigation of Butte's labor prob-

* The IUMMSW was the successor to the Western Federation of Miners.

lems. Three days later, the union communicated its specific demands to Secretary Wilson, adding three mine safety items to its original list and suggesting to Wilson that the union would abide by a federal determination concerning the practicability and reasonableness of its demands.

Assistant attorney general William C. Fitts simultaneously warned Secretary Wilson of the seriousness of the labor situation in Butte, as well as the likelihood that it would interfere with the war effort. Fitts also mentioned that the Justice Department was searching for possible violations of federal law. At this juncture Secretary Wilson learned that Butte's AFL craft unions had suddenly walked off the job, further disrupting copper and zinc production. To find a way out of this confusion, Wilson sent W. H. Rogers, a federal mediator and a former United Mine Workers official, to Butte.

Upon his arrival in Butte, Rogers found the labor situation unusually threatening. Immediately declaring settlement of the miners' strike impossible, he urged a concerted effort on the part of Gompers and the AFL to compel the craft unionists to return to work. In concert with Anaconda officials, Rogers worked out a scheme to undermine the strike. First, they enticed the skilled workers in the craft unions back to the job with an attractive offer, endorsed by Gompers, international union officials, and Rogers. They then offered less determined and more hard-pressed individual miners an illusory wage increase.

Although all the craft unionists had returned to work by mid-July, the vast majority of miners rejected the limited concessions that Rogers had arranged with the mine owners. Despite charges of subversion, antipatriotism, and anarchy leveled against them by employers and newspapers, the miners maintained their nonviolent walkout. According to an informant of Montana congresswoman Jeannette Rankin, they still looked to President Wilson and the federal government to settle the dispute equitably. The same informant reported that the miners would suspend their strike if President Wilson commissioned Rankin to effect a permanent settlement. Washington, of course, had no such plans in mind.

Throughout September the strike crippled copper and zinc production in Montana. Pleading with federal authorities to enforce a strike settlement based on abolition of the rustling card, the miners got nowhere. In Montana, as in Washington State, employers could break the outward manifestations of an IWW strike. Yet they failed to restore production levels. Dissatisfied miners returned to the mines only to malinger.

Arizona's wartime labor situation proved even more confused and complicated than Montana's. Equally essential to the war effort, Arizona's copper mines produced 28 percent of the nation's total supply. Unlike Montana's mines, Arizona's were scattered about the state in four widely separated and geographically isolated districts. Except for the Warren district in the Bisbee area, Arizona's mining regions had a notoriously polyglot work force: Americans, eastern Europeans, Mexicans, Mexican-Americans, Spanish-born workers, and even some Native Americans, who were mixed together in a cantankerous, divided, and discontented labor army. Miners' unions, moreover, had never had the success in Arizona they once had in Butte. The state's boom mining years began just as the WFM decayed, and when the war came in 1917 Arizona miners lacked any effective means of redressing basic job grievances.

Arizona was thus an ideal breeding ground for the IWW, which had just the leaders to organize there: Charles MacKinnon, Big Bill Haywood's brother-in-law, who carried both an IUMMSW card and a red card, a veteran of the 1906–7 Goldfield conflict, and a hard-rock miner with considerable influence in Arizona's mining camps; Frank Little, the one-eyed, part–Native American organizer-agitator, respected by the state's hard-rock miners for his courage and unyielding principles; and Grover H. Perry, secretary-treasurer of Metal Mine Workers' Industrial Union No. 800, an experienced IWW official who had already done notable organizing work among maritime workers on the Great Lakes and in Baltimore and who was now anxious to organize copper mines from his union headquarters in Phoenix.

The IWW moved ahead in Arizona in two ways. Where Moyer's union (the IUMMSW) was largely ineffective—as in Bisbee—Wobblies easily captured the old IUMMSW local from within, transforming it into a branch of the Metal Mine Workers' Industrial Union (in Bisbee the IWW even took over the IUMMSW's hall). Elsewhere in the state where Moyer's union retained influence, the IWW formed dual local unions and also infiltrated the IUMMSW locals, planning first to disrupt them and then to capture them from within.

In its organizing campaign the IWW made a simple, direct economic appeal to Arizona's miners. Emphasizing the IUMMSW's inability to raise wages as wartime prices soared, IWW leaflets demanded "shorter hours, more wages, and better conditions *today, while tomorrow we will be satisfied with no less than the complete ownership of the mills, mines, and smelters*" (italics added). Organizers called for the six-hour day, two men to each mining drill machine in order to reduce technological unemployment, the end of the speed-up, and the abolition of autocratic company labor policies. Aware of the polyglot composition of the miners, IWW organizers stressed that their union "provides for the admittance . . . of every person working in the mining industry, regardless of creed, color, or nationality." Metal Mine Workers' Union No. 800 promised workers a solidarity never before achieved in the hard-rock mining industry; it also offered Arizona's miners support from their fellow workers in Montana, Utah, Nevada, and even Alaska.

The IWW's appeal worked in Arizona. Helped along by the IUMMSW's inability to act, the IWW grew by leaps and bounds in Bisbee and added members in Arizona's other mining districts. Organized on January 29, 1917, Metal Mine Workers' Union No. 800 had over six thousand members by April and 125 paid organizers at work, mostly in Arizona, including Spanish-speaking organizers who distributed *El Rebelde,* the Spanish-language IWW paper.

Yet in Arizona, as had often been the case elsewhere in the nation, working-class discontent outran IWW plans. After April 1917, wages simply could not keep pace with price inflation, and neither IWW leaders nor IUMMSW officials could restrain Arizona's miners in their demand for higher wages. Spontaneous labor disputes thus erupted in the Jerome and Clifton-Morenci districts in May 1917. Federal mediation and expedient concessions by the affected mine owners, however, terminated these walkouts. For the moment, at least, Arizona's labor scene appeared placid.

Yet the state's labor problems had become too twisted to unravel. It was impossible without a scorecard to distinguish Wobblies, AFL men, and labor spies. Where employers thought that the IUMMSW was strong, they tried to use IWW locals to disrupt the stronger union. Where the IWW was strong, as in Bisbee, mine owners instigated the IUMMSW and the state Federation of Labor to act against the Wobblies. Throughout the state, Wobblies joined the IUMMSW, spies infiltrated the IWW, Justice Department agents hunted subversives, and mine owners and local businessmen formed loyalty leagues in order to suppress all trade unions. Only two constants prevailed: the employers' absolute refusal to deal with organized labor and the miners' unheard demands for a redress of their grievances through collective bargaining. Such a situation could only worsen before it improved.

Worsen it did, as Walter Douglas, president of the Phelps Dodge Corporation, found in the first week of June when he surveyed labor conditions at his Arizona mining properties. In a letter to secretary of the interior Franklin Lane, Douglas blamed his company's labor difficulties on IWW propaganda and the unpatriotic attempt of the president of the state Federation of Labor to unionize the mining industry at a time of national peril.

Until the Speculator disaster precipitated labor conflict in Butte, it appeared that employers might manage to control Arizona's tense labor situation. But after the Butte disaster, Arizona's copper miners could not be contained. Encouraged by events in Montana, Arizona's Wobblies decided to accelerate their drive in the Southwest. On June 26 the IWW called out its members working the mines in Bisbee, Globe, Miami, Swansea, and Jerome, Arizona.

Not to be outdone, IUMMSW locals initiated their own strikes for higher wages, shorter hours, and union recognition. By July 1, ten thousand men were out in the Clifton-Morenci district, where all large producers had been shut down; a day later eight thousand miners walked off their jobs in the Globe-Miami district. Spreading rapidly from one area to another, the strike movement by July 6 included 25,000 men and had succeeded in tying up every mining camp in the state. By then, the walkout was 90 percent effective in Bisbee, where the IWW controlled it, and 100 percent effective in Clifton-Morenci, where the IWW and the IUMMSW joined in an uncomfortable and unholy alliance.

In an investigation of the causes of these labor disturbances, a mediation commission appointed by Woodrow Wilson placed responsibility on the copper industry's heterogeneous, un-Americanized labor force, its heavy labor turnover, its anti-union policies, and its insistence on maintaining autocratic patterns of work discipline. Yet in Bisbee, where the commission had to account not only for industrial conflict but also for IWW dominance, the workers were largely American and almost all English-speaking, they were by and large settled family men, and they worked for Phelps Dodge, which, though autocratic and anti-union, provided the towns of Bisbee and Douglas with numerous company-financed advantages. The mediation commission simply blamed the IWW's rise in Bisbee on Phelps Dodge's destruction of the IUMMSW local there. Yet, as the commission's own evidence proved, in Clifton-Morenci and Globe-Miami, where less Americanized miners were more transient and the operators seemed just as anti-union and provided fewer company benefits, the IWW never achieved dominance.

It made little difference whether the strikes were inspired by the IWW. Regardless of which union initiated conflicts, the strikers asserted that if Americans could wage war abroad to spread democracy, they could also struggle at home to win the industrial democracy so long denied them by capitalist "autocrats," whose tyrannies were more real to the miners than those charged to Kaiser Wilhelm.

Labor Secretary Wilson's mediators consequently found the mine owners far from conciliatory or cooperative. They failed to obtain any substantial labor concessions from the copper companies, which insisted on handling labor relations in their customary autocratic spirit; as one company informed the Globe IUMMSW local, "First and foremost, we reserve the right and privilege to conduct our own affairs." Or, as Walter Douglas stated publicly, "There will be no compromise because you cannot compromise with a rattlesnake." The mediators thus had no option but to withdraw from the dispute in order to allow the main contenders to fight it out.

The Arizona labor conflict seemed to defeat everyone involved in it. Mine owners begged federal authorities for assistance, yet when Labor Department mediators offered it, employers refused to cooperate. Unable to defeat the copper companies, the IWW found itself also attacked by state officials, AFL affiliates, and federal agents. The AFL and the IUMMSW seemed equally impotent.

Arizona's mine operators, like the businessmen in Montana and Washington State, could neither break the IWW strikes nor restore full production. When President Wilson's mediation commission arrived in Arizona in the fall of 1917, it discovered that the state's copper mines had been totally or partially shut down for over three months, with a production loss of more than 100 million pounds of copper.

In the summer of 1917, from the Douglas fir forests of Puget Sound to the "richest hill on earth" at Butte, from the isolated mining towns of Arizona to the golden wheat fields of the Midwest, the IWW threatened the nation's war-making capacity. Many Americans thus wondered precisely what the IWW wanted before it would declare a truce in its class war.

# 15

## Employers Strike Back

On August 17, 1917, United States senator Henry Ashurst of Arizona arose on the Senate floor to denounce the IWW. "I have frequently been asked what 'IWW' means," he informed fellow senators, then added, "It means simply, solely, and only 'Imperial Wilhelm's Warriors.'"

War ordinarily engenders hatred for the enemy. This was particularly true in the America of 1917–18, when public authorities sought to inoculate against unpatriotic backsliding the millions of citizens who had emigrated from nations fighting on the enemy side. From printing press, pulpit, and President Wilson's war propaganda creation, George Creel's Committee on Public Information, propaganda flowed charging that the German nation was synonymous with evil, that the Kaiser was the devil incarnate, and that the German people were less than human.

The anti-German propaganda, which Creel's committee distributed in every community, equated disagreement with Wilson's war policies with incipient treason and saw evidence of German espionage in every action that hampered the American war effort. Since the IWW opposed the war in theory and took action in practice—namely, the lumber and copper strikes—that threatened war production, the nation's communications media declared the IWW ipso facto guilty of treason and espionage. In the spring and summer of 1917 America's press stimulated a new form of gold rush, the frantic search to discover German gold clinking in Bill Haywood's pockets.

From coast to coast—and most virulently in communities disturbed by IWW strikes—the tocsin sounded for repression of the Wobblies. Well after repression had become a fact, the *San Francisco Chronicle* commented on February 6, 1918, "The I.W.W. are worse than the Germans . . . the I.W.W. will never cease until persistently imprisoned or put out of existence." Across the nation, the *Wall Street Journal* noted, "The nation is at war, and treason must be met with preventive as well as punitive measures. When you hear the copperhead [i.e., IWW] hissing in the grass why wait until it strikes before stamping on it? Instead of waiting to see if their bite is poisonous, the heel of the Government should stamp them at once."

More thoughtful journals proved as frantic as the daily press in their denunciations of the IWW. The *Outlook* asserted that, whether or not German gold financed IWW intrigues, the Wobblies' industrial conflicts aided the enemy. "If the fullest military preparations are needed against an external enemy," the magazine advised, "they are no less needed against this internal enemy." Even the usually objective *Nation,* not known for its warlike enthusiasm, advised, "It seems likely that [IWW] leaders can . . . be arrested on substantial grounds of sedition or disorderly intent; and their arrest and summary punishment would give a salutary lesson to prospective lawbreakers."

In 1917 the halls of Congress echoed to denunciations of the IWW. Senators and congressmen from the Western states most affected by IWW strikes instigated the oratory. Miles Poindexter, a progressive senator from Washington whom the lumber barons once claimed had been elected by IWW votes, declared Wobbly leaders to be outlaws who should be handled firmly by public officials even in the absence of specific infractions of federal law. Only two congressional voices disputed the slanders and calumnies heaped on the IWW. Jeannette Rankin, who had voted against America's declaration of war and who was a political ally of Butte's mine workers, including the IWW element, and senator George Norris of Nebraska, another antiwar advocate who asked about the grievances that had provoked IWW strikes, alone sought to reason with their colleagues.

This mass wartime hysteria, which affected every class, sector, and region of the country, primed the employers' counterattack against the IWW. Although the bulk of anti-IWW propaganda may have been well intended and motivated by unselfish patriotic beliefs, this was only partially the case with Western employers, who used the rhetoric of patriotism to thwart the IWW menace to their wartime profits. Western businessmen missed no opportunity to make profits compatible with patriotism and organized labor synonymous with treason.

Before the IWW general strike hit the Northwest's lumber industry, employers believed they could deflect trade union penetration by obtaining government war contracts that would ensure federal protection for their economic interests. When the lumber strike began in Idaho in June, employers demanded federal Secret Service agents to protect their loyal employees from IWW intimidation. Early in July, before the beginning of the general strike, an association of Western lumbermen pleaded with their congressmen for federal protection in Idaho, Washington, and Montana. Later that month, with the IWW walkout fully effective, E. G. Griggs of the St. Paul and Tacoma Lumber Company demanded federal aid to defend Grays Harbor against what he deemed to be an "enemy invasion." In addition, scores of Northwest lumbermen wired panicky reports to Washington in which they stressed IWW interference with the government's supply of spruce for airplanes and shipbuilding, the desire of loyal employees to work if troops defended them against labor agitators, and the obvious links between the IWW and German espionage.

Unable to gain strikebreaking assistance from the Labor Department, Western businessmen found the Justice Department much more amenable to pressure. From their contacts with local United States attorneys, which were close and warm, employers learned that the Justice Department's local officials despised the IWW, disliked organized labor, and demonstrated scant sympathy for the worker's cause. Employers thus resorted to United States attorneys as the best channel through which to carry business suggestions to the highest echelons of the federal government.

These local attorneys faithfully conveyed to their Washington superiors the Western case against the IWW. In their pleas for federal action against the IWW, these local Justice Department officials exhibited—considering their profession—a striking disregard for the law. Representing the department in Seattle, Clay Allen simply advised that all IWW agitators and organizers be interned for the duration of the war, or, if aliens, that they be deported. He was not alone in this suggestion. U.S. attorney Francis Garrecht of Spokane reported ecstatically about the success of an internment policy implemented by military authorities in eastern Washington. Rather than turn IWW prisoners over to civilian officials as required by law, the military detained them in order to avoid habeas corpus proceedings and the release of their prisoners on bond. Conceding that this practice might have exceeded the power of the military and violated the letter of the law, he concluded, "The plan meets with public approval and covers the situation as nothing else can, and every effort should be made to continue in effect the arrangement here outlined."

While United States attorneys recommended stretching the law up to and beyond its breaking point, they also took delight in reporting elaborate "German plots." Their lack of evidence did not diminish the enthusiasm with which Justice Department attorneys in the West regularly informed attorney general Thomas Gregory of sinister German-IWW conspiracies. Clay Allen even urged the establishment of concentration-work camps in which to place IWW-German agents. Further illustrating his true beliefs, which were as much antilabor as anti-IWW, Allen asserted that the presence of federal troops in the Northwest served to quiet the legitimate (AFL) labor movement in Seattle, which, in his judgment, was "in the hands of men whose loyalty might properly be questioned."

That United States attorneys known for their intimate contacts with businessmen demanded repression of the IWW will occasion no surprise when it is realized that during these same years more moderate voices counseled similar action. Carleton Parker, a veteran West Coast labor reformer despised for his "radicalism" by some of the region's most prominent employers, proposed policies remarkably like those of attorneys Garrecht and Allen.

The Western businessman's battle against the IWW won other unexpected allies. Not only did federal attorneys and local labor reformers join the fight, but so did AFL affiliates. Wherever the IWW struck, AFL leaders such as Charles Moyer of the International Union of Mine, Mill and Smelter Workers (IUMMSW) and J. G. Brown of the Brotherhood of Timber Workers endorsed the action of workers who crossed picket lines or accepted jobs vacated by IWW strikers.

Employers not only pleaded for federal intervention, but also beseeched local and state officials to repress the IWW. At those levels business pleas received a more prompt reaction. In state after state, sheriffs, mayors, governors, committees of national defense, and other public organizations allied with employers to fight the IWW's threat. The states of Minnesota and Idaho, to cite but two examples, enacted so-called criminal syndicalism laws, which in effect outlawed IWW membership.

Washington State's council of defense, representing business, organized labor (meaning the AFL), and the public (whatever that meant), waged a multifaceted struggle against the IWW. It searched the state for evidence of disloyalty, it took into custody "irresponsible," "seditious," and "disloyal" IWW ringleaders, and it investigated the causes of labor disturbances. Where the state's power proved insufficient to the occasion, it unhesitatingly called for federal troops.

In wartime, state power generally proved incapable of coping with IWW activity. State militias, never noted for their efficiency, became unavailable in the summer of 1917, as they were federalized. Thus, governors planning to resort to military repression had to turn to Washington for aid. Montana's governor was the first to request and use federal troops to break an IWW strike, doing so on April 21 in the case of a labor dispute on the Great Northern Railroad at Eureka, Montana. Soon thereafter Arizona's chief executive requested similar assistance in order to control the strikes in his state's copper mines, and early in June Washington governor Ernest Lister asked the War Department for troops to patrol the Yakima Valley's farms and irrigation systems. In the end, state officials agreed with businessmen and United States attorneys that only federal power was capable of suppressing the IWW.

Until the federal government could be persuaded to act decisively against the IWW, many employers and private citizens preferred to act on their own. Loyalty leagues, citizens' alliances, and vigilante organizations cropped up in every Western community blighted by labor conflict.

Before America formally entered the war, the IWW felt the sting of this new generation of vigilantes. State militiamen and "off-duty" United States Marines raided IWW headquarters in Kansas City on April 3, 1917, destroying organization papers and office furnishings, as Kansas City's police placidly watched and then departed in company with the soldiers.

Kansas City marked only the beginning of vigilante activity. On May 30, IWW headquarters in Detroit had a similar visitation; on June 16, soldiers and sailors attacked Seattle headquarters. No Wobbly knew where or when vigilantes would strike next. Chicago headquarters had even been invaded secretly the night of May 24, and a number of dictaphone records, rolls of correspondence, and other items were stolen.

In order to protect itself from vigilante "justice," the IWW itself turned for assistance to federal authorities. Haywood sent two general executive board members and IWW attorney Fred Moore to Washington to lay the IWW's claim for justice before the president and the Justice Department. This was another of the Wobblies' wartime decisions that staggers the imagination. Having declared the war a capitalist bloodbath caused by businessmen eager to create an American empire, how could the IWW have expected sympathy from Woodrow Wilson, who had decided to sacrifice American lives to make the world safe for democracy, a goal Wobblies looked on with derision? Why, then, did Haywood turn to Washington to secure the IWW against vigilantism? Only one explanation seems plausible: Wobblies obviously had more faith in American society's commitment to fair play and to due process than their own rhetoric allowed. Believing themselves innocent of sedition, subversion, and espionage, Wobblies sought protection from the capitalist laws they condemned, the public officials they ridiculed, and the president they despised. Such faith would ultimately prove misplaced.

Left defenseless by public officials, Wobblies fell easy victim to vigilante justice. In the Midwestern wheat belt, commercial clubs provided Wobblies foolish enough to enter town a warm welcome. Beaten, arrested, jailed, tarred and feathered, the Wobbly harvester found refuge only at work among farmers more sympathetic to him than town dwellers.

Most grain-belt terrorism was spontaneous and sporadic, but that which occurred in the copper regions of Arizona and Montana was organized, continuous, and brutal. Unable at first to win quick federal repression of the IWW, copper interests decided, in the words of an Arizona vigilante, that "the citizens will have to handle the situation if the government will not." How Western citizens planned to handle the situation soon became evident.

Jerome, Arizona, had been one of the first areas in the state affected by IWW and IUMMSW strikes. There Wobblies fought AFL men, private detectives infiltrated the IWW local, and Justice Department agents observed everybody. Predictably, copper production lagged. Complicated by interunion rivalry, the labor problem in Jerome seemed beyond repair. Mine owners and local businessmen thus decided to alter the situation. On July 3, 1917, they organized the Jerome Loyalty League, which armed its members and threatened to arrest any individual who interfered with copper production. A week later the league went into action. "There was a picturesque occurrence at Jerome on July 10," the *Outlook* commented, "when hundreds of miners and other citizens, some with rifles and others with pick handles, cleared the town of the agitators whom they considered undesirable." So thorough indeed was this deportation of Jerome's "undesirables" that several private detectives were caught in the dragnet and banished to the California desert with the Wobblies.

The IWW, of course, protested. Its spokesmen in Jerome demanded that the federal government protect the constitutional right of copper miners to work and live where they desired. Instead of investigating the Loyalty League's action, however, the Justice Department probed the IWW deportees, seeking evidence to indict them on criminal charges.

Given the green light by a favorable public response to the Jerome deportations and the unwillingness of federal authorities to intervene on behalf of the deportees, Arizona's vigilantes attacked elsewhere. The town of Bisbee, like Jerome, had had its copper production tied up by industrial conflict. Again like Jerome, Bisbee had its share of private detectives and Justice Department agents. But in Bisbee, unlike Jerome, the copper miners, almost to a man, belonged to an IWW local, thus compounding the industrial impasse.

Since Bisbee's miners had walked out on June 28, county sheriff Harry Wheeler, an ex–Rough Rider, and governor Thomas Campbell had requested federal troops to break the strike. The War Department, however, offered only an observer, Lieutenant Colonel James J. Hornbrook, who reported "no violence or disorder" in Bisbee. Mine operators, local businessmen, and county officials assessed the problem quite differently. They saw violence, German gold, and treason everywhere.

To defend national security from what he took to be a clear and present danger, on the night of July 11 Wheeler set into operation a carefully contrived conspiracy. The sheriff imposed military discipline on a select group of so-called posse captains and deputized almost two thousand other anti-IWW townsmen. So thorough was the organization that, with the cooperation of the telephone, telegraph, and railroad companies, the conspirators shut Bisbee off from the outside world. No messages could reach or leave the city without the permission of Wheeler or one of his confidants. Thus prepared, at dawn on July 12 Wheeler's two thousand deputies, wearing white armbands to distinguish them from their intended victims, began a vast Wobbly hunt. By 6:30 A.M. the deputies had corralled more than twelve hundred men, the majority of whom were allegedly Mexicans, enemy aliens, and IWW, German-financed subversives. The armed posse marched its captives to a central distribution point at the Warren ball park. There, with rifles and bayonets gleaming in the early morning sun, the vigilantes placed their prisoners on cattle cars (obligingly provided by the El Paso and Southwestern Railroad) for transportation beyond Arizona's borders.

Several days later Sheriff Wheeler, neither disclaiming responsibility nor making any excuse for his actions of July 12, piquantly described the results of Bisbee's deportation: On July 11, he said, the IWW members defied the mayor and marshal of Bisbee, on July 12 he got rid of them, and on July 14 Bisbee had more men working in the mines than it had had on July 1.

While the sheriff gloated, his victims found themselves stranded in the desert at Hermanas, New Mexico, unable to return to their homes and families in Bisbee, where armed vigilantes still threatened their lives. As involuntary refugees from America's class war, the Bisbee deportees located temporary refuge in an Army camp at Columbus, New Mexico.

At the New Mexico camp Army officers also took a careful census of the deportees. Instead of uncovering an army of Mexicans, Germans, and subversives, they discovered that almost half the deportees were American citizens, most of whom had registered for the draft; only a handful were technically enemy aliens (that is, German- or Austrian-born); Mexicans were an insignificant minority; and a substantial number of the refugees had wives, children, property, bank accounts, and even Liberty Bonds in Bisbee. Among the deportees were also businessmen, AFL members, and a Bisbee lawyer.

Protestors immediately appealed to Governor Campbell, the Justice Department, and President Wilson to restore the refugees' rights. Haywood was not alone in wiring President Wilson on July 13 to demand that Bisbee's "Prussianized" methods be curbed and that the deportees be supported adequately until they could be restored to their homes and families. Two Labor Department mediators, Cochise County's state representative, Arizona's AFL officials, and countless private citizens united in the plea for federal action against Bisbee's vigilantes.

Federal officials soon disabused the refugees and their sympathizers of any confidence in constitutional guarantees. Every request from the deportees for federal action was brushed aside. Except for perfunctory condemnations of Bisbee vigilantism by President Wilson and Governor Campbell, public officials did nothing to restore the refugees' basic civil rights. The Justice Department simply denied them federal relief, and assistant attorney general William Fitts contended that the refugees had absolute freedom of action: They could subsist on military rations or, unprotected by federal power, they could return to Arizona.

Failing to obtain relief by citing constitutional rights, the IWW resorted to rhetorical intimidation. On July 31 the deportees' leaders wired Haywood that "if action is not taken by Federal Government forthwith in sending deported men back to homes in Bisbee, men themselves will take action in returning with arms if necessary." Actually, on the preceding day Haywood had wired President Wilson to threaten a general strike of metal miners and harvest workers if the government did not return the deportees to their homes. In a final effort to gain relief, the deportees promised the president that they would dig copper if the federal government operated the nation's mines and smelters.

Protests, threats, and demands for nationalization of the copper industry availed the IWW naught. From the president the IWW could expect neither sympathy nor aid. Nor could it expect more from the Justice Department, which continued to deny that federal laws or constitutional rights had been contravened by Bisbee's vigilantes.

The deportees finally deserted Columbus in mid-September. Most avoided Bisbee, but a few, such as A. S. Embree, tried to return home, where the vigilantes expected him. They wasted no time in jailing the militant Wobbly, who from prison continued to demand his constitutional right to live with his wife and children where he chose—only to be told by the Justice Department that the federal government was impotent to act.

Yet federal officials at this time (mid-September) had indeed acted in the matter of the IWW—not, to be sure, in defense of the Wobblies' basic constitutional rights. Federal officials had instead initiated an intensive nationwide effort to suppress the IWW and break its strikes in the lumber, copper, and harvest districts.

The Bisbee deportation precipitated two major decisions by the Wilson administration. First, Haywood's threats of a general strike convinced Wilson and the Justice Department that "IWW-ism," not vigilantism, must be repressed. Second, the blatantly unconstitutional actions taken by Bisbee's vigilantes provoked protests from Gompers and other prominent American patriots that Wilson could not ignore. In order to mollify the protestors and to establish the federal government's commitment to harmonious industrial relations, Wilson appointed a special mediation commission to investigate wartime industrial conflicts and to suggest equitable remedies. The president's first decision would demonstrate the effectiveness of federal power when it determined to crush radical labor organizations; the second decision would illustrate the government's weakness when it attempted to protect the basic rights of powerless workers.

Among the matters Wilson's mediation commission chose to investigate was the Bisbee deportation. It found this inquiry no easy task, for as late as the last week in October 1917, when the commissioners planned to open their Bisbee inquiry, the city remained under vigilante law. Sheriff Wheeler refused to cooperate with the federal investigators, whose witnesses the sheriff's men intimidated or stopped from appearing at the hearings. Even after the commission concluded its hearings and recommended that American citizens be allowed to enter and leave Bisbee freely, Wheeler and his local vigilantes refused to heed the requests of federal authorities.

If Bisbee's citizens played fast and loose with the rights of Americans, Butte's would do them one better. In the Montana city, too, an IWW-endorsed strike had curtailed copper production, and Butte's mine owners, like those of Bisbee, had thus far unsuccessfully sought federal repression of the IWW.

Immediately after news of the Bisbee deportations reached Butte, Montana copper miners, fearing similar treatment at the hands of local vigilantes, asked congresswoman Jeannette Rankin to obtain federal protection for them. During the last two weeks in July Butte remained placid and no deportations occurred. But on July 30 Rankin received disturbing information. A Butte informant reported to her that the mine operators intended, with the help of private gunmen and United States soldiers, to deport the strike's leaders. In fact, the employers had only one leader in mind.

Frank Little had arrived in Butte just a few days earlier to promote IWW activities. Hobbling about on crutches as the result of a leg broken in an accident and enduring constant pain from a rupture sustained in a beating he received during an Arizona labor conflict, Little brought his own personal antiwar crusade to Montana. Heedless of his own comfort and safety, the IWW agitator advised his supporters to continue their strike for improved conditions of life and work and to join him in refusing to endorse an imperialistic, capitalistic war. Previously, most local Wobblies had avoided the use of antiwar propaganda, but Little, much to the disgust of Butte's establishment, espoused his antiwar gospel wherever an audience congregated. Little's prominence within the IWW, his wide following among hard-rock miners, and his blatantly "unpatriotic" speeches made him a choice target for vigilante justice.

On the night of July 31 Butte's vigilantes paid Frank Little an unexpected visit. Asleep in his room next door to the Independent Miners' Union hall, he awoke to find his bed surrounded by armed masked men. Not yet fully awake and still undressed, he was seized by six men and carried from his room. At 3 A.M. on August 1, after an auto ride during which they tortured Little, the vigilantes brought him to his destination: a railroad trestle on Butte's outskirts. Wasting neither sympathy nor time, the masked men placed a rope around Little's neck, fastened the rope end to the trestle, and sent the crippled, tortured Wobbly swinging off to eternity.

State and local authorities did nothing to apprehend Little's murderers, and federal officials lacked any basis for action, for in this case, at least, no federal law had been violated. Even if the federal government had had a basis for intervention, it seems unlikely that Butte's vigilantes would have suffered any more than their Bisbee counterparts. In fact, the lynchers won sympathy from prominent politicians and from much of the nation's press. Many Americans seconded the verdict of Montana's senior senator, H. L. Myers, who blamed Washington, not Butte, for Little's murder. "Had he been arrested and put in jail for his seditious and incendiary talks," the Senator wrote, "he would not have been lynched."

While vigilantes usurped the law, local officials looked the other way, and federal authorities maintained that they could not punish lynchers or deporters, the IWW miners in Butte, as had those in Arizona, stressed that they had consistently sought to avert disturbances and riots. "We are going to the bottom of this thing," an IWW attorney commented about the lynching of Little, "but in a legal way." From the morning of the lynching until Little's solemnly impressive funeral on August 5 (the largest ever held in Butte), Butte remained absolutely peaceful. Instead of retaliating against the vigilantes by taking up arms or accelerating its strike activities, the IWW simply proclaimed

Sunday, August 19, as a day of protest. Beseeching other labor organizations to join the IWW protest, Haywood announced his organization's new motto: "We never forget. Organize and act."

While Haywood called on his followers to organize and act, other Americans prepared to end once and for all the IWW's menace to industrial peace and the status quo. Throughout July 1917, as vigilantes hunted Wobblies, Western businessmen, congressmen, and governors insistently hammered upon the theme that only federal action could stamp out the IWW. The Westerners maintained that local legal repression and private vigilantism had proved ineffective in coping with subversion that was interstate in scope and directed from the IWW's Chicago headquarters. Whether in the halls of Congress, statehouses in Montana, Nevada, California, and elsewhere, or simply in letters to the Departments of Labor, Justice, and Interior, Westerners demanded a federal solution to the IWW problem.

By mid-July 1917 these efforts to thwart the IWW had reached a new level of organization and intensity. On July 13, after numerous private meetings, the governors of California, Arizona, Utah, Nevada, Idaho, Colorado, Oregon, and Wyoming adopted a common plan of action to control the Wobblies, which they communicated to President Wilson. The president, in turn, referred the Western governors' representative, George Bell, chairman of the California Commission on Immigration and Housing, to the Secretaries of Labor, Justice, and Interior, and to the Council of National Defense, the last of which heard Bell's plea for federal suppression of the IWW. At a July 18 session of the Council of National Defense, Bell presented the Western governors' anti-IWW scheme. Bell urged Washington officials to act decisively. No riots had yet erupted, he conceded, and no conspiracy had yet struck, yet he demanded preventive action: Punish Wobblies for what they planned to do, not for what they actually had done. Bell and the Western governors recommended that the federal government intern "subversive" Wobblies in concentration camps for the duration of the war, to be held incommunicado without recourse to the law and without publicity; that federal censorship remove all mention of the IWW, whatever the circumstances, from newspapers and magazines; and that after IWW leaders had been interned and censorship established, the federal government compel employers to improve working conditions during the war emergency.

When Washington failed to implement this program promptly, Bell and the governors flooded the White House with telegrams demanding immediate repression of the IWW and full censorship of all news dealing with labor affairs. Throughout July and August the president, the Labor Department, and the Justice Department came under increasing pressures from Western businessmen and politicians. At the end of August the governor of Montana appeared in Washington personally to present the case for suppression of the IWW.

Well before the end of August, however, federal officials were indeed planning "prompt and courageous" action against the IWW. Where Bell's proposals for concentration camps and national censorship won little favor in Washington, a lower-key campaign for repression of the IWW initiated in Minnesota received a warm response from Justice Department officials. Like the states to its west, Minnesota had been plagued by IWW threats to its three primary industries: iron mining, lumber, and agriculture. Although its Commission of Public Safety, directed by former governor John Lind, had largely stifled IWW agitation in the lumber and mining region, it had failed to curb IWW activities in the widely scattered and sparsely populated agricultural districts. To achieve this last goal, Lind worked with Hinton Clabaugh, head of the Justice Department's Chicago investigation office, in an effort to obtain evidence proving that the IWW had violated federal wartime statutes. Finally convinced that they had uncovered the necessary evidence, Lind, Clabaugh, and several of their associates met secretly in Chicago on July 26 to plan future action against the IWW. Like other IWW opponents, they would resort to federal power. Unlike Bell and the Western governors, Lind and Clabaugh recommended no illegal or extralegal procedures; indeed, they discovered adequate grounds for repression in the existing legal structure. Justice could prosecute Wobblies for violations of wartime statutes, Labor's immigration service could detain and then deport alien Wobblies, and the Post Office could deny mailing privileges to the IWW.

Few public figures of any influence pleaded the IWW's cause in Washington or sought to enlighten the Justice Department about the motives behind the drive to repress the IWW. Among the handful of dissenters, two stand out: George W. Anderson, United States attorney for Massachusetts, a sensible New England Yankee representing a state largely untouched by the IWW in 1917, and Burton K. Wheeler, then a young Montana U.S. attorney and aspiring politician, who would later become nationally famous as a progressive senator, vice-presidential candidate of the 1924 Progressive party, and isolationist critic of Franklin Roosevelt's foreign policies. Untroubled by the IWW threat, Anderson warned the Justice Department, "I think the Federal Government should be critically careful not only to keep within the law . . . but to see to it that it is not made an unwilling and perhaps unconscionable partner in one of the lowest and meanest mercenary tricks ever played in any aspect of the class struggle." When he learned about the proposals of Bell and the eight governors, Wheeler immediately contacted Attorney General Gregory. "At this time," he wrote, "I consider it proper to call to your attention that the requests [for press censorship] contained in the telegrams to the President are fathered by a desire of the interests, employing labor that may be more or less involved with the general unrest among their employees, to keep the true condition of affairs from the public at large."

Neither sensible suggestions nor reasoned reports about the IWW received much attention in Washington during the hysterical summer of 1917. Too busy battling the Kaiser's forces overseas, President Wilson and his closest advisers could not trouble themselves to probe deeply into the roots of Western labor conflict. Aware that IWW strikes interfered with war production, Wilson found it easy to believe reports that stressed that the IWW had struck the lumber and copper industries not to raise wages or improve working conditions but to obtain German gold and subvert the war effort. Therefore, the Wilson administration succumbed to the Western businessmen's anti-IWW crusade. In August 1917 the president appointed federal judge J. Harry Covington to undertake a special investigation of the IWW that might acquire evidence to be used to prosecute the Wobblies. Almost simultaneously, Assistant Attorney General Fitts assuaged New Mexico senator Albert Fall's anxieties about the IWW. "I must tell you," Fitts wrote, "that under the direction of the Attorney General something quite effective is under way with respect to the I.W.W. situation. I do not think you or any of your western friends will be disappointed if the results which we hope to obtain are achieved."

# 16

## Decision in Washington, 1917–18

No irate lumber baron, no apoplectic copper mine owner, and no outraged state official had to convince the federal government of the seriousness of the IWW menace to national security. Wartime production statistics indicated that IWW strikes had curtailed lumber and copper production and made it necessary for the federal government to act decisively against the Wobblies. Yet the *form* of that action divided the three federal departments most responsible for coping with the Wobblies. Although the Labor, War, and Justice Departments each had its own exclusive policy for restraining the Wobblies, all three eventually learned to work in harness. By the fall of 1917 they cooperated closely enough to deprive rank-and-file Wobblies of their leaders, separate the leaders from their followers, and supply Western employers with an ample and malleable labor force.

It is not surprising that no concrete policy for handling the IWW emerged in Washington in the spring of 1917. Although a firm, even domineering president when necessary, Woodrow Wilson had lost interest in domestic affairs. Preoccupied with waging an international war to make the world safe for democracy, busily involved in forging a diplomacy to preserve the peace after the war ended, he by and large left the home front in the hands of industrious subordinates.

The departments involved in the formulation of wartime labor policy were governed by their own particular requirements. The War Department's interest was clearest: to speed up the production of supplies for its troops in the field. Except for its secretary, Newton Baker, the War Department—staffed largely by professional military men or amateurs sympathetic to the military—proved most responsive to Western pressures to repress the IWW. The Labor Department's objectives were more complicated: Also wanting to break production bottlenecks caused by labor discontent, it was not noticeably amenable to the suggestions of Western employers. Unlike War, Labor intended that strikers return to the job only after employers improved working conditions and allowed their employees to join loyal, government-sanctioned AFL unions. The Justice Department's concern with wartime industrial conflict was more ambiguous than that of the War or Labor Department. Having no soldiers to supply, lacking any desire to promote the cause of strikers or of AFL unions, but empowered to investigate violations of federal law, Justice served, at least in theory, as handmaiden to War and Labor. But partly because of the links between United States attorneys and local businessmen, and partly because officials high in the Justice Department had intimate connections with the corporate business world, it often served the needs of American soldiers and Western employers more faithfully than it subscribed to the goals of federal labor mediators.

Even within the three departments, disunity and disagreement prevailed. Secretary of War Baker, for example, was much more objective than his underlings about the IWW menace, which sometimes caused military commanders stationed in the states to disregard War Department orders. A somewhat comparable situation prevailed in the Justice Department, where Attorney General Thomas Gregory and his closest advisers restrained the federal attorneys who served Western employers more scrupulously than they served the law. On the surface, Labor seemed to be the most united of the three departments; from Secretary of Labor William B. Wilson on down, department officials promoted the cause of labor and of the AFL. But here, too, some officials proved amenable to employers, and some department agents were more irrationally and bitterly hostile to the IWW than the worst of businessmen and generals.

For a time the moderating influence exerted by Baker, Gregory, and William B. Wilson contained the groups in Washington that sought outright repression of the IWW. But the pressures for more forceful federal intervention against the IWW proved irresistible.

Not employers' demands but Washington's own estimate of war requirements determined the extent and nature of federal involvement in labor disputes. Federal intervention against the IWW followed a singular and ultimately repressive course not because of the existence of an anti-IWW conspiracy, nor because of discriminatory action by federal officials. Unsure of what Wobblies wanted, aware that the IWW's propaganda called for revolution, and fearful that the IWW, whatever its actual motives, might actually sabotage the war effort, federal officials honestly believed they had only one recourse: to restrain the Wobblies from interfering with national security. Perhaps the best way of doing so was to call in troops as a preventive force.

By 1917 the War Department had had considerable experience in using soldiers to quell domestic labor disturbances. In 1877 federal troops had repressed strikes, riots, and demonstrations arising from that year's railroad labor conflicts. Fifteen years later federal soldiers went to northern Idaho to break a miners' strike, and in 1894, despite opposition from Illinois governor John Peter Altgeld, president Grover Cleveland dispatched federal troops to the Chicago area to crush the American Railway Union's Pullman boycott. When the occasion demanded, federal authorities could always justify the employment of troops to preserve the domestic peace. World War I seemed such an occasion.

Almost as soon as America entered the conflict, and before IWW strikes affected war production, federal troops were assigned to protect railroads and other "public utilities" (initially defined as dams, water works, and gas and electric plants) from enemy espionage. Not entirely by coincidence, the first railroads and utilities so protected were in Montana and Washington State—states farthest removed from the area of German espionage and closest to the scene of IWW activity. Little rationalization was required to broaden Washington's 1917 definition of public utilities or to define certain other Western industries as vital to the war effort.

By July 1917 federal troops patrolled the mining regions of Arizona and Montana, the farms of eastern Washington, and the timber districts of western Washington and Oregon. No labor violence had occurred in any of these districts, and no evidence of German espionage or intrigue could be uncovered. Nevertheless, federal officials acted to prevent what they thought *might* be done by Wobblies active in the West.

Although federal troops broke AFL strikes as well as those of the IWW in the course of military intervention, this was never Washington's intention. Yet professional military men frankly did not know how to react to labor disputes. Accustomed to strict discipline among their men and obedience to their orders, they expected labor unionists and strikers to behave with the regularity and good order exhibited by troops. When workers instead proved unruly and disobedient, when they picketed, protested, and demonstrated, soldiers intervened.

With Washington 2,000 miles away, those on the firing line—soldiers, employers, United States attorneys, and state and local officials—claimed to have knowledge of the real situation, indeed to understand, as Washington apparently could not, the danger the IWW posed to national security. Western attitudes seemed to permeate federal agents in the region and were used in many districts to rationalize the unsanctioned establishment of martial law, under which alleged Wobblies were apprehended and interned by military authorities who removed them from the jurisdiction of federal courts. Although the

Justice Department and the Secretary of War disowned responsibility for these tactics, their disclaimers did imprisoned Wobblies scant good.

On one occasion in that troubled summer of 1917, the IWW threatened to retaliate against military harassment. James Rowan, representing Western loggers and harvesters, called for a general strike to begin in Washington State on Monday, August 20, with the walkout to continue until the military released its class war prisoners. The Army wasted no time in answering Rowan's threat. On Sunday, August 19, federal troops moved into Spokane and raided the local IWW headquarters, where they seized Rowan and twenty-six other Wobblies, all of whom were later interned. Although the IWW then canceled its general strike, the soldiers continued to guard IWW headquarters and to arrest other Wobblies.

With military intervention thus hampering the IWW, strikes in the copper and lumber industries weakened. The IWW was put on the defensive, now devoting as much energy to eluding capture as to waging the class war.

Despite the restoration of apparent stability, troops remained on duty from 1917 to 1919, and in Butte until 1920. They had proved so effective in preserving the peace that Western governors, United States attorneys, and local employers hated to see them withdrawn. Every Westerner committed to smashing the IWW pleaded with the War Department to maintain some of its soldiers on stateside duty. But merely ensuring labor peace did not in itself eliminate the IWW's influence among Western workers, nor did it ensure that workers would be content. That responsibility fell to the Justice and Labor Departments.

By 1917 Wobblies were familiar problem children to the Justice Department. Since the IWW's creation in 1905, department officials had unsuccessfully sought to establish a basis for federal action against the Wobblies. Before 1917, however, federal investigators failed to uncover evidence sufficient to justify criminal prosecution of the Wobblies.

The war crisis presented the Justice Department with the legal basis on which to prosecute the IWW. A presidential proclamation of April 6 authorized the detention of enemy aliens, and federal officials believed that a considerable number of IWW leaders fit that category. Congressional legislation made interference with conscription and war-related industrial production a statutory crime. Rumors circulated in the nation's capital that German agents financed the IWW—ample grounds for prosecution even under prewar statutes. By July 11, 1917, Attorney General Gregory, himself now a believer in the allegations that German gold was subsidizing the IWW, decided to amass the evidence necessary to prosecute the Wobblies.

For several days Justice Department officials carefully weighed their options, determining precisely what evidence United States attorneys and special agents should accumulate against the Wobblies. Finally, on July 16 assistant attorney general Charles Warren, the well-known historian of the Supreme Court, prepared a circular for distribution to all United States attorneys, which Gregory then moderated in tone in order to shield the department from public criticism. On the following day the department mailed Warren's circular to all its attorneys and special agents. In this circular the department recommended that an extraordinary effort be undertaken to ascertain the future plans of all Wobblies, as well as the names, descriptions, and history of the IWW's leaders, the sources of its income, the nature of its expenses, copies of all IWW publications, and any data that might possibly incriminate the Wobblies. The circular also suggested that alien Germans belonging to the IWW and participating in unlawful acts be promptly apprehended, so that the department could obtain warrants for their detention under the president's April proclamation. To help the attorneys and agents get the evidence Washington desired, the circular directed their attention to Section 3 of Titles I and IV of the Espionage Act of June 15, 1917.

An intensive nationwide investigation of the IWW failed to disclose German gold in Wobbly pockets or provide evidence that either the IWW as an organization or its members individually had violated the 1917 conscription or espionage acts. "So far as this Department has been able to discover, after the most careful and painstaking investigation," William C. Fitts informed the United States attorney for Oregon on July 28, "the I.W.W. organization is a matter for the States themselves to control under such laws as they deem proper to enact and to enforce." Yet in closing his letter, Fitts in fact held out the glimmer of hope for future federal action against the IWW.

The summer of 1917 saw the optimistic hope for revolution that had exhilarated Wobblies at Chicago headquarters during the first part of the year turn to fear and foreboding. Looking out of the IWW office onto West Madison Street that July, Chaplin, Haywood, and other office workers watched detectives daily change guard. Whether going to a restaurant for a snack or walking home after a day at the office, Chaplin and Haywood were constantly trailed by supposedly unobtrusive secret agents. Early in August IWW headquarters learned of a Post Office Department ruling that declared the organization's Italian- and Hungarian-language newspapers, for unspecified reasons, unmailable.

Yet not even the most astute Wobbly realized the extent of the danger about to befall the IWW. Nor did they have to wait long to discover it. Less than a month after the Justice Department found no incriminating evidence against the IWW, the federal government satisfied the fondest wishes of Western employers and public officials. Without informing any Western governors of a change in Justice Department policy toward the IWW, Attorney General Gregory notified President Wilson on August 21, 1917, that his department, acting through the usual channels, planned to strike against the IWW. Only three days later, the Justice Department's investigators discovered what had eluded them since the war began: "evidence" that the Wobblies' objective was to cripple the national war effort. On the morning of September 5, 1917, Justice Department agents and local police officers in Chicago, Fresno, Seattle, Spokane—indeed, in every city where the IWW had an office and where influential Wobblies congregated—invaded local IWW headquarters and the homes of Wobbly officials. Operating under perhaps the broadest search warrants ever issued by the American judiciary, federal agents seized everything they could find: minute books, correspondence, typewriters, desks, rubber bands, paper clips, and (in Chicago) even Ralph Chaplin's love letters.

"The expected has happened," Haywood reported two days later, adding, "The situation . . . is not serious yet. . . . No one is under arrest at the present time and we expect to have the office open for our usual transactions of business very soon." Knowing full well that the Justice Department had failed to locate German gold or IWW-associated espionage in June or July, Haywood and other Wobblies believed that their organization's papers, then being avidly scanned by federal agents and attorneys, would serve only to establish more fully the IWW's innocence. On the very day that Haywood labeled the situation less than grave, the United States attorney for Philadelphia, writing to Gregory about what his agents had confiscated from local Wobbly offices, noted, "Our purpose . . . as I understand it, [is] very largely to put the I.W.W. out of business."

Which is precisely what the Justice Department intended. Federal investigators had a field day sorting through IWW papers. For thirteen years the Wobblies had been publishing and distributing radical, sometimes revolutionary, literature; its officers corresponded luridly with each other about sab-cats, firebombs, and emery dust in machines; antiwar and antigovernment tirades filled the organization's newspapers, pamphlets, and correspondence. Like the Bible, the IWW's basic gospels provided ample support for almost any position one might wish to adopt; they preached violence and nonviolence, sabotage destructive and constructive, antipatriotism and patriotism, war and peace. Not overly concerned about when the items might have been written or about their complete context, the Justice Department could prove through the Wobblies' own words that they interfered with eleven different congressional acts and presidential proclamations involving the war effort, their strikes consti-

234 We Shall Be All

tuted a criminal conspiracy to interfere with the constitutional rights of employers executing government contracts, they influenced other Wobblies to refuse to register for conscription and others to desert the armed forces, they conspired to cause insubordination in the armed forces, and they conspired to defraud certain employers. The Justice Department easily succeeded in persuading a Chicago federal grand jury to indict 166 IWW members on the five above counts, and also for conspiring with Frank Little (a dead man) and "diverse other persons" (unknown, thus unnamed) to violate federal law. Other federal grand juries returned similar indictments in Fresno, Sacramento, Wichita, and Omaha.

Curiously enough, the indicted Wobblies did not flee into exile, nor did they go into hiding. No secret cells were established, no conspiratorial plans were laid. Instead, on September 29, only a day after the Chicago grand jury handed down its indictments, IWW attorney George Vanderveer and General Secretary-Treasurer Haywood advised all indicted Wobblies to surrender themselves for arrest. Even Vincent St. John and Ben Williams, both of whom had left the organization before America went to war, turned themselves in. In a California construction camp one Wobbly did not discover until December that he was among the 166 indicted leaders. Learning the news from an IWW publication, he immediately notified the Justice Department, "Have a U.S. marshal call and I will be here as I have committed no crime and I do not care to be a fugitive."

Only an overwhelming belief in their own innocence and an unquestioning faith that the laws they denigrated would protect them could explain the behavior of IWW leaders in September 1917. Perhaps they felt that a fair public trial proving the IWW's innocence would end forever the threat of legal repression and lend the IWW respectability as a labor organization. They had previously won courtroom victories in Boise, Salem, Duluth, and Everett. Why not an even greater legal triumph now?

What Ralph Chaplin observed as the IWW prisoners left the federal building in Chicago before being transported to Cook County jail should have served as a precursor of the future and as a warning about the course a wartime trial of labor radicals would take. Across the street from the federal building a cheap North Clark Street movie theater's marquee proclaimed, "Special Feature—The Menace of the I.W.W.," and it announced in big, bright red letters, "The Red Viper." The marquee simply reflected what the nation's press, politicians, and many of its citizens had already established in their own minds: that the IWW was guilty not of dissent in wartime or of revolutionary propaganda-making, but of crime and treason.

The men who insisted that America remained "a land of laws" and who were charged with enforcing those laws considered Wobblies to be degenerate and, in fact, beyond the pale of the law. William Fitts, on loan to the Justice Department from a Wall Street law office, was notorious for his anti-IWW prejudices. Convinced at first that Germany subsidized the IWW (although he later conceded this to be false), Fitts considered all the IWW's activities to be nefarious. He cooperated in 1918 with Gompers and with Ralph Easley, former National Civic Federation leader, to mount a nation-wide propaganda campaign among organized workers to enlighten them about the IWW's un-American, immoral, and illegitimate behavior. Nine months after the Justice Department began to repress the IWW firmly, Fitts thought further suppression in order. Writing to a former Washington State congressman, he commented, "Fear is the only force that will keep the wretches in order."

Had putting the IWW out of business and "keeping the wretches in order" been the only aim of federal authorities in 1917, their job would have been manageable. It took no great skill to imprison organization leaders, close down IWW presses, deny use of the mail to Wobblies, detain and deport aliens, or keep radical labor under control. But suppression of an organization could not transform discontented workers into efficient laborers. While military and legal repression of the IWW stifled the outward manifestations of labor discontent, it failed to overcome deep-seated working-class frustration and basic dissatisfaction with wages and working conditions. In order to end labor discontent in the West, the federal government ultimately turned to the Labor Department, the AFL, and a special presidential mediation commission.

From the start of the wartime labor troubles, the Labor Department had approached the IWW problem with caution and common sense. Though as hostile to IWW influence and gains as any other federal agency, Labor personnel sensibly took the view that discontent among the workers arose from economic and social exploitation, not from Wobbly agitation.

Cooperating closely with Gompers and the leadership of the AFL, Secretary of Labor Wilson and his colleagues sought to reach the roots of labor discontent. On August 10, 1917, Gompers stated the problem bluntly for President Wilson: Either the government and Western employers would bargain with representatives of the bona fide organized, constructive labor movement, or they would have to confront the "so-called" IWW. If lumbermen and mine operators negotiated with the AFL, Gompers and the Labor Department promised that the IWW would disappear.

Throughout July 1917 the Labor Department unsuccessfully attempted to bring together Western lumbermen and AFL officials. The Labor Department had influential allies. The Washington State Council of National Defense shared its assessment of the IWW problem. Shaped largely by reformer Carleton Parker, council labor policies aimed at separating rank-and-file lumber workers from their IWW leaders. This could be done, the council's members reasoned, by establishing the eight-hour day and greater job security in the lumber industry. When employers refused to go along with its recommendations, the council urged President Wilson to pressure lumbermen in the interest of patriotism to offer an equitable settlement to their employees.

Although the president remained aloof from domestic labor conflict, the Council of National Defense on August 10 authorized Secretaries Baker and Wilson to urge lumbermen to do their nation a patriotic service by operating their industry at peak efficiency, a condition that could be reached only by bargaining with legitimate (read: AFL) labor unions and by granting the eight-hour day. But the lumbermen were unable to conceive of the eight-hour day as a patriotic obligation, particularly when the Southern lumber industry continued to operate on a longer workday. Destroy the IWW, lumbermen countered, and spruce production would reach, indeed surpass, normal levels.

Yet when the IWW leaders were indicted and imprisoned, spruce production still failed to satisfy wartime needs. By October, however, the lumber production problem was passing out of the hands of the Labor Department and into those of the military. As early as May 1917 General John "Black Jack" Pershing, sharing the lumbermen's assumption that Western labor discontent had been fomented by the Kaiser's agents within the IWW, had delegated a junior officer to survey labor conditions in the spruce industry. That officer, Lieutenant Colonel Brice P. Disque, was to play a singular role in the fall of 1917 and the following spring in winning the eight-hour day for lumber workers. Not a career officer, Disque at first acted like a typical Progressive-era social reformer, one perceptibly influenced by Carleton Parker and Samuel Gompers. The colonel proved so satisfactory to Gompers that the AFL president informed his West Coast associates that Disque would be sympathetic to organizing mill and forest workers into AFL affiliates. On October 16, when Gompers wrote this, he had good reason for his optimism.

Before departing for the West Coast to meet with lumbermen, Disque had obtained most of his knowledge about labor affairs from Parker, Gompers, Walter Lippmann, and Felix Frankfurter. These influential reformers reinforced the colonel's own belief that the IWW could best be curbed by improving working conditions in the lumber industry.

Once on the West Coast among the lumbermen whom he was supposed to cajole into granting improved working conditions, Disque underwent a slight but significant transformation. More and more he came to share employers' prejudices against organized labor, AFL as well as IWW. Away from Gompers's influence, Disque lost interest in helping the AFL to organize the lumber industry in order to preserve labor peace and increase production. As a result of this change in his attitude, the labor situation in the Northwest remained tense.

Like the IWW, the AFL, the Labor Department, and the War Department before him, it appeared Disque had failed to win the eight-hour day or restore labor tranquillity. But he had succeeded, unlike the others, in allaying the fears of lumbermen, who distrusted most federal officials, whom they accused of being reformers and radicals. The same employers who steadfastly protested Washington's establishment of an eight-hour day consented to allow the colonel leeway to resolve all labor issues, including the eight-hour day.

When Disque finished rationalizing lumber industry labor practices, neither the AFL nor the IWW threatened employers' economic power. In recompense for giving their employees the eight-hour day, uniform wages, and decent bed and board, employers obtained a more docile labor force. Disque closed the woods to labor organizers and trade union members by organizing a company union—the Loyal Legion of Loggers and Lumbermen (or, as it was called, the 4Ls)—with practically compulsory membership and a no-strike policy. Meanwhile, his junior officers and troops acted as recruiters for the 4Ls and as military police empowered to harry Wobblies and AFL organizers out of the forests.

What originated in wartime as an emergency program formulated by the Labor Department and the social reformers within its orbit to improve conditions in the lumber industry and to supplant the IWW with the AFL became, in the hands of an Army officer, a plain, old-fashioned union-busting arrangement. Disque taught employers a valuable lesson some had been unable to learn by themselves: that granting workers the shadow of industrial democracy without the substance kept them contented and productive.

Forced in the end to defer to the military in coping with the IWW in the Northwest, the Labor Department and its reform allies intended to do better in the Southwest. Since the eruption of the copper strikes in Arizona, the Labor Department had fought to root the IWW out of the region by winning higher wages and union (AFL) recognition for the copper miners. Mine operators, of course, were no more amenable than lumbermen to federal labor conciliation. To every Labor Department attempt to meliorate the copper industry's labor strife, employers asserted that "we must have a free hand in the employment of our men and authority in the direction of work."

Gompers planned to rescue federal officials from their predicament. He devised a scheme that, so he thought, would spread industrial democracy domestically and simultaneously increase copper production. On August 22, responding to a query from Newton Baker, Gompers suggested that the Council of National Defense eliminate the IWW by providing new federally sanctioned labor agencies to study and adjust industrial disputes. At the end of the month the Council of National Defense, under intense pressure from Gompers, Baker, and President Wilson, resolved to appoint a special commission to investigate the deportation of workers from their homes.

What ostensibly began as an investigation of illegal deportations became under Secretary Wilson's astute management an opportunity to mediate the substantive issues causing labor discontent in the West, particularly in industries threatened by the IWW. To cloak the true purpose of the commission, which was primarily to curb the Wobblies, Secretary Wilson suggested that it also investigate disputes not related to the IWW. Moving ahead rapidly on his own, on August 31 the Labor Secretary presented President Wilson with recommended appointees to a five-man commission. He suggested two businessmen—J. L. Spangler, a Pennsylvania Dutch coal mine operator with a reputation for fair dealing with the United Mine Workers, and Verner Z. Reed, a Colorado entrepreneur of unusually liberal and catholic leanings (he was also a liberal Catholic)—and two trade unionists, John E. Walker, a former United Mine Workers' official, then president of the Illinois Federation of Labor and a moderate socialist, and E. P. Marsh, a more conservative unionist and president of the Washington State Federation of Labor. Secretary Wilson himself would be the fifth commission member, and he would serve as chairman. More important than any of the commission members, however, was the man Wilson selected as his secretary: Felix Frankfurter.

Then a young Harvard Law School professor serving his first tour of duty in Washington as a junior Labor Department official, Frankfurter lost no time in establishing his own preeminence among the commission appointees. Just as thirty years later he would lecture his colleagues on the Supreme Court and lesser lawyers about the subtleties of the American Constitution and the Supreme Court's role in interpreting it, in October 1917 Frankfurter taught President Wilson's mediators, including the Secretary of Labor, the refinements of industrial conciliation and the means of destroying the IWW.

Frankfurter accepted the Gompers–William B. Wilson–Newton Baker assessment of wartime industrial conflicts involving the IWW. Like them, he believed that labor conflict arose from tangible grievances, not from German or IWW intrigues; like others, he, too, maintained that the IWW must be curbed. Consequently, Frankfurter urged the five presidential mediators to undertake an in-depth investigation of Arizona copper miners' grievances, to establish conciliation machinery to abolish the actual grievances, to impress upon employers their responsibility to compromise with employees in the interest of national security, and to devote particular attention to convincing antiwar workers that their labor could play an essential part not only in winning the war and spreading democracy abroad but also in establishing industrial justice at home.

Officially appointed by the president on September 19, 1917, the mediation commission operated on the basis of Frankfurter's guidelines. Because it intended to eliminate IWW spokesmen as partners in any ensuing labor agreements with the mine owners, AFL and International Union of Mine, Mill and Smelter Workers (IUMMSW) affiliates in Arizona readily accepted commission recommendations. Although the president declared the Wobblies to be illegitimate and un-American trade unionists, employers remained as recalcitrant as ever about bargaining with workers. Even though the commission now offered to settle disputes with government-sanctioned AFL unions, operators declined to negotiate with labor.

Frankfurter, however, came to his elders' rescue. The young attorney's influential contacts proved remarkable in their variety and power. Not only did he have entry to the world of labor and social reform, but his connections extended to Wall Street financiers, War Department bureaucrats, foreign diplomats, and Bernard Baruch, director of the war production effort. When Arizona's mine managers balked at commission proposals, Frankfurter used his personal influence to the fullest extent. Writing to a Wall Street friend, Sam Lewisohn, an owner of considerable mining property in Arizona, Frankfurter urged Lewisohn to instruct his mine managers to abide by commission recommendations concerning the labor question. To his friends in the British Embassy, Frankfurter suggested pressure on Scottish capitalists with copper mine interests in America to compromise on the labor issue. He resorted to acquaintances in the Justice and War departments for authority to threaten recalcitrant mine operators and owners with the seizure of their properties.

As a result of Frankfurter's private initiatives, on October 20 the commission succeeded in settling the labor dispute in the Globe-Miami district; subsequently it arranged similar settlements for the Clifton-Morenci and Warren districts. All three settlements disposed of the IWW by establishing the principle that industrial conflict must be suspended for the duration of the war and that copper production must assume priority over workers' wages or employers' profits. Employers consented to deal with miners' grievance committees elected secretly and to bargain with union representatives when local grievance procedures failed to settle disputes. Employers nevertheless retained open-shop conditions and won federal support for their wage policies, which previously had been endorsed by the War Industries Board. Both parties to the commission's settlement consented to binding arbitration by Department of Labor agents if labor grievances could not be adjusted locally. A simple procedure eliminated the Wobblies from the terms of the agreement: Any employee who since the copper strike had uttered comments disloyal to the United States or who belonged to an organization that refused to recognize contractual obligations (meaning the IWW) was declared ineligible for reemployment in the mines.

This agreement should have occasioned considerable rejoicing among mine owners and managers, for it terminated the IWW menace to copper production. But employer cooperation proved more apparent than real. Labor Department mediators promptly discovered that an immense number of miners had been designated as disloyal or as Wobblies, which in either event rendered them ineligible for reemployment. In addition, wherever possible the mine operators purged AFL members as well as Wobblies, rejected out of hand consideration of their employees' grievances, subverted the elected grievance committees, and refused to adjust wages to the cost of living.

In response to this continued employer autocracy, the IWW reemerged in Arizona. The federal government suddenly found itself face to face with another Wobbly labor offensive. Reporting on the Arizona labor situation in March 1918, Labor Department conciliator Hywel Davies warned the Labor Department that a spirit of disloyalty and anarchy was festering in Arizona, awaiting only the proper psychological moment to erupt. "The industrial mass is not disloyal," he reported, "but idleness furnishes the . . . opportunity for the anarchist to develop his deviltry." Hence, a Labor Department official sent to Arizona to mediate and to conciliate advised his Washington superiors to allow the Justice Department to deport alien Wobblies and to prosecute "disloyal" citizens. After the IWW had been totally suppressed, Davies suggested, then the Labor Department together with Gompers could flood Arizona with AFL organizers and Labor Department agents, who would recruit workers into loyal trade unions that were satisfactory to employers.

Events in Butte demonstrated abundantly that federal labor policies were governed as much by anxiety about the IWW as by an objective interest in improving working conditions and in establishing industrial justice. Montana's labor problems differed in no essential respect from Arizona's. Thus the factors that had brought Frankfurter and his commission associates to Arizona's copper districts should have led them to Butte, where the Metal Mine Workers' Union and congresswoman Jeannette Rankin pleaded for a mediation commission investigation of labor conditions. But the Butte strike had been broken by the time the mediation commission began its operation. Copper production in Montana was fast returning to normal, and a Labor Department conciliator reported on November 20, 1917, "There is not much left of the Butte Metal Miners' Union." By December, Frankfurter learned from Eugene Meyer of the War Industries Board that Butte's operating capacity seemed satisfactory. Unable to interest the federal government in an investigation of labor conditions once production had returned to normal, the Metal Mine Workers' Union on December 20, 1917, officially ended its walkout.

The IWW thus proved an excellent barometer of federal interest in Western working conditions. When IWW membership flourished and IWW strikes crippled full production, federal concern with decent working conditions and industrial justice rose sharply. When IWW membership declined and its ability to strike collapsed, federal interest in decent treatment for workers fell precipitously.

It was to be expected, then, that when the IWW reawakened in Butte in the spring of 1918, federal concern about the city's working conditions also came to life. Immediately upon news that a reorganized Metal Mine Workers' Independent Union, dominated by Wobblies and their fellow travelers, in June 1918 had petitioned the National War Labor Board for a hearing on working and union conditions in Butte, Frankfurter, the Labor Department, and Hywel Davies went to work. At Frankfurter's suggestion, Davies traveled to Montana. Before arriving in Butte, he wired Frankfurter, "The imperative need of the hour is action by the A. F. of L. President Gompers understands the whole trouble.' Once in Montana, Davies discovered conditions much as he had just left them in Arizona. Employer autocracy and the IUMMSW's debilitated condition had opened the breach for an IWW resurgence. Montana's Wobblies, according to Davies, also spread disloyalty and anarchy. He boiled the Butte problem down to a single question: "Shall the legitimate or the illegitimate labor union dominate?" His preferences were clear. "An outlaw organization, camouflaging under another name [i.e., the IWW in Butte], can be eliminated," Davies prescribed, "only when the opportunity for a more decent relationship is provided, and it is in this particular case the joint duty of the Employers to join hands with the A. F. of L."

Working with Gompers, accommodating Butte's mine owners, and maintaining federal troops on duty in Montana enabled federal authorities to hold the IWW on a tight rein. Wherever and whenever the IWW threatened war production in 1917 and 1918, the federal government reacted with a combination of military repression, judicial prosecution, and industrial conciliation. By the end of 1917 rank-and-file Wobblies as well as their leaders were in an unenviable predicament. Remaining loyal to their organization and its objectives, they courted deportation or arrest. Walking out on strike, even without a commitment to revolutionary rhetoric or unmotivated by opposition to the war effort, they found themselves declared illegitimate trade unionists and thus ineligible for reemployment under improved working conditions. Surrendering their red cards and enrolling in the AFL, rank-and-file Wobblies learned that AFL membership conferred few benefits and weak federal guardianship, except when IWW activities increased. Knowing neither which way to go nor precisely what to do, Wobblies no longer could turn to experienced leaders for guidance. By December 1917 every first-line IWW leader was behind bars and restricted, by Post Office Department regulations and Justice Department surveillance, from communication with members on the outside.

No wonder at the beginning of 1918 the IWW faced extinction. Wobblies had always expected to meet resistance from employers and from the AFL; they had learned to live with it. A full-scale federal anti-IWW crusade was something else, especially when it offered carrots as it struck with sticks.

# 17

## Courtroom Charades, 1918–19

On April 1, 1918, in an impressive white marble federal courthouse in Chicago, Judge Kenesaw Mountain Landis, who would later become famous in the aftermath of the 1919 Black Sox scandal as baseball's first commissioner, ascended the bench to inaugurate the initial wartime trial of the Wobblies. In the courtroom that day was a young reporter and radical who had just returned from Russia, where he had witnessed the Bolshevik Revolution and written *Ten Days That Shook the World,* the classic journalistic account of that shattering event. Since his participation in the 1913 Paterson strike shortly after his graduation from Harvard College, John Reed had grown increasingly radical, until he crowned his intellectual journey to the left with firsthand reports of the Bolshevik Revolution and with membership in the newly established American Communist party (1919). In Chicago to report the IWW trial for left-wing American publications, Reed hoped to do as well by the Wobblies as he had done by the Bolsheviks.

Reed's dispatches from Chicago transformed the impending courtroom struggle into an American folk myth. He described Judge Landis thus: "Small on the huge bench sits a wasted man with untidy white hair, an emaciated, face in which two burning eyes are set like jewels, parchment-like skin split by a crack for a mouth the face of Andrew Jackson three years dead." Turning to the defendants, Reed wrote, "I doubt if ever in history there has been a sight just like them. One hundred and one lumberjacks, harvest hands, miners, editors . . . who believe the wealth of the world belongs to him who creates it . . . the outdoor men, hardrock blasters, tree-fellers, wheat-binders, longshoremen, the boys who do the strong work of the world. . . . To me, fresh from Russia, the scene was strangely familiar. . . . The IWW trial . . . looked like a meeting of the Central Executive Committee of the All-Russian Soviet of Workers and Deputies in Petrograd!"

Reed's likening of the Wobblies to Russia's successful revolutionaries only worsened their public image. Given Americans' increasing paranoia about bolshevism, the Wobblies on trial in Chicago would become the first victims of the Great Red Scare that began with the repression of the IWW in 1917 and culminated in attorney general A. Mitchell Palmer's 1919 raids.

As for the defendants, their hopes for an acquittal were simply pipe dreams. How could they expect to receive justice at the hands of citizens who applauded vigilantes and lynchers? Yet the prosecution and the defense pursued their mutual legal charades in Judge Landis's courtroom, although the outcome of the trial had been largely predetermined by the ubiquitous environment of public hysteria and by the pretrial strategies of the contenders.

Almost six months elapsed between the September 1917 raids on IWW headquarters and the actual trial, which opened on April 1, 1918. During that period the defenders and the prosecutors devised the tactics and strategy that shaped the course of the entire legal struggle not only in Chicago but also in courtrooms in Sacramento, Wichita, and Omaha.

Not all the indicted Wobblies agreed on a course of legal action. Most outspoken among the dissenters was Elizabeth Gurley Flynn, who, sometime between the September raids and her indictment, severed her connection with the IWW. Flynn maintained that since the federal government insisted on observing the mechanics of due process, the IWW should take advantage of the prosecution's fairness. She asserted that the government could not substantiate its blanket indictment of 166 Wobblies; after all, she noted, it was incredible that the prosecution had ample evidence to present against each defendant charged with having committed a hundred separate crimes. Flynn suggested that each defendant move for a severance of his case (i.e., request a separate trial), thus, through a nationwide series of pretrial proceedings, stymieing the prosecution. Indeed Flynn herself, with Carlo Tresca, Arturo Giovannitti, and Joseph Ettor, moved for severance.

Logic buttressed Flynn's recommendations. At least twenty-two of the defendants originally indicted in Chicago were either dead, no longer members of the IWW (some had never formally belonged in the first place), inactive, or in military service. Each of these (or their attorneys) certainly had adequate grounds to demand a dismissal or, at a minimum, a severance. For the remaining defendants separate trials might have increased the likelihood they would be judged on their own individual guilt or innocence, and not on the basis of guilt by association with the feared Haywood and the dead Frank Little.

Although logic favored Flynn's legal strategy, certain inescapable realities suggested a different course. First, the IWW lacked the legal and financial resources to conduct a battery of individual cases, whereas the federal government had unlimited resources. Second, most Wobblies lacked the influential and respectable friends whom Flynn and her associates claimed as sympathizers. Third, the defendants saw their trial as a matter of conscience, not crime; certain that they had committed no criminal acts and that they had been indicted for their beliefs, which they refused to recant, they chose to stand together as a matter of principle.

Lacking the options available to Flynn, the remaining IWW defendants pursued what had for them become customary legal defense procedures. Before the Chicago federal grand jury returned indictments against the arrested Wobblies, Haywood's office formed a general defense committee composed of members with previous experience in managing legal matters. The general office also proposed a voluntary fifty-cent membership assessment for defense work, as well as the establishment of local defense committees to operate in conjunction with the national one. In November 1917 the general executive board replaced *Solidarity* with the *Defense News Bulletin,* a journal devoted primarily to the IWW's legal campaign, which was published regularly until July 1918, when it was suspended. Haywood lost no time in obtaining competent legal assistance. Fortunately, he did not have far to seek; George Vanderveer, famous among Wobblies for his defense of the Everett prisoners and for his efforts on behalf of Seattle's disinherited (which gained him his reputation as "Counsel for the Damned"), took charge of the legal defense.

Although intensified wartime hysteria boded ill for the Wobblies, they retained several important friends. Most influential, though least useful, among the IWW's allies was Frank Walsh, who, with William Howard Taft, was shortly to become cochairman of the National War Labor Board. Early in November Haywood had asked Walsh for assistance in creating a nonpartisan defense league to work in conjunction with the IWW's own committees. However sympathetic Walsh was to the Wobblies—and that he was sympathetic there can be no doubt—his official ties to the Wilson administration and his desire to maintain them militated against his cooperating publicly with the IWW. But Walsh offered Haywood and Vanderveer confidential advice and put them in contact with helpful sympathizers. Foremost among this latter group was Roger Baldwin, founder of the National Civil Liberties Bureau, who, throughout February 1918, pleaded with President Wilson, Labor Secretary Wilson, and War Secretary Baker to drop the prosecutions of the Wobblies as a matter of expediency as well as in the interests of civil liberties. Louis F. Post, an official in the Labor Department's Immigration and Naturalization Service and also publisher of *The Public,* a reformist journal, defended the Wobblies' civil liberties both in the pages of his publication and in Washington. Alexander Lanier, a captain in military intelligence, shared Baldwin's and Post's reservations about the prosecutions. In a long, carefully reasoned letter to President Wilson (later published in *The New Republic*), Lanier point by point destroyed the government's entire legal case against the IWW.

Defense efforts notwithstanding, many Wobblies expected the worst. Writing from his jail cell in Tombstone, Arizona, A. S. Embree acknowledged that "our men can be killed and jailed." Writing to a Wobbly friend from Chicago's Cook County jail, James Rowan confessed, "Of course we expect nothing else than to be jailed for taking part in a strike . . . for we know that a rebellious slave is the worst criminal in the eyes of the master." At the same time, these men were not altogether without optimism  Finding solace in the successful November Revolution in Russia, Rowan remarked, "What they can do in Russia, we can do in this 'Land of the Free.'" More philosophically, Embree noted, "The end in view is well worth striving for, but in the struggle itself lies the happiness of the fighter." Wobblies indeed acted on the prescription of the Italian communist Antonio Gramsci: "Pessimism of the Intelligence. Optimism of the Will."

Although the defendants themselves were pessimistic about their legal fate, Vanderveer labored with unabated optimism to defend them. Fully expecting to win dismissal of the Chicago indictments before the trial opened, during arraignment in December he argued that the Justice Department's evidence had been seized illegally, in violation of the First and Fourth Amendments to the Constitution, and hence that the indictments should be quashed. His legal points overruled, Vanderveer resorted to different arguments with George Creel and President Wilson. He reminded both men that several of the Chicago defendants had previously severed their connections with the IWW, while others had never been members in the first place. He suggested that the government's prosecution of the IWW was assumed throughout the world of labor to be an attack on labor's right to organize, and that unless the defendants were released and working conditions improved, industrial unrest would intensify. This line of argument, however, proved equally unrewarding. Nevertheless, Vanderveer still expected victory when the case came to trial. Investigation had convinced him that none of the four counts in the indictment would stand up in court, for never had the IWW as an organization opposed conscription, and neither had any Wobblies refused conscription on organizational grounds, nor been found guilty of insubordination while in the armed services. The industrial counts seemed even more ludicrous to Vanderveer, who felt certain that he could prove to a jury's satisfaction that IWW strikes were undertaken solely to improve working conditions, never to interfere with the war effort.

But Vanderveer's optimistic assessment ignored the intense pressures to destroy the IWW generated by Western businessmen and the mass popular war hysteria. It was unlikely that a jury composed of ordinary American citizens—the type even then sanctioning vigilante action against the Wobblies—would acquit alleged traitors. The facts of life in wartime America simply made Vanderveer's optimism baseless.

In preparing its case against the IWW, the Justice Department left little to chance. Ostensibly, Charles F. Clyne, federal attorney for the Northern Illinois District, was handling the prosecution, but in fact the department turned the case over to three special prosecutors. Of the three, Frank K. Nebeker and William C. Fitts had been prominent corporation attorneys in peacetime, Nebeker for mining and smelting enterprises in the Mountain States and Fitts as a partner in an influential Wall Street law firm. When Clyne eventually proved unable to cope with Vanderveer in open court, Nebeker was put in command of the trial.

The Justice Department placed every conceivable roadblock in the IWW's path. While pressing the case against the Chicago defendants, the government made further IWW arrests in Wichita, Omaha, and Sacramento. This effectively immobilized the defense operations of second- and third-line IWW leaders and added to the newspaper coverage that reinforced the popular conviction that the Wobblies were disloyal. On Monday, December 20, three days after the Chicago defendants had been arraigned, federal agents invaded general defense headquarters in Chicago, seizing literature, subscription lists, and mailing lists. Long after the original warrant on which the agents had acted expired, federal officials continued to occupy Chicago defense headquarters. Simultaneous raids interfered with defense activities in Seattle, Sacramento, and other cities. Meanwhile, the Justice Department, in conjunction with postal authorities, barred IWW literature from the mails. Not even private correspondence completely escaped federal censorship or control. Nebeker at times even sought to interfere with newspapers and magazines that published stories possibly favorable to the IWW's defense. Congress, too, assisted the Justice Department's prosecution, for as the Chicago trial began in the spring of 1918, several congressmen introduced bills to declare the IWW illegal and to make membership in it a crime. Unsuccessful though they were, the bills' backers did succeed in further poisoning the public atmosphere against the IWW.

The Justice Department was indeed fortunate that public hysteria had convicted the Wobblies before the jury heard the prosecution's evidence, for the prosecution, in fact, had no evidence. Although for public consumption the

Justice Department had consistently held that the IWW as an organization was not on trial, its case clearly hinged on the organization's record rather than on specific crimes committed by individual Wobblies. From the beginning of its investigation, the prosecution had based its case against the defendants largely on the existence of an anticapitalist and antiwar conspiracy by the IWW, the evidence for which derived from the Wobblies' own publications. In March, on the eve of the trial, the prosecution still could do no better. In a twenty-three-page summary of the IWW's criminal record Fitts prepared for the attorney general, for example, he could not cite a single instance of a specific crime committed by a Wobbly. Instead, Fitts restricted his legal brief to quotations and citations from IWW newspapers and pamphlets on sabotage, all of which led him to conclude that "the seditious and disloyal *character and teachings* of the organization necessarily brought it into conflict with other federal laws" (italics added). The evidence amassed by the prosecution proved, if anything, the innocence of individual Wobblies.

Lacking the evidence it thought necessary to convince a federal judge, or perhaps a judicious elite, of the Wobblies' guilt, the department realized that a jury composed of twelve randomly chosen citizens would probably reflect the nation's war hysteria. What abstract justice could not accomplish for the prosecution, flesh and blood Americans would.

On April 1, 1918, 113 Wobblies were brought before Judge Landis, and each was charged with over one hundred separate crimes for a grand total of well over ten thousand violations. Before the prosecution could present its evidence or the defense could rebut it, however, a jury had to be selected. Nebeker directed the prosecution—with Clyne retiring to the background—and after almost a full month of examination he chose a jury eminently satisfactory to the Justice Department. Exactly a month to the day—April 1 to May 1—after the defendants initially came before the bench, formal presentation of the government's case began. How fitting that a trial that was to become a judicial farce, if not a circus, should commence on April Fool's Day, and that formal presentation of evidence against a radical, allegedly revolutionary labor organization should begin on May Day!

The setting of the trial was a strange mixture of incongruities. The stern and dignified Judge Landis presided over a courtroom in which spittoons were prominently in evidence. The Justice Department's legal celebrities competed for attention with a motley assortment of journalists, among them Carl Sandburg, Art Young, David Karsner, and John Reed. Some of these men were eager to grind out lurid copy about the dangerous Wobbly traitors, while others were more interested in exploring the implications of such a trial for free speech, dissent, and labor activities in a wartime democracy.

Yet despite the drama of the personalities and the setting, the trial proved a disappointing anticlimax to the hysterical propaganda and the massive federal raids that preceded it. Nothing original or startling came to light during the trial. Evidence that the prosecution had been unable to secure previously was not suddenly introduced from the witness stand or in Nebeker's opening and closing arguments. For every anticonscription or antiwar Wobbly that Nebeker cited, Vanderveer produced others, larger in number, loyally serving in the armed forces. In fact, one of the original 113 defenders, A. C. Christ, appeared in court in military uniform on April 1; the government, however, wisely dismissed Christ's case along with that of eleven other defendants.

The Chicago trial was Boise, Paterson, and Everett all over again, but on a larger and grander scale. Previous prosecutors had promised to prove the guilt of individual Wobblies, and, unable to do so, had instead indicted the organization on the basis of its philosophy and its publications; this was Nebeker's gambit in 1918. Failing to prove specific individual crimes, he read to the jury from the IWW preamble, from *Solidarity*, from Flynn's translation of Pouget's *Sabotage*, and from the private correspondence of various Wobblies. In the last analysis the Justice Department asked the jury, as representatives for an entire nation, to condemn a philosophy, an attitude toward life, and, most important, an organization.

The defense, for its part, followed established precedent. Easily surmounting a court ruling that declared evidence concerning exploitive working conditions inadmissible, Vanderveer brought IWW soapboxers to the witness stand to testify about their life experiences, and they inevitably focused on just such exploitive working conditions. Big Jim Thompson gave the same speech in the Chicago courtroom that he had given in hundreds of lumber camps and hobo jungles and on city street corners. "Red" Doran presented his famous illustrated chalk talk—a crudely metaphorical analysis and indictment of capitalism—which may have excited working-class audiences but only bored the jury and the courtroom. The trial's high point was Haywood's testimony, which extended through two days of repetitive questioning. As Carl Sandburg had observed several months earlier, Haywood was inclined to discuss the alleged ten thousand crimes "with the massive leisure of Hippo Vaughn pitching a shutout."

The only surprise in the defense's strategy came when Vanderveer declined to offer a closing argument to the jury. No adequate explanation has ever been suggested for that decision, and, given the lack of sources, any explanation must remain highly conjectural. Nevertheless, it does not seem improbable that Vanderveer had nothing to say in a summation that he had not already said or established more effectively during his examination and cross-examination of witnesses. Moreover, it appears likely that Vanderveer honestly believed the prosecution had failed to adduce evidence that would lead a jury to convict any individual defendant; since the organization, in theory, was not on trial, the defense had no reason to present a final rebuttal. In other words, Vanderveer probably assumed that whatever decision the jury reached, it could hardly be based on the evidence offered by the government.

Be that as it may, in mid-August, after nearly four months of testimony, Landis instructed the jury on the intricacies of determining the guilt or innocence of one hundred defendants charged on four separate counts with having committed more than ten thousand crimes. The jurors thus had to make four hundred distinct determinations. Difficult as that may have seemed, it apparently proved astonishingly easy, for in less than one hour the jury returned with a verdict of "guilty" for every defendant on each and every count. The speed and the substance of the verdict shocked the Wobblies. "I did not think," Vincent St. John wrote to Frank Walsh, "that mob justice would prevail in a U.S. court."

After having demonstrated judicial objectivity and restraint for five long months, Judge Landis revealed his real emotions on August 31, when he sentenced most of the defendants with as little mercy as possible. Seventeen defendants received some measure of clemency, but their connection to the IWW was at best debatable. Landis meanwhile sentenced thirty-five Wobblies to five years in prison, thirty-three to ten years, and fifteen, including Haywood, St. John, and Chaplin, to twenty years, or the legal maximum. Total fines levied in the case exceeded $2 million. Among those sent to the federal prison at Leavenworth, Kansas, was Ray Fanning, a nineteen-year-old Harvard sophomore who was not even an IWW member. As the sentences were announced, Ben Fletcher, a Baltimore and Philadelphia waterfront organizer and the only African American among the defendants, added some strained gallows humor to the somber proceedings as he observed, "Judge Landis is using poor English today. His sentences are too long." (Earlier in the proceedings Fletcher had sardonically informed Haywood, "If it wasn't for me, there'd be no color in this trial at all.")

Landis's harsh sentences sat well with the press and with popular opinion in an emotional climate that was soon to nourish A. Mitchell Palmer's Red Scare. In the past, more conservative American labor factions had usually united with more radical ones in time of legal peril. This had been the case in Boise, Lawrence, Paterson, and Everett. But not in Chicago. Although scores of British labor organizations made formal protests, not a single AFL affiliate opposed the Justice Department concerning the IWW verdict.

Deserted by press, public, and organized labor, the convicted Wobblies could turn for support only to the small body of civil libertarians clustered around Roger Baldwin and the National Civil Liberties Bureau, such former comrades as Elizabeth Gurley Flynn, isolated sympathizers such as Captain Lanier and Louis F. Post, and their old friend Frank P. Walsh. Yet none of these sympathizers could rescue the Wobblies from the substantial terms at Leavenworth inflicted on them by Landis.

But the Chicago Wobblies were not alone in their tribulations and prison sentences. With Haywood and the others convicted, the Justice Department, its boosters, its camp followers, and its lonely opponents turned their full attention to the West.

Although the IWW cases in the West were directly related to the federal crackdown on the organization and to the specific needs of the prosecution in the Chicago trial, local pressures and passions, particularly in California, added an extra fillip to the repressive legal campaign. Most of the Wobblies held prisoner in the Western states had been arrested during the September–November 1917 raids. The more important among them, however, had been transferred to Chicago to stand trial there with other first-line IWW leaders; some of the evidence confiscated in the West was used in Chicago. Now in August 1918, its main trial successfully completed, the Justice Department could cater to Western businessmen, politicians, and inflamed citizens by prosecuting local Wobblies. (Politics was never far beneath the surface; administration Democrats were keenly conscious of the importance of Western votes to their national success.)

By far the most interesting and revealing of the secondary IWW trials opened in Sacramento in December 1918. Sacramento demonstrated more clearly than Chicago the lengths to which the Justice Department went in order to get Wobblies and their sympathizers.

IWW defense efforts in California encountered customary obstacles. Federal agents raided local defense headquarters seven times in six months, seizing all IWW records and papers; agents arrested the defense committee's secretaries, one of whom they held incommunicado for eight months. No Wobbly or IWW sympathizer altogether evaded the authorities. When Theodora Pollok, a young woman with the best family connections, appeared at the Sacramento police station to arrange bail for several prisoners, police arrested her, confiscated her funds, and subjected her to a medical examination intended for prostitutes.

Theodora Pollok's links to the IWW are interesting to trace. The daughter of a prominent Baltimore family whose influential friends in Washington could plead her case before the highest federal officials, including Woodrow Wilson, Pollok, like so many other well-bred and well-educated young women of her generation, despised the restraints imposed by society on the Victorian (American) woman, and she sought release in a life of strenuous social reform. Asthmatic and tubercular, she was compelled to move to California for her health. She became active in IWW legal defense work, which resulted in her taking out a red card and later being arrested in Sacramento. Although she could scarcely be classified a saboteur, a subversive, or an assassin, the prosecution refused to dismiss its charges against her, despite the remonstrations of President Wilson, Attorney General Gregory, Labor Secretary Wilson, and lesser federal officials.

The prosecution had good reason for refusing to dismiss its case against Pollok. As U.S. Attorney John Preston admitted in one of his franker moments, the government's evidence against the other Sacramento defendants was barely more substantial than what it had against Pollok. Better, Preston's reasoning went, try and convict an innocent woman than weaken the case against fifty-four dangerous Wobblies.

Despite his lack of evidence, Preston secured grand jury indictments in February 1918. He had to postpone the trial of the Sacramento defendants until after the Chicago trial ended, however, for an acquittal in Sacramento would naturally have undermined the government's chances for conviction in Chicago. From February until December 1918, when the Sacramento trial finally began, the Bureau of Investigation sought to build a case against the California defendants. It did, but only of the most circumstantial kind. Using IWW publications and the private correspondence of several Wobblies, the bureau proved that members of the organization advocated sabotage.

The Sacramento prosecution thus came into court with what it apparently thought was incriminating evidence; at least it cited specific instances of criminal acts alleged to have been committed by individual defendants. Yet, as in Chicago, the bulk of the correspondence cited by the prosecutors dated from the years 1913–15, before the period covered by the indictment. The evidence of IWW crimes for the war years proved even more circumstantial than that for the prewar period, and it was founded in large degree on the testimony of paid informants.

Most of the Sacramento Wobblies, unlike those in Chicago who had expected to win justice in a capitalist court, remained true to their IWW faith. Asserting that judges and courts were purely institutions designed to place a legal veneer on the exploitation of the ruling American capitalist class, all but three of the Sacramento Wobblies declined to hire an attorney or to defend themselves in court. Only Pollok and two other less notable defendants dissented from the strategy of a "silent defense" and chose to be represented by counsel and offer a defense in court.

Whether they elected counsel or not, whether they defended themselves before the jury or not, the Sacramento defendants met similar fates: conviction by a jury that deliberated less than an hour before handing down its verdict on January 16, 1919. All of the "silent defenders" were sentenced to prison terms, ranging from one to ten years. The three vocal defendants had to wait until June 18, 1919, before being sentenced. Only a medical report by a Stanford University physician, concluding that imprisonment would kill Pollok, and the trial judge's own conscience, if not that of the Justice Department, saved her from a term in prison. Instead, the judge fined her $100, while he sentenced her two codefendants to two months in jail.

Just before the end of the Sacramento trial, another twenty-seven Wobblies received prison terms in Wichita, Kansas. In Kansas, as elsewhere, the evidence amassed against the Wobblies consisted entirely of organization publications and private correspondence, not overt illegal acts. As usual, after a trial lasting less than three weeks, a local jury found all the defendants guilty; the judge then sentenced twenty-six of them to prison terms ranging from one to nine years.

More fortunate but equally maltreated was a group of sixty-four Wobblies arrested in Omaha, Nebraska, on November 13, 1917. Arriving in Omaha to attend a special convention called by the Agricultural Workers' Industrial Union, the Wobblies instead met federal agents. United States Attorney Thomas Allen realized at once that he had no legitimate case against the arrested men. Turning to Attorney General Gregory for advice, he was counseled to delay legal action until after the trial in Chicago; at the same time Gregory ordered him to hold the Wobblies until the next regular session of the Omaha federal grand jury. In June 1918, eight months after their arrest, these Wobblies were still in jail, awaiting presentment before a grand jury. Certain that he had no case against his prisoners, whom he conceded were innocent, Allen offered the Wobblies a "compromise": They could plead guilty and be sentenced to the length of time they had already served in jail. The Wobblies, of course, rejected the "compromise."

But in the Omaha case for the first time Washington officials equivocated. Perhaps some of them had pangs of conscience about the propriety of sentencing another large group of probably innocent men to prison. Not until April 1919 did the department reach a decision; after having kept the Wobblies locked up for a year and a half, it decided to dismiss all charges. By April 1919 almost all the first- and second-line IWW leaders were in federal prison; those still at large were either free on bail, fugitives from justice, victims of the immigration authorities, or on the verge of being tried on criminal syndicalism charges in various state courts.

The law had clearly proved to be an effective instrument of repression. When vigilantes had deported miners from Bisbee or had lynched Frank Little in Butte, the American conscience had been troubled. But when the Justice Department arrested suspected criminals, indicted them before grand juries, tried them before impartial judges and randomly selected petit juries—that is, when the formal requirements of legal due process were observed—the American conscience rested easier. As long as most Americans deemed membership in the IWW to be tantamount to treason, there was little danger that due process would release an army of Wobbly bandits on a helpless community. Where the federal government doubted the effectiveness of the courtroom as an instrument of repression, it could remit alien or naturalized Wobblies to immigration authorities, who were not compelled to observe due process in their deportation proceedings. Whatever the method chosen—be it legal trial or administrative deportation—the government accomplished its essential objective: repression of the IWW.

Although the federal trials and deportations did not force the IWW out of existence, the whole basis of its existence changed. Before September 1917 it had been a flourishing labor organization, daily gaining new recruits and funds; afterward, its leaders were imprisoned, its ranks decimated, and its treasury depleted by legal expenses. Before 1917 it had been a fighting labor organization, waging industrial war against lumber barons, mine owners, and wheat farmers; afterward, it became primarily a legal defense organization, combating writs, government lawyers, and judges.

# 18

## Disorder and Decline, 1918–24

In 1917–18 the IWW seemed to pose a distinct threat to the established order in America. Claiming from 100,000 to 250,000 members, it had tied up the woods of the Northwest and paralyzed the copper mines of Montana and Arizona. Three years later, in 1921, Ben H. Williams, who had briefly returned to the IWW as editor of *Solidarity*, observed in a valedictory editorial announcing his absolute divorce from the IWW, "'Isolation' is a word that aptly describes the present position of the I.W.W. in the labor movement of the United States."

The IWW's failure to adapt to the realities of life in postwar America ensured its continued isolation from the mainstream of the labor movement as well as from the "new" radicalism. After the war a more sophisticated breed of American employer erected an anti-union dam composed in equal parts of welfare capitalism and an "American Plan" that channeled the labor movement away from a swift running course into a languid backwater. Simultaneously the course of radicalism flowed away from prewar reform socialism into the more turbulent riverbed of revolutionary communism, ultimately leaving the Wobblies and the Socialists cut off not only from the radical current but also from the mainstream of American history, which, in the 1920s, flowed swiftly with the capitalist current.

Before and during World War I the IWW had flourished in the copper and lumber industries partly as a result of obstinate employers and partly as a consequence of abominable working conditions. Although the war effort revolutionized neither employer attitudes nor working conditions, it nevertheless wrought perceptible—and, from the IWW's point of view, decisive—changes in both. This was particularly true in the case of the lumbermen, who before 1916 had been among the most combative and antilabor of American businessmen. Under pressure from Washington and from the Army, they had inaugurated the eight-hour day, increased daily wages, and improved living and working conditions. In response to federal initiatives, the employers acquiesced in the creation of the Loyal Legion of Loggers and Lumbermen (4Ls), a company union that offered lumber workers the shadow of industrial democracy. For the first time in the industry's history, its workers were granted, if not actual power, a voice in decisions affecting their lives. When the war ended in November 1918 the lumbermen did not forget what they had learned under duress: that accommodation was more effective than opposition in averting labor unrest. Hence in 1919 most employers retained the 4Ls as a civilian organization; still others considered adopting the company union scheme that the Rockefeller interests had instituted successfully at the Colorado Fuel and Iron Company in the aftermath of the 1914 Ludlow massacre.

Similar though somewhat less substantial improvements in labor-management relations took place in the copper industry. Here employers remained obdurately antilabor, yet after the war they continued to cooperate with Labor Department mediators, who still tried to foist AFL affiliates on recalcitrant employers as an alternative to the IWW. Although the copper companies declined to deal with AFL unions—except where powerful skilled unions of machinists, engineers, and building tradesmen left them no choice—they maintained the grievance machinery created during the war. In some cases— Phelps Dodge most notable among them—they expanded what had already been an elaborate paternalistic welfare labor policy.

After 1918 the Wobblies also found their appeal to migratory harvesters circumscribed. Here, however, the causes were different. Federal officials had not had to intervene during the war in order to ensure efficient production in agriculture, nor had farmer-employers altered their basic attitudes toward labor. But the labor force itself began to change. The Ford "flivver" was already working its wonders among migratory harvest hands. Where once migratory workers had been mostly unattached men who beat their way from job to job on "sidedoor coach," they were fast becoming more and more family units that traveled as far and as often as their battered secondhand cars carried them. For the migratory who rode the rods and camped in the jungles, an IWW red card had been a necessity of life, his insurance policy against coercion by detectives, brakemen, gamblers, and thugs. For the family of harvesters who traveled by auto as a self-contained unit, the red card was much less important. Meanwhile, in the wheat fields the widespread use of the combine reduced the total demand for labor and hence the size of the migratory army among whom the IWW had traditionally recruited.

Even where objective conditions remained the same—as on the Philadelphia waterfront—the postwar IWW isolated itself from the labor movement. Since 1913 an IWW local of longshoremen affiliated with the Marine Transport Workers' Industrial Union had maintained job control on the Philadelphia waterfront. Ably led, first by Ben Fletcher and then by Walter Nef, in effect the longshoremen achieved a closed shop and union-determined wages. After having loyally loaded ammunition and troop ships during the war, the longshoremen's local entered the postwar world more powerful than ever. With its closed shop and its $25 initiation fee (which was well above the IWW's constitutionally sanctioned maximum) intended to restrict entry into the union, it was the second largest postwar affiliate of the IWW. As such, it inevitably came into conflict with the putative leaders of the IWW, who, having no strong following of their own, clung to outdated revolutionary precepts that dated back to the organization's earliest and least successful days. These leaders asserted that the longshoremen's initiation fee contravened the IWW constitution and that the local's regular, orderly negotiations with employers subverted the IWW's revolutionary spirit. They thus presented an ultimatum to the longshoremen: Either reduce the union initiation fee to the constitutionally sanctioned $2 maximum or be suspended from IWW membership. Ben Fletcher, who had gone to prison for his principles and who, upon his release from Leavenworth, returned to Philadelphia to lead his fellow black workers, accepted the 1922 challenge of the IWW's general executive board and in 1924 led his longshoremen out of the IWW and into the AFL.

If changing economic realities and self-defeating organizational policies had not weakened the IWW, further government repression would have done so. Public surveillance of the Wobblies did not end with the conclusion of the wartime trials. Well after the close of the war, federal troops stayed on duty in Arizona and Montana, where they cooperated with mine owners and local authorities in curbing IWW activities. Naval and Army intelligence infiltrated spies into IWW locals and sent agents to the 1919 IWW convention in Chicago. Meanwhile, the Western states that had enacted criminal syndicalism statutes inaugurated their own prosecutions against Wobblies as federal prosecution abated.

This combination of economic change, government repression, and internal inadequacies rendered the IWW largely inactive and ineffective in the spring and summer of 1918. The organization had not held a national convention since 1916, and it would not convene another until May 1919. Its newspapers, journals, and pamphlets were censored and denied use of the mails; its basic records remained impounded in a Chicago warehouse. With all its most capable and experienced leaders in prison, administratively the organization was in chaos.

At a time when the Wobblies needed leaders as never before, and when the organization had to cope with new social and economic realities, there was no one with sufficient experience or talent to refashion the IWW in the radical manner required. Whether Haywood, Richard Brazier, Ben Fletcher, and almost two hundred other Wobblies serving time in federal prison could have saved the IWW from decline is at best debatable. Clearly, their years in prison insulated these men from the changes transforming America, just as those changes further isolated the IWW from the labor movement. Wobblies went into prison as representatives of America's most radical social movement; they would come out into a world in which Communists had replaced them on the revolutionary left. The world that had been and the world that was diverged so greatly that few of the imprisoned IWW leaders ever again assumed prominence in the organization they had helped establish. Given the number of problems that plagued the IWW in 1917 and 1918, it is remarkable that the organization survived at all. Yet survive it did. Indeed, it remained virile enough to frighten military men, Western employers, and local officials, though closer observers of the labor scene knew better.

If the events of 1918 seem peculiar, 1919 was strange indeed. It was one of those years, like 1789, 1848, or 1871, when rumors of impending revolution haunted conservatives and elated radicals. In Russia the Bolsheviks had held power for two years despite domestic chaos, civil war, and external invaders; led by Béla Kun, a communist faction had risen to power in Hungary; and the Bolsheviks also threatened to capture control of postwar Germany. In England an ambitious and growing Labour party proclaimed a postwar reconstruction program that called for the total socialization of British society. In 1919, left-wing Socialists had broken with the Socialist Party of America in order to found an American Communist party. Although America's Communists split into three factions and were compelled by federal action to go underground, not to emerge as a united party until 1922, many citizens took the Bolshevik threat to America seriously. More frightening to most Americans than bolshevism was labor unrest, which was sometimes equated with revolution in the public, as well as the business, mind. In America the year opened with a general strike that paralyzed Seattle for five days in January and ended with the September Boston police strike and the massive nationwide steel strike that lasted into the winter of 1919–20. In between, over 300,000 coal miners, under the leadership of John L. Lewis, walked out of the mines. More ominous still, that spring and summer bombs were sent to prominent businessmen and public figures, including attorney general A. Mitchell Palmer.

In reality, the IWW was in no position to take credit for major strikes, let alone to lead them. This was demonstrated at its 1919 convention, which met in Chicago in May. Thirteen unions and forty-six delegates representing an undetermined number of members attended the sessions. Among the delegates, hardly a link to the IWW's substantial past could be discovered, except perhaps John Pancner's wife. The names of the secretary-treasurer and the members of the general executive board were unfamiliar. The decisions rendered by the convention seemed still less familiar. Delegates from the Agricultural Workers' Industrial Union (AWIU), a body that had once prided itself on its realism and its experienced, skilled leadership, introduced a resolution forbidding national officials, except for editors, to hold office for two consecutive terms. The convention adopted this resolution. The convention also dismantled the general recruiting union, an institution Haywood had worked so hard to perfect, and it threatened to deny all IWW members then in prison, or even under indictment—virtually the entire prewar leadership—the right to hold office. In a letter sent from his Leavenworth cell to secretary-treasurer Thomas Whitehead, Haywood protested these actions. But the 1919 convention seemed unconscious of the IWW's past. Strong leadership had never been the IWW's long suit; now its new leaders made weak leadership a certainty, partly by restricting tenure in office to one term and partly by isolating the organization from most of its former leaders.

The convention decisions came at a particularly inopportune time, for the IWW was in no position to endure another wave of repression such as had almost decimated it during the war. Yet the industrial conflicts and the bomb scares of 1919 set the stage for A. Mitchell Palmer's repressive raids and the beginning of the great Red Scare. Wobblies, it must be said, did their own little bit to bring on the scare.*

Before the year ended, Wobblies engaged in armed conflict. Centralia, Washington, was a lumber town in a region with a long history of IWW activity. Like most towns in the area, it had a small IWW hall downtown where Wobblies congregated to chat about old times, read radical literature, and discuss when the revolution would come. That particular hall soon became famous. Centralia's American Legionnaires planned to celebrate Armistice Day, 1919, with a parade that included an unusual touch of patriotic fervor: destruction of the local IWW hall. Knowing what was coming and acting on legal advice, the Wobblies prepared to defend their hall against attack. When the Legion-

---

* The Red Scare of 1919–20 was ignited by fears stirred by Russia's Bolshevik Revolution, fanned by the mailing of anonymous letter bombs to public officials (including Attorney General Palmer) in April 1919, and stoked by the strike wave of that year. The paranoia of government officials reached its peak on January 2, 1920, when a national dragnet coordinated in 32 cities by the U.S. Justice Department arrested more than 4,000 persons, more than 500 of whom were ultimately deported.

naires' line of march approached IWW headquarters, its participants met an
unexpected welcome, for inside, as well as on adjoining rooftops, armed Wobblies prepared to fire on them. A brief and bloody gunfight followed, during
which the more numerous Legionnaires stormed the hall and drove the Wobblies into flight. Bloodied and enraged, the Legionnaires pursued the fleeing
Wobblies, cornering one of them on the town's outskirts. Wesley Everest, the
trapped Wobbly and a distinguished war veteran, attempted to hold off his
pursuers in a gun battle that John Dos Passos was later to describe in his nov-
el *1919*. Outnumbered and encircled, Everest had no choice but to surrender
to the Legionnaires, who promptly and unceremoniously castrated and then
lynched him.

The Centralia incident coincided with the initiation of Palmer's Red Hunt,
a sport in which Wobblies were frequently found to be favorite prey. Fearing
Wobbly-induced violence in his state also, the governor of California wired
Palmer, "Will you please at once take all steps possible to the end that America may be kept wholly American." Palmer agreed to do so, and indeed he tried.
So did his young associate in the Red Hunt, J. Edgar Hoover. Hoover, in fact,
sought to make deportation of alien Wobblies an automatic and mandatory
procedure, and proposed the selective arrest of Wobblies in groups of five
hundred in order to cripple the organization permanently.

In Washington and other states, the IWW had to go underground to survive. A year later the Supreme Court of Washington declared its state's criminal syndicalism law to be constitutional, thereby outlawing all Wobblies and
causing their former attorney to comment, "The Wobs are nearly extinct, the
Supreme Court decisions, the one handed by the State outlawing them, and
the refusal of the U.S. to give them a hearing [a reference to an appeal in the
Haywood case] have put them out of existence." Outlawed and forced underground in most Western states, the Wobblies came into close touch with many
communists, and many came to believe that the IWW was the radicalism of
the past and communism the wave of the future.

From 1920 to 1924 three issues divided the IWW: the status of its political
prisoners, its relationship with the Communist party at home and the Comintern abroad, and the distribution of power within the organization between
centralists and decentralists, industrial unionists and anarchists. The first issue determined what role the old leadership would play in the postwar IWW,
the second decided whether the Wobblies would continue to function as an
independent radical entity, and the third irreparably split the organization.

Few organizations could have survived the leadership drain the IWW suffered almost from the day of its birth. Early in its history it had lost Debs, Si-

mons, DeLeon, and Moyer; later, Trautmann, William Z. Foster, and others dropped out; and on the eve of as well as throughout World War I, Elizabeth Gurley Flynn, Joe Ettor, Carlo Tresca, Arturo Giovannitti, and James P. Cannon, among others, bade the organization farewell. To this small but select group of voluntary dropouts was added the mass of leaders sentenced to federal penitentiary terms. Such a drain was simply too great a handicap for an organization as inherently weak as the IWW.

Had most of the IWW officials imprisoned in 1918 returned to assume control of the organization when their jail terms ended, there might have been a slim chance for a resurgence of the IWW in the 1920s. From the first, however, imprisonment frayed the nerves of the already edgy Wobbly inmates and vitiated the little solidarity they had brought into prison with them. At Leavenworth the Wobblies quarreled often and bitterly over how they should behave: One faction counseled acquiescence to prison authorities in order to abet the efforts of the general defense committee; another faction advised resistance and even a "general strike" against prison work assignments.

While the prisoners quarreled on the inside, on the outside the general defense committee, the American Civil Liberties Union (the renamed National Civil Liberties Bureau), and the Workers' Defense League (directed by Elizabeth Gurley Flynn) waged a legal struggle on two fronts. On one front, attorneys appealed the Chicago, Sacramento, and Wichita verdicts, planning, if necessary, to carry their appeals to the Supreme Court. On the other, the general defense committee, in alliance with a wide variety of middle- and working-class reformers, lobbied within the Justice Department and the White House for pardons. The IWW meanwhile scraped its slender financial resources together and raised cash collateral sufficient to bring forty-six Wobblies, including Haywood, out of Leavenworth on bond pending the appeals. Coming out in August 1919, these men promptly went to work for the general defense committee, now directed by Haywood, speaking throughout the country in an effort to raise defense funds.

These legal defense endeavors all ended in failure, which further exacerbated differences within the IWW. As long as Woodrow Wilson sat in the White House and A. Mitchell Palmer controlled the Justice Department, the commutation campaign met a stone wall. In Wilson's view, to pardon or commute the sentences of the Wobblies would be to concede that they had been imprisoned in the first place for political reasons; moreover, to release them from prison would be tantamount to certifying them as loyal, patriotic Americans, a concession the self-righteous Wilson could never make.

Warren Harding's election to the presidency, however, promised relief and a new look at the clemency petitions. Harding did prove more flexible than Wilson, but his willingness to bend ironically proved more destructive to the IWW than Wilson's obduracy. At first the Justice Department continued to oppose clemency for the Wobblies, advising the new president, "The defendants . . . apparently voice the same contempt for the law that they did when they fought for Germany . . . and they would probably again turn to sowing seeds of discontent and preaching revolution if their sentences were commuted."

When the Supreme Court declined to review the IWW cases, the Wobblies were confronted with yet another crisis. Only thirty-seven of the forty-six Wobblies then out on appeal bond surrendered for confinement; among the nine who disappeared, and hence jumped bond, were Haywood, Vladimir Lossief, and George Andreytchine, all of whom later showed up in Soviet Russia. Haywood's flight, in particular, stunned the Wobblies. For more years than they would have cared to admit, Haywood had symbolized the IWW's cause and spirit in the public mind; Big Bill had seemed the prototypical Wobbly, the rebel ideal type, ever ready to throw down the gauntlet to capitalist injustice. Now unexpectedly refusing to be martyred for the cause he personified, Haywood had betrayed friends and fellow workers (those who had provided collateral for his bond), and deserted the IWW and the United States for communism and exile.

Like most of Haywood's friends and acquaintances, most historians of the IWW have found his decision to jump bail inexplicable. By and large, they maintain that he naively saw in Soviet Russia the revolution and the new society he had so much wanted to create in America; hence he leaped at the opportunity to help the Russian Communists build a workers' state. Actually, the reasons for his decision are much more prosaic. The time Haywood served at the Cook County Jail and at Leavenworth in 1917–19 undermined his failing health. By the time he left prison on bail he was probably suffering from ulcers and diabetes. Soon he would suffer psychological setbacks as well. Both his advice and his offers to serve the IWW rejected at the 1919 convention, Haywood came out of Leavenworth a physically sick and psychically wounded man. This was evident in his tenure as secretary of the general defense committee. Apparently drinking heavily, Haywood let the defense office fall apart. So chaotic did its operations become that the IWW's general executive board felt compelled to remove Haywood from office. Thus, before he fled to Russia, Haywood had been practically disowned by the IWW.

Haywood's experiences in Russia suggest that exile hurt him at least as much as it did the IWW. Scarcely a Bolshevik, he did not fit into Lenin's or Leon

Trotsky's schemes. The IWW's antiorganizational approach proved as unacceptable to Russia's new rulers as it had been to America's. For a time Haywood directed a labor project in the Kuznets district, but it is clear that by 1923 his dream of building a Wobbly-style utopia in Russia had soured. Tired and sick, he retired to Moscow's Lux Hotel. Some time later he married a Russian national, a liaison about which there is very little real information. When the American communist leader Alexander Trachtenberg made his pilgrimages to Russia in the 1920s, he usually found Haywood in his Moscow hotel. Much later, Trachtenberg remembered Haywood as having been a desperately lonely man, an alien in Moscow's new society, who found solace in whisky and in the old Wobbly associates who, somehow or other, occasionally drifted into his hotel room. They would join their former chief in drink and song, going interminably through the *Little Red Song Book* until they collapsed in a drunken stupor. These were apparently the high points of Haywood's quiet Moscow exile. Frequently hospitalized, he tried to keep abreast of labor developments at home and found time to complete his unsatisfactory and distorted autobiography. Finally, on May 28, 1928, Haywood died unmourned in a Moscow hospital. Soviet officials placed part of his ashes beneath a plaque in the Kremlin wall alongside those of John Reed. The remainder were shipped to Chicago's Waldheim Cemetery and placed next to the graves of the Haymarket Riot martyrs.

The Wobblies who returned to prison to join their fellow workers in Leavenworth faced their own crises. In 1922 the clemency campaign had finally achieved some success with President Harding, who in December commuted the sentences of eleven Wobblies who agreed to withdraw from the IWW. Then, in June 1923, Harding offered to commute the sentences of the remaining IWW prisoners, except for the Sacramento defendants, if they would agree to remain law-abiding and in no way to encourage law-breaking. By implication, Harding's proposal assumed that the Wobblies had broken the law and had been justly convicted. This caused eleven of the eligible Wobblies to decline the offer and to harass the Wobblies who accepted Harding's proposal. The split between the Leavenworth prisoners on this issue was reflected in IWW convention discussions and in organization journals. Those on the outside favored the recalcitrants and castigated the other prisoners as traitors to the organization. But even the recalcitrants did not have much longer to wait for relief, for on December 15, 1923, President Coolidge commuted the sentences of all the remaining wartime prisoners.

The Wobblies who left prison in 1923 returned to an organization that no longer particularly desired them. For understandable reasons, the Wobblies distrusted Chaplin and the others who had accepted commutation in June 1923; for inexplicable reasons, they also distrusted the prisoners who came out in December. Unwanted in positions of leadership by the organization for which they had gone to prison, the freed Wobblies devoted much of their time to internecine battles that disrupted annual conventions and further weakened the organization.

Some of the leading prewar Wobblies did have somewhere else to go: the Communist party. As early as 1920 three men well known and admired by many Wobblies had moved toward communism: William Z. Foster, James P. Cannon, and John Reed. Furthermore, Moscow's reestablished Third International (Comintern) as well as its newly created Red International of Labor Unions (RILU, or Profintern) pleaded with IWW leaders to join the common world-wide revolutionary front represented by the Bolsheviks. Several Wobblies found the Bolshevik invitation appealing.

For many other Wobblies, however, communism offered few attractions. Still dedicated to syndicalism and to nonviolent direct action, they found repugnant a movement based on control of the state and the violent seizure of power. Committed to the concept of industrial democracy, they found alien the Bolshevik principles of the dictatorship of the proletariat and democratic centralism. Opposed to all forms of coercion and bureaucracy, they looked upon the Soviet system with deep suspicion.

Disagreements over communism further aggravated the IWW's internal disorders. Communism became topic number one in the IWW; when Wobblies weren't fighting over it in their halls or in the streets, they debated the issue in their newspapers and conventions. At annual conventions IWW delegates debated whether to send delegates to RILU conferences, their decisions usually coming only after extremely close votes. George Williams, the IWW delegate dispatched to Moscow in 1921, was repelled by what he observed in the Soviet Union and, in a report to the IWW, asserted that the Bolsheviks intended to capture the IWW for communism. He also charged that a communist takeover would leave the Wobblies with neither an organization nor principles.

Acting on Williams's report, in 1922 the IWW's general executive board rejected IWW participation in the Profintern. Restating traditional IWW syndicalist doctrines (which the 1922 leaders believed to be industrial unionism), the general executive board explained why Wobblies and Communists had nothing in common. "The history of American unionism testifies to the destructive influence of labor politics and politicians," the IWW statement as-

serted. "Experience has proven that when politics moves into a union economic effectiveness moves out, and hope for the workers moves out with it."

In fact, no matter what the IWW did on the issue of communism it stood
to lose. Had it entered the Profintern and formed a coalition with the American Communists, it would undoubtedly have been subverted as a distinct organization and swallowed up by the more organized, more industrious, and
better-financed Communists. Choosing, as it did eventually, to oppose communism, and in language even more violent than that later used by post–World
War II "cold warriors," it succeeded only in isolating itself from the center of
revolutionary ferment in the 1920s and 1930s without entering the mainstream
of American society.

By the time of its 1924 convention, then, the IWW stood on the verge of
collapse, needing only the slightest nudge to push it over into the abyss of
nonexistence. The 1924 convention completed the disruption of the IWW.
Delegates arrived in Chicago to find two separate sessions scheduled—one
called by the existing officials, the other announced by James Rowan and the
West Coast lumber workers' union. On the fifth day of the regularly scheduled convention, delegates voted to suspend the IWW's entire national leadership, including the bulk of the general executive board and the Lumber
Workers' Industrial Union No. 120, the IWW's largest affiliate. After the convention, the contending factions, in a fashion reminiscent of 1906, struggled
in the streets and in the courts for control of IWW headquarters at 1001 West
Madison Street. When the new leaders enthroned by the 1924 convention secured title to headquarters, they ensured their own future impotence by denying Richard Brazier and Forrest Edwards, two prominent and outstanding
prewar Wobblies, roles in reconstructing the IWW.

Reflecting years later on the impact of the 1924 schism, Mary Gallagher sur-
mised, "My personal opinion has been that the whole split was engineered to
break up the I.W.W. as completely as possible." Contrary to her notion, the
IWW division did not occur as the result of a conspiracy, though the end was
the same as if it had: total collapse. In California, where for a brief time the
IWW had increased its membership, scores of Wobblies dropped away, never
to return. Rowan went back to Washington State in 1925 to resume his fight
against the IWW leadership by calling on timber workers and other Wobblies
to join his Emergency Program to save the IWW. By 1926, however, Rowan's
movement was almost bankrupt, and in 1930 it claimed at best two hundred
followers. Old-time Wobblies, who had remained loyal out of habit or conviction, silently slipped away from the IWW. At the 1925 convention only eleven
delegates representing seven unions met. Another convention would not be

held until 1928, when seven unions would send a total of eight delegates; then there would be another three-year hiatus until seven Wobblies representing eight unions convened in 1931. By then, IWW conventions seemed more like college homecomings in which alumni exaggerated the good old days than like the sessions of a radical labor organization.

# 19

## Remembrance of Things Past: The IWW Legacy

Perhaps the most remarkable feature about the IWW has been its extended old age. After a ten-year period of infancy and adolescence extending from 1905 to 1915, it enjoyed three years of maturity, followed by almost half a century of declining virility and approaching senility. No longer a vital presence on the American radical scene after 1919, only a shell of its former self after 1924, the IWW could on occasion momentarily recapture the essence of its remarkable past.

But even in decline the IWW waged several major industrial conflicts significant enough to attract public attention and to recall its prewar struggles. For a brief time in 1923–24 the IWW experienced a resurgence in California, particularly among maritime workers, who were long a prime source of Wobbly recruits. Three years later an industrial conflict in Colorado returned the IWW to national attention. The IWW made rapid progress in recruiting Colorado coal miners, particularly after A. S. Embree, a leading prewar organizer just released from prison in Montana, arrived to direct the effort. The IWW's opponents reacted as expected: Ignoring the miners' tangible economic grievances and their actual demands, employers, newspapers, and AFL leaders focused on the IWW's alleged subversive character. Vigilantes, local police, state police, and finally national guardsmen harassed, arrested, beat, and shot miners and their sympathizers. Against this opposition the strikers could not resist beyond February 1928.

Bankrupt and decrepit at the peak of prosperity, the IWW could scarcely be expected to withstand the severe depression about to grip the nation. With the depression, the IWW floundered. Apart from minor involvements on the fringes of the labor warfare of the 1930s in bloody Harlan County, Kentucky, among coal miners, and in Washington State's Yakima Valley among hop pickers, where Wobblies endured their usual indignities, the IWW was more isolated than ever from the mainstream of radicalism and the labor movement. Communists, not Wobblies, now led unemployed workers in protest demonstrations and hunger marches. Symbolically, Ralph Chaplin was silenced at a Chicago street-corner meeting by young Communists who drowned out his voice by loudly singing *Solidarity Forever,* Chaplin's most famous song. When Franklin Roosevelt became president and for the first time in American history the federal government actively encouraged the emergence of independent unionism, the IWW was too weak to benefit. In fact, it criticized both Section 7a of the National Industrial Recovery Act and the 1935 Wagner (National Labor Relations) Act for placing the government in an area where it did not belong: labor-management relations. The IWW's critique of the Wagner Act was remarkably like that issued by the National Association of Manufacturers!

Incapable of competing with communism's variety of revolution, the IWW was equally unable to contend with the industrial unionism of the Congress of Industrial Organizations (CIO). In steel, autos, rubber, lumber, and textiles and on the high seas, CIO unions gained the areas of potential industrial unionism long since relinquished by the Wobblies.

Some Wobblies realized that times had changed and that their former organization had lost its purpose, as John Pancner's personal decision in the 1930s indicated. No member had stayed with the IWW longer, nor suffered more frequent imprisonments, than Pancner (he had been one of the 1918 federal prisoners), yet during the labor crisis of the 1930s he joined the CIO, affiliating with a United Auto Workers (UAW) local in Detroit and remaining a loyal UAW-CIO man. While Pancner was not alone among Wobblies in making that decision, the prominence of his role in the IWW and his loyal twenty-five-year commitment to that organization gave his action a special significance.

The CIO's success diminished any prospects Wobblies might have had for a rebirth of their organization. With skilled workers firmly committed to the AFL, the mass-production workers enthralled and rewarded by the CIO, and most of the unorganized laborers hostile to any form of unionism, the Wobblies had no place to go except back into their "haunted halls."

When World War II ended in 1945 and the cold war began the following year, the IWW was little more than a historical relic. *Time* magazine sarcastically described its 1946 convention as a family reunion of thirty-nine men and a grandmotherly-looking woman, who met in an office building on the North Side of Chicago to pass resolutions that denounced capitalism, fascism, nazism, the CIO, and the AFL. "With that off their chests, the Industrial Workers of the World went home."

The federal government meanwhile had not entirely forgotten the Wobblies. Victimized by an earlier red scare, Wobblies again fell prey to the antiradical hysteria ignited by the cold war and fanned by Senator Joseph McCarthy. After doing battle with American and foreign Communists for three decades, the remaining Wobblies in 1949 found themselves included on attorney general Tom Clark's list of subversive organizations. Unable to hire a lawyer or to send a member to appear before the Subversive Activities Control Board in Washington to challenge the attorney general's decision, the IWW was shorn of the right to act as a collective-bargaining agency for American workers under the terms of the Taft-Hartley Act. (In addition, Wobblies refused, on principle, to sign loyalty oaths.) Ostracized by organized labor and the government, the IWW had become an organization of charming but tired old men and a handful of alienated college students who were unsure about where to take their dissatisfaction with American society.

✳ ✳ ✳

In their analyses of the IWW's eventful history, several scholars have concluded that had it not been for America's entry into World War I and the repression of the organization that ensued, the IWW might well have usurped the CIO's subsequent role in organizing mass-production workers. These scholars believe that the base established by the IWW among harvesters, loggers, and copper miners would have become sufficiently stable, had war not intervened, for the Wobblies later to have penetrated other unorganized sectors of the economy.

This rendering of history leads one to conclude that the IWW's ultimate failure was more a result of external repression than of internal inadequacies. Nothing, of course, need be inevitable. Yet given the internal deficiencies of the IWW, the aspirations of most of its members during the organization's heyday, and the dynamics of American capitalism—what might better be called the American system—the Wobblies' attempt to transform American workers into a revolutionary vanguard was doomed to failure. Wobbly doctrine taught workers how to gain short-range goals indistinguishable from those sought by ordinary, nonrevolutionary trade unions. Able to rally exploited workers behind crusades to abolish specific grievances, the IWW failed to transform its followers' concrete grievances into a higher consciousness of class, ultimate purpose, and necessary revolution—to create, in short, a revolutionary working class in the Marxist sense. This was so because the IWW never explained precisely how it would achieve its new society—apart from vague allusions to the social general strike and to "building the new society within the shell of the old"—or how, once established, it would be governed. Wobblies simply suggested that the state, at least as most Americans knew it, would disappear.

Even had the IWW had a more palatable prescription for revolution, it is far from likely that its followers would have taken it. In fact, IWW members had limited revolutionary potential. At the IWW's founding convention Haywood had alluded to lifting impoverished Americans up from the gutter. But those lying in Haywood's metaphorical gutters thought only of rising to the sidewalk, and once there of entering the house.

This placed the IWW in an impossible dilemma. On one hand, it was committed to ultimate revolution; on the other, it sought immediate improvements for its members. Like all people who truly care about humanity, the Wobblies always accepted betterment for their members today at the expense of achieving utopia tomorrow. This had been true at Lawrence, McKees Rocks, and Paterson, among other places, where the IWW allowed workers to fight for immediate improvements, a result that, if achieved, inevitably diminished their discontent and hence their revolutionary potential. Even at Paterson, where IWW-led strikers failed to win concessions, some Wobblies discerned the dilemma of their position: the leaders' desire for revolution coming up against their members' desire for palpable gains.

Internally, the Wobblies never made up their minds about precisely what kind of structure their organization should adopt. By far the most capable IWW leaders favored an industrial union structure under which largely independent, though not entirely autonomous, affiliates organized by specific industry would cooperate closely with each other under the supervision of an active general executive board. But many lesser leaders, and more among the rank and file, were captivated with the concept of the One Big Union (the mythical OBU) in which workers, regardless of skill, industry, nationality, or color, would be amalgamated into a single unit. Incapable of negotiating union-management agreements owing to its protean character, the OBU would be solely the vessel of revolution. Considering the inherent difficulties involved in organizing unskilled workers on a stable basis, organizational form and structure was an issue of the utmost importance. Yet it remained a problem that the Wobblies never resolved satisfactorily.

Its mythology concerning rank-and-file democracy—comprising what today is known as "participatory democracy"—further compounded the IWW's internal deficiencies. The IWW had been most successful when led by strong individuals like Haywood, who centralized general headquarters in 1916, or Walter Nef, who constructed a tightly knit and carefully administered Agricultural Workers' Organization. Too often, however, jealous and frustrated Wobblies, lacking the abilities of Haywood or Nef but desiring their power and positions, used the concept of "participatory democracy" to snipe at the IWW's leaders on behalf of an idealized rank and file. And without firm leadership the organization drifted aimlessly.

Even had the IWW combined the necessary structure, the proper tactics, and experienced, capable leaders, as it did for a time from 1915 to 1917, its difficulties might still have proved insurmountable. There is no reason to believe that before the 1930s any of America's basic mass-production industries could have been organized. Not until World War II was the CIO, an organization with immense financial resources, millions of members, and federal encouragement, able to solidify its hold on the nation's mass-production industries. And even then the CIO made no headway among migratory workers or Southern mill hands. What reason, then, is there to think that the IWW could have succeeded in the 1920s or earlier, when it lacked funds, counted its members by the thousands, not the millions, and could scarcely expect government assistance? To ask the question is to answer it.

Yet had the IWW done everything its academic critics ask of it—established true industrial unions, accepted long-term officials and a permanent union bureaucracy, signed collective agreements with employers and agreed to respect them—done, in other words, what the CIO did, what would have remained of its original purpose? Had the founders of the IWW been interested in simply constructing industrial unions on the model of the CIO, the advice of their scholarly critics would be well taken. But the IWW was created by radicals eager to revolutionize American society, and to have asked them to deny their primary values and goals would have been to ask too much.

Whatever the IWW's internal dilemmas, the dynamics of American history unquestionably compounded them. Unlike radicals in other societies who contended with established orders unresponsive to lower-class discontent and impervious to change from within, the Wobblies struggled against flexible and sophisticated adversaries. The years of IWW growth and success coincided with the era when welfare capitalism spread among American businesses, when all levels of government began to exhibit solicitude for the worker, and when the catalyst of reform altered all aspects of national society. This process became even more pronounced during World War I, when the federal government used its vast power and influence to hasten the growth of welfare capitalism and conservative unionism. Reform finally proved a better method than repression for weakening the IWW's appeal to workers.

Although the IWW ultimately failed to achieve its major objectives, it nevertheless bequeathed Americans an invaluable legacy. Young Americans who practice direct action, passive resistance, and civil disobedience, and who seek an authentic radical tradition, should find much to ponder in the Wobblies' past. Those who distrust establishment politics, deride bureaucracies, favor community action, and preach participatory democracy would also do well to remember the history of the IWW. Indeed, all who prefer a society based on community to one founded on coercion cannot afford to neglect the tragic history of the IWW.

In this history, two lessons stand out. The first underscores the harsh truth of Antonio Gramsci's comment, quoted earlier, that in advanced industrial nations revolutionaries should take as their slogan: "Pessimism of the Intelligence; Optimism of the Will." The second lesson emphasizes the irony of the radical experience in America and elsewhere in the Western industrial world. As a result of their commitment to ultimate revolution as well as to immediate improvements in the existence of the working class, radicals the world over quickened the emergence of strong labor unions and acted as midwives at the birth of the welfare state. But success, instead of breeding more success, only produced a new working class enthralled with a consumer society and only too willing, even eager, to trade working-class consciousness for a middle-class style of life. The ultimate tragedy, then, for all radicals, the American Wobblies included, has been that the brighter they have helped make life for the masses, the dimmer has grown the prospect for revolution in the advanced societies.

Yet no better epitaph could be written for the American Wobbly than A. S. Embree's comment from his prison cell in 1917: "The end in view is well worth striving for, but in the struggle itself lies the happiness of the fighter."

# Bibliographic Essay

## Recent Works on the History of the IWW

No historian has yet attempted a scholarly general history of the IWW since the publication of *We Shall Be All* in 1969. That is not to say that the Wobblies have lacked historians. Numerous studies have appeared in the past few decades that explore important events in the history of the IWW, the lives of its most prominent leaders, and the legacy that the organization left behind. Indeed, those who want to learn more about the history of the IWW now have a rich historiography available to them.

For an introduction to that recent scholarly literature, students should consult the symposium on the thirtieth anniversary of the publication of *We Shall Be All* that appeared in the journal *Labor History* 40 (August 1999), pp. 345–69. Contributions to that symposium by David Montgomery, Elizabeth Jameson, Marcel van der Linden, Joseph McCartin, and Melvyn Dubofsky reassess Dubofsky's original study in light of recent historical scholarship. For a thorough discussion of works on the IWW that appeared in the first eighteen years after the publication of *We Shall Be All*, students should begin with Melvyn Dubofsky's "Note on Literature Published Since 1970," a bibliographical essay appended to Dubofsky's *We Shall Be All* Second Edition (University of Illinois Press, 1988). Readers interested in works on IWW history published since the mid-1980s might begin with some of the following works.

Few new interpretations of IWW history have been advanced in the years since the publication of *We Shall Be All*. Yet one recent and provocative reinterpretation of Wobbly history is to be found in Howard Kimeldorf's *Battling for American Labor: Wobblies, Craft Workers, and the Making of the Union Movement* (University of California Press, 1999), a book that revolves around case studies of Philadelphia longshoremen and New York City restaurant workers. Kimeldorf's argument that syndicalism did not vanish from the ranks of labor with the collapse of the IWW, but rather took root in unexpected ways in the unions of the American Federation of Labor, is bound to spark renewed debate on the Wobbly legacy among a new generation of labor historians. Readers wanting to view Wobbly history as Wobblies themselves interpreted it should consult *Solidarity Forever: An Oral History of the IWW*, compiled by Stewart Bird, Dan Georgakas, and Deborah Shaffer (Lake View Press, 1985). The reissue of Patrick Renshaw's 1967 volume, *The Wobblies: The Story of the IWW Syndicalism in the United States* (Ivan R. Dee, 1999), allows readers easier access to the best general history of the IWW published before *We Shall Be All*. A fascinating account of the turbulent times that gave birth to the Wobblies is to be found in J. Anthony Lukas's *Big Trouble: A Murder in a Small Western Town Sets Off a Struggle for the Soul of America* (Simon & Schuster, 1997). The book aspires to deliver more than a history of the events and personalities tied to the 1905 murder of the ex-governor of Idaho, Frank Steunenberg, which is its central concern. Lukas's book offers a broad-ranging, if digressive, exploration of American culture and class conflict at the moment when America's twentieth-century industrial order was just taking shape.

If general treatments of IWW history have been rare in recent years, monographs examining facets of IWW history have been plentiful. Most of the recent work on the IWW or aspects of its history has been influenced by the focus on community, culture, ethnicity, gender, and race that has been a central feature of post-1960s labor history.

Rich community studies now allow us to explore the hardscrabble Western working-class milieu in which the IWW had its origins. Three excellent treatments are David M. Emmons, *The Butte Irish: Class and Ethnicity in an American Mining Town, 1875–1925* (University of Illinois Press, 1989); David Brundage, *The Making of Western Labor Radicalism: Denver's Organized Workers, 1878–1905* (University of Illinois Press, 1994); and Elizabeth Jameson, *All that Glitters: Class, Conflict and Community in Cripple Creek* (University of Illinois Press, 1998). Emmons's book examines a mining city whose labor movement proved pivotal to Wobbly history at more than one juncture. Brundage helps shed light on the ways in which Irish Land League radicalism and the Knights of Labor helped set the stage for the later emergence of the IWW in Denver. And Jameson tells the compelling tale of a community that was the site of two explosive labor conflicts—in 1894 and 1903–4—that shaped the distinctive radicalism of the IWW's forerunner, the Western Federation of Miners.

Those interested in the ethnic subcultures that nurtured the Wobblies may consult a number of recent works in addition to the work of Emmons and Brundage on the Irish. The works of Philip Mellinger and Gunther Peck especially have shed much new light on the conditions endured by immigrant workers in the West. See Mellinger's *Race and Labor in Western Copper: The Fight for Equality, 1896–1918* (University of Arizona Press, 1995) and his article "How the IWW Lost Its Western Heartland: Western Labor History Revisited," *Western Historical Quarterly* 27 (1996), 303–24. Peck's articles, "Padrones and Protest: 'Old' Radicals and 'New' Immigrants in Bingham, Utah, 1905–1912," *Western Historical Quarterly* 24 (1993), 157–78, and "Reinventing Free Labor: Immigrant Padrones and Contract Laborers in North America, 1885–1925," *Journal of American History* 83 (1996), 848–71, and his book, *Reinventing Free Labor: Padrone and Immigrant Workers in the North American West, 1880–1930* (Cambridge University Press, 2000), have brilliantly illuminated the dynamics of the labor market in which immigrants to the American West found themselves trapped. Case studies of ethnicity and class in particular communities in which the IWW was active can be found in Philip J. Dreyfus, "The IWW and the Limits of Inter-Ethnic Organizing: Reds, Whites, and Greeks in Grays Harbor Washington, 1912," *Labor History* 38 (1997), 450–70; and A.

Yvette Huginnie, "A New Hero Comes to Town: The Anglo Mining Engineer and 'Mexican Labor' as Contested Terrain in Southeastern Arizona, 1880–1920," *New Mexico Historical Review* 69 (1994), 323–44. For new insights into the Italian immigrant communities that supported the IWW, see Michael Miller Topp, "The Transnationalism of the Italian-American Left: The Lawrence Strike of 1912 and the Italian Chamber of Labor of New York City," *Journal of American Ethnic History* 17 (1997), 39–63; and Patrizia Sione, "Patterns of International Migrations: Italian Silk Workers in New Jersey, USA," *Review (Fernand Braudel Center)* 17 (1994), 555–76.

Those interested in exploring the role of gender in shaping the experience of workers to whom the IWW appealed may also turn to a number of new studies. Among them are Ardis Cameron, *Radicals of the Worst Sort: Laboring Women in Lawrence, Massachusetts, 1860–1912* (University of Illinois Press, 1993); Vincent DiGirolamo, "The Women of Wheatland: Female Consciousness and the 1913 Hop Strike," *Labor History* 34 (1993), 236–55; Colleen O'Neill, "Domesticity Deployed: Gender, Race, and the Construction of Class Struggle in the Bisbee Deportations," *Labor History* 34 (1993), 256–73; and Bonnie Stepenoff, "'Papa on Parade': Pennsylvania Coal Miners' Daughters and the Silk Worker Strike of 1913," *Labor's Heritage* 7:3 (1996), 4–21.

More recent attention has been focused on the question of race and the IWW as well. David Roediger offers one insightful view of the ways in which the most famous Wobbly in the South, Covington Hall, dealt with race and gender in his essay "Gaining a Hearing for Black-White Unity: Covington Hall and the Complexities of Race, Gender, and Class" in his book *Towards the Abolition of Whiteness: Essays on Race, Politics, and Working Class History* (Verso, 1994). Several studies of the Philadelphia waterfront, where the IWW built a powerful biracial union under the leadership of the black Wobbly Ben Fletcher, now illuminate one important but heretofore dimly understood chapter in IWW history. Those interested in the IWW's organizing among these dockworkers should consult Howard Kimeldorf and Robert Penney, "'Excluded' by Choice: Dynamics of Interracial Unionism on the Philadelphia Waterfront, 1910–1930," *International Labor and Working-Class History* 51 (1997), 50–71; Kimeldorf's "Radical Possibilities? The Rise and Fall of Wobbly Unionism on the Philadelphia Docks," in *Waterfront Workers: New Perspectives on Race and Class,* edited by Calvin Winslow (University of Illinois Press, 1998); Lisa McGirr, "Black and White Longshoremen in the IWW: A History of the Philadelphia Marine Transport Workers Industrial Union Local 8," *Labor History* 36 (1995), 377–402; and Peter Cole, "Shaping Up and Shipping Out: The Philadelphia Waterfront during and after the IWW Years, 1913–1940" (unpublished Ph.D. dissertation, Georgetown University, 1998).

Those interested in the distinctive working-class culture and the movement lore cultivated by the Wobblies should begin with Archie Green's *Wobblies, Pile Butts, and Other Heroes: Laborlore Explorations* (University of Illinois Press, 1993). An argument that one aspect of Wobbly culture, the IWW's antireligious bent, stymied its growth where religious institutions were well entrenched is advanced in Kevin J. Christiano's "Religion and Radical Labor Unionism: American States in the 1920s," *Journal for the*

*Scientific Study of Religion* 27(3) (1988), 378–88. IWW movement culture may be studied in Wobbly songs and poems. *Juice Is Stranger Than Fiction: Selected Writings of T-Bone Slim*, edited and introduced by Franklin Rosemont (C. H. Kerr, 1992), contains selections from perhaps the best-known Wobbly bard after Joe Hill. The work of another IWW poet is discussed in Donald Winters's "Covington Hall: The Utopian Vision of a Wobbly Poet," *Labor's Heritage* 4 (1992), 54–63. And of course Joe Hill's songs continue to live on in the periodic reissue of the Wobblies' "little red songbook," the most recent being *Songs of the Workers to Fan the Flames of Discontent*, 36th ed. (Industrial Workers of the World, 1996).

Several biographies of IWW leaders have also appeared in recent years. Dubofsky's own *"Big Bill" Haywood* (St. Martin's Press, 1987) provides a short and evocative treatment of the most famous Wobbly's life. In *Iron in Her Soul: Elizabeth Gurley Flynn and the American Left* (Washington State University Press, 1995), Helen C. Camp provides a fresh reexamination of the Wobblies' famous "Rebel Girl." The life and thought of William Z. Foster, who played brief yet important role in IWW history before emerging as America's best-known Communist leader, has attracted the most recent interest from scholars. Works on Foster include Victor G. Devinatz, "The Labor Philosophy of William Z. Foster: From the IWW to the TUEL," *International Social Science Review* 71 (1996), 3–13; Edward P. Johanningsmeier, *Forging American Communism: The Life of William Z. Foster* (Princeton University Press, 1994); and James R. Barrett, *William Z. Foster and the Tragedy of American Radicalism* (University of Illinois Press, 1999).

Some of the richest work on IWW history continues to be generated in local case studies. Among them are Thomas J. Dorich, "'This Is a Tough Place to Work': Industrial Relations in the Jerome Mines, 1900–1922," *Journal of Arizona History* 38 (1997), 233–56; and Joseph W. Sullivan, "'Every Shout a Cannon Ball': The IWW and Urban Disorders in Providence, Rhode Island," *Rhode Island History* 54 (1996), 51–64. Regional studies have also shed light on underappreciated aspects of IWW history. A treatment of the IWW's organizing among Great Plains harvesters that incorporates the ideas of such social theorists as Michel Foucault is to be found in Ted Grosshardt, "Harvest(ing) Hoboes: The Production of Labor Organization through the Wheat Harvest," *Agricultural History* 70 (1996), 283–301. A book that amply demonstrates the Wobblies' lasting legacy among one region's workers is Nigel Anthony Sellars, *Oil, Wheat, and Wobblies: The Industrial Workers of the World in Oklahoma, 1905–1930* (University of Oklahoma Press, 1998). And an argument that the geographic mobility of Northwest loggers did not hinder their ability or willingness to join the IWW is advanced in Richard A. Rajala's "A Dandy Bunch of Wobblies: Pacific Northwest Loggers and the Industrial Workers of the World, 1900–1920," *Labor History* 37 (1997), 205–34.

New studies have also shed more light on the extent of repression directed against the Wobblies. John Clendenin Townsend's *Running the Gauntlet: Cultural Sources of Violence Against the I.W.W.* (Garland, 1986) explores the general theme of repression. In "The Case of the Wandering Wobblie: *The State of Oklahoma v. Arthur Berg*," *Chronicles of Oklahoma* 73 (1995–1996), 404–23, Von Russell Creel tells the sad tale of one

Wobbly organizer who received a ten-year jail term in 1923 under Oklahoma's criminal syndicalism law. There are now two treatments of the terrible events that shook Centralia, Washington, in 1919: Tom Copeland's *The Centralia Tragedy of 1919: Elmer Smith and the Wobblies* (University of Washington Press, 1993) and John M. McClelland's *Wobbly War: The Centralia Story* (Washington State Historical Society, 1987). Richard Melzer "Exiled in the Desert: The Bisbee Deportees' Retention in New Mexico, 1917," *New Mexico Historical Review* 67 (1992), 269–84, explores the deeply unsympathetic reactions of the New Mexicans who found miners from Bisbee stranded on cattle cars in the vicinity of Columbus, New Mexico, after their deportation by Arizona vigilantes. Francis Shor, "The IWW and Oppositional Politics in World War I: Pushing the System Beyond Its Limits," *Radical History Review* 64 (1996), 74–94, emphasizes that it was the IWW's avowed radicalism that brought upon it federal repression during World War I.

Perhaps the most significant development in Wobbly historiography since Dubofsky's book first appeared has been the publication of numerous studies on the international history of the IWW. Verity Bergmann's *Revolutionary Industrial Unionism: The Industrial Workers of the World in Australia* (Cambridge University Press, 1995) and Erik Olssen's *The Red Feds: Revolutionary Industrial Unionism and the New Zealand Federation of Labor, 1908–1913* (Oxford University Press, 1988) have deepened our understanding of the dissemination of Wobbly syndicalism across the Pacific. J. Peter Campbell's "The Cult of Spontaneity: Finnish-Canadian Bushworkers and the Industrial Workers of the World in Northern Ontario, 1919–1934," *Labour/La Travail* 41 (1998), 117–46, and Mark Leier's *Where the Fraser River Flows: The Industrial Workers of the World in British Columbia* (New Star, 1990) have done the same for Canada. And insight into the impact of the IWW among Mexicans may be found in Norman Caulfield's "Wobblies and Mexican Workers in Mining and Petroleum, 1905–1924," *International Review of Social History* 40 (1995), 51–76. A strong argument for the necessity of seeing Wobbly history through an international perspective is advanced by Marcel van der Linden in "On the Importance of Crossing Borders," *Labor History* 40 (August 1999), 362–65.

Finally, students may now find numerous resources related to IWW history on the Internet. The modern-day IWW, though but a shadow of the IWW of the past, maintains an elaborate Web site that may be accessed at <http://www.iww.org>. This site contains links to a number of interesting documents pertaining to Wobbly history as well as other recent articles and books dealing with various aspects of the story of the IWW.

# Index

MELVYN DUBOFSKY, Distinguished Professor of History and Sociology at Binghamton University, SUNY, held the John Adams Chair in American History at the University of Amsterdam, The Netherlands, during the spring of 2000. He is the author of numerous books and essays on U.S. labor and twentieth-century history, including biographies of John L. Lewis (co-written with Warren Van Tine) and "Big Bill" Haywood, *The State and Labor in Modern America,* and *Hard Work: The Making of Labor History.*

JOSEPH A. McCARTIN is an associate professor of history at Georgetown University in Washington, D.C. He has written widely on the modern U.S. labor movement, politics, and the state. His book *Labor's Great War: The Struggle for Industrial Democracy and the Origins of Modern American Labor Relations, 1912–1921* was awarded the 1999 Philip Taft Labor History Prize.

# The Working Class in American History

University of Illinois Press
1325 South Oak Street
Champaign, IL 61820-6903
www.press.uillinois.edu